The Journey of Passion

Women and Gender in China Studies

VOLUME 16

The titles published in this series are listed at *brill.com/wgcs*

The Journey of Passion

Desire, Identity, and Community in Romance Genres of Imperial China

By

Ying Zou

BRILL

ISSN 1877-5772
ISBN 978-90-04-69334-0
ISBN 978-90-04-69335-7 (PDF)
DOI https://doi.org/10.1163/9789004693357

Library of Congress Control Number: 2026936354

Brill and Koninklijke Brill BV are part of De Gruyter Brill.
www.degruyterbrill.com

Questions about General Product Safety Regulation: productsafety@degruyterbrill.com

Cover illustration: Daiyu Weeping over Fallen Blossoms by the Flowers' Grave, Illustration for the *Zengping butu Shitou ji* 增評補圖石頭記, 2 volumes (Shanghai: Shangwu yinshuguan, 193–?); Source: Beijing shifan daxue tushuguan, downloaded from Wikimedia Commons.

Contents

Acknowledgments

This book has been a long time in the making, with periods of progress and pause along the way. In its final stages, I am reminded of all those who stood by my side throughout this journey, and I would like to take this opportunity to express my deep gratitude to each of them.

I thank the late John C.Y. Wang for his support and guidance during my research and writing, and I regret not having published this book sooner, before his passing. I am deeply indebted to Ban Wang for recognizing the value of my topic at the initial stages of this project and for advising me to explore the intimate connection between feelings and ethics, an approach that became foundational to my research. The many pleasant conversations with him – in his office, suffused with the fragrance of tea, and in the cafeterias at Stanford – remain vivid memories. His faith in me and my work has been crucial to the completion of this book.

I owe a special debt to Xiaozhen Hu, who first aroused my interest in the study of women's *tanci* writing and thereby foreshadowed this book's central themes. I thank her for her unfailing kindness and willingness to help. I am also grateful to Maram Epstein, Louise Edwards, and Wilt Idema for their valuable advice on the presentations and articles that make up parts of this book, and for their generosity in helping me embark on the research that ultimately culminated here. Special gratitude goes to Yiqun Zhou, who has continually inspired me with her scholarly acumen and engaged me in discussions ranging from academic matters to personal concerns. She is both a mentor and a friend.

Many thanks go to friends and colleagues in both the United States and China, among them Jeeyoung Peck, Ning Ma, Xiaoqiao Lin, Chengjuan Sun, Xiaojing Sun, Sun Yu, Yang Huilin, Leng Chengjin, Zhu Wanshu, Xu Zhengying, Wang Xin, Wu Zhen, Zheng Zhiliang, Xu Jianwei, Xu Nan, Zeng Xiangbo, Chang Peijie, Chen Tao, Hong Yue, Wang Yan, and Ma Dongyao, who shared their wisdom and assisted me in matters large and small. I owe a great debt to Zhang Ming, my advisor at Peking University, for planting some of the most significant seeds of this study by introducing me to *The Peony Pavillion*, which I first read, as an undergraduate, in the season of falling petals. His warm care and encouragement have remained a constant source of support over the years.

I would like to thank the two anonymous readers consulted by Brill, whose comments and corrections were enormously helpful in improving an earlier version of the manuscript, and especially Louise Edwards, the editor of the series in which this book appears, who read the manuscript with great care and offered insightful suggestions on the introduction that helped expand the scope of the book. My thanks are also due to the production staff at Brill, Iulia Ivana in particular, for their editorial assistance, and to copyeditors Tom Marling and Jon Wilcox, whose conscientious and meticulous work is greatly appreciated. I gratefully acknowledge the financial support of the School of Liberal Arts, Renmin University of China.

An earlier version of Chapter 4 was published as "Talent, Identity, and Sociality in Early Qing Scholar-Beauty Novels," *T'oung Pao*, Sept. 2016. Part of Chapter 6 was published as "Cross-dressing and Other Disguises in *Zaisheng yuan*," *Late Imperial China*, Dec. 2012.

Most of all, I am blessed by the support of my family. Words are insufficient to express my gratitude; I dedicate this book to them.

Introduction

This book focuses on the evolution of the traditional romantic discourse represented by the *caizi-jiaren* 才子佳人 (scholar-beauty) model, in particular the workings of gender, desire, and the shaping of identity embodied in these romantic narratives. Although, as a specifically technical term, the "*caizi-jiaren* novel" refers to a type of vernacular romance in the mid to late seventeenth century, the scholar-beauty romance, as a cultural discourse as well as a story type, had begun to rise in mid-Tang China (766–835), and increasingly thrived in the late imperial period, and thereupon was made up of various narrative forms spanning from classical tales (written in literary Chinese) to drama and vernacular fiction. In general, a *caizi-jiaren* story concerns the love affair between a handsome and talented young scholar and a beautiful and often chaste woman, who is equal to or better than her male counterpart in terms of literary talent or moral quality. My goal, however, is not to give a full account of a whole tradition of the *caizi-jiaren* romance, but to focus on some significant turning points in the development of the *caizi-jiaren* model. I consider the *caizi-jiaren* model in Patricia Parker's sense – neither as "fixed generic prescription nor as abstract transhistorical category" but as "an organizing principle" for the interpretation of a poetic form.[1] Hence, I will engage these texts through the framework of intellectual and emotional history. The goal of this book is to determine what changed in literati thinking about desire and their identity, while at the same time I attempt to account for the changes that took place.

In conceptualizing the term "*qing*" 情 (feelings or passion), an idea that is not restricted to the description of romantic relations, but can be extended to the more general notion of emotion, the *caizi-jiaren* romance is characterized by the conceiving of emotional relationships, and the amorous exploits of idealized heroes and heroines.[2] These romantic narratives both elevate everyday life and the value of individual freedom and also highlight the pursuit of sublime emotions and cultural ideals. The struggle to strike a balance between private feelings and public morality shapes these fictional narratives. In view

1 Patricia Parker, *Inescapable Romance: Studies in the Poetics of a Mode* (Princeton, NJ: Princeton University Press, 1979), 4–5.

2 See for instance Paolo Santangelo's discussion on *ai* 愛 and *qing* 情, which covers the representations of various affections including passion, desire, sexual attraction, and love-affection. Paolo Santangelo, "Introductory Notes," in Paolo Santangelo and Gabor Boros, *The Culture of Love in China and Europe* (Leiden: Brill, 2020), 7–8.

of the constitutive feature of emotion in the conception of the self, narratives of romance serve as an important site for working out discourses of agency and compulsion, or new modes of subjectivity and sociality. In its intersection with historical processes and social changes, the *caizi-jiaren* romance constructs various forms of feelings, thereby providing alternative versions of discourses about the self, gender, and ethics, which are different from the modern Western models.

The linkage between emotion and selfhood, and between desire and subjectivity, underwent changes and development in the Chinese cultural tradition before colonialism and Westernization. Emotion is relevant to historicity and social constructiveness in that it is intimately tied to the specific regime and social customs, and thus evolves along with the development of history. In premodern China, there are shifting paradigms at work in the romantic structure. Regardless of whether the tension between the perception and experience of *qing* occurs in medieval classical tales or in Ming-Qing drama and fiction, the modes of emotion change in distinctive ways. When new emotional relations fail to be drawn into the social morality, the original emotional discourse is rendered invalid, to the extent that people desperately need a new system of emotional expression. The variations of emotionally expressive styles shed light on the historical changes in the correlations between emotion and self and between culture and power. Not only are there differences in the precise working out of emotional bonds in different social and cultural contexts, but also in various individual conditions. Therefore, my research aims to show the trajectory of these paradigmatic shifts, and examine the workings of desire, the changing of ethical evaluations in the romantic discourse of premodern China, and further to explore the role which emotional discourses play in the understanding of social and political life by reflecting on these transformations within their historical and ideological contexts. What I find equally interesting is how emotions are specifically reshaped in the constructions of self, and how people take actions and make changes as affective and ethical beings in their own plights. In order to demonstrate this, the core of this book consists of close readings of certain romantic narratives, each of which addresses particular ethical and emotional issues in relation to particular conditions.

By doing so, I hope to shed light on the intricacy of private and public, self-identity and community, thereby contributing to the ongoing studies of discourses of desire, subjectivity, and gender in premodern China. Recent studies have attempted to demonstrate how the representation of desire and sexuality works as a means to create a discourse of private selfhood. This signals a tendency toward separating the pursuit of personal emotions and fantasy from the public realm of morality. Stephen Owen reads romance as the construction of private spaces independent of the public sphere.[3] From another perspective, Paul Rouzer sees in the Tang romantic tales the representation of homosocial modes of desire, and new codes of public behavior among the community of male elites. However, his singular emphasis on the social construct involving the bonds between ruler, courtier-minister, and literatus risks reduplicating the gap between the private and the public, between sexuality and social forces. In fact, his social and political reading of Tang romance inspires us to further explore the sophisticated relations between desire and morality, self and community, in late imperial China as well as the mid-Tang period, although he asserts that the link between literary romance and political relations was dissolved with the advent of a more "late imperial" world of desire and sexuality, in which "eroticism becomes increasingly depoliticized."[4] Manling Luo, in the same vein, examines the reception of romantic values within the late medieval literati community as a means of identifying and perpetuating themselves as the literate elite, with an emphasis on the paradoxical nature of the literati storytellers' maneuvers in delineating their sexual identity, which arose from the inherent tension between romantic life and social values.[5]

Scholars of late imperial Chinese literature have been developing a productive understanding of the paradox of *qing* and public order present in the Ming and Qing fiction. Wai-yee Li makes a valuable attempt to explore the paradox of love and enlightenment in late imperial fiction. She perceives the radical subjectivity and the subversive implications in the structure of desire, which she thinks of as a quality of the individual "falling outside any system of order."[6] Other scholars follow Li's project in tracing the late imperial fascination with *qing* in wider historical contexts and gender strategies. They tend to show that

3 Stephen Owen, *The End of the Chinese "Middle Ages": Essays in Mid-Tang Literary Culture* (Stanford, CA: Stanford University Press, 1996), 130–73.

4 Paul Rouzer, *Articulated Ladies: Gender and the Male Community in Early Chinese Texts* (Cambridge, MA: Harvard University Asian Center, 2001), 309.

5 Manling Luo, *Literati Storytelling in Late Medieval China* (Seattle: University of Washington Press, 2015), 133–36.

6 Wai-yee Li, *Enchantment and Disenchantment: Love and Illusion in Chinese Literature* (Princeton: Princeton University Press, 1993), 256. Anthony Yu also shares Li's view by seeing desire as the defining trait and distinctive problem of the human, which is in essence divorced from, or challenges, the social. Qiancheng Li, on the other hand, elucidates how late imperial Chinese literature is characterized by the juxtaposition of *qing*, sexual desire in particular, as a fundamental force in life and the inner self, and its opposite, or religious – especially Buddhist – detachment. See Anthony Yu, *Rereading the Stone: Desire and the Making of Fiction in Dream of the Red Chamber*, Princeton, NJ: Princeton University Press, 1997; Qiancheng Li, *Transmutations of Desire: Literature and Religion in Late Imperial China*, Hongkong: The Chinese University of Hongkong Press, 2020.

men and women of late imperial China were torn between private desire and social order.[7] Maram Epstein analyzes the competing discursive constructions of desire between the "aesthetics of authenticity" and orthodoxy.[8] More recently, she further reflects on the Western tendency to privilege romantic love as the core of individual selfhood, and thus turns to reexamine the role of filial piety in producing subjectivity in light of the tensions between the personal/improper and the ritually sanctioned/appropriate. Epstein in her original study provides a flexible understanding of filial duty as a social code that people can manipulate to achieve affective interiority and recognized personhood, in seeing filial piety as a technology of self, a means of creating autonomous sites of resistance to both family and state.[9]

As the scholarship mentioned above has revealed, the uneasy coexistence of the veins of personal emotional pursuit and the moralistic characterizes Chinese narrative discourses of desire and sexuality. Yet the issue is how we interpret this deeply embedded yet paradoxical combination of private desire with moral norms in premodern Chinese romance, a tension that also occurs in the intellectual discourses of the periods of focus in this study. The multiplicity and ambivalence of emotions precisely call such dualistic frameworks into question, and invite us to perceive the world around us as characterized by openness and fluidity. Although interiority and individualism in these

7 See Martin Huang, *Desire and Fictional Narrative in Late Imperial China* (Cambridge, MA: Harvard University Asia Center, 2001); Keith McMahon, *Misers, Shrews, and Polygamists: Sexuality and Male–Female Relations in Eighteenth-Century Chinese Fiction* (Durham, NC: Duke University Press, 1995); Maram Epstein, *Competing Discourses: Orthodoxy, Authenticity, and Engendered Meanings in Late Imperial Chinese Fiction* (Cambridge, MA: Harvard University Asia Center, 2001).

8 Epstein, *Competing Discourses*.

9 See Maram Epstein, *Orthodox Passions: Narrating Filial Love during the High Qing* (Cambridge, MA: Harvard University Asia Center, 2019), 256–61. Notwithstanding the importance of filial piety as one type of emotional expression in late imperial China, nevertheless, it is the cult of *qing* that provides a remarkable source for altering the conventional filial duties into a possibly affective ethics. In fact, Wang Yangming 王陽明 (1472–1529) already identified parent–child love as the basis of the principle of filiality and thrust for filial practices, although *qing* was reclaimed as an aspect of filial piety during the early and mid-Qing; see Wang Yangming, "Xu Ai lu" 徐愛錄, in *Chuan xi lu* 傳習錄 (Zhengzhou: Zhongzhou guji chubanshe, 2008), 25–26. The discourse of *qing* presents an escape from the regulatory norms of feelings, and thus it may offer support for the existing polity of emotion, but also may endanger its basis. Likewise, the acts of filial self-sacrifice exhibit more complex responses to identity categorization, often including both ideological and counterideological tendencies. We should be cautious, therefore, that the overemphasis on the role of the filial piety in producing individual selves and personhood will be likely to trap us in the danger of seeing all those who fully internalize ritual ideals as free subjects with interiorized affective cores.

romantic narratives tends to become progressively more focused upon over time, culminating in the Ming and Qing (1368–1911) in particular,[10] they are not meant to undercut Confucian moralization, but rather insist on a critical self-reflection, or self-questioning. Therefore, I attempt to reexamine the relationship between *qing* and its moralizing tendency, and that between personal identity and sociality, in light of a more nuanced view that grows out of the romantic representation of literati identity. I see these seemingly conflicting forces as unfolding in a dynamic process of critical inquiry and self-reflection, as literati made choices about how to respond to the changing world around them, or in their negotiation with state power or the particular historical situation which they encountered.

In the Confucian context, how to reconstruct ethical values or a moral vision during periods of historical transformation forms a fundamental issue. The paradoxical mode of thinking present in the romantic narratives represents the way in which literati both affirmed new emotional needs, or self-interest, and contemplated their boundaries. This was not an ambiguous attitude torn between self-interest and public order, but an unfolding process of reclaiming one's subjectivity or agency. In this respect, romance serves as a critical medium that relies on unceasing self-scrutiny to sustain its moralizing vigor. The identity crises and moral anxieties of the literati in response to changing times were projected into the romantic narratives of various periods, which were thereby enriched by the dialectics of self-affirmation and self-questioning. Such a process of self-reflection fosters openness to subjectivity, producing emotion-relevant nuances of expression and action that exhibit the individual's anxiety, plight, and struggle – complex emotional responses that are difficult to articulate in a legible manner, but which cultivate a possibility of challenging identity categorizations and creating a variety of new personhoods.

In this respect, the pornographic genre that similarly dealt with desire, gender, and morality may be seen as the foil of the *caizi-jiaren* romance, as is revealed in the juxtaposition of the erotic episodes concerning the Precious Mirror of Love (*fengyue baojian* 風月寶鑒) and the purer representation of *qing* that happens in Prospect Garden (*daguan yuan* 大觀園) in *The Dream of the Red Chamber* (*Honglou meng* 紅樓夢), the renowned masterpiece written in the mid-eighteenth century. In contrast with the romances of genuine feelings that give rise to a new consciousness of the ramifications of desire and the

10 Although the history of the Qing dynasty ended in 1911, my discussion in this book mainly concerns works written before 1840 – when the first Opium War broke out – a year generally regarded as the beginning of the late Qing.

evolving subject, erotic fiction tends to concentrate on the negative process of self-ruination, such as in portrayals of the danger of excess lust that ends in the utter repudiation of sexual desire, or in descriptions of the deadly consequences that arise when a man who pursues desire is ultimately consumed by his own desire, as in the case of *The Carnal Prayer Mat* (*Rou putuan* 肉蒲團) and *The Plum in the Golden Vase* (*Jin Ping Mei* 金瓶梅), two of the most notorious pornographic novels in the Ming-Qing period.[11] Generally speaking, Chinese pornography frames the representation of sexuality in terms of the principle of karmic retribution and Buddhist salvation, providing moral lessons through a disavowal of desire and self. Although these immoral texts claim to denounce the very licentiousness with which their pages are filled, at the same time, their goal is to arouse the interest of readers, and they are largely written by and for men. More often than not, ironically, they result in reinforcing, rather than challenging, the gender hierarchy and the dominant patriarchal ideology, which may have been the main force behind the rise of erotic fiction in late imperial China.[12] This irony is partly due to the rupture between desire and morality, which *caizi-jiaren* romance modifies by inserting *qing* that endows the self with moral agency. By promoting an ideal of authenticity and refined sensibilities, therefore, romance marks the contrast with erotic fiction, which features the materialization of desire and the dissolution of self, and thus serves as the unspoken other for the reconfiguration of desire, subject, and ethics in the literati consciousness.

In pursuit of both self-interest and social responsibility, therefore, literary men demonstrate a distinctive mode of writing the self in the *caizi-jiaren* romance, posing a new construction of subjectivity that is based upon group identity or community identity rather than any single entity. They also employ romance to express a sense of male sociality within communities of like-minded literary men, thereby shaping a sense of self and cultural distinction by means of communal ties and delineating a socio-literary world with

---

11 See Martin Huang's and Keith McMahon's readings of these two novels; Huang, *Desire and Fictional Narrative*, 86–110; McMahon, *Misers, Shrews, and Polygamists*, 46–51.

12 For the discussion on the paradoxical features of eroticism, see Santangelo and Boros, *The Culture of Love*, 115–35. As far as gender ideology is concerned, Martin Huang has perceptively suggested that erotic stories occasionally represent women's sexuality and suppressed subjectivity, while in the context of homoerotic relationships, women's bodies emerge as a site where desire both subverts and duplicates the gender power structure. Keith McMahon has also keenly pointed out that the erotic romances distinguish themselves from the chaste ones by depriving the heroine of her mobility outside the home and of her exclusive right to one man, albeit they retain the chaste romances' vestiges of the independent and superior women. Huang, *Desire and Fictional Narrative*, 111–36; McMahon, *Misers, Shrews, and Polygamists*, 126–49.

its own competences and forms of sociability. In these romances, the literary community stands in the private–public or the individual–state continuums, playing a pivotal role in both containing the threat of excessive self-interest and promoting the relative autonomy of the literary elite in the face of the political and moral challenges. As such, these works suggest a double-edged agenda, in the sense that the romantic construction of a literary communal ideal made possible both a redefinition of personhood and a renewal of a moral vision, and eventually an adaptation to the new historical circumstances. Therefore, I seek to go beyond dualistic approaches and explore further the multiplicity of desire and self-fashioning situated in the public sphere and power relations. I will read the *caizi-jiaren* romance in the light of the more dynamic modes of gender and desire, with a focus on the working of desire as a dialogue with moral systems and public power, and gender's relation to cultural expression.

The works discussed here, in fact, were experienced not solely as models for male personhood. In the *caizi-jiaren* romance, new forms of subjectivity always come into being along with a new female ideal. As Nancy Armstrong claims, the discourse of individuality developed first as a specifically female form of subjectivity.[13] As a symbol of *qing*, the female plays an important role in the construction of a new principle of identity and a new relationship between self and society in late imperial China. In particular, female agency and personhood is complex and tortuous in that female characters channel their desires not only against constraints and conventions but also through them, encountering both possibilities and limitations. In this sense, the heroines are both products and agents of the social order and moral norms. In reading these texts I thus do not aim to discover either a frame of repression or a form of liberation. Instead, I see the idealization of women as an aspect of the larger cultural project of literary elite self-fashioning in reaction to changing historical circumstances. In this process of self-fashioning, endowed with an inner depth and an ability to act on her own, the heroine functions as the appropriate vehicle for the hero to work out his own autonomy of self and community. I try to demonstrate that, by foregrounding the heroine's fulfillment of her desire and self, male authors not only promote a project of self-construction through the use of female agency, but also define what a self-conscious woman desires. Men represented women as they wished them to be, and thus exerted an impact on the self-expression of the educated gentry woman in late imperial China, who, we know, was a common reader and lover of these romances. In particular, women *tanci* 彈詞 authors wrote in the tradition of *caizi-jiaren* romance,

13 See Nancy Armstrong, *Desire and Domestic Fiction: A Political History of the Novel* (New York: Oxford University Press, 1987), 14.

despite its hostility to their own desires, but at the same time enabled a distinctively female voice to be heard. Women's writing (and rewriting) of romance not only represented their self-perceptions, but also explored the profound plight that they encounter in patriarchal society. In this sense, romantic discourse reinvented or constructed identities and subjectivities, regulated conduct, and defined the way self, gender, and power were represented.

My arguments here also engage with certain recent explorations in the theory of the subject and gender. Michel Foucault explores how power works through knowledge and discourse to create a subject that inhabits a modern institutional culture, and through the penetration and inscription of the subject as subjectivity.[14] Even more significant is that he employs the genealogical method in his writings, as he states in *Discipline and Punish* that the book is "intended ... as a genealogy of the present scientific-legal complex."[15] Foucault's extensive use of historical methodology in his treatment of sexuality led to the negation of a prior and essentialized form of sexuality and desire, inviting us instead to think of desire as being grounded on power and writing. It is in this sense that he sees modern sexuality as not being logically prior to its written representation, but to the "veritable discursive explosion" of talk "around and apropos of sex" that began in the seventeenth century.[16] Foucault's studies have led scholars to focus on the role that social structures and historical changes play in defining desire and its objects. Discourses of gender and desire do not transcend history, but are imbedded in the social site of production.

Contemporary feminist critique has also contributed greatly to this understanding, by showing how the conception of the subject ignores the historical conditions that women confronted. In that respect, Nancy Armstrong's *Desire and Domestic Fiction: A Political History of the Novel* adds more feminist approaches to Foucault's perspective. Armstrong acknowledges that Foucault's theory encourages a historical understanding of gender as an integral dimension of sexuality, but she also argues that one must refine Foucault's productive hypothesis to include the issue of gender if one intends to describe the formation and behavior of such a discourse of sexuality in British culture.[17] Therefore, she discusses how the rise of domestic fiction in eighteenth-century England facilitated the formation of a highly elaborate form of femaleness, and

---

14 See Michel Foucault, *Discipline and Punish: The Birth of the Prison*, trans. Alan Sheridan (New York: Vintage, 1977).

15 Ibid., 23.

16 See Michel Foucault, *The History of Sexuality*, vol. 1: *An Introduction*, trans. Robert Hurley (New York: Vintage, 1978), 17.

17 Armstrong, *Desire and Domestic Fiction*, 11.

accordingly developed the most basic qualities of human identity, and how a specifically modern form of desire came into being along with a new image of woman. Armstrong stresses the relationship between the sexual and the political on the ground that domestic fiction virtually introduced a new form of political power – "men generally retained their political identity in writing that developed the qualities of female subjectivity and made subjectivity a female domain."[18] This literature created and popularized the ideal of the romantic, domesticated heterosexual couple – a new sexual politics of the household that underpinned middle-class hegemony – as the foundation of modern society. In framing sexual relations as the site for reconfiguring power relations across the axes of class, culture, gender, and generation, Armstrong argues that gender is a cultural and political construct that operates as a key instrument of governance and class formation, and that the development of the conception of individuality, first and foremost, presupposes the discursive construction of the female subjectivity.[19]

Foucault's analysis of how the self is constructed through power relations and disciplinary modes also leads to the possible dismissal of subjectivity as illusion, as well as the disclaiming of the notion of the good, thereby stimulating a meaningful discussion about the connections between a sense of self and social morality. Charles Taylor, who strives to dislodge the viable elements of Foucault's thought from a perspective that seems to downplay social improvement, for example, advocates the harmonization of personal identity and moral visions.[20] Taylor follows Foucault in adopting a historical and nonessentialist understanding of identity, but at the same time grants greater weight to the collective than to the personal dimensions of identity. In *Sources of the Self*, Taylor presents his own version of the history of people's self-conceptions, by excavating the various historical embeddings of our conceptions of agency. According to Taylor, "our agency is a dialogical consciousness," in the sense that there is no self prior to social relations, or before it comes into being in dialogue with others.[21]

Furthermore, he stresses that "to be an agent is to be oriented to a basic good or set of goods."[22] Foucault's great understanding of the complex workings of power has resulted in a retreat from normative frameworks that, from

---

18 Ibid., 4.

19 Ibid., 10.

20 Charles Taylor, *Sources of the Self: The Making of the Modern Identity* (Cambridge, MA: Harvard University Press, 1989).

21 Charles Taylor, *Human Agency and Language* (Cambridge: Cambridge University Press, 1985), 8.

22 Taylor, *Sources of the Self*, 47.

Taylor's perspective, one unavoidably has and draws on. Instead, Taylor advocates the need to recognize "a plurality of goods," with a belief in a lively sense of the conflict among goods, and the exploration of the human predicament as a locus of moral sources.[23] In his historical explanation of the rise of a modern self, therefore, Taylor uses an interpretive approach to give an account of people's self-interpretations and their visions of the good. He claims that "history cannot therefore be driven by laws that are completely external to those agents' self-understandings."[24] In his historical sketches in *Sources of the Self*, he traces how people conceive of themselves in particular moments of history, how they interpret their complex social existence, and how they conceptualize the good. He sees individuals as being in possession of various linguistic and cultural components that provide them with an orientation to the good – "language does not only serve to depict ourselves and the world, it also helps constitute our lives."[25]

Like those of Charles Taylor, one of Judith Butler's preoccupations has been to address the ways in which agency is not a transcendental capability of the subject.[26] While Butler has developed Foucault's ideas that desire, sexuality, and subject are not naturally occurring but discursively constructed categories, Butler's studies on sex and gender also theorize modes of self-formation by arguing that performativity is the reiteration of norms by which one becomes intelligible as a subject.[27] More recently, her account of the binding of desire and subjectivity has articulated a theory of agency that "takes into account the double workings of social power and psychic reality" – that is, subjects and desires are not outside frameworks of social norms, although they are not reducible to these processes of normalization.[28]

Together, these theories contribute to the reflection on subjectivity and the quest for agency, and most importantly bring the historicist elements front and center. Foucault offers new insights into the dynamics of power and the suspicion of subjectivity, and in particular his analyses of how subjects are

---

23 Ibid., 511–13.

24 Taylor, *Human Agency and Language*, 3.

25 Ibid., 10.

26 Judith Butler, *Bodies That Matter: On the Discursive Limit of "Sex"* (New York: Routledge, 1993), 94–95.

27 As for the concept of performativity, see Judith Butler, *Gender Trouble: Feminism and the Subversion of Identity* (New York: Routledge, 1999).

28 Judith Butler, Ernesto Laclau, and Slavoj Zizek, *Contingency, Hegemony, Universality: Contemporary Dialogues on the Left* (London: Verso, 2000), 151. Butler's recent works that engage questions of agency also include *Undoing Gender* (New York: Routledge, 2004) and *Giving an Account of Oneself* (New York: Fordham University Press, 2005).

produced call into question essentialist assumptions about sex and gender. Foucault makes it possible for me to consider historicizing the subject under discussion and explaining the production of self-conceptions in premodern Chinese romantic discourse in terms of their relevance to particular historical junctures. Taylor's thinking about the relationship between our moral sources and our identities gives us a viable means of reflecting on what transforms identity. His insistence on a dialogical and cultural understanding of identity encourages me to think how the expressive inner self is integrated with public life in Chinese tradition. Thus, my study intends to capture the ways in which agency resides in the *caizi-jiaren* mode through crucial transitions and developments in the ideas of desire, selfhood, and community. On top of that, the construction of both individuality and ethical ideals are often interwoven with the images of women. Recent feminist critiques mentioned above encourage me to explore the formation of a female subject and the formulation of female desire in terms of their own complex history, as well as the role normative frameworks play in women's self-construction and self-interpretations and the possibility of the articulation of both the plights and aspirations of women confronted as writers.

Along with these perspectives, I see my readings of the romantic narratives in this study as giving a picture of how desires and passionate attachments are not formed and realized beyond social practices, even though they are not fully reducible to social norms. Gender issues also add to our understanding of social issues, and complicate our reflection on human agency as it engages both constraints and possibilities. Accordingly, my investigation aims to keep gender in dynamic relation with other factors that influence how men and women write about desire and emotional attachment in fiction and the stories that they tell. In particular, the extent to which the fashioning of a modern self in China was conditioned not only by colonial encounters with the West but also by intertwined relations to a Confucian intellectual world that was unremittingly readjusting itself.

In this sense, this analysis of premodern Chinese romance also provides useful data for the study of emotion, which, although it has been generally neglected by poststructuralist theory, has progressively advanced in the past three or four decades. Posing as a root-and-branch critique of the Western conception of the subject and of subjectivity, poststructuralism denies the existence of intention, experience, choice, and desire, and sees the "self" not as something that could be free or imprisoned but as a mere product of certain discursive structures and disciplinary orders, thereby completely dismissing the role of feelings in the construction of the self. By contrast, emotion research has opened up an extraordinary opportunity to rethink the very nature of the self beyond that afforded to it by poststructuralism – that is, as completely decided and constructed by power and culture – and to restore agency and meaning to individuals as bearers of subjective experiences and feelings and who pursue the making of choices. Admittedly, even if the incorporation of emotion makes possible a new conceptualization of the self, the theorists of emotion have been profoundly impacted by poststructuralism in making the case for emotion as a discursive practice.

Through the years, theories of emotion, both in the fields of anthropology and literary criticism, have debated whether feelings are universal and biological phenomena or culturally produced, and on the importance of the person either as collectively constructed or individual in emotional experiences. Despite his acknowledgment of the culturally variable elements of the romantic experience, William Jankowiak apparently focuses more attention on the universality of romantic passions, for example, the private experience of love as a cross-culturally identifiable emotional state, the pathways of interrelation between love, sex, and marriage, and the gender differences in romantic expression.[29] Jankowiak usefully reminds us of the pervasiveness of love in China and Chinese literature; however, to avoid oversimplified conclusions, some historical dimensions are required to understand both the continuity and the transformations of Chinese romantic emotions, as well as the complexity and richness of their manifestations. The cultural specificity of the emotional experiences present in the *caizi-jiaren* narratives challenges Jankowiak's generalized view of love as the individual power to undermine social order and the family, and the gender cliché that for men romantic fantasies stem from physical attraction but for women they stem from an evaluation of the partner's inner character or social status. Romantic love in premodern China was intimately intertwined with a broad range of emotional relationships other than sexual desire, such as filiality and loyalty. Their interactions demonstrate the particular ways in which personal choice was integrated into the institution of marriage through a variety of meaningful conflicts, and therefore offer the opportunity for more nuanced analyses of the phenomenon of love as it is experienced and expressed in different cultural and historical settings.

---

29 William Jankowiak, *Romantic Passion: A Universal Experience* (New York: Columbia University Press, 1997), 1–20; Renato Rosaldo, *Culture and Truth: The Remaking of Social Analysis* (Cambridge, MA: Beacon Press, 1989); Michelle Z. Rosaldo, *Knowledge and Passion: Ilongot Notions of Self and Social Life* (Cambridge: Cambridge University Press, 1980); Michelle Z. Rosaldo, "Toward an Anthropology of Self and Feeling," in *Culture Theory: Essays on Mind, Self, and Emotion*, ed. Richard A. Shweder and Robert A. LeVine (Cambridge: Cambridge University Press, 1984), 137–57.

Patrick Colm Hogan follows Jankowiak in addressing the manifestations of romantic love in Chinese literature, represented by Li Qingzhao's 李清照 (1084–1155) lyrics, and endeavors to integrate this into his overall exploration of the significance of literature to the interdisciplinary study of emotion.[30] His discussions are particularly valuable on certain common characteristics of romantic literature, the mutual relevance of ethics and emotion, and the emotional engagement with literature across cultures all over the world. To demonstrate the generalizability, however, he stresses the features of Chinese romance that are seemingly consistent with Western principles and practices, and fails to seek the specificities of China's trajectory, which are also what the Western theorizing about the history of emotions has largely ignored.

One notable exception is Paolo Santangelo and Gabor Boros's valuable study of emotions and love imagery in traditional Chinese philosophy and literature in parallel with those in European culture in *The Culture of Love in China and Europe*.[31] Santangelo productively offers both general outlines of the evolution of the notion of love and a wide ranging survey of its various facets in literary texts, concerning such themes as genuine love, supernatural transcendence, moral sentiments, the language of seduction, and so on, aiming to sketch the picture of the "regimes" and "counterregimes" of emotions in Chinese literary culture.[32] Consequently, he also makes room for us to detail the subtle process of emotional engagement in the mechanics of identity formation and associated ethical construction in Chinese romantic literature, and to rethink in depth the complexity of the self and agency.

In this recent trend, the so-called affective turn, the development of an awareness of emotions in social and cultural context has increasingly accentuated the critical role feelings play in the historical process, thereby accounting for changes in the way people think about self, affection, and personality.[33] Michelle Rosaldo draws on the influential writings of Clifford Geertz, who suggests that emotional experience is malleable and constituted by culture, to propose a constructionist notion of emotions.[34] She insists that "what individuals

30 Patrick Colm Hogan, *What Literature Teaches Us about Emotions* (Cambridge: Cambridge University Press, 2011).

31 Santangelo and Boros, *The Culture of Love*.

32 Santangelo, "Introductory Notes," 10.

33 On the "affective turn," see Patricia Ticineto Clough and Jean Halley, eds., *The Affective Turn: Theorizing the Social* (Durham, NC: Duke University Press, 2007); Jan Plamper, "The History of Emotions: An Interview with William Reddy, Barbara Rosenwein, and Peter Stearns," *History and Theory* 49, no. 2 (May 2010): 237–65.

34 Clifford Geertz, *The Interpretation of Cultures* (New York: Basic Books, 1973); Rosaldo, *Knowledge and Passion*; Rosaldo, "Toward an Anthropology of Self and Feeling."

can think and feel is overwhelmingly a product of socially organized modes of action and of talk."[35] In Rosaldo's view, affect is culturally ordered and does not exist in isolation from thought.[36] She reinforces her stance with feminist concerns, which make possible a critique of the received Western common sense that women are inherently more emotional than men, and thus are supposed to be excluded from public life. Like Rosaldo, other theorists of emotion step in to fill the traditional gap in which emotions are separated from rationality and thought.[37] As is stated in Michael Hardt's preface to *The Affective Turn: Theorizing the Social*, "Affects straddle these two divides: between the mind and body, and between actions and passions."[38]

Furthermore, Abu-Lughod and Lutz justify this constructionist stance on emotions by distancing themselves from the culture concept and yet following Foucault's concept of discourse and power by raising the question of "emotion as discursive practice."[39] They believe that discourses differ from culture in that they are potentially mutable, and thus can be changed over time. They argue that emotions are essentially discursive and construct yet another place in which power is covertly exercised over us. "Like Foucault," Lutz states, "I am interested in how the emotions – like other aspect of a culturally postulated psyche – are the place in which the most minute and local social practices are linked up with the large scale organization of power."[40] In this, Abu and Lutz seek to conceive of individuals who could be free of culture and power, and are able to criticize or resist them.

As a matter of fact, a review of the historical development of Chinese romantic discourse will contribute to an alternative conceptualization of self, which is different from both the autonomous individual self and the illusory self completely determined by culture and discourse. Such a self is an evolving construct generated through a process of self-exploration, self-reflection, and self-alteration, and above all fosters the concept of intersubjectivity that emphasizes the self as a product of both socialization and emotional affiliation

35 Rosaldo, "Toward an Anthropology of Self and Feeling," 147.

36 Ibid., 137.

37 See Lila Abu-Lughod, *Veiled Sentiments: Honor and Poetry in a Bedouin Society* (Berkeley: University of California Press, 1986); Catherine A. Lutz, *Unnatural Emotion: Everyday Sentiments on a Micronesian Atoll and Their Challenge to Western Theory* (Chicago: University of Chicago Press, 1988).

38 Ticineto Clough and Halley, *The Affective Turn: Theorizing the Social*, xi.

39 Lila Abu-Lughod and Catherine A. Lutz, "Introduction: Emotion, Discourse, and the Politics of Everyday Life," in *Language and the Politics of Emotion*, ed. Lila Abu-Lughod and Catherine A. Lutz (Cambridge: Cambridge University Press, 1990), 10.

40 Lutz, *Unnatural Emotion*, 7.

with others. It is a self that can be molded by culture and discourse, a self that can make change, and which therefore is often provisional and personally variable, but at the same time achieves agency and historical significance, as revealed in the heroine's meaningful struggles to resist the gender-biased view of self in the woman-authored *tanci* work *Karmic Bonds of Reincarnation* (*Zaisheng yuan* 再生緣), as well as in the protagonists' complex attempts at both self-affirmation and self-questioning in *The Dream of the Red Chamber*. As such, an exploration of the course of the development of the *caizi-jiaren* genre will show how emotion functions as a medium of negotiating between the individual and their social/cultural construction, and how the flow of feelings engages with identity formation and is fundamentally infused with the history of thought.

Based on the trajectory of the shifting modes of the *caizi-jiaren* story type, this investigation will cover a broad range of texts spanning from the ninth century through the eighteenth century – from Tang *chuanqi* 傳奇 tales through Ming-Qing drama, fiction, and *tanci* – aiming to show how the conventions of romance address cultural and ideological changes in the representation of desire, self, and women. My focus is on the presentation of this sexual fantasy mainly as it is transmitted in fictional texts written by men, but also in a few cases by women, their *tanci* works in particular. In Tang *chuanqi*, romances usually take place on the margins of society (represented by haunted chambers or brothels), most typically between a wayfaring scholar and a courtesan. These stories address a variety of identity crises that Tang literati were faced with in terms of the infeasibility of the marriage system, the unpredictability of city life, and the pressures of officialdom. The increasing maturity of the imperial examination system made possible the literati's autonomy, while a profound crisis of culture lay in the inability of the examination system to provide moral validation. In particular, in the latter half of the eighth century, as the Tang coped with decentralization and rebellion, literary intellectuals began to look to the common needs of the people, and at the same time to rebuilding the ideological and moral grounds of the imperial state and the role of literati in it. In these Tang tales, desire represents a kind of ambiguity or deviance, hinting at the difficulties in, and the ultimate impossibility of, expressing *qing* and the self in the existing mode of expression. The presentation of the hero's and the heroine's perspectives often betrays an ironic tone, and different viewpoints circulating in the literati's interpretive community also set these perspectives in ambiguous opposition to each other. These numerous voices serve not merely to address doubt and anxiety about romance, but also reflect a process of ongoing negotiation, in the sense that these romantic tales end in the failure to resolve the profound conflicts between private desire and social decorum, thus imbuing the narratives with a sense of open-endedness that is seldom seen in the later romantic tradition. Although they also imaginatively solve the moral gap by way of suspending desire or passion in an aesthetic realm less constrained by moral qualms or by subjecting the passions to a disciplinary code of manners, either way evinces that contemporary men of letters saw desire and sensitivity as falling outside of social decorum and morality, and thus passion could only be disciplined by moral codes that were external to it in nature.

Song (960–1279) *chuanqi* tales began to reshape the relationship between *qing* and morality, developing a discourse of correspondence between heavenly principles (*tianli* 天理) and human feelings (*renqing* 人情), rather than the conflicts between them. Song romances often endow the heroine with moral power, which ensures her some kind of subjectivity. This mode of writing was informed by the emergence of Neo-Confucianism, whose focal point was the shift from the reliance on external classics to a focus on the innate moral mind. Song literati tended to believe that each individual could realize the pattern of heaven that was in their own nature, and this worked as the ultimate foundation for moral life. Hence, the rise of Neo-Confucianism is regarded as a signal of the emerging early modernity. A newfound attention to human affairs and the autonomy of the individual dominated Song intellectual life. Accordingly, Song romantic tales attempt to reconceptualize the self as grounds for morality. They downplay the sense of anxiety and tension that occurs in Tang romance, inspiring a diverse and uncertain world where normative models are at best a matter of interpretation.

When it comes to *caizi-jiaren* drama and fiction in the Ming-Qing period, the imaginary space tends to move from the social periphery to the boudoir, or gardens connected to the boudoir in some way. The heroine and her desire become more domesticated, and thus vindicated. That is to say, the *caizi-jiaren* romance is legitimized and integrated into the social order through the moralization of desire and love. In comparison with Song intellectual trends, the late Ming witnessed a further emphasis on the present and the internal – not the innate moral mind, but the spontaneity of *qing*. Emotions were thought of as emanating from a core of authenticity that made moral perceptions possible. The literati elite who were impacted by Xinxue 心學 (Learning of the Mind) insisted on the existence of an inborn moral sense that led to virtuous impulses of "sentiment." In late Ming romantic narratives, passion and one's moral nature actually converge, and the individual's own *qing* itself is a source of virtue. Moral awareness became available to the mind via natural sentiment. The belief that everyone was capable of feeling produced a new optimism about the strength of inborn sentiment as the foundation of a better social order. Late Ming literati not only used romances to represent a new elite sensibility or taste, but also invested them with a new seriousness, elevating conjugal love as a new cultural and moral ideal. For example, *The Peony Pavilion* (*Mudan ting* 牡丹亭), generally acknowledged as having established a new model of *caizi-jiaren* romance in the late imperial period, attempts to construct a new selfhood through the power of *qing*. Replete with subjectively rich moments, this romantic play both engenders a kind of interiority and explores the possibility of self. Its heroine is exclusively concerned with her own commitment to an ideal of passion and self, although she fulfills her dream in the end through the reintegration of the self to a larger social whole. As such, late Ming romance generally looks inward, but at the same time extends the concept of *qing* into human relations or social bonds other than the domestic sphere, thereby rebuilding the relationship between self and society, and realizing the ideal of a "world of *qing*."

After the Ming–Qing transition, the *caizi-jiaren* romance is further idealized, yet in a modified way, or parodied and rejected with the aim of reshaping the literati elite's social and cultural identity. Some of these narratives contextualize the reconciliation of self-interest and morality in the larger cultural trend of the post-Ming reflection on the late Ming's celebration of *qing*. Early Qing scholar-beauty novels emerged as a new type of emotional refuge, which set the stage for the elaboration of the new emotional style of sentimentalism. They demonstrate a new interest in self-fashioning and resocialization in the immediate aftermath of the dynastic transition. These works reflect on the late Ming understanding of *qing* and move to a new sense of self through an emphasis on innate *cai* 才 (talent), and in this way sexual relations are channeled into newly responsible ends. They also highlight a kind of male friendship based on talent and the establishment of local community as a stage for cultural and social practices. The focus on male sociality in these romances combines community solace over the fall of a Han empire with an interest in self-fulfillment; the resulting expression is a complex balance between the autonomy of elite communities and their accommodation with the new regime. Early Qing scholar-beauty novels take on a new emotional ideal, in which intense friendship and affectionate marriage are linked.

On the other hand, *The Dream of the Red Chamber* evinces a tendency to undercut the very ideals of *qing* and self-construction that it embraces. It is less about the repression and liberation of human desire than about the revelation of how it is created. The representation of women in this novel resists a reductive typology insofar as their portrayals no longer just index collective ideals, but illustrate the diversity of desire and positions, whereby the novel displays a process of simultaneously fabricating and demystifying individuality. In *The Dream of the Red Chamber*, emotions are seen as the most authentic part of life, an experience that facilitates subject and identity formation, and simultaneously as something to be transcended and which offers us the capacity for reflection or action. It is in this respect that *The Dream of the Red Chamber* reflects a profound sense of epistemological uncertainty in the eighteenth-century intellectual culture, in which the late Ming sentimentalist discourse, together with its optimistic hopes for self-fashioning and social ethics, was repeatedly brought into question, although the sentimentalist conceptions of the previous era lived on in a certain way.

Not until the second half of the eighteenth century does the romantic lover in the domesticated space change into the adventurous woman on the road, while the theme of love in conventional romances is replaced by the heroine's adventurous pursuit of a public career at court, a new theme represented in many women's *tanci* works as well as some novels by male literati such as *Flowers in the Mirror* (*Jinghua yuan* 鏡花緣). Women's *tanci* works of this era outwardly follow the tradition of the *caizi-jiaren* romance. Yet they rewrite conventional romantic archetypes to exhibit the ways in which women attempt to act upon their own initiative through social norms, and also the profound plight that the patriarchal system imposes on the female individual who has various desires, both public and private. It is through social participation and the experience of this plight that the heroine becomes a subject. This kind of writing, furthermore, facilitated the formation of a "reading community" among women who wrote and read *tanci*, and a special "textual relationship" among these women. All of this indicates that subjectivity was an ongoing construction. Women authors in this unique mode of romance developed a mode of dialogue – both the voice of the principal narrator and that of her interlocutor present different versions of a self and reflect on how to inscribe the female self in narrative. These women's *tanci* works thus maintain a collective, unending fantasy, which raises particularly problematic questions about individual psychology, personal fulfillment, and gender identity.

Here, the imaginary space is not a simple metaphor, but signifies broader paradigmatic shifts and leads to the dialectics of within and without, open and closed. These shifts are no doubt results of extensive transformations occurring in society and intellectual culture that characterize the focal periods of this study. The unfolding process of self-questing, the exploration of the ramifications of desire, and the unremitting self-questioning were part of a larger cultural project, fostered by a questioning and new awareness of the place of the individual and emotion within the social matrix. In examining various forms of agency in the shifts of the *caizi-jiaren* mode, I explore the early modernity of certain late-imperial phenomena, as well as a variety of discourses reflecting on its inherent limits and dilemmas. I trace a path through the controversies about the connections between the different conceptions of the self and their moral sources, and show how these discourses developed out of earlier pictures of human identity through both negation and continuation.

This study consists of six main chapters. Chapter 1 surveys the history of the Confucian understandings of the self and desire (as a category serving to shape our understandings of the self), and their relationships with social morality, thereby providing the intellectual contexts in which romance culture bloomed, and a general picture of how the development of these discourses assumes a role in the ramifications of self-representation in various romances. Chapter 2 deals with Tang romances as well as some later romantic tales in classical Chinese. Through re-reading three key texts – Jiang Fang's 蔣防 (792?–835?) "The Story of Huo Xiaoyu" (*Huo Xiaoyu zhuan* 霍小玉傳), Yuan Zhen's 元稹 (779–831) "The Story of Yingying" (*Yingying zhuan* 鶯鶯傳), and Bai Xingjian's 白行簡 (776–826) "The Story of Li Wa" (*Li Wa zhuan* 李娃傳) – I argue that Tang *chuanqi* narratives address doubt and anxiety about romance, as well as imply an attitude of openness toward the emotional interests of the characters, by presenting a variety of conflicting discourses of love and morality. How ways of representing women and love were both inherited and changed in later romantic tales will also be briefly examined.

Chapters 3 and 4 consider the scholar-beauty drama and fiction in late imperial China as examples of the canonization of the *caizi-jiaren* pattern, which makes use of passion for social harmony rather than addressing the problem of passion. In this part, I demonstrate how these texts shape a collective self-identity by uniting sensibility with morality, defining femininity and female subjectivity, and addressing a common cultural narrative. Chapter 3 investigates three of the most beloved examples of scholar-beauty drama – Wang Shifu's 王實甫 (1260–1336) *The Story of the Western Wing* (*Xixiang ji* 西廂記), Tang Xianzu's 湯顯祖 (1550–1616) *The Peony Pavilion*, and Meng Chengshun's 孟稱舜 (ca. 1599–1684) *Mistress and Maid* (*Jiaohong ji* 嬌紅記) – illuminating the various ways in which they construct a common self through the power of *qing*. These plays render *qing* as a kind of life force that is naturalized and ultimately integrated into social morality. Therefore, they give less prominence to the conflicts between desire and morality than to those between generations or between good and evil, thereby demonstrating that spontaneous yet socially responsible love can be moral as well. I argue that the plays present both cases of individuating emotional relations and those of arousing empathic emotions in the recurrence of the standard romantic plot.

Whether these plays celebrate subjectivity or the intersubjective relationships of lovers, however, romantic love is seen as a source of virtue, and thus a force for realizing and reshaping social morality, and for reforming human nature.

Chapter 4 examines how early Qing scholar-beauty novels evoke the sense of self with new frankness through the replacement of *qing* with *cai*, and further express a sense of community and male sociality based on talent. Moreover, the discussion concerns how gender tropes work in scholar-beauty novels, and how the talented woman figure serves as both the agent and the product of the early Qing Han elite's self-fashioning project in reaction to the Manchu conquest. In exploring the possible historical explanations of developments in scholar-beauty novels, this chapter demonstrates how the newfound focus on talent, mutual appreciation, friendship, and community helped establish an emotional refuge for literary men to construct personal identities, promote cultural autonomy, and eventually reintegrate into the new political order of the fledgling Qing dynasty.

Chapters 5 and 6 take up two masterpieces of the eighteenth century, Cao Xueqin's 曹雪芹 (1715–1763) *The Dream of the Red Chamber* and Chen Duansheng's 陳端生 (1751–1796) *tanci* work *Karmic Bonds of Reincarnation*, both of which continue to work within the narrative confines of the *caizi-jiaren* romance, but to some degree also parody or reject the ideal of romance in prior scholar-beauty drama and fiction. Chapter 5 explores the subtlety with which *The Dream of the Red Chamber* represents the workings of female desire and proffers a chorus of multiple perspectives. By analyzing the skillful manipulation of multiple points of view that switch between the author, the Stone, and the hero, Baoyu, I illustrate how *The Dream of the Red Chamber* produces an active and dynamic process of acquiring self-knowledge, a self-conscious process of critical inquiry that subverts and problematizes dualistic classification, such as truth/fiction, self/other, real/unreal, and so on. The question of how Baoyu invents a new language of emotions represented by *yiyin* 意淫 is stressed, in the sense that this term is utilized to represent as a form of deep empathetic bonding, fostering non-egoistic imaginations of emotion-rich situations. I also demonstrate that the construction of the utopian community by means of the poetry club in *The Dream of the Red Chamber* plays a part both in claiming a cultural identity through the negotiation with late Ming and early Qing philosophical and literary culture, and raising questions concerning the relationship of communal utopias with public order.

Chapter 6 concerns women writers' self-exploration in their own *tanci* works, focusing in particular on the most distinguished such work, *Karmic Bonds of Reincarnation*. By focusing on topoi such as the garden, self-portraiture, and cross-dressing, I explore how *Karmic Bonds of Reincarnation* rewrites conventional romance not only to illuminate, but also to construct, the interior being of its female characters. Such a construction of interiority fashions a female subject who not only transgresses sexual and social norms, but also experiences the profound plight imposed on the female by the patriarchal system, and further shapes a collective fantasy within a female reading/writing community. I argue that, through the agent of fantasy, the woman writer both interiorized the phenomenon of cross-dressing within a female perspective and improvised a personal variation on romantic discourses and prevailing gender norms, such that the trope took on new meanings for female authors/readers, opening up possibilities for self-exploration and self-alteration.

The texts discussed in this study foreground the ways that fantasy and desire work to animate moral norms, which we are constrained by, but with which we must also live, in order to invigorate critical and ethical reflection. In focusing on romances that raise significant issues about desire, agency, and gender, I have elected to consider texts by men and women writers, since gender issues intersect with social issues in ways that complicate simple binary oppositions between men and women. The material here has been structured so that the texts provide us with shifts in narrative dynamics that can be best understood by exploring works across a broad historical period. In exploring this range of material, I venture to relate Chinese fiction to broader questions about intellectual and cultural changes, and thus reflect on Confucian society from a historical perspective, rather than read it as merely an unchangeable whole. My hope for this study is that an examination of romance's negotiation with morality will complicate our understanding of traditional China's discourses of self, emotion, and society, and of agency beset by both contradictions and compromise, and at the same time contribute to the debates concerning women's agency in premodern China. Although other studies have touched upon romance and female agency as tangential subjects, my study provides a sustained and analytical reading of these issues, and attempts to capture new ways to read canonized literature, in the hope that premodern Chinese romance can also be studied in the contexts of contemporary debates on desire, emotion, self, and ethics and of the new and more complex views that have emerged from these debates.

CHAPTER 1

Desire, Self, and Society: a Historical Review

One of the critical concerns in Neo-Confucian thought is the question of self. In the earlier Chinese tradition, Confucius and Confucianism had attached much importance to self-cultivation and self-fulfillment. From the twelfth to seventeenth centuries – the period in which Neo-Confucianism was prevalent – a process of internalization, along with other significant changes in society and culture, took place in the intellectual field. Both the emergence of Lixue 理學 (Learning of the Principle) in the Southern Song (1127–1279) and the rise of Xinxue 心學 (Learning of the Mind) in the mid-Ming (ca. 1450–1522) are often taken as major transitions to a new stage of scholarly thought. Despite a diversity of views within the discourse spanning the Song to the Ming dynasties, the central concern about self was nonetheless shared by those whose philosophical positions differed in other respects. Overall, as a cumulative and self-referential tradition, Neo-Confucianism sought to maintain ideological continuity in unremittingly redefining the self's relation to the world. In this chapter, I examine this Confucian self by describing its genesis and revisiting the internal history of Neo-Confucianism in terms of the conceptions of self and its moral sources.[1] I do not conduct a full survey of Confucian thought but instead I focus on the significant turning points in the Confucian tradition, particularly those corresponding with the critical shifts in the *caizi-jiaren* model that are addressed the following chapters, such as those of the mid-Tang period, the Song dynasty, and the late Ming and early Qing. For this purpose, I will first contextualize these thoughts by reexamining the ideological foundations of the imperial state and the role of literati in them, and then trace some of the key concepts that are repeatedly present through these turning points, which define the notion of a person's inwardness or true core: the mind (*xin* 心), authenticity (*zhen* 真)/sincerity (*cheng* 誠), and nature (*xing* 性)/feelings (*qing* 情).

Confucianism from the outset had been deeply preoccupied with the problem of self or personhood. In the *Analects* (*Lunyu* 論語), when Confucius is asked what it takes to be truly human, he answers, "Now the man of perfect

1 The Buddhist and Daoist conceptions of self are not the focus of my discussion, although they deserve to be another topic of study. Concerning the expression of self, also consult Robert E. Hegel and Richard C. Hessney, eds., *Expressions of Self in Chinese Literature* (New York: Columbia University Press, 1985).

HTTPS://DOI.ORG/10.1163/9789004693357-003

virtue, wishing to be established himself, seeks also to establish others; wishing to be enlarged himself, he seeks also to enlarge others. To be able to judge of others by what is nigh in ourselves – this may be called the art of virtue" 夫仁者，己欲立而立人，己欲達而達人。能近取譬，可謂仁之方也已.[2] In other words, Confucius defines one's "self" in relation to others, and reciprocity is a fundamental premise of his view of self-cultivation. There can be no fulfillment for the individual in isolation from his fellow men.

Furthermore, Confucius emphasizes that self-cultivation is a gradual process of learning.[3] Both cultural engagement and moral self-control are essential to self-cultivation, and yet the ultimate self-realization is a spontaneous and joyful self-discipline, that is, a status in which "I could follow what my heart desired, without transgressing what was right" 從心所欲，不踰矩.[4] As Wm. Theodore de Bary has aptly pointed out, "for Confucius the individual exists in a delicate balance with his social environment, reconciling his own self-respect for others, his inner freedom with the limiting circumstances of his own situation in life."[5] For a Confucian, learning aims, ultimately, to enable the individual spontaneously to do the morally correct thing regardless of the circumstances.

This kind of voluntary effort, or joyful self-examination, is further articulated by Mencius as a psychological process, that is, cultivating the sincerity inside oneself. "All the ten thousand things are there in me. There is no greater joy for me than to find, on self-examination, that I am true to myself." 萬物皆備於我矣。反身而誠，樂莫大焉.[6] The perfect fit between the reality of who we are and what we become conscious of ensures that the moral behaviors – that are predicated on the inward goodness – are true to our real selves. This focus

---

2 Yang Bojun 楊伯峻, ed., *Lunyu yizhu* 論語譯註 (Beijing: Zhonghua shuju, 1980), 6.30, p. 65; James Legge, *The Chinese Classics, with a Translation, Critical and Exegetical Notes, Prolegomena, and Copious Indexes*, vol. 1: *Confucian Analects, the Great Learning, and the Doctrine of the Mean* (Taipei: SMC Publishing, 1991), 194.

3 "I find inspiration by intoning the songs, I learn where to stand from observing ritual propriety, and I find fulfilment in playing music" 興於詩，立於禮，成於樂. Here, poetry stands for culture in general. Confucius's concept of music (*yue* 樂) was always linked with rites (*li* 禮), and thus they were often spoken of together. Therefore, this observation refers to an inspiration toward wholeness, toward an ideal of self-completion through art. See Yang Bojun, *Lunyu yizhu.*, 8.8, p. 81; Roger T. Ames and Henry Rosemont, Jr., trans., *The Analects of Confucius: A Philosophical Translation* (New York: Random House, 2010), 122.

4 Yang Bojun, *Lunyu yizhu*, 2.4, p. 12; Legge, *Confucian Analects*, 147.

5 Wm. Theodore de Bary, *Learning for One's Self: Essays on the Individual in Neo-Confucian Thought* (New York: Columbia University Press, 1991), 3–4.

6 Yang Bojun 楊伯峻, ed., *Mengzi yizhu* 孟子譯註 (Beijing: Zhonghua shuju, 1992), 13.4, p. 302; translation from D.C. Lau, trans., *Mencius* (London: Penguin Books, 1970), 182.

on unity later becomes a universal Neo-Confucian claim about the constitution of reality, which is grounded in the coherence of self and others, and of self and things as well. Song Neo-Confucians asserted that "sincerity" (*cheng*) is the principle that links self-cultivation to the larger organism of the external world. For them, "sincerity" serves as the guiding force illuminating inner truth and hence facilitating self-cultivation.

The Neo-Confucians sought to provide literati with a way of thinking for themselves by declaiming "learning for oneself" (*wei ji er xue* 爲己而學). According to Peter Bol, Neo-Confucianism began on the margins, as the attempt to find an alternative to the orthodoxy of that day.[7] He contends that Neo-Confucianism shifted the focus of self-cultivation away from cultural activities to the cultivation of moral conduct, and that such a change was inevitably linked to the transformation of the elite group in Chinese society known as the *shi* 士.[8] In the seventh century, the *shi* were an elite patronized by great aristocratic clans, whereas in the tenth and eleventh centuries the *shi* were the civil bureaucrats, and they finally became the more numerous, but rarely illustrious, local elite families in the Southern Song. "A crisis of faith in the ability of culture to influence human behavior" began to take shape after the An Lushan rebellion of 755.[9] Bol claims that some literary men such as Han Yu 韓愈 (768–824) began to seek to recover the original moral efficacy of literary writing, and thus launched the classical prose movement. Han Yu viewed the Way of the sage as the ultimate source of the value of literary writings and the object of learning, which provided a man with a worth independent of family status.[10] Han Yu's ideas about how every literatus could write in his own style gave classical-style writers of the eleventh century an intellectual

---

7 See Peter K. Bol, *Neo-Confucianism in History* (Cambridge, MA: Harvard University Asia Center, 2008), 3.

8 Peter K. Bol, *"This Culture of Ours": Intellectual Transitions in T'ang and Sung China* (Stanford, CA: Stanford University Press, 1992), 32–75.

9 Ibid., 109.

10 The classical prose movement, or *guwen yundong* 古文運動, which flourished in the late eighth and early ninth centuries, advocated a form of prose modeled on the classics as a reaction against the "parallel prose" prevalent from the Six Dynasties to the Tang dynasty. The proponents of this movement, such as Han Yu and Liu Zongyuan 柳宗元 (773–819), claimed that literature should return to a simpler and classical style, so as to illuminate the Way (*wen yi ming dao* 文以明道). On this movement, see William H. Nienhauser, Jr., *The Indiana Companion to Traditional Chinese Literature* (Bloomington: Indiana University Press, 1986), 494; Bol, *"This Culture of Ours"*, 127; Ge Xiaoyin 葛曉音, "Lun Tang Song de guwen gexin yu rudao yanbian de guanxi" 論唐代的古文革新與儒道演變的關係, in *Han Tang wenxue de shanbian* 漢唐文學的嬗變 (Beijing: Beijing daxue chubanshe, 1990), 156–79.

agenda. Writing in the classical style demonstrated the attempt to learn for oneself rather than follow the socially acceptable style of literary writing that the imperial examination required. The masters of the classical prose movement in both the mid-Tang and the Northern Song, in fact, discussed the relationship between the Way and prose (*wen* 文) precisely through an emphasis on the writer's subjectivity – the writer should cultivate himself in the pursuit of the Way, and then present the Way in prose.[11]

After a transitional era that began in the latter half of the Tang and continued into the Northern Song, the late Song saw the literati's pursuit of a new solution to maintain their elite identity, due to a growing incapability on the part of the Song government to provide the elite with governmental service. At the same time, the Song government was increasingly unable to exercise institutional discipline over the elite. The downward mobility of the elite compelled them to compete for land and other resources in order to support their families, often furthering their own interests at the expense of others.[12] It was both against such a self-interested tendency and the pursuit of self-identity alternative to the political one that Zhu Xi 朱熹 (1130–1200) shifted moral authority away from the political system and toward the individual, with a new conception of the self as grounds for morality in society and politics.

Zhu Xi's theory is based on the premise that the principle is inherent in every kind of thing. For Zhu Xi, all principles are present even before the formation of the physical universe, so they are both abstract and eternal.[13] As such, Zhu Xi endorsed and further elaborated Cheng Yi's 程頤 (1033–1107) doctrine that "nature (*xing* 性) is the principle," indicating that all things that are inherently united embody the principle, and the principle is likewise endowed in all human beings as their nature. Simultaneously, Zhu Xi emphasizes that "Without the mind, the principle has no place to attach itself" 理無心，則無着處.[14] While he distinguishes physical nature from general human nature, from Zhu's perspective, the principle cannot be manifested without physical endowment, in that we cannot know the principle except through the mind, while it is also because of our physical endowment that the mind is not properly manifested. The mind originates from the principle, so it is originally good – this part Zhu Xi calls the "mind of the Way" (*daoxin*

11 See Zhu Gang's 朱剛 discussion in "Wen yi zaidao" 文以載道, in *Tang Song "guwen yundong" yu shidafu wenxue* 唐宋"古文運動"与士大夫文學 (Shanghai: Fudan daxue chubanshe, 2013), 27–42.

12 See Bol, *"This Culture of Ours"*, 58–75.

13 Zhu Xi, *Zhuzi yulei* 朱子語類 (Changsha: Yuelu shushe, 1997), 1.1.

14 Ibid., 5.77.

道心); but the part of the mind which is concealed by physical endowment is the "mind of man" (*renxin* 人心). Hence, in order to make our original mind become visible, we need to cultivate our inner selves.

Such a focus on the mind can be thought of as a kind of subjectivism. In his "Guanxin shuo" 觀心說 (Essay on the Viewing of the Mind), Zhu Xi claims:

> The mind is that with which man rules his body. It is one and not a duality, is subject and not object, and controls the external world instead of being controlled by it. Therefore, if we examine external objects with the mind, their principles will be apprehended.
>
> 夫心者，人之所以主乎身者也，一而不二者也，爲主而不爲客者也，命物而不命於物者也。故以心觀物，則物之理得。[15]

Here, the mind mediates a person's perception of the principle in things and of one's own nature, thereby providing an innate moral sensibility. When the individual begins to investigate or examine external objects, he may think an object valuable because it embodies the principle. Yet the principle is not a significance expressed or embodied in the object, but in the mind. Hence, Zhu Xi views the individual as a self-determining moral agent. The moral agency here is the mind, or more specifically the mind which controls human appetites and desires, follows principle or the inherent nature, and ultimately makes possible active communication with heaven, earth, and others. It is the mind that works as the unifying center of the person and the agency.

Elsewhere, Zhu Xi goes further to suggest the intricate relations between *xin*, *xing*, and *qing*, saying that "the mind unites the emotions and the nature, but it is not equal to nature and emotion so that it cannot be distinguished from them" 心統攝性情，非儱侗与性情爲一物而不分別也.[16] He explains, "Once *xing* emerges into concrete form, it is *qing*" 性才發，便是情.[17] Although Neo-Confucians often followed Zhu Xi's formulation of the elemental distinction between *xing* as the fixed, latent aspect of being, and *qing* as the emergence and actualization of *xing*, they simultaneously tended to believe that *xing* and *qing* are contingent and interwoven.

15 Zhu Xi, *Huian xiansheng Zhu wengong wenji* 晦庵先生朱文公文集 (Beijing: Beijing tushuguan chubanshe, 2006), 4.4957–60.

16 Zhu, *Zhuzi yulei*, 5.85.

17 Ibid., 5.82.

The discussion of human nature in relation to emotions can be traced to Han Yu.[18] In his oft-quoted "Yuan xing" 原性 (On the Origins of Human Nature), Han Yu suggests that human nature is what men receive at birth, while emotions arise in response to contact with the external world. For the higher grade of human nature, it "abides in the Mean" although it is stirred by emotions (*dong er chu qi zhong* 動而處其中), whereas for the lower grade, it merely follows emotions (*zhi qing er xing* 直情而行). Yet human nature can be improved through education or government.[19] Han Yu's idea is further developed by his disciple, Li Ao 李翺 (772–841), who elevates *qing* to a status of being inseparable from *xing*, or the materialization of *xing*. He argues:

> Neither the nature nor the emotions exist independently of one another. Nonetheless, without the nature the emotions would have nowhere to be born from. For the emotions are born from the nature: they are not emotions of themselves, but rely on the nature to be emotions. The nature is not a nature of itself but shows its brightness through the emotions. … Is the sage without emotions? The sage is absolutely still and without movement, arrives without traveling, shows his spirit-like power through not speaking, and gives light without shining.
>
> 性與情不相無也，雖然無性則情無所生矣，是情由性而生；情不自情，因性而情；性不自性，由情以明。……聖人者豈無其情耶？聖人者，寂然不動，不往而到，不言而神，不耀而光。[20]

In other words, emotions derive from nature, and thus are also inherent within us; at the same time, one can attain true nature only through detaching oneself from emotional responses. Li Ao presents us with a dialectical relation between *qing* and *xing* – although emotions are the outer forms of human nature, true nature has to keep emotions in balance. Han Yu's and Li Ao's arguments foreshadow the thoughts of Neo-Confucians from the Song all the way

18 For a detailed survey of the development of the relationship between *xing*, *qing*, and *yu*, see Huang, *Desire and Fictional Narrative*, 24–35; Yu, *Rereading the Stone*, 56–82.

19 Han Yu, *Han Yu quanji jiaozhu*, 2686; discussed in Charles Hartman, *Han Yu and the T'ang Search for Unity* (Princeton, NJ: Princeton University Press, 1986), 204–205; Bian Xiaoxuan 卞孝萱 and Zhang Qinghua 張清華, *Han Yu pingzhuan* 韓愈評傳 (Nanjing: Nanjing daxue chubanshe, 1998), 263–67.

20 Li Ao 李翺, *Li Wengong ji* 李文公集, Sibu congkan 四部叢刊, 2.1a–13b; for an English translation and discussion, see T.H. Barrett, *Li Ao: Buddhist, Taoist, or Neo-Confucian* (New York: Oxford University Press, 1992), 96–97.

to the early Qing – a kind of "materialism" that considers intrinsic principles as merely being brought to realization through the medium of material reality.[21]

For Song Neo-Confucians, the unity of the principle is both there in the external world and in our mind. They defined *xing* by recourse to its constituent components: "The character *xing* consists of *sheng* 生 and *xin* 心. It is because human beings have the principle complete in their minds that it is called nature" 性字從生從心，是人生來具是理于心，方名之曰性.[22] Zhu Xi further highlights that both *xing* and *qing* conform to the mind (*xin*) ("both the character *xing* and *qing* have the radical *xin*"; 性、情字皆從心).[23] Hence, the mind is able to grasp the coherence of the principle that all people possess innately. On the other hand, the term *qing* refers to common feelings shared by oneself and others, and is often stretched to signify the entire ground of concrete existence. Sometimes, in the Chinese tradition of thought, *qing* may also appear as the essential nature of things, or the basic conditions of the entire world or cosmic order.[24] Neo-Confucians tended to see *qing* as emotional responses filtered through an awareness of coherence as well. Zhu Xi endorses Mencius's view that "*qing* enables people to do good" (*qing keyi wei shan* 情可以爲善), although he interprets it as "the correct *qing* flowing from our nature is originally all good" 那情之正，從性中流出來者，元無不好也.[25] Therefore, the mind also serves as the locus of the link between one's internal coherence and emotional responses to the external world. Accordingly, Neo-Confucians believe in a state of sincerity (*cheng*), in which emotional responses are consonant with the innate coherence of the principle. Zhu Xi asserts that *cheng* means being true to the mind's intimation to the good. He clarifies the term *cheng* in *The Doctrine of the Mean* as follows: "Sincerity is spoken of as the mind, and this is fundamental" 誠以心言，本也.[26] He further explains that "only the ultimate sincerity can fully develop one's nature" 惟天下至誠，爲能盡其性, by "making one completely recognize one's nature and deal with it correctly" 知之無不明而處之無不當也.[27] This is how the internalization emerges

---

21 See Andrew Plaks's discussion on the term *qing* in Wai-yee Li and Yuri Pines, eds., *Keywords in Chinese Culture* (Hong Kong: Chinese University Press, 2020), 324–29.

22 Chen Chu 陳淳, *Beixi zi yi* 北溪字義 (Beijing: Zhonghua shuju, 1983), 6; translation with modification from Wing-tsit Chan, trans., *Neo Confucian Terms Explained: The Pei-hsi tzu-i* (New York: Columbia University Press, 1986), 38.

23 Zhu, *Zhuzi yulei*, 5.83.

24 See Andrew Plaks's exposition on this matter, in "Before the Emergence of Desire," in Li and Pines, *Keywords in Chinese Culture*, 324–29.

25 Zhu, *Zhuzi yulei*, 5.85; translation from Wing-tsit Chan, trans. and comp., *A Source Book in Chinese Philosophy* (Princeton, NJ: Princeton University Press, 1963), 631.

26 Zhu Xi, *Sishu jizhu* 四書集註 (Changsha: Yuelu shushe, 1987), 48.

27 Ibid., 46–47.

in Zhu Xi's theory, in which one can realize one's innate potential to be a moral subject in the larger organism of the world.

In fact, Neo-Confucians all believe that human beings can cultivate and realize what they can experience personally because they possess it innately. For Zhu Xi, however, the mind is meant to understand its own nature or principle, whereas for the Ming thinker Wang Yangming 王陽明 (1472–1529), an advocate of the Xinxue School, the mind was the principle itself, and the goal of self-cultivation is to cultivate the mind's awareness of coherence, thereby attaining the state in which the mind is capable of interacting with the world around it spontaneously and morally – his teachings are concerned with the real foundation of ethical behaviors. Compared with Zhu Xi, Wang Yangming's inward turn was even more evident.

The relation of the human mind and nature in Zhu's thought is further addressed and expanded by Wang Yangming. Wang's thought exemplifies the same tension as that of Zhu Xi, that is, how to redefine the role of the *shi* during rapid social change. Many of the phenomena of the Song-Yuan period reappeared in the mid-late Ming when Wang Yangming lived – the growth of commerce that created a new prosperity, new sources of power, and local elite activism – yet there also appeared new divisions between the court and literati as well as new value systems.[28] The early Ming dynasty was interested in establishing a state ideology, thereby providing a model for a new social order and encouraging social stability in an impoverished country that had undergone decades of war. In these circumstances, Neo-Confucian teachings were subsumed into a national orthodoxy that restrained literati minds.[29] Not only did the early Ming state promote Neo-Confucian learning and combine it with the imperial examination system, but it also transferred the Neo-Confucian vision of the self-supervising local community into legislations aimed at making it universal and obligatory.[30] When these legislations began to fail, however, Neo-Confucians attempted to distance themselves from the court and recover the original transformative power of Neo-Confucianism, thereby regaining their social mission through a revival of literati voluntarism. They sought to escape from the state's ideological control and saw themselves as the proper moral source.

---

28 See Timothy Brook, *The Confusions of Pleasure: Commerce and Culture in Ming China* (Berkeley: University of California Press, 1998).

29 See Benjamin A. Elman, "The Foundation of 'Dao Learning' as Imperial Ideology," in *Culture and the State in Chinese History: Conventions, Accommodations, and Critiques*, ed. Theodore Huters, R. Bin Wong, and Pauline Yu (Stanford, CA: Stanford University, 1997), 58–63.

30 Bol, *Neo-Confucianism in History*, 4–5.

Wang Yangming, as the most important representative of the Xinxue School, provides a more complete exposition of the sayings of the Song thinker Lu Jiuyuan 陸九淵 (1139–1193), who says, "The mind is the principle" (*xin ji shi li* 心即是理).[31] Wang maintains that one's spirituality or consciousness is the ruler of all creatures and spirits in the universe – "there is nothing under heaven external to the mind" (*tianxia wu xinwai zhi wu* 天下無心外之物).[32] This is an even more radical subjectivism relative to Zhu Xi's. The external world cannot exist independent of thought. Thought and valuation are now situated in the mind in a new and stronger sense, in fact, the mind is now the exclusive locus of such realities. For Wang Yangming, there is no other world of abstract *principles*, as Zhu Xi emphasized, rather, the principle, which is rooted in emotions, resides in the mind:

> The substance of the mind is nature, and nature is identical with principle. Consequently, as there is the mind of filial piety toward parents, there is the principle of filial piety. If there is no mind of filial piety, there will be no principle of filial piety. … Are principles external to the mind?
>
> 心之體，性也，性即理也。故有孝親之心，即有孝之理；無孝親之心，即無孝親之理矣。……理豈外於吾心邪？[33]

According to Zhu Xi, there is the principle of filial piety first, and then there is the mindset of being filial to parents. On the contrary, Wang Yangming insists that, if there is no mind, there will be no principle. Zhu Xi regards the principle as being inherent within us, but not the same as the abstract principle itself. However, Wang pushes Zhu's idea further to the extent that the principle is not only inherent in the mind, but that the mind is the governor of the principle, and that self is the moral source per se.

The key term in Wang Yangming's philosophy is "intuitive knowledge." Wang Yangming thinks of the "true self" (*zhenji* 真己) as "innate moral knowledge" (*liangzhi* 良知), and thus "the master of the body" (*quke de zhuzhai* 軀殼的主宰).[34] Through unremittingly internalizing self-cultivation, Wang

31 Lu Jiuyuan, *Lu Xiangshan quanji* 陸象山全集 (Beijing: Zhongguo shudian, 1992), 11.95.

32 Wang, *Chuan xi lu*, 334; translation from Wing-tsit Chan, trans., *Instructions for Practical Living and Other Neo-Confucian Writings by Wang Yang-ming* (New York: Columbia University Press, 1963), 222.

33 Wang Yangming, "Da Gu Dongqiao shu" 答顧東橋書, in *Chuan xi lu*, 162; Chan, *Instructions for Practical Living*, 94.

34 Wang Yangming 王陽明, *Chuan xi lu zhushu* 傳習錄注疏, annot. Deng Aimin 鄧艾民 (Shanghai: Shanghai guji chubanshe, 2012), 81.

suggests, one can get direct access to inner truth, and ultimately attain spontaneous illumination. Wang's discourse of innate moral nature is replete with ideas of spontaneity and genuineness, although the inner naturalness requires careful nurturing or a process of internalization.

However, Wang Yangming discusses how to manifest the original nature of the mind (*xin zhi de* 心之德) with a greater focus on sincerity (*chengyi* 誠意). In interpreting the line from *The Doctrine of the Mean* "Only those who are absolutely sincere can fully develop their nature and know the transforming and nourishing process of heaven and earth" 惟天下至誠，為能盡其性，知天地之化育, he asserts that the restoration of the original substance of the mind is precisely to maintain one's sincerity, and thus one can realize unity with heaven and earth.[35] The sense of a coherence with all things is, in Wang's view, natural to the human mind:

> That the great man can regard heaven and earth and the myriad things as one body is not because he deliberately wants to do so, but because it is natural to the humane nature of his mind to do so. Forming one body with heaven-and-earth and the myriad things is not only true of the great man. Even the mind of the small man is no different.
>
> 大人之能以天地萬物為一體也，非意之也。其心之仁本若是，其與天地萬物而為一也。豈惟大人，雖小人之心亦莫不然。[36]

Here, the belief in the coincidence of all things in the universe is internalized as the fundamental nature of the mind, and hence made the foundation for individual morality and social action. Therefore, suffice it to say that the affirmation of "genuineness" finds for moral behavior an internal basis, that is to say, it is true to our real selves, but at the same time the attribute of "sincerity" confirms the principle of coherence between self-cultivation and external world.

Like Zhu Xi, Wang Yangming bases his philosophy on the presupposition that human nature is originally good. Nevertheless, Wang advocates that there is nothing external to our mind, so we can manifest our original nature in our immediate intuitive reaction to things. Therefore, Wang insists that intuitive knowledge cannot be extended through contemplation and reasoning, but through our daily experience in dealing with ordinary affairs and human

---

35 Ibid., 13; Chan, *Instructions for Practical Living*, 13.

36 Wang Yangming, "Daxuewen" 大學問, in *Chuan xi lu*, 230; Chan, *Instructions for Practical Living*, 272.

feelings. He says, "There is no event outside of human feelings and human affairs" 除了人情事變則無事矣.[37] In other words, there is, within our immediate experience, a sense which discloses the moral order to us. This is a deeper turn inward, or a deeper concern for what is within.

When Wang Yangming discusses filial piety with his students, he emphasizes that one will naturally follow the principle only if one has deep love as the root; one cannot seek for the principle of filial piety in the parent.[38] For Wang, therefore, what finally secures moral order is that realm of instinctual piety – more supple and resilient than abstract law – where the affections of the subject are invested. It is through our natural instincts of benevolence and compassion that we are brought into harmony with others. In this way, an ethics of order and observance is transformed into an ethics of sympathy. The emphasis on sensibility suggests a stronger internalization. Yet, its ultimate goal is to achieve a common general humanity, and thus involves a decentering of the subject instead. Indeed, Wang's idea of sensibility and benevolence lays the groundwork for a moral life more deeply felt, and hence it is an attempt to cope with the problems of living a proper life amid the social changes induced by economic expansion, the venality of officials, and injustice in general. Of course, Wang still speaks of the state of equilibrium and harmony, which is achieved through watching over one's desires and feelings. We have to await his successors to see *qing* promoted to the position of main virtue. Feeling or sentiment becomes the key term in the theory of the "cult of *qing*" that came on stage in the late Ming, an era that exemplifies the profound mutual influence of the literary and intellectual spheres.

Wang Yangming's subjective approach opened up many possibilities for individual development and self-expression. The later Wang Yangming School explored these possibilities in a variety of ways. Wang Gen 王艮 (1483–1541) is considered the founder of the Taizhou branch of Wang Yangming's teaching. Like earlier Confucians, Wang Gen views reciprocity as the basis of all social relations. Yet, his reciprocity is justified in terms of a kind of self-love. Such ideas can be found in one of his essays:

> Those who know how to preserve the self will love the self like a treasure. If I can love the self, I cannot but love other men; I can love other men, they will surely love me; and if they love me, my self will be preserved. … And if my self cannot be preserved, with what shall I preserve my prince and father?

---

37 Wang, *Chuan xi lu*, 69; Chan, *Instructions for Practical Living*, 34.

38 See Wang, *Chuan xi lu*, 6–7; Chan, *Instructions for Practical Living*, 8.

> 知保身者，則必愛身如寶。能愛身，則不敢不愛人。能愛人，則人必愛我。人愛我，則吾身保矣。……吾身不能保，又何以保君父哉？[39]

Wang Gen's thought endorses our normal impulse of self-love. Although, for him, it is still important that we are endowed with the capacity for a general benevolence, it is even more important to realize that true self-love and social care are the same. Society is regarded as an interlocking one, depending on individuals' mutual preservation and support. It is also in this sense that the self and society are one continuum, and thus humans are called to a broader perspective, to embrace the whole.

At the same time, Wang Gen denies those extravagant gestures of self-sacrifice and self-denial to be the proper means of loyalty and filial piety. He claims that one's duty to heaven and one's parents, from whom one receives life, is to nourish, preserve, and reproduce that life in its most fundamental biological form.[40] As mentioned earlier, Wang Yangming attaches importance to everyday experiences, and yet his emphasis in intuitive knowledge is on the mind. Nevertheless, Wang Gen's conception of the self is strongly physical. In effect, he sees the substance of man's heavenly nature as manifested in humans' ordinary desires and wants, in that what is nearest at hand is divine.[41] From his point of view, one can attain sagehood by going about one's daily tasks. Thus, both the bodily self and the ordinary life are affirmed.

Wang Gen's celebration of the ordinary needs of people is taken to the limit by He Xinyin 何心隱 (1517–1579), who strongly affirms man's desires. He maintains that desires are in the inborn nature of man, and thus are to be preserved and satisfied rather than denied and suppressed.[42] Furthermore, he argues that it is impossible for the human being to be without desire, for even the wish to be without desires is a desire. Therefore, to overcome selfishness does not require the eradication of desires, but merely the reduction of them.[43] Even when one subordinates his life to a spiritual ambition, this act is merely that of choosing among desires rather than that of eradicating them, and accordingly a means to self-fulfillment instead of self-denial.

The affirmation of the ordinary life of people is not only an inward turn, but also a downward turn. It represents the "popular" aspect of the thoughts

39 Wang Gen, "Mingzhe baoshen lun 明哲保身論," in *Mingru Wang Xinzhai xiansheng yiji* 明儒王心齋先生遺集 (Beijing: Zhonghua shuju, 1911), 1.12b–13a.

40 Ibid., 2.9a–b.

41 Ibid., 3.4b.

42 He Xinyin, "Guayu" 寡欲, in *He Xinyin ji* 何心隱集 (Beijing: Zhonghua shuju, 1960), 2.40–41.

43 He Xinyin, "Bian wuyu" 辯無欲, in *He Xinyin ji*, 2.42.

of Wang Yangming and his followers. When Wang Yangming maintains that every man possesses intuitive knowledge, he also shows that everyone, in his original nature, is a sage. Therefore, his followers often say that "the streets are full of sages." When it comes to Wang Gen and He Xinyin, their advocacies of the ordinary life and the common man's direct access to sagehood claim a large number of commoners. They speak not only to the elite – the major audience of Zhu Xi's doctrine – but also the lower classes. That is why the Taizhou School is seen as a "mass" movement.[44]

Another crucial figure is Li Zhi 李贄 (1527–1602), who carries the individualism in the thought of the Wang Yangming School to its height, and greatly extends this intellectual concern into the literary field. Li Zhi further develops Wang Gen's idea that the elementary needs of the human being are the very substance of the Way. He says, "Wearing clothes and eating foods are the principles of ethics" 穿衣吃飯，即是人倫物理.[45] He believes that common human nature is rooted in undeniable appetites and basic needs. He even associates sensual desires with the "original mind" (*benxin* 本心), and self-interest with "endowed nature" (*bingfu zhi ziran* 稟賦之自然).[46] Like He Xinyin, he takes self-interest as being natural and inevitable. However, he thinks that one has to respect others' self-interest while realizing one's own, because individuals differ:

> The Way, which is like the road, does not have only one path; nature, to which the mind gives birth, is not merely one kind either. … Others are not the same as you. You hope that other people have [the feelings] that you have, and that they have none you do not have. This does not mean that your mind is inconsiderate, but this is only what is peculiar to yourself instead of what is common to people all over the world. If one wants to put the whole world into order with a universal law, this is doubtful.
>
> 夫道者，路也，不止一途；性者，心之所生也，亦非止一種已也。……人之與已不相若也。有諸已矣，而望人之同有；無諸已矣，而望人之同無。此其心非不恕也，然此乃一身之有無也，而非通於天下之有無也。而欲為一切有無之法以整齊之，惑也。[47]

---

44 Wm. Theodore de Bary, ed., *Self and Society in Ming Thought* (New York: Columbia University Press, 1970), 171.

45 Li Zhi, "Da Deng Shiyang" 答鄧石陽, in *Li Zhi wenji* 李贄文集 (Beijing: Shehui kexue wenxian chubanshe, 2000), 1.4.

46 Li Zhi, *Li Zhi quanji zhu* 李贄全集注 (Beijing: Shehui kexue wenxian chubanshe, 2010), 6.526, 14.255.

47 Li Zhi, "Lun zheng pian" 論政篇, in *Li Zhi wenji*, 3.81–82.

Thus, while one has to hold one's self-interest, one must not project one's private feelings on others, but recognize such self-interestedness as universal, thereby securing a larger place for human desires and selfhood. In interpreting his own conception of "conquering one's self and restoring rites" (*keji fu li* 克己復禮) in another essay, Li Zhi refers to the "self" as one's preconceived opinions and rationalizations rather than private desires and feelings, and "rites" as partaking of the norms of common customs and desires.[48] In fact, he insists that true rites are a matter of conforming to the instinctive desires of human beings, rather than to external forces.[49]

Li Zhi's discussion of human nature, which is also premised on the concept of the "childlike mind" (*tongxin* 童心), valorizes the value of sincerity (*zhen*). Li Zhi's elevation of the sincerity is reminiscent of the sayings of Luo Rufang 羅汝芳 (1515–1588), one of notable thinkers in the Wang Yangming School, who also valorizes the "mind of the newborn baby" (*chizi zhi xin* 赤子之心), regarding the utterly intuitive response as the base and motivation of moral action.[50] The childlike mind, in Li's view, is originally pure, and it can be lost only due to the intrusion of senses and moral doctrines.[51] To maintain one's "childlike mind" is to protect one's innate sincerity, and to eliminate affectation. The "childlike mind" serves as the expression of the "true self," as he asserts, "If one loses the childlike mind, one loses the sincere mind" 若失卻童心, 便失卻真心.[52] Likewise, he associates the "childlike mind" with vernacular and folk literature, promoting it as a more spontaneous and sincere literature.[53]

Another noteworthy aspect of Li Zhi's thinking is his promotion of the husband–wife relationship to the extent of its transcending those of the father–son and the ruler–subject. He argues that the husband–wife relationship comprises the beginnings of human life, and that all other relations derive from this. Thus, he denies the idea that the supreme ultimate or supreme principle is the origin of the world.[54] On many occasions, Li Zhi endorses the love and companionship of husband and wife. He sympathizes with Xun Can's 荀粲 (210–238) pining for his wife after her death, seeing Xun as being highly perceptive of human feelings.[55] He also celebrates Zhuo Wenjun

48 Li Zhi, "Si wu shuo" 四勿説, in *Li Zhi wenji*, 3.94.

49 Ibid., 3.95.

50 Huang Zhongxi, *Mingru xue'an* 明儒學案, in *Huang Zong xi quanji* 黃宗羲全集 (Hangzhou: Zhejiang guji chubanshe, 1985), 8.6.

51 Li Zhi, "Tongxin shuo" 童心説, in *Li Zhi wenji*, 3.91–93.

52 Ibid.

53 See John C.Y. Wang, *Chin Sheng-t'an* (New York: Twayne Publishers, 1972), 5–8.

54 Li Zhi, "Fufu lun" 夫婦論, in *Li Zhi wenji*, 3.84–85.

55 Li Zhi, *Chu tan ji* 初潭集, *juan* 1, in *Li Zhi wenji*, 5.9.

卓文君 (ca. 179–139 BCE), in that she recognizes Sima Xiangru's 司馬相如 (179–118 BCE) "heart of zither," and places a priority on the conjugal relationship over the father–daughter one.[56] His endorsement of emotions does not necessarily reject the celebration of virtue, but provides virtue with a natural or sincere foundation.

The valorization of the male–female relationship was even more prevalent in the late Ming literati culture, which saw a heightened focus on *qing* as sentiment or love. This phenomenon has generally been termed the "cult of *qing*" movement, which sees our bent toward the good as being internalized in sentiment. We can look for moral sources in the sentiment, or love, we find within. In one of the prefaces to Feng Menglong's 馮夢龍 (1574–1646) *A History of Love* (*Qingshi* 情史), Feng says:

> Had heaven and earth had no *ch'ing* they would not have produced the myriad of things. Had the myriad of things had no *ch'ing* they would not have eternally given each other life. Life gives birth to life, and never is extinguished because *ch'ing* itself never becomes extinguished. … I intend to establish a school of *ch'ing* to teach all who are living, so that a son will face his father with *ch'ing* and a vassal will face his lord with *ch'ing*. One can, then, deduce the relations of all the various phenomena from this single point of view. … At that time, robberies and thefts will cease to happen, and evil and treason never arise; the Buddha will have no further use for his mercifulness and forgiveness, and the sage no further use for his teaching benevolence and righteousness.
>
> 天地若無情，不生一切物。一切物無情，不能環相生。生生而不滅，由情不滅故。…… 我欲立情教，教誨諸眾生：子有情於父，臣有情於君，推之種種相，俱作如是觀。…… 盜賊必不作，奸宄必不起。佛亦何慈悲，聖亦何仁義。[57]

Thus, for Feng, our *qing*, synonymous with "love" or moral sentiments that everyone is capable of feeling, is an integral part of the whole universe. To be good, it is important to identify our own sources of goodness, not only in ourselves, but in other humans, and even in the creator itself. In this way, the whole universe is regarded as good and benevolent, and society as an intimate community is bound together by affective ties. With the innate and transformative power of *qing*, people will have no need for buddhas and sages, the

56 Li Zhi, *Cang shu* 藏書, *juan* 37, in *Li Zhi wenji*, 3.719.

57 Feng Menglong, *Qingshi* 情史 (Changsha: Yuelu shushe, 2003), 1; Hua-yuan Li Mowry, *Chinese Love Stories from "Ch'ing-Shih"* (Hamden, Connecticut: Archon Books, 1983), 13–14.

teachings of which are external to our nature, but each will be one's own savior. As the basis of ethical behavior and the origin of all virtues, *qing* reconceptualizes all human relations as fundamentally grounded in affect, including those of the father–son and the ruler–subject. Optimism about human nature fosters a belief in the power of positive natural sentiments, and a new confidence in a better social order.

Of course, Feng does not think that feeling can simply replace principle; but he does hold that principle in itself is insufficient for social unity, and that to become a regulative force in society it must be animated by love and affection. In the final critical summary of chapter 1 ("Chastity") he articulates the relationship between principle and love.

> With regard to all matters of loyalty, filial piety, chastity or heroism, if one tries to act solely from principle, then one's actions will certainly be forced; if, however, one tries to act on the basis of genuine *ch'ing*, then his actions will certainly be sincere. Thus it has been ever since time began. The relation between a husband and his wife is of all relations the most intimate. He who is feelingless to his wife can never be a faithful husband; she who is feelingless to her husband can never be a virtuous wife. An ordinary intellectual only knows that reason restrains *ch'ing* but does not know that *ch'ing* maintains reason.
>
> 自來忠孝節烈之事，從道理上做者必勉強，從真情上出者必真切。夫婦其最近者也，無情之夫，必不能為義夫；無情之婦，必不能為節婦。世儒但知理為情之範，孰知情為理之維乎。[58]

Principle and sentiment, in this sense, go together: the social order is to be renewed on the basis of virtue and the custom of *qing*. Feelings of benevolence and love give shape to moral judgement and render moral action pleasurable. Here his inspiration is clearly Wang Yangming, whose doctrine of "intuitive knowledge" promotes the goodness of human nature and the potential of emotional responses to maintain the principle, which, to Wang, became available to the mind via inborn sentiments. Although Wang is primarily concerned with the relations of the mind, nature, and the principle in his discussion on filial practices, he sees virtue as an outgrowth of natural sentiments with an emphasis on profound love as the root of morality (*shen'ai zuo gen* 深愛作根). Furthermore, Feng promotes the centrality of *qing*, or feeling, to superior virtue and social bonds. For Feng, hence, affection in its moderate degree is innocent, amiable, and morally good. Feng Menglong is essentially concerned with

58 Feng, *Qingshi*, 21; Mowry, *Chinese Love Stories from "Ch'ing-Shih"*, 38.

the possibility of being a moral agent in the world through finding something within the self, thereby achieving a state of "genuineness" (*zhenqie* 真切), or spontaneously responding to the principle, and a sense of connection between self and its social and moral contexts. It is love and sincerity (*qing* and *cheng*) that secure this kind of unity and make possible both self-transformation and social morality. Ultimately, for Feng, *qing* is about building a new kind of community, which is maintained by subjective, yet moral, feelings[59] – "Those without love are transformed into sentient beings, and private feelings are transformed into public feelings, and thus fortunately throughout the world people get along with each other through emotional relations, and hopefully the frivolous mood of society will change" 無情化有，私情化公，庶鄉國天下，藹然以情相与，於澆俗冀有更焉.[60] Feng Menglong's ultimate goal is to transform society through the unity of true feelings and social morality, seeing social responsibility as the duty of people from all over the world.

In comparison with Feng's emphasis on the maintenance of social community, Li Zhi's assertion of genuineness and individualism made him a precursor of the late Ming literary "expressive movement."[61] Li Zhi's claim that each individual is different had a great impact on Yuan Hongdao 袁宏道 (1558–1616), both a literary theorist and one of the best essayists of the late Ming, frequently depicting natural scenes with human touches or scenes of secular life in the city. Yuan and his brothers, who formed the Gong'an School, all emphasized individuality and spontaneity, while attacking the imitation of ancient writers. Although the advocacy of individuality in the literary field was far from novel, Yuan's is more radical, and based on the celebration of ordinary life. In his preface to the collected poems of his younger brother, Yuan contends that most of his younger brother's works uniquely express his personal nature and are not restricted by convention.[62]

59 Epstein's notion of the primacy of filial love during the High Qing is helpful for the understanding of this subjective quality of filiality. In fact, the sentimental conceptions of filial obligations had origins in both Wang Yangming and Feng Menglong and continued to shape social relations and lives in the early and middle Qing. For some of the late Ming literati, both romantic love and that between the parent and child were one and the same universal, natural feeling, the root of morality and foundation of all social bonds. This novel view of emotions functioned as a force for good in human affairs – both in the marriage based on affection and the household of benevolent parent–child relations. See Epstein, *Orthodox Passions*, 1–3.

60 Feng, *Qingshi*, 1.

61 James J.Y. Liu, *Chinese Theories of Literature* (Chicago: University of Chicago Press, 1975), 78–79.

62 Yuan Hongdao, *Yuan Zhonglang quanji* 袁中郎全集 (Shanghai: Shijie shuju, 1935), 5; Liu, *Chinese Theories*, 80.

In another preface to a friend's collection, he brings out the concept of "gusto" (*qu* 趣), which echoes Li Zhi's notion of the "childlike heart," to characterize genuine self-expression and sensuality. He believes that gusto more profoundly owes to nature than to learning.[63] This concept of "gusto" therefore can be considered as a dimension of "personal nature," focusing on instinct and emotion. Since the individual is different and original, he has to follow what is within rather than find his models without. In this sense, art is neither imitation of ancient models nor a mere emotional response to the external world, but a kind of ineffable inner expression.

Therefore, such an expressive view of both human life and art leads to the idea that only the folk songs sung by women and children in the streets are poetical, because they sing from the heart, and the natural expression of feeling is poetry. He explains:

> These are still the works of "true people," who are without knowledge or learning; hence, they are full of true voices ... they are words uttered in accordance with the free bent of one's nature, and can express people's joy, anger, sadness, pleasure, appetites, and desires.
>
> 猶是無聞無識真人所作,故多真聲。……任性而發，尚能通於人之喜怒哀樂嗜好情欲，是可喜也。[64]

In this regard, Yuan Hongdao shows his agreement with Li Zhi, who applies the concept of the "childlike heart" to the writer, and regards popular works of drama and fiction as great literature. It can be said that the late Ming literati culture saw the rise of a rejuvenated orientation to both a daily involvement with the world and the untainted, childlike origins of individuality.

The affirmation of true self and *qing*, in particular the elevation of sensual desires, however, simultaneously raises the question of discontinuities between natural, emotional reaction and moral intention, and between inner transcendence and inevitable mundaneness. Late Ming literati, on the one hand, evoked a kind of profound inwardness and the rhetoric of self-justification through their writing; on the other hand, however, they were keenly aware of the problems and paradoxes in the celebration of genuineness. Several researchers

63 Yuan, *Yuan Zhonglang quanji*, 5; Liu, *Chinese Theories*, 81.
64 Yuan, *Yuan Zhonglang quanji*, 6; Liu, *Chinese Theories*, 80–81.

have aptly pointed out the sense of anxiety and ambivalence on the part of late Ming writers behind their pursuit of spontaneity and freedom.[65]

To some degree, this literary "movement" in the late Ming resembles the "Expressivist turn" in eighteenth-century Europe, in which an admiration for folk poetry also emerged.[66] However, the late Ming's individualism neither developed to the extent that the full autonomy of the self was affirmed, nor attempted to unite radical autonomy and expressive unity (or unity with nature). On the contrary, many literary men of the late Ming ultimately adopted an attitude of self-questioning and self-control. For example, Tang Xianzu's later plays hold a very different view of *qing* from that in *The Peony Pavilion*, suggesting that true freedom of self can be attained only through the transcendence of desires and emotional attachment. Yuan Hongdao also expresses deep self-criticism toward sensual desire. In his earlier years, he claimed that the pursuit of sensual pleasure was his primary concern, but he renounced sensual excess and showed profound repentance for these earlier claims in his later writings.[67] Although the late Ming literati primarily attempt to maintain a balance between emotional attachment and moral pursuits, and to seek transcendence of this kind of division and the realization of their social responsibilities, the pervasive concern with genuineness in late Ming culture also breeds the potential for self-division and epistemological uncertainty. The danger lies in that the excessive pursuit of sensual pleasure and inner truth tends to subjectivize values to the extent that they become merely a kind of mental taste, and thus morally problematic. "Early Qing retrospection on the late Ming, therefore, underlies the deleterious effects of the quest for the true self."[68] Thinkers of the early Qing believed that the Ming had been weakened by liberalism and anti-intellectualism which reduced morality to mere feelings. Consequently, a movement toward rapprochement with Zhu Xi became the order of the day in both scholarship and morality. Yet this turn to Zhu's philosophy was not a simple one but a higher reconciliation, in which the ideas of the Xinxue School were partly retained.[69]

---

65 See Huang, *Desire and Fictional Narrative*, 5–22; Wai-yee Li, "Looking for the True Self," in Li and Pines, *Keywords in Chinese Culture*, 342–59.

66 For the "Expressivist turn" in eighteenth-century Europe, see Taylor, *Sources of the Self*, 368–90.

67 See Martin Huang's discussion on "desire, anxiety, and ambivalence during the late Ming," in Huang, *Desire and Fictional Narrative*, 5–22.

68 See Li, "Looking for the True Self," 335–36.

69 See Benjamin A. Elman, *From Philosophy to Philology: Intellectual and Social Aspects of Change in Late Imperial China* (Cambridge, MA: Harvard University Press, 1984).

In the midst of general trends toward profound reflection on late Ming liberalism, scholars such as Huang Zhongxi 黃宗羲 (1610–1695), Gu Yanwu 顧炎武 (1613–1682), and Wang Fuzhi 王夫之 (1619–1692) intended to restore the relations between the idea of self and the conduct of social affairs, speaking of heavenly principles as an aggregate of individual social or biological needs. They all articulated an ideal state of harmony between *xing* and *qing*, between the private and the public. As Gu Yanwu puts it, "When the private desires all over the world are harmonized, they become the public interests all over the world" 合天下之私，以成天下之公.[70] This kind of sociality of self-interests can be found as well in Wang Fuzhi's 王夫之 (1619–1692) statement that "the publicness of human desire is the ultimate heavenly principle" 人慾之大公即天理之至矣.[71] He also discusses the workings of *xing* in the context of *qing* by stating that "*xing* is something that keeps things in proper measure, whereas what constitutes its state of equilibrium is *qing*; *qing* is that which keeps *xing* in balance" 性者節也，中之者情也，情中性也.[72] For these scholars, a good society is based on the true needs of the self, and thus it is a community of authentic individuals, although they tried to eschew radical subjectivity.

This philosophical notion of individuality further emerged in the thoughts of the eighteenth-century thinker Dai Zhen 戴震 (1723–1777), who criticized Neo-Confucianism for its attitudes toward emotions and desires, and yet maintained the universality and sociality of desire. He argues that "when an individual is among people, it is called *qing*. Principle is the state when *qing* is neither excessive nor insufficient."[73] For him, desires and feelings are positive forces for moral cultivation and self-fulfillment, for they bring one into contact with the external world and society. At the same time, they need to be properly integrated into a social context or public, thereby connecting the individual to the universal community. Dai Zhen is likewise against a transcendent principle that is external to one's self and emotional expression, while he conceives of

---

70 Gu Yanwu, "Yan siqizong" 言私其豵, in *Rizhi lu jishi* 日知錄集釋, annot. Huang Rucheng 黃汝成 (Shanghai: Shanghai guji chubanshe, 2006), 3.148.

71 Wang Fuzhi, *Sishu xunyi* 四書訓義, *juan* 3, in *Chuanshan quanshu* 船山全書 (Changsha: Yuelu shushe, 1988–1996), 7.137.

72 See Andrew Plaks's discussion on this question in "Before the Emergence of Desire," 328; see also Huang, *Desire and Fictional Narrative*, 53–55.

73 Dai Zhen 戴震, *Mengzi ziyi shuzheng* 孟子字義疏證, Siku quanshu 四庫全書, 6.153; see also Ann-ping Chin and Mansfield Freeman, trans., *Tai Chen on Mencius: Explorations in Words and Meaning* (New Haven, CT: Yale University Press, 1990), 95.

the individual as a social unit and systematically articulates the social and biological needs of each individual in society.[74]

The rise of Evidential Learning, represented by Dai Zhen's ritual studies (*lijiao* 禮教), on the other hand, put into question Neo-Confucian premises on the innate coherence of things.[75] Evidential Learning advocated a kind of knowledge that reached factual conclusions through the careful study of the evidence, rather than through an apparent correlation between innate morality and external things. In short, the illumination of the coherence of a subject in the mind was no longer the aim of learning, but instead the inherent value of unity had become suspect.[76] Of course, although the supporters of Evidential Learning viewed learning differently, they suggested as well that the literati should obtain intellectual discipline and cultivation by means of learning. Just like their Neo-Confucian predecessors, they asserted the independence of intellectual life from political power while seeking support and recognition from the bureaucracy and the court.[77]

In conclusion, Chinese intellectual tradition from the mid-Tang through the mid-Qing showed a self-referential tendency, in particular a concern with the autonomy and responsibility of the individual. Literati attempted to keep creating a tension between the ruler and themselves, strengthening the role of the social and political elite that saw itself as responsible for government and society. They were intent upon showing people how to think for themselves, and upon finding ways of acting for the common good on their own. Such a position was grounded on their faith in a morality that was not something created by political power but by the cultivation of universal qualities endowed in all human beings alike. We can thus find two major intellectual developments

---

74 See Minghui Hu, *China's Transition to Modernity: The New Classical Vision of Dai Zhen* (Seattle: University of Washington Press, 2015), 3–4.

75 In the early Qing, the Kangxi emperor, in order to consolidate his power, criticized the excesses of the late Ming self-indulgence and revived Zhu Xi's Neo-Confucianism in examination education, and thus ensured that it remained a core element of literati society. In this way, together with the two great Qing emperors that followed him, he ended the distinction between politics and morality and the tension between the literati and ruler. However, Qing literati still presented themselves with independence to oppose political power. By the end of Kangxi's reign, in fact, intellectual culture had parted with the Neo-Confucianism of the Song to the Ming dynasties and settled on a new way of learning. On the social-historical context in which the Evidential Learning arose, see Bol, *Neo-Confucianism in History*, 100.

76 See Bol, *Neo-Confucianism in History*, 278.

77 Minghui Hu argues that Dai studied the ritual apparel system to formulate a new political subjectivity by creating a value outside the imperial state. See Hu, *China's Transition to Modernity*, 200.

traceable in this tradition: increasing internalization and the significance of ordinary life.[78] As scholars have argued, late imperial Confucian society was experiencing a subtle process of secularization.[79]

Nevertheless, on the other hand, literati intellectuals profoundly reflected on the ambiguities in the quest for the true self, a kind of dialectics between moral transcendence and mundane desires, and between inner self and public life. Hence, traditional Chinese intellectual life never aimed to develop a wholly free, self-determining subject, but rather to establish its underlying principle as the fusion of the general and the particular, of self and society, in other words, to realize one's specificity in social relations. Although the late Ming intellectual trend toward the emphasis on desire and feelings diverges greatly from Song Neo-Confucianism, which asserted the primacy of reason and principle, how to sustain a moral life that is spontaneous and unfeigned were central concerns of both Song and Ming thought. Qing philosophers' reflections on late Ming liberalism were grounded in not only a negation of ungoverned desires and selfishness, but also a continuation of the use of emotions and desires as positive drives to live a moral life, and a new application in the integrity of the individual as a unique expression of a larger moral process. Hence, Chinese literati seemed to increasingly seek the inner moral resources, and meanwhile never escaped from social responsibility, but constantly looked for new ways to enter (or re-enter) the public realm. These endeavors resulted from a profound belief in the fundamental importance of the coincidence between the inner self and the external social world. Although the late Ming literati's promotion of genuineness and emotions offered them the strength to reflect on and reinterpret Confucian classics and ritual, they did not arrive at a kind of self-division in the sense of an essential disjunction between the self and its social, political, and moral contexts, but fostered both the belief that benevolence and affection were one and that natural sentiment serves as the root of morality and optimism for a harmonious social order. For all the

78 To some extent, these developments exhibit the characteristics of what Charles Taylor calls the "modern self" in the process of its constitution. Three important facets of the modern self, according to Taylor, are reflectivity and inwardness, the affirmation of ordinary life, and the use of nature as moral source, see Taylor, *Sources of the Self*. In saying this, I do not mean to read Western values into Chinese thought, nor to equate the Western "modern self" to the Confucian concepts of personhood, but merely to show that certain commonalities in terms of a person's relation to the world and others cannot be ignored. Similar intellectual transformations did take place across different cultures, yet in their own characteristic ways.

79 See Yu Yingshi, *Zhongguo jinshi zongjiao lunli yu shangren jingshen* 中國近世宗教倫理與商人精神 (Taibei: Lianjing chuban shiye gongsi, 1987); John B. Henderson, *The Development and Decline of Chinese Cosmology* (New York: Columbia University Press, 1984).

inconsistency or contradictions evoked, the main force that links the self to others, and to social participation, remained a core element of literati voluntarism and literati values.

This particular intellectual tradition allowed the literati to serve simultaneously as participants in the imperial system and as individuals who distanced themselves from it, and yet who took responsibility for the world around them. In this respect, mid to late Ming Neo-Confucians stood out as they took principled stands against the abuse of imperial authority often at the expense of their own lives, and they systematically mobilized and organized the literati community.[80] In the early seventeenth century, literati organizations sought to utilize new ways of networking independently of the political system to influence government and reform politics.[81] When it comes to the mid-Qing, although the breakdown in intellectual unity and the increasing relativism among literati intellectuals provided grounds for them to identify with different ideological positions, they still operated within the framework and crucial assumptions of the Confucian literati values, with an attempt to find a new vision of social morality. All of these Confucian engagements aimed to both reinvigorate individual moral effort and present new ways of becoming involved in public life for literati.

In fact, the change I have been tracing above – both a process of increasing internalization and an unceasing concern about public discourse – took place not only in the intellectual and social field, but throughout the entire culture. It is parallel to, and interwoven with, the transformation of literary discourse, the rise of the novel and drama, the new valuation of the centrality of inborn sentiments to virtue, and the changing understanding of self and sociality. For example, the rise of a new expressive interest in poetry and literary essays manifested the new consciousness of the human–nature relationship; in literary works, there was a tendency toward an idealization of marriage

---

80 Since the Southern Song, in fact, the Neo-Confucians worked to create communities of literati who shared their vision and provided local leadership, for example, in the forms of Neo-Confucian academies and shrines. In the sixteenth century, the reemergence of local literati communities facilitated the revival of Neo-Confucian voluntarism. See Bol, *"This Culture of Ours"*, 58–75; Kandice J. Hauf, "The Community Covenant in Sixteenth Century Ji'an Prefecture, Jiangxi," *Late Imperial China* 17, no. 2 (1996): 1–50.

81 Toward the end of the Ming, literati organizations, such as the Donglin Academy and the Restoration Society, redirected intellectual culture and exercised a decisive influence over government. This kind of organization had no parallel in the Song and Yuan. See Heinrich Busch, "The Tung-lin Shu-yuan and Its Political and Philosophical Significance," *Monumenta Serica* 14 (1995): 1–163, Willian S. Atwell, "From Education to Politics: The Fu She," in *The Unfolding of Neo-Confucianism*, ed. Wm. Theodore de Bary (New York: Columbia University Press, 1975), 333–68.

based on both affection and ritual, and a throng of particular details of circumstances and happenings; the novel increasingly dealt moralistically with romantic attachment, became concerned with the reconciliation as well as the conflicts of self and society, and offered an imagination of community or networks among likeminded men; we also see a growing importance of natural sentiments for the cultivation of sensitivity and virtue: deep love as well as the devotion to virtue; the extremes of expression fill the texts of the period, not just novels and plays, but a variety of essays and *pingdian* 評點 criticism. The relations between the thoughts on desire, mind, and morality and their literary expression are not clear-cut – neither is fully independent of the other, but both derive from, as well as contribute to, social change.

CHAPTER 2

A Query about Desire: Tang *Chuanqi* Tales

In this chapter, I will examine Tang *chuanqi* 傳奇 tales that focus on love and courtship.[1] The representation of women and female desire in these narratives allowed the contemporary men of letters an expedient way of exploring tensions between emotion and ritual, and between self-interest and social conventions. By defining women's desire, the literatus not only made expanded claims to his own sensitivity and individuality, but also addressed his anxiety and moral concerns.

The emergence of *chuanqi* tales in the Tang (618–907) may be explained by various sociocultural factors. For example, the rise of a culture of literary examination made literary talent a vital medium for defining status; it also cultivated a need for self-promotion by circulating writings (including prose writings), in order to deliver literary products into the hands of the prominent.[2] Moreover, the ascent of the literati to the social scene was concomitant with the institutionalization of official courtesans, who were becoming indispensable at the imperial examination's annual celebration and other official gatherings.[3] The Tang dynasty saw the blooming of courtesan culture, as well as urbanization and prosperity in Chang'an and Luoyang. There also was a keen interest in the fantastic, associated with the rise of the urban setting on the part of writers in the capital elite circle.[4]

---

1 The "*chuanqi* tale" is a subgenre of fiction that appeared during the Tang dynasty and became highly prevalent between 780 and 820. Tang *chuanqi* tales are usually short in length and written in classical language. In contrast to an earlier form of classical-language fiction known as *zhiguai* 志怪 (records of anomalies), Tang *chuanqi* tales primarily focus on the subject of human characters, although they occasionally concern the supernatural beings as well. For a detailed explanation of the term, see Nienhauser, *Indiana Companion to Traditional Chinese Literature*, 356–59; William H. Nienhauser, Jr., "Tang Tales," in *The Columbia History of Chinese Literature*, ed. Victor Mair (NY: Columbia University Press, 2001), 579–94.

2 Chen Yinke [陳寅恪], "Han Yu and the Tang Novel," *Harvard Journal of Asiatic Studies* 1 (1936): 39–43; Cheng Qianfan 程千帆, *Tang dai jinshi xingjuan yu wenxue* 唐代進士行卷與文學 (Shanghai: Shanghai guji chubanshe, 1980); Liu Kairong 劉開榮, *Tangdai xiaoshuo yanjiu* 唐代小說研究 (Hongkong: Shangwu yinshuguan, 1964), 18–36; Victor H. Mair, "Scroll Presentation in the T'ang Dynasty," *Harvard Journal of Asiatic Studies* 38, no. 1 (1978): 35–60.

3 Song Dexi 宋德熹, "Tangdai de jinü" 唐代的妓女, in *Zhongguo funü lunji xuju* 中国妇女論集續集, ed. Bao Jialin 鮑家麟 (Taibei: Daoxiang chubanshe, 1991), 67–121.

4 Linda Feng, *City of Marvel and Transformation: Chang'an and Narratives of Experience in Tang Dynasty China* (Honolulu: University of Hawai'i Press, 2015).

HTTPS://DOI.ORG/10.1163/9789004693357-004

The *chuanqi* narrative reached its peak in the middle of Tang, after the An Lushan 安祿山 and Shi Siming 史思明 rebellions (755–763), which had aggravated the decline of the old aristocracy.[5] During the post-rebellion period, politics and society had shifted their focus away from the court and the old clans to local educated gentry who attempted to play a role in national politics. These social changes that the rebellions brought about paralleled the transformation of the intellectual culture of the age. The classical prose movement, from which the *chuanqi* form drew its stylistic inspiration, was also launched in this cultural environment (see the previous chapter). This was an era in which leading intellectual figures were also literary figures, and they were writing about how responsible scholars ought to engage in *wen* 文 (literature) and *xue* 學 (learning). They believed in the role of literature in illuminating or clarifying the Way, a Way which was understood as coinciding with that of Yao 堯 and Shun 舜 rather than the rites of the Zhou 周 dynasty (1046–256 BCE).[6] This anti-ritual tendency partook of a sense of subversion, insofar as it shifted attention from the aristocratic ritual traditions to the interests of the lower-official class and focused on a belief in *xing* and *qing* as something individuals embodied and could act on.

Peter Bol maps out the competing discourses surrounding the reform programs of the Tang literati, which aimed to halt what was considered the era's intellectual and moral decline.[7] In this, the relationship between morality and human desires became a critical issue of debate.[8] As Bol has observed, the prevailing ethics of the mid-Tang saw human desires as a threat to morality.[9] However, the elite's redefinition of its self-identity in the new social world, and the development of private interests, complicated matters. For example, Han Yu suggests that realizing morality does not necessarily mean ceasing to desire, but creating an integrated order that satisfies the interests and desires of men.[10] Han Yu's disciple, Li Ao further elevates *qing* to a status of being inseparable from *xing*: "Nature is not nature in and of itself but shows its brightness through emotion" 性不自性，由情以明.[11] Certain Tang romantic tales capture this moment in which elite culture was changing significantly. Indeed, some

---

5 Cheng Yizhong 程毅中, *Tangdai xiaoshuo shihua* 唐代小說史話 (Beijing: Wenhua yishu chubanshe, 1990), 18–19; Li Jianguo 李劍國, *Tang Wudai zhiguai chuanqi xulu* 唐五代志怪傳奇敘録 (Tianjin: Nankai daxue chubanshe, 1993), 30–50.

6 See Zhu, *Tang Song guwen yundong yu shidafu wenxue*, 27–42.

7 Bol, *"This Culture of Ours"*, 78–107.

8 Ibid., 108–47.

9 Ibid., 131.

10 Ibid., 124–31; see also my discussion in Chapter 1.

11 Li Ao, *Li Wengong ji*, Sibu congkan 四部叢刊, 2.1a–13b; Barrett, *Li Ao*, 96–97.

authors of *chuanqi* tales, such as Yuan Zhen, were also important figures in the classical prose movement.[12] His interest in both forms suggests the involvement of scholars who advocated classical prose writing in the development of the *chuanqi* tales. Like the classical prose movement, the writing of *chuanqi* tales was probably directed toward a new audience in the local elite that was in its formative stage in the late eighth century, or at least was attempting to arouse a new awareness in the old elite class. These authors developed their own literary interests in order to reimagine their roles and collective identities. As a kind of discursive working out of social identity, Tang romantic tales as a whole address the problems of the age: they attempt to find something that is universal and innate in human nature, and thus which transcends the differences of class or group; for this reason the questions of passion and virtue, which result from uncertainty over private desires and interests, are frequently staged in these tales.

In this chapter, I intend to show how desire intersects, and works together, with moral discipline. I argue that, through the ironic representation of the hero's and the heroine's perspectives, Tang romantic tales present various conflicting discourses of love, which ultimately attempt to realize the romantic relationship through the act of publicizing or socializing private desire, suspending desire or passion in an aesthetic way less constrained by moral qualms, or subjecting passion to a disciplinary code of manners and thus extirpating it. Tang *chuanqi* narratives highlight doubt and anxiety about romance and make disciplining the passions – not merely arousing them – the focal point of the emerging genre of romance. Their endeavors to define the limits of love and passion both raise and problematize the question of virtue and social norms, although one has to await the development of romantic discourse in the late imperial period for the completion of the integration of passion into moral philosophy, and the promotion of love to a main moral virtue. While more often than not these attempts end in failure, the conflicting cultural

---

12 Liu Kairong examines the relations between Tang *chuanqi* tales, the classical prose movement, and the political struggles in the mid-Tang, and claims that *chuanqi* tales represent the striving for political power in the partisan conflict between Niu Sengru 牛僧儒 and Li Deyu 李德裕. However, the *chuanqi* authors often belong to different political factions – for example, Bai Xingjian belonged to the Niu party and Yuan Zhen to the Li party – and yet had shared concerns for the common questions of passion and virtue. This indicates that their writings were not only related to political considerations, but also to general issues raised by the classical prose movement. See Liu Kairong, *Tangdai xiaoshuo yanjiu*, 18–36. For the political implication of Tang *chuanqi* tales, also see Bian Xiaoxuan 卞孝萱, *Tangren xiaoshuo yu zhengzhi* 唐人小說与政治 (Xiamen: Lujiang chubanshe, 2003); Yu Gang 俞鋼, *Tangdai wenyan xiaoshuo yu keju zhidu* 唐代文言小說与科舉制度 (Shanghai: Shanghai guji chubanshe, 2004).

discourses of romance and morality leave many curious ironies in these tales. The tensions between didacticism and personal intensity of feelings or desire, and between the seemingly objective narrator and the individuals' insights, are left unresolved. These conflicts and tensions reflect a dynamic process of ethical construction and ideological negotiation – between the tentative pursuit of universality and free choice and the power of the ritual system and moral compulsion – on the part of the authors of *chuanqi* tales in the mid-Tang, a group of new literary men whose sympathies lay with the young and aspiring scholar-official heroes in the tales.

This chapter examines three key texts – Jiang Fang's "The Story of Huo Xiaoyu", Yuan Zhen's "The Story of Yingying", and Bai Xingjian's "The Story of Li Wa" – to show how these tales foreground female desire and womanly virtue, and furthermore, how desires in these tales are either represented as a haunting curse, defused through the aesthetic suspension of private desire, or tamed by the suppression of romance.

1 Uncontrollable Desire: "The Story of Huo Xiaoyu"

"The Story of Huo Xiaoyu" is often read in terms of the construction and endorsement of a paradigmatic discourse of romance.[13] Nevertheless, the uncertainty over romance and passion embedded in the story cannot be readily ignored. At first glance, the story creates a touching romantic affinity between the protagonists, the talented poet Li Yi 李益 and Huo Xiaoyu 霍小玉, daughter of the deceased Prince Huo and his maid. After Prince Huo's death, Huo Xiaoyu, together with her mother, is driven away and enters her mother's former profession of courtesanship. Both Li Yi and Huo Xiaoyu are looking for a suitable companion, and both choose the other freely. Their mutual appreciation lies in the parallel between Li Yi's exceptional literary talent and Huo Xiaoyu's unsurpassable beauty. This parallelism works on two levels. First, Huo Xiaoyu's beauty can be seen as the externalization of Li Yi's talent, hence a self-evident demonstration of his worth. Second, what Huo Xiaoyu longs for is merely "a young man who is her equal in quality" (*getiao xiangchengzhe* 格調相稱者): "she asks no money – she yearns only for a man of gallantry and feeling" 不邀財貨，但慕風流.[14] Here, presented as the sole aspect of female

13 See Owen, *The End of the Chinese "Middle Ages"*, 130–48; Luo, *Literati Storytelling in Late Medieval China*, 2015.

14 Lu Xun 魯迅, ed., *Tang Song chuanqi ji* 唐宋傳奇集 (Tianjin: Tianjin guji chubanshe, 2002), 99; for Owen's translation, see Owen, *The End of the Chinese "Middle Ages"*, 178–79.

desire, male (literary) talent is endowed with a value independent of political and social relations. As such, romance provides literary men with an autonomous "private world" by defining women's desire and value.[15] In this sense, Li Yi and Huo Xiaoyu create a perfect romance, setting a model for the *caizi-jiaren* tradition, which was further developed in later romantic literature in China.

However, this seemingly perfect romantic world is also depicted as problematic, even from the beginning. With the help of a matchmaker, Li Yi is led to meet Huo Xiaoyu at her house. As Stephen Owen rightfully points out, "One of the most important aspects of the culture of romance is its site."[16] The Tang love stories most often happen in a secluded place, removed from the conventions of family and the real world. Xiaoyu's dwelling seems unfathomable – like desire itself – to the extent that Li Yi is assailed with hesitancy and apprehensions when he enters the house for the first time:

> In the courtyard there were four cherry trees, and from the one in the northwest corner there was hung a cage with a parrot in it. When it saw Li Yi come in, it spoke, "A man is coming – quick, pull down the curtains!" By nature Li Yi was proper and reserved, and his heart was still apprehensive and beset by doubts. When he heard the bird speak out so suddenly, he was overcome with panic and didn't dare go further.
>
> 庭間有四櫻桃樹；西北懸一鸚鵡籠，見生入来，即語曰："有人入來，急下簾者！"生本性雅淡，心猶疑懼，忽見鳥語，愕然不敢進。[17]

Li Yi's hesitance to enter Xiaoyu's house suggests the author's doubts about romance. The romantic world is represented here as both enticing and potentially dangerous. Entering a romantic space means excluding oneself from reality and social connections. When Li Yi enters Xiaoyu's house, the door is locked behind him.[18] This ensures the isolation and enclosure of the romantic space, which accommodates the private desire that is separated from the

15 Stephen Owen sees romance as the demonstration of an interest in the creation of private spaces independent of public sphere. See Owen, *The End of the Chinese "Middle Ages"*, 141.

16 Ibid., 137.

17 Lu, *Tang Song chuanqi ji*, 100; Owen, *The End of the Chinese "Middle Ages"*, 180.

18 Manling Luo points out that Li Yi is locked in Huo's house twice. But for the second time, he is actually locked in the carriage (instead of in Huo's house) by the knight-errant in yellow robes, who manages to force him to go to Huo Xiaoyu's again. See Manling Luo, "Discourse Formation in Tang Tales: Literati Identity Construction and the Writing of Chuanqi" (PhD. dissertation, Washington University at St. Louis, 2005), 96–97.

outside world. Romance is rendered as a suspension from the temporal and spatial reality.

Outside of this secluded enclosure, however, romance runs into conflict with social demands. Xiaoyu realizes the discrepancy between their statuses and thus the predestined outcome that Li Yi will inevitably makes an advantageous marriage with another woman immediately after he passes the imperial examination. She thus proposes a compromise – that they condense a lifetime of love and pleasure into eight years, after which she will shave her head and become a nun. Although Li Yi vows never to abandon her, after passing the imperial examination he leaves Xiaoyu's house to take up an official post and follows his mother's order to marry Miss Lu, a woman from a distinguished family. From then on, he cuts off his connection to Xiaoyu, and never returns to Xiaoyu's house until immediately before her death. It is because the romantic world of private desire cannot be reconciled with the public world of social propriety that, once Li Yi steps into public life, he is unable to return to an uncompromised romantic space.

An even more profound tension between self-interested desire and social norms is brought out by Xiaoyu's constancy in the pursuit of love. Even though Li Yi cuts off his connection to her and hopes that she will give up on him, Xiaoyu stubbornly persists in seeking to reach Li Yi, using up her fortune obtaining news of her beloved. From this point on, Xiaoyu's desire traverses the boundary of the enclosed private space and reaches into the public realm. Her story begins to be circulated in the city. Xiaoyu eventually sells a purple-jade hairpin, which her father, Prince Huo, had given her when she became an adult. This hairpin is then recognized by an old jade carver, who himself had made the hairpin for Prince Huo. The maid tells Xiaoyu's story to the carver, who is moved to tears. Afterwards, he leads the maid to the mansion of Princess Yanxian, who is also greatly moved and gives the maid money to take back to Xiaoyu. Here, the interesting question is what moves the old jade carver and the princess. Do they lament the romance itself or its disastrous consequences? The author leaves intriguing ambiguity here. The old jade carver says, "To think that the sons and daughters of the nobility could fall into such misfortune and end up like this! The years left to me will soon be done, and to see such reversals from splendor to decline is a pain not to be borne" 貴人男女，失機落節，一至於此。我殘年向盡，見此盛衰，不勝傷感.[19] Xiaoyu is the daughter of a prince. Under normal conditions, she might well not be involved in such a romance, but rather have a decent marriage like that of Miss Lu. Nevertheless, not only has she been removed from her family, but also her

19 Lu, *Tang Song chuanqi ji*, 101; Owen, *The End of the Chinese "Middle Ages"*, 185.

uncontrollable desire for romance strips her of her least and last connection to that family – she gives up her father's gift, the hairpin, as well as the property given to her by the family. In this sense, the old jade carver's lament seems more a sympathetic criticism of Xiaoyu's love story than an endorsement.

Not only does Xiaoyu use up her possessions, but her intense emotions also consume her health. Immediately before her death, she scolds Li Yi with resentment:

> Fair of face and in the flower of my youth, I perish swallowing my resentment. I have a loving mother at home, yet I will not be able to care for her. My fine silken clothes and the music of pipes and strings will from this point on be forever ended. I must carry my suffering to the underworld, and all of it was brought on by you. Li Yi, Li Yi! We must now say farewell for good. But after I die, I will become a vengeful ghost and allow you no peace with your wives and concubines for the rest of your days.
>
> 韶顏稚齒，飲恨而終。慈母在堂，不能供養。綺羅弦管，從此永休。征痛黃泉，皆君所致。李君李君，今當永訣！我死之後，必為厲鬼。使君妻妾，終日不安！[20]

Her passion, which is initially devoted to the romantic encounter, ultimately causes her resentment and demise. There is nevertheless a moral danger attendant on this kind of self-justifying constancy. Both her pledge to become a nun after Li Yi's marriage and her ultimate death make the romantic heroine abandon her familial obligations. As she points out herself, she is no longer able to care for her mother after she dies. In other words, she is unable to fulfill her filial duty as the protagonist of an absolute romance.

Yet the conflict between private desire and the family deepens in the revenge of Xiaoyu's spirit. As she announced in advance, the tale closes with her soul haunting Li Yi's marriage, taking the form of inculcating in him a severe sense of jealousy and paranoia. Private emotions refuse to stay under control in Xiaoyu's story, asserting themselves again and again. Xiaoyu's obstinate will exposes an inherent destructive drive, which leads to family disruption as well as irrational self-destruction. Likewise, distrusting the fidelity of his wives, Li Yi threatens them and drives them away. He falls into restlessness for the rest of his life, and his family is cursed forever. The danger of female desire – particularly its intense dissatisfaction – is given form in Xiaoyu's spirit. Li Yi's anxiety about his inability to control the feelings and desires of his wives illustrates

---

20 Lu, *Tang Song chuanqi ji*, 102; Owen, *The End of the Chinese "Middle Ages"*, 189.

his recognition of this danger. Romance now becomes a nightmare, in which Li Yi constantly precludes any possible romance. Such an ending, haunted by the fear of uncontrollable desire, echoes Li Yi's first entry into Xiaoyu's house, in which he seems anxious and uncertain about the unfathomable romantic sphere.

By foregrounding the female protagonist and her desire, the tale highlights the dilemma between private desire and social propriety. Although Xiaoyu's story originally seems a pleasant romance with a perfect match between talent and beauty, it turns out to be a tragedy of personal resentment and enduring anxiety. The tale ultimately demonstrates that passion, particularly when it is ungovernable, compromises integrity and freedom. What is brought into conflict in the story is not only the romantic plot and social narrative, but also the discourses of ideal romance and aggressive desire. In fact, on the evening before Xiaoyu is to be buried, Li Yi "sees" her again: "her appearance as lovely and desirable as she used to be … looking around at Li Yi [she] said, 'I am embarrassed to see that there is still such feeling in you that you have come like this to see me on my way. Even in the dark realms below I could not help being moved to sigh.'" 容貌妍麗，宛若平生……顧謂生曰："愧君相送，尚有餘情。幽冥之中，能不感嘆." [21] In this illusion, Li Yi preserves Xiaoyu as an ideal romantic heroine, as he saw her at the beginning of the story. At that time, we are told that Xiaoyu loves Li Yi's poetic lines "When I opened the curtains, wind stirred the bamboo, / and I thought it was my old friend coming" 開帘風動竹，疑是故人來.[22] This couplet both stages and shapes the romance, in which Xiaoyu plays the role of the poetic female persona. Owen is right in saying that this "prefigures her fate: to spend a long span in just such a state of unfulfilled anticipation, awaiting in vain the return of her old love."[23] Yet Huo Xiaoyu ends up overfulfilling her romantic role – she is not only a desiring woman who always waits for her lover, but also a seeker whose unfulfilled desire and hatred are so intense as to curse her lover forever. Although Li Yi attempts to appease her anger and to return her to the status of lovely romantic heroine, he fails – Xiaoyu becomes a vengeful ghost in the end, as she has told Li Yi she will.

The discussion above indicates the complexities of Tang narratives. There is no unanimous reading of Huo Xiaoyu's story, which provides multiple points of view. On the one hand, the story presents a public support of romance: within the tale, literary men of delicate feelings sympathize with Xiaoyu's deep

21 Lu, *Tang Song chuanqi ji*, 103; Owen, *The End of the Chinese "Middle Ages"*, 189.

22 Lu, *Tang Song chuanqi ji*, 100; Owen, *The End of the Chinese "Middle Ages"*, 181.

23 Owen, *The End of the Chinese "Middle Ages"*, 138–39.

passion and knights-errant condemn Li Yi's heartlessness. A man in a yellow shirt in particular, in the company of Li Yi's literati friends, manages to bring the romance to a conclusion by coercing Li Yi back to witness Xiaoyu's emaciation and death, inflicted by his inconstancy in love. As such, an internal audience is constructed within the story, who pass judgment on the protagonists and dramatize a sympathetic attitude toward romance. Yet, as Owen claims, it is because the audience cannot choose romance for themselves that they identify with romantic stories.[24] They can witness the performance of the protagonists, sobbing, and then freely exit from the show. In fact, the author not only demonstrates how Xiaoyu devotes her life to romance, but also how Li Yi becomes lost in deep sadness and lasting anxiety. When Li Yi learns of Xiaoyu's serious sickness, "feeling shame, he gives up with a heavy heart and eventually refuses to go" 慚恥忍割，終不肯往.[25] This description indicates that Li Yi is in an awkward plight – he pays for the tension between romance and social propriety. We are also told that after Xiaoyu dies, Li Yi weeps day and night with deepest sorrow and apparent sincerity. Soon after Xiaoyu's death he marries Miss Lu, as demanded by his mother, but the narrator points out that he has no joy in his new marriage, for his heart is filled with sadness and remembrance. Although the reader seldom hears Li Yi's voice, the author's strategic representation of his response suggests his point of view. The inclusion of these descriptions counterbalances the weight of public opinion, and thus bespeaks the story's refusal to commit to any single perspective of narration.

In the end, the author neither fully sides with Xiaoyu nor with Li Yi – he merely presents a dilemma. We see the narrator play the game from behind a screen of detachment, hence there is an ironic subtextual perspective. There is a discrepancy between the simplistic surface of public opinion (the enthusiastic sympathy with romance) and the underlying complexities of authorial judgment. To some degree, "The Story of Huo Xiaoyu" endorses the values of romance, but at the same time shows its doubts about the indulgence in absolute romance and ungovernable passion. This mode of irony is often embedded in Tang *chuanqi* tales to the extent that they produce a sense of openness in the interweaving of different viewpoints, as they seek to figure the gap they perceive between private desire and social obligation.

---

24 Ibid., 142.

25 See Lu, *Tang Song chuanqi ji*, 102.

2 The Ambiguity of Desire: "The Story of Yingying"

"The Story of Yingying" is characterized by gaps and ambivalence. Some scholars try to interpret its textual inconsistency in terms of an authorial motive of self-exculpation. They read the story as an autobiographical record of the author's youthful adventures by constructing the equivalence between the author, the narrator, and the male protagonist.[26] However, such a reading can find little support from historical evidence, and fails to adequately explain the author's psychological ambivalence, for the story ends up undermining the hero's attempt at self-justification, as Owen has pointed out.[27] Indeed, "The Story of Yingying" evokes a sense of irony and complexity by sustaining competing viewpoints of the hero, the heroine, and the author, and by providing both a moralistic and a romantic viewpoint, thereby addressing the problem of self-interest as well as the fundamental tension between romance and propriety.

The author's intensive attention to the ethical difficulty of romance is first represented in his protagonists' moral struggles. He foregrounds the uneasy tension between romance and propriety in his presentation of both Scholar Zhang's 張生 and Yingying's 鶯鶯 attempts at the containment of this tension. Thus, we inevitably see two opposing versions of the same romance going on here. In fact, both Zhang and Yingying try to control the development of their relationship in their own ways.

Yingying's desire to direct the illicit romance to a proper marriage is apparent from the beginning. Although Madame Zheng's motives in holding a banquet at which Yingying is introduced to pay respects to Zhang are already dubious, it is Hongniang 紅娘, Yingying's maid, who first brings up the possibility of a proper marriage. When Zhang becomes infatuated with Yingying

---

26 Wang Zhi 王銍 (1130–1143) was the earliest to identify "The Story of Yingying" as an autobiographical account of an affair of Yuan Zhen; see Zhao Lingzhi 趙令畤 (1061–1134), "Bian chuanqi Yingying shi" 辯傳奇鶯鶯事, in *Houqing lu* 侯鯖録, Zhibuzuzhai congshu 知不足齋叢書 ed., 5.1a–7a. Among studies by modern scholars, the most influential may be Chen Yinke's 陳寅恪 "Du Yingying zhuan" 讀鶯鶯傳, in *Chen Yinke xiansheng lunwen ji* 陳寅恪先生論文集 (Taibei: Sanranxing chubanshe, 1974), 2.527–36. For more information regarding the autobiographical reading of "The Story of Yingying," see Yin Zhanhua 尹占华, "'Yingying zhuan' shi Yuan Zhen ziyu – jian yu Wu Wenbin Xiansheng Shangque"《莺莺傳》是元稹自寓——兼與吴伟斌先生商榷, *Xibei shida xuebao* 西北師大學報 48, no. 4 (2001): 65–69; James Hightower, "Yuan Zhen and 'Yingying zhuan,'" in *Harvard Journal of Asiatic Studies* 33 (1973): 90–123.

27 Owen, *The End of the Chinese "Middle Ages"*, 149.

and tells Hongniang what he feels, Hongniang flees in embarrassment. Yet, the next day, Hongniang – possibly entrusted to convey her mistress Yingying's wish – suggests that Zhang seek Yingying's hand in marriage. But this suggestion is declined by Zhang, who wishes immediately to fulfill his passion without waiting for the time-consuming process of an arranged marriage. Thereupon, Zhang composes two poems – "spring verses" – to express his love for Yingying at Hongniang's suggestion. This poetic seduction works, in the same way that Huo Xiaoyu is drawn to Li Yi. It again suggests the romantic bond between beauty and talent, and the relations between desire and language. Nevertheless, what is different here is that Yingying is not only a beauty, but also a talented writer. She responds positively to Zhang's "spring verses" with her own poetry, which anticipates a romantic rendezvous by representing herself as the heroine of her own romance. But when Zhang climbs over the wall into her chamber, she gives him a severe upbraiding with a highly moralistic tone. The inconsistency of Yingying's responses displays her conflicting impulses – she is caught between morality and passion. As most readers can deduce, her eloquent denunciation of Zhang only betrays her attempt to conceal, or justify, the romantic impulse reflected in her poem. In delivering that moral lesson, in fact, her emphasis on "ritual" (*li* 禮) may be a subtle hint at the desire for a proper union. Zhang, however, seems to lose hope and discontinues the relationship. Then, a few nights later, Yingying goes to Zhang's room voluntarily. Now she takes the initiative to deepen their relationship. As Owen states, "One of the most important aspects of the culture of romance is its site. The central ceremony of a proper marriage is meeting the bride and bringing her to the groom's home, hence into his family."[28] In this regard, the site Yingying chooses for her romance suggests her desire for a "proper" marriage.

Yingying's intention is further hinted at with the development of the story. We are told that, since the first night, Yingying had been absent for some ten days. Only after she receives Zhang's poem "Meeting the Holy One" (*Hui zhen shi* 會真詩) does she let him see her again and join her in the western chamber for nearly a month. Why does Yingying hold up their meetings, and then continue their rendezvous upon receiving Zhang's poem? A large space is opened here for interpretation. Yingying may be playing the role of the goddess of Wu Mountain in Song Yu's "Gaotang fu" 高唐賦 (Rhapsody on the Gaotang Shrine), in which the goddess visits the king of Chu in a dream and then departs after their sexual union; inviting Zhang to participate in this ancient story.[29] Yet it is also possible that Yingying wants to rewrite the ending of the ancient

28 Ibid., 137.
29 Ibid., 160–61.

romance – in which the goddess suddenly evaporates into the air – to show that, unlike the goddess, she is actually accessible on a regular basis. Of course, she might otherwise simply feel shame regarding her improper behavior, but is overwhelmed at last by the romantic passion expressed in Zhang's poetry. Whatever her real motive, the important thing is that she hopes to "regularize the relationship."[30] In other words, she wants to integrate romance into the social norm. For her, this is the only way that she can sustain her romance without threatening social conventions and her self-esteem. Moreover, as Owen indicates, the potential fusion of romance and social order is also embodied in the sites of their sexual encounters – the first night in Zhang's room and, this time, in the western chamber – which is referred to in the romantic poem composed by Yingying.[31]

Although Yingying's motives are ambiguous, her seemingly contradictory behavior reflects her dilemma between private desire and social propriety, and her attempt to resolve it by proposing a proper marriage. Nevertheless, Zhang has no intention of regularizing the situation. Indeed, immediately after Yingying suggests regularizing their relationship, Zhang leaves for the capital for an unstated reason. The text announces that "Yingying seemed to raise no complaints, but the sad expression of reproach on her face was very moving" 崔氏宛無難詞，然而愁怨之容動人矣.[32] A few months later, Zhang visits Puzhou again and stays with Yingying for several months. During Zhang's second visit, Yingying remains silent, not only withholding speech, but also withholding her moods and emotions. Yingying's elegant silence creates new ambiguity here. This may be a kind of protestation of an abandoned woman, which seems to conform to the social convention of "being sad without complaint" (*yuan er bu nu* 怨而不怒). Indeed, an exemplary woman of good family was expected to withhold her appearance (including her speech and her talent) in public. Not until the eve of Zhang's departure for the capital to take the imperial examination does Yingying "express" what she feels in a deliberately respectful and seemingly consoling way. With a dignified expression and a calm voice, she says gently to Zhang, "It is quite proper that when a man

30 Lu, *Tang Song chuanqi ji*, 198; Owen, *The End of the Chinese "Middle Ages"*, 197. There are textual variations here. One version is "Zhang often asked about how Madame Zheng felt. She [Yingying] said, 'I cannot do anything about it.' So she hoped he would marry her" 張生常詰鄭氏之情。則曰："我不可奈何矣。" 因欲就成之. The other version has the variant "知" for "我". In this case, Yingying's speech would be a statement about her mother's intentions: "she knows there is nothing she can do about it, so she hopes you will regularize the relationship." See the editorial note in Lu, *Tang Song chuanqi ji*, 200.

31 Owen, *The End of the Chinese "Middle Ages"*, 156.

32 Lu, *Tang Song chuanqi ji*, 198; Owen, *The End of the Chinese "Middle Ages"*, 197.

seduces a woman, he finally abandons her. I don't dare protest. It was inevitable that having seduced me, you would end it – all this is by your grace. And with this our lifelong vows are indeed ended. Why be deeply troubled by this journey?" 必也君亂之，君終之，君之惠也；則殁身之誓，其有終矣，又何必深感於此行？[33]

Unlike Huo Xiaoyu, who directly denounces Li Yi's betrayal, Yinying conveys her intention by disguise. She tells him that his betrayal was proper, but we can readily see through to her unstated meaning: she is the victim of the seduction; and she innocently believes that she can depend on their lifelong vows. In this highly rhetorical speech, Yingying plays a proper social role of an abandoned woman, while suggesting the possibility of sustaining their relationship through marriage.

Such an attempt to unite romance with social propriety is more obviously displayed in Yingying's letter, which demonstrates a delicate manipulation of unexpressed desires and epistolary propriety:

> From your letter I am given to understand that you are occupied by the pursuit of your studies in the capital. The path to progress in studies does indeed depend on not being disturbed. Yet I feel some resentment that I, a person of so small account, have been left behind forever in a far place. Such is fate. What more is there to say? ... And when I come to dream, my thoughts usually are of the misery of separation, which stirs me until I am choked with sobbing. When we are twined together, absorbed in our passion, for a brief while it is as it once used to be; but then, before our secret encounter comes to its culmination, the soul is startled awake and finds itself sundered form you. Although half of the covers seem warm, yet my thoughts are on someone far, far away. ... Long ago, connected to you as a cousin, I happened to be together with you at a banquet. Having inveigled my maid-servant, you consequently expressed your private feelings. Young people are unable to maintain a firmness of heart. ... In the folly of my passion I thought that I would remain in your care forever. How could I have foreseen that, "once having seen my lord," it would be impossible to plight our troth. Since I suffer the shame of having offered myself to you, I may no longer serve you openly as a wife. This will be a source of bitter regret that will last until my dying day. I repress my sighs, for what more can be said? If by chance in the goodness of your heart you would condescend to fulfill my secret hope, then even if it were on the day of my death, it would be for me like being reborn. But, perchance, the successful scholar holds love to be but of little account and sets it aside as a lesser thing in order to pursuer things of greater importance, considering his

33 Lu, *Tang Song chuanqi ji*, 198; Owen, *The End of the Chinese "Middle Ages"*, 198.

previous mating to have been a vile action, his having taken enforced vows as something one may well betray. If this be so, then my form will melt away and my bones will dissolve, yet my glowing faith with not perish. My petals, borne by the wind and trailing in the dew, will still entrust themselves to the pure dust beneath your feet. Of my sincerity unto death, what words can say is all said here. I sob over this paper and cannot fully express my love. … This jade ring is a thing that I have about me since I was an infant. I send it to you to wear among the ornaments that hang at your waist. … My message is that I would have you, sir, be as pure as the jade, that my own poor aspirations are as unbroken as the ring. That my tear stains are on the bamboo, and that my melancholy sentiments are like this twisting and tangled thread. Through these things I convey what I feel, and will love you always.

伏承使於京中就業，進修之道，固在便安。但恨僻陋之人，永以遐棄，命也如此，知復何言？……乃至夢寢之間，亦多感咽。離憂之思，綢繆繾綣，暫若尋常；幽會未終，驚魂已斷。雖半衾如暖，而思之甚遙。……鄙昔中表相因，或同宴處，婢僕見誘，遂致私誠，兒女之心，不能自固。……愚陋之情，永謂終託。豈期既見君子，而不能定情，致有自獻之羞，不復明侍巾幘。沒身永恨，含歎何言？倘仁人用心，俯遂幽眇；雖死之日，猶生之年。如或達士略情，舍小從大，以先配為醜行，以要盟為可欺，則當骨化形銷，丹誠不泯；因風委露，猶託清塵。存沒之誠，言盡於此；臨紙嗚咽，情不能申。……玉環一枚，是兒嬰年所弄，寄充君子下體所佩。……意者欲君子如玉之真，弊志如環不解，淚痕在竹，愁緒縈絲，因物達情，永以為好耳[34]

Yingying's letter first shows her "understanding" of Zhang's choice of abandoning her for social advancement. However, despite her emphasis on this "fate," she expresses her desperate romantic longing day and night. The specific expressions of sentiment, which beautifully accord with epistolary etiquette, explain the intensity of her feelings. At the same time, she reflects upon their relationship and their moral responsibilities, and thus makes her last effort to persuade Zhang to marry her. The sophisticated rhetoric of Yingying's letter aims to touch Zhang from both emotional and moral perspectives. The jade ring, which Yingying presents Zhang as a gift to convey her complicated feelings, has a variety of connotations related to ritual order, moral integrity and loyalty represented by its firmness and warm glow, and devoted and authentic love symbolized by its purity and prevailing beauty. Furthermore, Yingying utilizes the term "zhi" 志/aspiration to make clear her goal towards proper marriage as well as romantic attachment. She strives to reconcile passion with

---

34 Lu, *Tang Song chuanqi ji*, 198–99; Owen, *The End of the Chinese "Middle Ages"*, 199–200.

marriage, in the hope that virtuous innocence and sincerity can override conventional proprieties. No doubt her painstaking effort to resolve her dilemma between private desire and social morality is compelling, and yet it is doomed to fail, for it ultimately is up to Zhang to provide the solution. But Zhang apparently has his own version of romance.

At the outset of the story, Zhang explains himself to those who question him about his self-restrained behavior when confronted by sexual temptation. He justifies himself as an authentic romantic hero who reserves his passionate desire merely for "things of unusual beauty" (*wu zhi you zhe* 物之尤者). In doing so, Zhang paves the way for introducing his "unusual" version of romance. In Zhang's view, his first meeting with Yingying is characterized by his infatuation with her unusual behavior – her unusual beauty, silence, and resistance for unstated reasons. Yingying's beauty so infatuates him that he asks for her maidservant Hongniang's help. But when Hongniang suggests that he propose to Yingying, he declines. He grounds his choice of romance rather than marriage in the immediacy of his passion. He states that his passionate desire does not allow him to wait for the time-consuming process of marriage arrangement. Thus he reminds us of the irreconcilable gap between romance and marriage. Romance should be spontaneous, timeless, and resistant to social conventions such as those of "a regular matchmaker and the exchange of betrothal presents and names" 因媒氏而娶，納彩問名. Likewise, he accepts an alternative solution recommended by Hongniang – we are told that he immediately composes two "spring verses" to seduce Yingying. The kind of spontaneity represented in his act of poetic writing corresponds to the immediacy he seeks in romantic love.

From this point on, Zhang's story involves various kinds of poetic experience. He receives Yingying's poem, and tries to fulfill the poetic scene depicted in it. Viewed through Zhang's eyes, their first night is constructed as extremely mythic:

> The evening was the eighteenth of the month, and the crystalline rays of the moon slanting past his chamber cast a pale glow over half the bed. Zhang's head was spinning, and he wondered if she might not be one of those goddesses or fairy princesses, for he could not believe that she came from this mortal world. ... She had not said a word the entire night. Zhang got up as the daylight first brought color to the scene, and he wondered to himself, "Could that have been a dream?" In the light there was nothing left but the sight of some makeup on his arm, her scent on his clothes, and the sparkles of her teardrops still glistening on the bedding.

是夕旬有八日也，斜月晶瑩，幽輝半床。張生飄飄然，且疑神仙之徒，不謂從人間至矣。有頃，寺鐘鳴，天將曉，紅娘促去。崔氏嬌啼宛轉，紅娘又捧之而去，終夕無一言。張生辨色而興，自疑曰："豈其夢邪？" 及明，睹妝在臂，香在衣，淚光熒熒然，猶瑩於茵席而已。[35]

By rendering Yingying a goddess and their sexual encounter a dreamlike scene, this account once again echoes Song Yu's aforementioned tale of the goddess of Wu Mountain. Zhang's incomplete poem, "Meeting the Holy One," further strengthens this connection. The whole experience is represented as otherwordly and elusive.

This act of poeticizing romantic experience is also demonstrated in the way in which Zhang deals with Yingying's letter. Her letter, written to win him back in a polite yet touching way, is shown to his friends by Zhang, and thus circulated among the literati. Consequently, a private act is turned into public discourse – it evokes endless literary responses, not only from Zhang's friends, but also in various later *chuanqi* tales. In this way, the letter is not regarded as an instrument of communication (an earnest plea for a proper marriage in a humble gesture); rather, its literary splendor is an end in itself. In "The Story of Yingying," the letter elicits poetic responses from Zhang's friend, Yang Juyuan 楊巨源 – a historical literatus and poet from Puzhou 蒲州, where the story takes place, and Yuan Zhen's good friend in real life – and from Yuan Zhen himself in his role as narrator of the story. Yang Juyuan's poem focuses on Zhang's literary talent and amorous sensibility:

清潤潘郎玉不如，	Pure luster of this young Pan Yue – even the jade cannot compare;
中庭蕙草雪銷初。	sweet clover grows in courtyard as snow first melt away.
風流才子多春思，	The amorous young talent is filled with spring desires –
腸斷蕭娘一紙書。	poor Miss Xiao, her broken heart in a letter of just one page.[36]

This quatrain exemplifies the perfect romance between talented scholar and sentimental beauty without pointing to the tensions of the love affair. Yingying is reduced to an empty name of the common romantic heroine, "Miss Xiao"; her highly self-conscious and moral letter is flattened, described as "just one page." Yang also covers up the truth that breaks Yingying's heart by paralleling Zhang's "spring desires" and Yingying's "broken heart." In so doing, Yang

35 Lu, *Tang Song chuanqi ji*, 198; Owen, *The End of the Chinese "Middle Ages"*, 196.
36 Lu, *Tang Song chuanqi ji*, 199; Owen, *The End of the Chinese "Middle Ages"*, 201.

diminishes the difference between the hero's and the heroine's perspectives so as to more effectively employ Yingying as the appropriate heroine of a romance that both he and Zhang celebrate.

In contrast to the brief account of the romantic plot in Yang's quatrain, Yuan Zhen's poem, which is said to be a continuation of Zhang's "Meeting the Holy One," is highly descriptive. The detailed depiction of the lovers' first night together echoes and complements Zhang's representation of his dream-like experience in the narrative. But more importantly, through allusions to the erotic tradition in Chinese poetry, Yuan stages the lovers' encounter in the mode of a mortal man meeting a goddess – which focuses on their intense passion and ultimate separation – thereby justifying the lovers' inevitable separation.

鴛鴦交頸舞，	Mated ducks, their necks twined in dance,
翡翠合歡籠。	Kingfishers encaged in passion's embrace.
眉黛羞偏聚，	Her black brow knit in modesty,
唇朱暖更融。	Her carmine lips, warming, grew softer.
氣清蘭蕊馥，	Breath pure as the fragrance of orchids,
膚潤玉肌丰。	Her skin glossy, her marble flesh full.
無力慵移腕，	Worn out, too tired to move her wrist,
多嬌愛斂躬。	So charming, she loved to curl up.
[...]	
方喜千年會，	No sooner made glad by this millennial meeting,
俄聞五夜窮。	She suddenly heard nights hours end.
流連時有恨，	At the moment resentful, she lingers on,
繾綣意難終。	Clinging with passion, desire unspent.
慢臉含愁態，	A sad expression on languid cheeks,
芳詞誓素衷。	In sweet lines she vowed the depths of love.
贈環明運合，	Her ring-gift revealed a union fated,
留結表心同。	A love-knot left showed hearts were the same.
[...]	
乘鶩還歸洛，	She rode her cygnet back to the Luo;
吹簫亦上嵩。	He played his pipes as he climbed Mount Song.
[...]	
海闊誠難渡，	The sea is so vast, truly hard to cross;
天高不易衝。	And the sky is high, not easy to reach.
行雲無處所，	Goddess moving in cloud, nowhere now to be found;
簫史在樓中。	And Xiaoshi is there in his high chamber.[37]

37 Lu, *Tang Song chuanqi ji*, 199; Owen, *The End of the Chinese "Middle Ages"*, 202.

By centering exclusively on the sensual details of the erotic encounter, the poem disguises the moral dilemma in the narrative and celebrates the aesthetic aspects of love. What is more remarkable is its poetic revision of the plot. In the poem, Yingying's gifts, the ring and love-knot, are presented immediately after the sexual scene as the memento of their passionate but transient love, while in Yingying's letter, these gifts are an implicit call for a proper and permanent marriage. Moreover, at the end of the poem, Zhang is figured as Xiaoshi, who is immersed in his dreamlike trance, and endlessly awaits the disappearing goddess. By contrast, Yingying's sadness is obscured, replaced with an aura of mystery and uncertainty.

Both Yang's and Yuan's responses participate in Zhang's lyrical representation of his romance. For all the differences in the romantic models they employ, they both demonstrate a profound separation from the letter that inspires their compositions. In fact, one more poetic response, from Yuan's good friend, Li Shen 李紳, who was also a real Tang literatus and poet, is introduced at the end of the narrative, wherein they talk about the story, and Li thinks of it as outstanding (*zhuoran chengyi* 卓然稱異), to the extent that he composes "Yingying's Song" to make it widely known. Although the narrative does not display the detailed content of the poem but merely the title, we can judge from Li Shen's high opinion of the story that his perspective is in accordance with Yang's and Yuan's. The letter is a narration that provides a chronological account of the romantic story as well as the psychological and moral complications accompanying it, whereas the poems tend to aestheticize the love affair as timeless, a momentary suspension from time and moral obligations. The contrast between these two figurations parallels that between Yingying's version of romance and Zhang's.

Nevertheless, this arresting poetic transformation is followed by an obtrusive move to a moralistic objection, as Zhang justifies his abandonment of Yingying in terms of his aversion to a dangerously contaminating beauty. Yingying's enigmatic image and her unpredictability, which attracted him before, now frighten him. Just as Huo Xiaoyu's constancy makes her both the perfect heroine of romance and the uncontrollable vengeful spirit, Yingying's inconsistency renders her both an unusual beauty and a powerful threat. From poetic infatuation to sudden moralization, however, the text moves too fast to be credible. Moreover, Zhang asks to see Yingying again after having abandoned her and rebuked her for her destructive potential. This also seems puzzling. In actuality, Zhang refuses to turn his romantic heroine into a proper wife, thereby removing the threat that the romance poses to social morality. And it is because Yingying has been married off and is no longer a threat to his romance narrative that Zhang can see his lover again. More importantly, the text makes it clear that Zhang tries to see Yingying because he happens to pass through the place where she is living. The spontaneity and immediacy are again emphasized, echoing his first entrance into the romance.

However, Yingying refuses to see him again. Learning of Zhang's pain at such a rebuff, she writes a poem professing lingering love and longing. But she never sees him. When Zhang is about to leave, she composes another poem urging Zhang to love his new wife with the passion he once felt for her. Yingying's two poems once more display her conflicting emotions between romantic yearning and moral responsibility, and her inability to overcome the conflict. Yet for Zhang, although Yingying's rejection pains him, he can now complete his "Meeting the Holy One," or realize the poetic scene portrayed in Yuan Zhen's poem by playing the role of Xiaoshi who awaits his beloved in his chamber in vain.

The discrepancy between Zhang's story and Yingying's lies in their profound mutual misunderstanding. They approach the romance, as well as the acts of writing and reading, from different angles. Yingying attempts to direct her romance to narrative completion with her favored ending, marriage, while Zhang tends to concentrate his romantic experience on poetic scenes. When Yingying makes every effort to incorporate her romance into the social norms of respectability and fulfillment, Zhang resolutely separates his passionate desire from social conventions. By mystifying Yingying and her desire, Zhang adores her aesthetically but rebukes her morally. It can be said that this gap between private desire and social norms, together with the tentative solutions to this gap, induce the split in the text. The split in the text originates from a split in the self, as the literatus betrays his dubious attitude toward desire by foregrounding the ambiguity of Yingying's image and behavior.

Nevertheless, the story presents not only the hero's and the heroine's points of view, but also the perspectives of audience and the narrator. It has been argued that Tang tales' conclusions often thematize and imagine sociality in the form of recounted gossip circulated among literati networks or within a knowledgeable readership.[38] Friendship networks and scenes of social exchange here are deployed to create communal discourses and collective literati identities.[39] Although the historical fidelity of these framing scenes or representations of literati sociality are difficult to verify due to the limitations of the extant historical sources, the meticulous placement of the story in the context of social talk and the reliability of its sources of information underscores the question of authenticity.

---

38 See Sarah M. Allen, *Shifting Stories: History, Gossip, and Lore in Narratives from Tang Dynasty China* (Cambridge, MA: Harvard University Asia Center, 2014), 25–69.

39 Luo, *Literati Storytelling in Late Medieval China*.

At the end of "The Story of Yingying," the "I" narrator – identified as Yuan Zhen – appears, portraying his discussions with his friends and colleagues about the affair, and explaining his moralistic motivation to recount this love story. Here, the narrator is on Zhang's side, affirming his repudiation of Yingying. However, can we see this "I" narrator as the self-identifying author? Partly, perhaps. If this story were created by Yuan Zhen, then the appearance of the poet Yuan Zhen as a character in the story – who completes Zhang's "Meeting the Holy One" in sixty lines – is equally intriguing. It problematizes the simple equation of the "I" narrator with the character Yuan Zhen, and Yuan Zhen as the character in the story with Yuan Zhen as the author. The character Yuan Zhen, Zhang's friend, approves of Zhang's romantic view, while the "I" narrator disapproves of the love affair – this contrast demonstrates the author's hidden motives and double view, which attempts to strike a balance between the moralistic and romantic perspectives. Within the larger frame of the question of the story's authenticity, consequently, there is a further query about whether Yingying's perspective or Zhang's is true. In this light, the story's oversimplified moralistic ending is unable to resolve the textual problematic in all its complexities. The circulation of the story as a topic of social talk suggests that the matter of human nature involving aberration and normality, and emotions and rites, has become a significant subject of discussion among a certain group of literary men.

More importantly, the story's ambivalences and complexities are demonstrated in its tendency to generate multiple and even conflicting versions of the same "true" characters and stories. The author restrains himself from smoothing out the underlying gaps and inconsistencies in the story, thereby representing anxiety, desire, and motives in an ironic light. If this narrative stance is not an intentional, authorial irony, then at least it shows romance's potential for self-ironization. Although Yingying and Zhang approach the dilemma between romance and propriety in different ways, they both try to deploy social moralities to cover their self-interest. In this sense, we see the failure of the Confucian moralizing discourse. But finally, the power of romance is downplayed too, for both the hero and the heroine end up with a sad separation and marriage to other people.

Moreover, distancing himself from both the hero and the heroine, the author endeavors to dispel the possibility of being accused of having self-serving motives by transforming the moral-psychological response to the problem of self-interest into a valorization of the literal, or the image, as an end in itself.[40] However, this emphasis on literary forms and genres extends beyond a

---

40 Wai-yee Li argues that the mixture of genres in the story implies an ideal of inclusiveness. See Li, "Mixture of Genres and Motive for Fiction in 'Yingying's Story,'" in *Ways with Words:*

purely all-encompassing aesthetic pursuit. Admittedly, Zhang's two distanced self-justifications both employ the question-and-answer form used in traditional rhapsody, a literary form designed to exhibit skill in argumentation. Both Yingying's and Zhang's self-images coincide with conventional images of lovers in such genres as rhapsody and palace-style poetry.[41] Zhang also tends to act out romantic scenes in literature. Nevertheless, this construal of the literal as its own end is not limited to a literary practice of mixing genres, but significantly recasts self-interest as merely a subject for fiction, thereby compromising fiction's problematic motivation. In doing so, the romance exposes itself as merely a textual construction, insisting that what is real is only what is conveyable by multiple signs, or images. In this regard, "The Story of Yingying" plays the game of romance in a more light-hearted way than "The Story of Huo Xiaoyu," which is so deeply trapped between conflicting claims as to become an irrecoverable tragedy. The intense tension embedded in the latter is partly released in the story under discussion through the intriguing play of gaps and inconsistencies.

"The Story of Yingying" has had a lasting impact on Chinese literature and culture. It has inspired a long list of adaptations, and thus propelled the development of romantic discourses. In particular, some later *chuanqi* tales follow the manipulation of various literary writings in "The Story of Yingying," even to the extent of directly copying the poems and Yingying's letter in the story with only a few revisions, in order to present themselves as exhibitions of poetry and literary prose, or a kind of linguistic indulgence in love and desire. The canonical status of this story is also demonstrated by its tentative exploration of the entry of romance into the domestic sphere, although it only testifies to the impossibility of this containment. The ultimate integration of the romance into family is left to its dramatic transformation in the late imperial period, *The Story of the Western Wing*.

3 The Treatment for Passion: "The Story of Li Wa"

In an enlightening study of "The Story of Li Wa," Paul Rouzer has pointed out that the story is an "anti-romance."[42] This is true in the sense that the story

---

Writing about Reading Texts from Early China, ed. Pauline Yu, Peter Bol, Stephen Owen, and Willard Peterson (Berkeley: University of California Press, 2000), 185–92.

41 As Owen observes, Yingying enacts various images, ranging from the mysterious goddess and the abandoned woman to the self-effacing wife. See Owen, *The End of the Chinese "Middle Ages"*, 160–61.

42 Rouzer, *Articulated Ladies*, 241.

demonstrates the great danger of romance, as romantic passion almost destroys a promising young man. Moreover, the heroine is represented as either a professional courtesan or a virtuous woman, rather than a romantic lover. Scholars also note the story's symmetry in terms of the hero's fall and rise.[43] Yet, I would further argue that this structural balance is also reflected in the counterpoise between the "romantic" world and a moral life. The former is marked as ersatz and ephemeral, while the latter is ultimately realized and perpetuated.

Upon the first encounter of the hero and the heroine, the issue of money comes to the fore. Once the scholar falls in love with the heroine, Li Wa 李娃, on the street, he is well prepared to pay. The intrusion of financial compulsion reminds us that the unalloyed romantic relationship represented here is illusory. When the scholar enters Li Wa's house, its luxury is repeatedly mentioned – dazzling curtains and couches, sumptuous quilts and pillows, elegant rooms, foods with a rich variety of flavors – which suggests the economic necessities of maintaining this "romantic" world. Although during the scholar's first visit Li Wa and her "mother" (the procuress) seem to show little interest in money, they do not deny the financial code of the pleasure quarters. As Li Wa says when she offers to pay for the first night's expenses, "Anything more can wait for another day" 其餘以俟他辰.[44] Indeed, as time passes, the scholar squanders his money and is driven out. This contrasts with "The Story of Huo Xiaoyu," in which Huo asks not for money but for a man of talent and feeling, so that the romantic world is protected from financial pressures. In this sense, "The Story of Li Wa" shows that the hero falls victim to a romantic delusion from the very start.

Indeed, the scholar is so overwhelmed with romantic passion that he considers its realization to be his life's ambition (*pingsheng zhi zhi* 平生之志).[45] Nevertheless, a male literatus's ambition ought not to be romantic passion, but rather an illustrious public career. The scholar's misapplication of the word "*zhi*" 志 indicates his misrecognition of the relationships between romance and one's public career. This misrecognition is further urged by the reply of Li Wa's "mother": "Between man and woman strong desire exists. If their feelings are engaged together, even the 'bidding of father and mother' cannot control them" 男女之際，大慾存焉。情苟相得，雖父母之命，不能制也.[46] Here, there is an obvious allusion to the *Liji* 禮記 (*Book of Rites*), in which one

43 See Glen Dudbridge, *The Tale of Li Wa* (London: Ithaca Press for the Board of the Faculty of Oriental Studies, Oxford University, 1983), 37–39; Kominami Ichirou 小南一郎, "Li A den no kouzou" 李娃伝の構造, *Touhou gakuhou* 東方学報 62 (1990): 284–91.

44 Lu, *Tang Song chuanqi ji*, 148. The translation is from Dudbridge, *The Tale of Li Wa*, 125.

45 Lu, *Tang Song chuanqi ji*, 148.

46 Ibid.; Dudbridge, *The Tale of Li Wa*, 127.

passage explains: "In food and drink and in sexual relations exist the greatest desires of mankind" 飲食男女，人之大慾存焉.[47] This passage, which introduces the necessity of ritual and ethical restraint, is now exploited to naturalize the primacy of human desires.[48] Furthermore, the "bidding of father and mother" is cited from Mencius, who believes that men and women who associate with each other without the bidding of parents will be despised by family and society.[49] The Han commentator Zhao Qi 趙岐 (?–201) clarifies: "People should not follow their desires when their feeling is evoked, but should act in accordance with ritual" 人不可触情從慾，須禮而行.[50] But the scholar fails to realize this orthodox statement about desire and morality. Instead, he attempts to construct a family based on romance.

Immediately after the "mother" consents to his moving in, the scholar surrenders to his role as her son-in-law: "I would gladly make myself your menial servant" 愿以己為厮養.[51] From then on, he rents a vacant court in the Li house, moving into the family home and acting as husband and son-in-law. His entrance into the Li house mimics the ceremony of a "proper" marriage, in which the wife is brought to the husband's home. Thus, he constructs a "pseudo-family" for himself, and takes it seriously.[52] It is this fictive familial relationship, based on romantic delusion, that traps the scholar in the scheme of Li Wa and her "mother." Li Wa's "mother" invites the scholar to visit the temple of the Spirit of the Bamboo Grove, claiming that this is to pray for offspring; later, stopping off at Li Wa's "aunt's" home on their return, the scholar and Li Wa are told that Li Wa's "mother" has taken ill causing Li Wa to leave hurriedly while Li Wa's "aunt" delays the scholar with talk of the mother's impending (false) funeral in the role of (fictive) "son-in-law," so that he fails to follow Li Wa, allowing her and her "mother" to make an escape with his worldly possessions. With their escape, ironically, these efforts to perpetuate familial relationships all disappear overnight and the scholar is left penniless and alone. This transience, which often marks the nature of romance and the pleasure quarters, produces a moral failure. In this sense, the hero's attempt to domesticate romance is doomed to fail, for family is not supposed to be a space of spontaneous passion, but rather a ritualized institution.

---

47 *Liji*, *juan* 21, in *Shisanjing zhushu* 十三經注疏 (Taibei: Xin wenfeng chuban gongsi, 2001), 11.1073.

48 Dudbridge, *The Tale of Li Wa*, 127n85.

49 *Mengzi zhushu* 孟子注疏, *juan* 5, *xia*, in *Shisanjing zhushu*, 20.268.

50 Ibid., 20.269.

51 Lu, *Tang Song chuanqi ji*, 148; Dudbridge, *The Tale of Li Wa*, 127.

52 See Rouzer, *Articulated Ladies*, 243.

Moreover, the author tells us that, after he takes up residence in the Li house, the scholar gets more and more obsessed with his pseudo-family and pleasure-seeking, and thus he no longer keeps in touch with his relatives and fellow literati. His misuse of his passion and the concept of "family" make him a "non-person," since a person is defined first and foremost by social connections in a Confucian society. This tragic outcome is played out more thoroughly in his fall to the bottom of society. After he is abandoned, he falls seriously ill in his indignation and sorrow. Later, he is moved into a funeral parlor, where he regains his health, and becomes a dirge-singer. Before long, his singing skills as a mourner become incomparable, for his emotional sensitivity and life experience endow him with this special talent. But ironically, while mourning is a ritual which normally defines familial relationships, the scholar makes a living mourning strangers. According to the prevailing social norms, his talent is supposed to be used for a public career rather than for entertainment. Such a misuse of passion and talent again prevents him from being reintegrated into the family.[53] When the scholar displays his marvelous singing skills at a contest held by two competing funeral parlors, he wins over the entire audience, except his father. Learning that the scholar has become a dirge-singer, his father leads him to the east of the Apricot Garden and beats him nearly to death. By doing so, his father cuts off his familial bonds.

In fact, when the scholar is brought to the funeral parlor, he enters a "liminal zone," a time and space of withdrawal from normal society.[54] The father's "execution" further erases the scholar's identity, making him an utter "non-person": covered in sores and wounds, he is abandoned even by the funeral parlor employees; after he recovers, he makes a living as a beggar. The progression of the hero's adventure in Chang'an – the encounter with Li Wa, the establishment of his fame as a dirge-singer, and hopeless begging in the city – frees him from the constraints of social bonds and responsibility, but also causes his loss of personal identity. When he gives rein to his private desire, or willfully asserts himself, he deviates from social order and falls into a process of dehumanization. In this sense, personal identity cannot be defined by romantic passion or talent itself, but by public recognition.

---

53 Rouzer addresses this from another perspective. He points out that "the direct expression of emotion supposedly makes for successful poetry," rather than touching on songs. See Rouzer, *Articulated Ladies*, 244.

54 See S.-C. Kevin Tsai, "Ritual and Gender in the 'Tale of Li Wa,'" *Chinese Literature: Essays, Articles, Reviews* 26 (Dec. 2004): 114.

Many scholars have noted that the father's choice of location in which to beat his son is meaningful.[55] The Apricot Garden is a place both for those who pass the exams to hold celebrations and for courtesans and literati to meet. The evocation of this place reminds the scholar, or the reader, of the "correct" relationships between romance, family, and public career. The romantic world is only a site that betokens a literatus's public success – a reward for those who successfully pass the exams, or a demonstration of the talent of the promising examinees – rather than one that can be perpetuated in the family. But the scholar takes a wrong path: he devotes himself to romantic passion. Modern readers often have difficulty understanding the father's cruel act of beating his son nearly to death.[56] However, the author indicates that it is in essence the romantic delusion that causes the scholar's degradation and dehumanization. As Li Wa says when she rediscovers the scholar begging in extreme hunger and cold, "We led him to fail his ambition and lose his due place in family and society. The relation of father and son is an endowment of nature, yet we caused [a father] to break off his affection, to take his son's life and abandon him" 令其失志，不得齒于人倫。父子之道，天性也。使其情絕，殺而棄之.[57] In this way, the story demonstrates the danger and harm of the discourse of romance. Thus, the scholar's degradation reaches its lowest point.

The second half of the story, however, focuses on the restoration of the hero to a proper social position. It is Li Wa who rescues him from the miserable life of a wandering beggar, and who helps him return to elite society. However, this is not only a rebirth of the hero, but also a transformation of the heroine, Li Wa, who accordingly transforms from a courtesan to an exemplary woman and noble duchess. By instructing the scholar to recreate his identity, Li Wa introduces herself into elite society. But what is at stake in such an accomplishment?

Upon their second encounter, Li Wa is so moved by the sight of the scholar's "non-person" situation as a beggar that she decides to take him in. When the "mother" asks her to get rid of the scholar, Li Wa justifies her own decision:

> This is the son of a good family. Once he drove tall carriages, bore trappings of gold. When he came to our house it was all squandered within a year. Together,

55 See Rouzer, *Articulated Ladies*, 244–45; Seno Tachihiko 妹尾達彥, "Todai kohanki no chouan to denki shosetsu – 'Li A den' no bunseki o chuushin to shite" 唐代後半期の長安と伝奇小説——李娃伝の分析を中心として, in *Hino Kaizaburou Hakase shouju kinen lonshuu: chuugoku shakai seido bunkashi no shomondai* 日野開三郎博士頌壽紀念論集：中國社會．制度．文化史の 諸問題 (Fukuoka: Chuugoku shoten, 1987), 488.

56 See Rouzer, *Articulated Ladies*, 244–45; Kominami Ichilou, "Li A den no kouzou," 281.

57 Lu, *Tang Song chuanqi ji*, 151; Dudbridge, *The Tale of Li Wa*, 165.

> mother and daughter, we set up a scheme of deceit, abandoned him and drove him out. This was scarcely human conduct. We led him to fail his ambition and lose his due place in family and society. The relation of father and son is an endowment of nature, yet we caused [a father] to break off his affection, to take his son's life and abandon him. The whole world knows it was because of me. This young man's relations fill the court. One day, when someone in power conducts a full investigation of what happened, disaster will overtake us! What is more, if we deceive Heaven and betray man, the ghosts and spirits will not assist us. Let us not leave ourselves a legacy of misfortune!
>
> 此良家子也，當昔驅高車，持金裝，至某之室，不逾期而蕩盡。且互設詭計，舍而逐之，殆非人行。令其失志，不得齒於人倫。父子之道，天性也。使其情絕，殺而棄之，又困躓若此。天下之人，盡知為某也。生親戚滿朝，一旦當權者熟察其本末，禍將及矣。況欺天負人，鬼神不祐，無自貽其殃也。[58]

This speech indicates that Li Wa acts out of a sense of guilt. What she fears are both moral retribution and practical revenge from the scholar's relatives. Here, love is not emphasized in terms of their relationship. In fact, in the whole story, there is no sign that absolutely suggests that she loves him. Although we are told that when the scholar has used up his money the mother treats him more and more indifferently while Li Wa's affection becomes more sincere, Li Wa's subsequent assistance in the scheme to abandon the scholar hints that this affection does not transcend her profession as a courtesan. When she runs into him again, she is stung by her own conscience. The moral obligation she feels paves the way for her acceptance by the hero's family and elite society. From then on, she takes up the role of mother instead of lover.[59] Like a mother, she not only nurtures his health, but also supervises his studies. Now, she identifies not with her own class interests, but with the patriarchal ideology and elite interests of establishing fame and identity.

Convincing the scholar to pick up his books, Li Wa carefully plans his path of reintegration into elite society. She spends a large amount of money on buying him books for exam preparation, compensating for the money he squandered on the pleasure quarters. She supervises his study with tireless effort. When he gets tired, she directs him to compose poems and rhapsodies, which were important for a male elite to succeed in social activities in Tang society. Under her meticulous direction, he makes great progress in his learning and

---

58 Lu, *Tang Song chuanqi ji*, 150–51; Dudbridge, *The Tale of Li Wa*, 164–65.

59 See Rouzer, *Articulated Ladies*, 246.

is anxious to have a try at the literary examination. However, Li Wa persuades him to further strengthen his learning, so that he can amaze the world with a tour de force. Just as Li Wa expects, he is placed in the top class at the first attempt. At this point, however, the story is not yet complete. According to Li Wa's advice, the scholar works even harder and attends another periodic examination, through which the emperor summons exceptional men from all parts of the state. This time, he is placed at the top of the list, and achieves the highest reputation in elite society. In this process of reestablishing the scholar, Li Wa exhibits great ambitions and strong desires. Yet, her desires only inhabit those of the scholar; her rise is only possible through his reintegration. She is acquisitive and rational. Her prudent calculation contrasts with the scholar's spontaneous passion and rush to self-gratification. As such, the story represents the complex mechanism of desire in terms of the relationships between literati and courtesans.

Having fulfilled her task of returning the scholar to elite society, Li Wa offers to leave him so that he can marry a girl from a prominent family. But the scholar refuses her so passionately – he threatens to commit suicide if she leaves him – that she agrees to accompany him to Jianmen and then go back. However, in Jianmen the scholar encounters his father, who hears the whole tale from his son and lets him marry Li Wa. In this way, Li Wa is wholeheartedly accepted by the elite family. Throughout the tale, Li Wa is portrayed as a person who always knows how to separate herself slightly from the object of desire and thus not only opens a space for rational calculation but also effectively balances the scholar's passionate inclination. After she is welcomed into the illustrious clan through the six rites of marriage, Li Wa performs all the rituals of the family and evinces a high degree of womanly duty. In this way, the tale depicts self-restraint and the conduct of ritual as contributing to the rise of Li Wa. These are exactly what are missing from a romance. In this sense, as a resourceful courtesan, Li Wa is successfully domesticated through the abandonment of romance and the denial of passion.

Through Li Wa's compromise with the patriarchy, the story arrives at a miraculous conclusion – it is Li Wa's "sincerity" that harmonizes private feelings and public discourse, and that makes it possible for the hero both to maintain his passion and desire and to be reintegrated into the elite class. Li Wa is ultimately characterized in the role of mother, a moral subject who provides a moral example or guidance for the hero. However, the seemingly perfect ending is unable to appease all anxiety, or to completely defuse the threat of instability embedded in the story. After all, the scholar does ignore his social responsibility and public career in pursuit of romantic passion. Even after he succeeds in the examinations and recovers his reputation, he is still passionately attached to Li Wa. These details remind the reader of the citation of Mencius by Li Wa's "mother," through which the author presents an alternative discourse competing with that of patriarchal authority. Ultimately, this "anti-romance" suggests the power of romance, and the anxiety about it, despite the tale's idealized resolution. At the same time, however, although the story primarily upholds the patriarchal ideology, it also highlights the failure, or the flaws, of the patriarchy. For example, Li Wa proves to be a better parent than the scholar's real father. Not only does she nurture his body, but she also educates him regarding how to be a respectful person in elite social life. She remakes the scholar in the way she wants him to be, and successfully transforms herself as well. Such a power of transformation renders her somewhat threatening, even though the author attempts to cloak the threat by converting Li Wa to the moral values of the patriarchy. At the very end, moreover, the scholar enacts his mourning duties for his parents so movingly as to bring forth natural omens, thereby receiving the emperor's gifts and promotion. Ironically, however, the scholar's moving mourning of his parents evokes his former lowly status as a professional mourner, a juxtaposition which functions to undermine the authority of the ritual. Thus through its parodies of marriage, the funeral, and parenthood, rituals central to Tang elite families, the tale serves as a more general critique of Tang society as a whole. It dramatizes the struggle between the assertion of a kind of universality or unity of sincerity and emotion that transcends class difference and the uncertainty about self-interest and personal expression that profoundly confronts the protagonists.

Is it financial relationships, rituals, or private feelings that constitute a family? What is the proper relationship between romance, family, and virtue? How "The Story of Li Wa" frames these questions aroused lasting interest in later periods. Hu Yinglin 胡應麟 (1551–1602) comments on the story, "That Li Wa later took in Li [the scholar] was merely sufficient to atone for her guilt over betraying and abandoning him. It is quite ridiculous for the author to praise her for being virtuous" 娃晚收李子，僅足贖其棄背之罪，傳者称其賢，大可哂也.[60] Feng Menglong also criticizes Li Wa:

> Why does [one say that] Li Wa is righteous? When she casts lingering looks at the scholar upon his dropping the whip, she is just afraid that he is not coming. When they stay at her house and make merry, she is only afraid that he will not linger. When it comes to the plan to swindle, she acts in collusion with the mother, lest he should go away. Is there such righteousness in the world?

60 Hu Yinglin 胡應麟, *Shaoshi shanfang bicong* 少室山房笔叢 (Beijing, Zhonghua shuju, 1958), 41.567.

> Fortunately, the scholar endures humiliation and suffers hardships. If one day he dies at the house, at the funeral parlor, under his father's whip, or in the snow and wind, Li Wa never has him on her mind. Is she willing to shed a single tear for him? She wraps him in an embroidered jacket only because she had lived in the pleasure quarters so long that she plans to go with him. But her love for him is not so strong as that of his for her. Once she is horrified and shocked by the sight [of his miserable situation], only then does she perform such a magnificent act. The scholar treats Li well, but it is still regrettably late, even though he is repaid in this way. And then, once Li re-establishes him, he repays her with the splendid title of the Duchess of Qian. The scholar is unfortunate to meet Li, but how fortunate is she to meet him again?
>
> 世覽《李娃傳》者，無不多娃之義。夫娃何義乎？方其墜鞭流盼，唯恐生之不來。及夫下榻延歡，唯恐生之不固。乃至金盡局設，與姥朋奸，反唯恐生之不去。天下有義焉如此者哉！幸生忍羞耐苦，或一旦而死于邸，死于凶肆，死于箠楚之下，死于风雪之中，娃意中已無郑生矣。肯為下一滴泪耶？繡襦之裹，盖由平康滋味，尝之已久，計所與往還，情更無如昔年郑生者，一旦惨于目而怵于心，遂有此豪举事耳。生之遇李厚，雖得此報，猶恨其晚。乃李一收拾生，而生遂以汧國花封報之。生不幸而遇李，李何幸而復遇生耶？[61]

Both Hu and Feng condemn Li Wa's initial betrayal and abandonment of the scholar. Feng even asserts his opinion that Li Wa does not love the scholar as intensely as he did her. *Qing* is highly valued in Feng's mind. For Hu and Feng, Li Wa is not a real lover, let alone a virtuous lover. In contrast, the author sees Li Wa more as a courtesan who is not without a sense of rectitude, rather than as a lover. Probably because of this, the author is less strict with the heroine than later critics.

According to Dudbridge, Yuan and Ming dramatic adaptations of the story exhibit new ideas on moralism and romance.[62] Two major changes are made in these adaptations: (1) A bond of true affection between Li Wa and the scholar is emphasized. From the start, Li Wa is represented as being sincerely engaged with her lover, while the mother is characterized as rapacious and ruthless. By letting the mother alone set up the trap to abandon the scholar, the adapted plays exempt Li Wa from the guilt of betrayal and make Li a victim of the mother's scheme, too. Thus Li Wa is exculpated and made into an innocent lover, as

61 Feng, *Qing shi*, 16.319–20.

62 Dudbridge, *The Tale of Li Wa*, 82–92.

well as a virtuous woman. (2) The theme of generational conflict, and its ultimate containment, is further emphasized. In these plays, the scholar refuses to acknowledge the connection with his father after he is established as a county magistrate. But Li Wa persuades the scholar to bow to his father by threatening her own suicide. Li Wa herself also rejects her "mother" violently, before also reconciling with her by the intervention of the scholar's father. These conflicts are ultimately contained or reconciled in a more integrated moral solution. These two changes indicate that it is love, or private feelings, instead of moral obligation, that becomes the thrust of the story. If the original "The Story of Li Wa" introduced a courtesan into the domestic sphere only by suppressing romantic passion, then later dramas attempted to valorize love and integrate it into the family. "The Story of Li Wa" demonstrates both the power of romance and the attempt to overcome it. Yet the gap in-between is left for later adaptations to bridge in a more effective and expedient way.

Taken as a whole, Tang *chuanqi* tales do not form a unanimous voice, but betray manifoldness and uncertainty through their delineation of the reception of the love story within the contemporary interpretive communities. They tend to display a process of ongoing negotiation concerning *xing* and *qing*, rather than the pursuit of consensus, in the circulation of gossip or social talk among literati networks. The inherent ambivalences and anxieties underlying the various voices and values remain unsettled in the tales, through which the open-endedness of the self is instead made possible. In the frame of literati sociality that often contextualizes love stories, friendly groups of literary men are linked by both the pursuit of aesthetic pleasures and intellectual exchanges, which bring about the possibility of a new way of thinking about emotion and moral issues based on a sentiment that allows them to view desire as morally positive.

The classical romantic tale as a genre underwent development and changes throughout later periods. However, the Tang stories discussed above establish basic stereotypes that are taken up by later versions. Lacking originality, Song romantic tales are merely a miscellaneous patchwork of the popular Tang stories. For example, "The Record of Tan Yige" (*Tan Yige ji* 譚意歌記) exploits "The Story of Yingying" and "The Story of Huo Xiaoyu" as the frame of the first half of the story, while its second half greatly reflects the influence of "The Story of Li Wa." In "The Record of Tan Yige," the heroine is rewarded with a good marriage for both constraining herself and treating others according to heavenly principles (*tianli* 天理). One of the characteristics of Song tales is that they tend to be moral comedies with endings of union and celebration. In many cases, Song tales attempt to develop a discourse of correspondence between heavenly principles and human feelings (*renqing* 人情), rather than the conflicts between them.[63] They represent a certain principle that is "so-of-itself" (*zhiran zhi li* 自然之理), that is, part of the natural order of things and the foundation for the moral and social system, as some Song thinkers suggested.[64] It seems that authenticity is not a matter for discussion or conscious reflection in these tales, since humans' basic values are what they share with heaven-and-earth as something that is natural. The tales discussed in this chapter assert a belief in a universal process of integrated and dynamic creation that involves both human beings and heaven-and-earth. In many Song tales, emotion is reevaluated as something that enables human interaction with the world. Emotion, and sometimes desire as well, plays a positive role in the organization of social life. It is not an obstacle to social harmony that has to be regulated or suppressed, but something that is natural about human beings. Therefore, what we often find in Song tales is the condition of harmony and equilibrium that is the proper state of self, society, and cosmos, as well as a kind of a joyful sensation of unity between the ultimate principle and human feelings (*zhili renqing* 至理人情), which contrasts with the typical mood or tone of anxiety and uncertainty present in the Tang tales discussed in this chapter.[65] In this respect, Song tales anticipate the coming late Ming drama, in which romantic passion is also integrated into marriage and family, albeit with a differing manner of internalization (that is made clear in following chapter).

In Song tales, more often than not, the difficulty of romance lies more in defects of personal integrity than in the conflict between private desire and social propriety. Likewise, there emerges a new stereotype, the heartless and dissipated lover. The hero of "The Story of the Mandarin-Duck Lamp" (*Yuanyang deng zhuan* 鴛鴦燈傳), Scholar Zhang, is a case in point. He is a dandy who betrays his lover and marries a courtesan. This story ends with a legal solution: the magistrate orders Zhang to marry both women, with the first lover being the legal wife.[66] Similar legal solutions can be seen in another tale, "Zhang Hao" 张浩, in which "human feeling" is affirmed by "heavenly principle" in the form of legal justice.[67]

---

63 See "Liuhong ji" 流红記, "Tan Yige ji" 譚意歌記, "Wang Youyu ji" 王幼玉記, in *Songdai chuanqi ji* 宋代傳奇集, ed. Li Jianguo 李剑国 (Beijing: Zhonghua shuju, 2001), 151–54, 184–89, 229–35.

64 For a discussion, see Bol, *"This Culture of Ours"*, 191–201; Bol, *Neo-Confucianism in History*, 63–65.

65 This kind of tone parallels with Ouyang Xiu's advocacy for *zhili renqing* and *ziran zhile* 自然之樂. See Zhu, *Tang Song guwen yundong yu shidafu wenxue*, 95, 155–59.

66 Ibid., 421–27.

67 Ibid., 242–44.

Ming-Qing romantic tales are also modeled on Tang tales in terms of structure and diction, although they add new plot designs and exhibit some different concerns. For example, one classical tale collection of the early Ming, *New Tales Told by Lamplight* (*Jiandeng xinhua* 剪燈新話), includes quite a few stories that take the disorder of the dynastic transition as their background. It is this disorder that leads to the failure of romance, which reflects an interest in the doings of fate. Another collection of the late Ming, *The search for Lamplight: A Sequel to Tales* (*Mideng yinhua* 覓燈因話), claims to be inspired by *New Tales Told by Lamplight*. However, it contains far more moral lessons. As for those tales representing love in the Ming–Qing transition, the mutual loyalty of lovers, as representative of anxieties about loyalty to the previous dynasty, is particularly valued.

In general, romantic tales after the Southern Song show a tendency toward low-brow literature. As scholars have claimed, the composition of these tales reflects the influence of vernacular short stories and plebeian ideology.[68] Daughters of shopkeepers and merchants increasingly play a leading part in these tales. Many of them are adapted into vernacular short stories, which attain a higher "mimetic level."[69] Compared with Tang romantic tales, they tend to make aesthetic experience less central, subordinating it to moral meaning, and thus give ideas priority over literary delicacy. Their ambiguous position between "elegance" and the "vulgar" suggests a contradiction between an old literary form and the new content of daily life.[70]

---

68 Cheng Yizhong 程毅中, *Song Yuan xiaoshuo yanjiu* 宋元小說研究 (Nanjing: Jiangsu guji chubanshe, 1998), 179–88; Liu Yongqiang 劉勇強, *Zhongguo gudai xiaoshuo shi xulun* 中國古代小說史敘論 (Beijing: Beijing daxue chubanshe, 2007), 205–18.

69 For a definition of mimetic level, see Northrop Frye, *Anatomy of Criticism: Four Essays* (Princeton, NY: Princeton University Press, 1957), 33–35. See also Patrick Hanan, "The Making of The Pearl-Sewn Shirt and The Courtesan's Jewel Box," *Harvard Journal of Asiatic Studies* 33 (1973): 124–53.

70 As Wu Cuncun 吴存存 has convincingly argued, the so-called "popular literature" that was written or rewritten by literary men, such as vernacular fiction, romantic tales, and plays, still partook of elite consciousness, rather than completely aligning with the commoners' interests, although they, to a certain degree, expressed a cross distinction of social and gender stratification. The perspectives of the lower social strata on emotion and sexuality are instead vividly represented in genres that are independent of romantic associations, such as popular songbooks, some erotic stories, etc., which features a variety of urban commoners, non-elite women in particular, portrays their marriage fates and daily lives, and the role played by women in the diversity of urban life. These authentic commoner texts reflect the social values that contradict the elite literature and the trend to challenge social norms. For the discussion on the importance and complexity of various class status in the course of fictional romantic affection, see Wu Cuncun 吴存存, "Pingmin de qingge – cong wanqing beifang pingmin changben kan xiaceng nüxing dui

On the other hand, a large number of Tang *chuanqi* tales were adapted into drama.[71] As is well known, the long plays that flourished in the Ming period were also called "*chuanqi*," which suggests these two genres' correlation in terms of subject matter and plot design. In fact, even Yuan *zaju* 雜劇 drama had been called "*chuanqi*."[72] This correlation is especially true for romantic tales and plays. In fact, all of the Tang tales discussed in this chapter were repeatedly reworked into *zaju* or *chuanqi* drama. The newly emergent genre of drama saw a blooming of romance culture. With lively performances and graceful lyrics, romantic plays won great popularity among both the literati circles and illiterate audiences from the Yuan dynasty onward. They represent a critical stage in the evolution of romantic discourse. Compared with Tang *chuanqi* tales, romance is more smoothly legitimatized and domesticated in Yuan and Ming drama through the moralization of love and female desire. In these later plays, the rigidity of etiquette and reservations about passion are implicitly set aside in favor of a more open and egalitarian manner, which, as the seventeenth century went on, becomes increasingly sentimental. It is to these romantic plays that we now turn.

---

xingbie he xingai wenti de liji yu qidai" 平民的情歌——從晚清北方平民唱本看下層女性對性別和性愛問題的理解與期待, *Xiqu yu suwenxue yanjiu* 9 (2021): 18–39; "Chunyi ce zhong de liangpian gaixie xiaoshuo" 春意冊中的兩篇改寫小說, *Zhongguo wenhua* 52 (2020): 91–103; "Suzhou Dialect, Social Status, and Gender in *Sancaifu*, a Rediscovered Mid-Qing *Chuanqi* Play," *Chinoperl: Journal of Chinese Oral & Performing Literature* 39, no. 1 (2020): 7–30.

71 See Lu Xun 魯迅, *Zhongguo xiaoshuo shilüe* 中國小說史略 (Beijing: Renming wenxue chubanshe, 1975), 54.

72 Xu Dajun traces the use of the term "*chuanqi*" in the field of Chinese literature and explores the relations between Yuan *zaju* drama and fiction, arguing that Yuan critics use the term "*chuanqi*" in regard to *zaju* with an eye to the subject matter, the literary value, and the act of literary creation, while the term "*zaju*" is used from the angle of the performance form. See Xu Dajun 徐大軍, *Yuan zaju yu xiaoshuo guanxi yanjiu* 元雜劇與小說關係研究 (Zhengzhou: Henan renmin chubanshe, 2006), 17–34.

CHAPTER 3

The Moralization of Passion in *Caizi-jiaren* Plays of the Late Ming

As Li Yu 李漁 (1611–1680) points out, "Nine *chuanqi* plays out of ten are about love" 傳奇十部九相思.[1] Although love as a dominant theme in Yuan and Ming drama largely follows the tradition of Tang tales, its representations in plays reflect marked differences. In pre-Yuan drama, stories about love affairs frequently occur between a young scholar and a courtesan. In the Yuan plays, in contrast, love between young scholars and girls of good families is celebrated to a greater extent. Moreover, whereas the Tang love story often ends in tragedy, love in Yuan plays – whether with a courtesan or between young lovers of comparable social position – eventually leads to a happy ending, despite tribulations and digressions. These changes suggest the domestication of romance, an effort to legitimize desire and rebuild the connection between desire and morality. As some scholars suggest, it is in these plays that the literary formula of the *caizi-jiaren* pattern is firmly established.[2] This basic pattern is emulated, modified, and parodied in later drama and fiction. More importantly, it opens up new areas of philosophical-literary discourse, that is, the rise of *qing*.

In fact, researchers have begun to examine the intriguing relationships between the late Ming cultural context and Yuan drama. They demonstrate that the canonization of Yuan drama was basically undertaken by the Ming elite through critical and editorial practice that transformed the dramatic scripts focusing on performance and music into a written genre with a standardized register of language and which reflected the values of elite society.[3] In this way, they not only legitimized the genre but also literati reproduction and appropriation of that drama. Stephen West's comparison of *Yuankan zaju sanshi zhong* 元刊雜劇三十种 (*Thirty Yuan Zaju Plays*) with Ming editions sheds

1 Li Yu 李漁, "Lianxiang ban" 憐香伴, in *Li Yu quanji* 李漁全集 (Hangzhou: Zhejiang guji chubanshe, 1992), 2.110.

2 See Zhang Shuxiang 張淑香, *Yuan zaju zhong de aiqing yu shehui* 元雜劇中的愛情與社會 (Taibei: Da'an chubanshe, 1991), 125–26.

3 Stephen H. West, "Text and Ideology: Ming Editors and Northern Drama," in *Ming Qing xiqu guoji yantao hui lunwen ji* 明清戲曲國際研討會論文集, ed. Hua Wei 華瑋 and Wang Ailing 王瑷玲 (Taibei: Zhongyang yanjiu yuan Zhongguo wenzhe suo, 1988), 235–84; Patricia Sieber, *Theaters of Desire: Authors, Readers, and the Reproduction of Early Chinese Song-Drama, 1300–2000* (New York: Palgrave Macmillan, 2003), 45–81.

HTTPS://DOI.ORG/10.1163/9789004693357-005

light on such agendas of the late Ming literati.[4] Patricia Sieber also examines quite a few late Ming collections of Yuan plays, including Li Kaixian's 李開先 (1502–1568) *Revised Plays of the Yuan Worthies* (*Gaiding yuanxian chuanqi* 改訂元賢傳奇), Zang Maoxun's 臧懋循 (1550–1620) *One Hundred Yuan Plays* (*Yuanren baizhong qu* 元人百种曲 or *Yuanqu xuan* 元曲選), Meng Chengshun's 孟稱舜 *Joint Selection of Famous Plays Old and New* (*Gujin mingju hexuan* 古今名劇合選), and others. Her study shows that in the act of anthologizing Yuan plays late Ming literati tended to invest Yuan drama with a romantic coloring by focusing on the romantic aspects.[5] Many of the plays published in the late Ming period and attributed to Yuan authors fell under the category of romance.[6] The late Ming elite's reproductive appropriation of Yuan drama attests to their desire to vindicate romance as a form of self-expression, an assertion about the autonomous ethical power on their part to make choices and judgments. They not only exploit these plays to represent a new elite sensibility or taste – as Patricia Sieber attempts to show – but also invested them with a new seriousness, elevating them as a new cultural and moral ideal. The effort to authorize desire itself, as well as the novel view of emotions such as love, mutual affection, and benevolence as a force for good in human affairs, reflects a variety of moral concerns and ideological constructions on the part of the late Ming, and post-Ming, literati.

Li Zhi's 李贄 (1527–1602) famous essay "Tongxin shuo" 童心說 (On Childlike Mind) begins with a quote about *The Story of the Western Wing*, and endorses it as a kind of literature with a "childlike mind" or "sincere heart."[7] For Li, "sincerity" is the highest good as well as the essence of good literature. Correspondingly, he strongly promotes vernacular literature, seeing it as being more spontaneous and less rationalistic. In another essay entitled "Za shuo" 雜說 (Miscellaneous Remarks), he celebrates *The Story of the Western Wing* as being a creation of nature (*zaohua zhi gong* 造化之工).[8] Furthermore, he emphasizes the spontaneous expression of emotion in a dramatic and passionate way:

---

4 West, "Text and Ideology: Ming Editors and Northern Drama," 273–83.

5 Sieber, *Theaters of Desire*, 45–81.

6 See *Gu mingjia zaju* 古名家雜劇, Guben xiqu congkan 古本戲曲叢刊, ser. 4, vols. 93–95 (Shanghai: Shangwu yinshuguan, 1958); *Gu zaju* 古雜劇, Guben xiqu congkan, ser. 4, vols. 4–8; *Zaju xuan* 雜劇選, Guben xiqu congkan, ser. 4, vols. 96–98; *Gujin mingju hexuan* 古今名劇合選, Guben xiqu congkan, ser. 4, vols. 101–120; Zang Maoxun 臧懋循 (1550–1620), ed., *Yuanqu xuan* 元曲選 (Beijing: Zhonghua shuju, 1989).

7 See Li, *Li Zhi wenji*, 1.91–93.

8 Ibid., 1.90–91.

> Those who can truly write never intended to produce literature in the first place. In the bosom [of a true writer], there are so many indescribable, strange things, in his throat there are so many things he wants to utter yet dare not, in his mouth there are often so many words he wants to say but has nowhere to say – when these have been stored up to the limit and accumulated for so long that they can no longer be checked, then, one day, when he sees a scene that arouses his emotions, when what touches his eye draws a sigh from him, he will "grab someone else's winecup to pour over his own grievances," give vent to his feelings of injustice, and lament the ill fates of a thousand years.
>
> 且夫世之真能文者，此其初皆非有意于為文也。其胸中有如許無狀可怪之事，其喉間有如許欲吐而不敢吐之物，其口頭又時時有許多欲語而莫可所以告語之處，蓄極積久，勢不能遏。一旦見景生情，触目興嘆，奪他人之酒杯，澆自己之塊壘，訴心中之不平，感數奇于千載。[9]

Although these ideas can be traced back to the *Zhuangzi* 莊子, the *Book of Poetry* (*Shijing* 詩經), and later poetic criticism in the Six Dynasties period,[10] Li Zhi's dramatic expression conveys a strong sense of individuality, rather than the harmony of man with nature upon which those ancient thoughts focused. To Li Zhi, the outpouring of emotion is a kind of innate need, and true literature is the spontaneous revealing of the instinctive desires of human beings. Subsequently, he makes the following observation on *The Story of the Western Wing*: "When I read this play, I imagine how he [the author] conducts himself. At that time, he must have had grievance against the monarch and his peers, and hence he uses the partings and reunions of lovers to bring it out" 余覽斯記，想見其為人，當其時必有大不得意於君臣朋友之間者，故借夫婦離合姻緣以發其端.[11] At first glance, this allegorical reading of romance belongs to a long-standing tradition, which commences with the *Songs of Chu* (*Chuci* 楚辭) and the preface to the *Book of Poetry*. Yet Li Zhi does not draw an analogy between heterosexual desire and the desire of the minister for his ruler, but rather highlights the disharmony between the individual and society by making an association between them.

In his 1614 edition of *The Story of the Western Wing*, *Xin jiaozhu guben Xixiang ji* 新校註古本西廂記 (*Newly Collated and Annotated, Ancient-Text-Based Story*

9 Ibid., 1.91. Translation from James J.Y. Liu, *Chinese Theories of Literature* (Chicago: University of Chicago Press, 1975), 79.

10 Including the Three Kingdoms period (220–280 CE), the Jin dynasty (265–420), and the Southern and Northern Dynasties (420–589).

11 Li, *Li Zhi wenji*, 1.91.

of the Western Wing), Wang Jide 王驥德 (1540–1623) refutes Li Zhi's philosophical and political approach to the play, seemingly constructing it as a self-contained world of elite sensibility. Despite his aversion to Li Zhi's use of *The Story of the Western Wing* to advocate an extreme position, however, Wang himself promotes a literature of moral education (*shijiao wenzi* 世教文字). He says,

> The ancient men have passed away. I pick up old stories and apply new music to them. I put the splendid dress on the persons of virtue and paint the faces of the evil in black and white. I put the stories on stage, letting the audience be admonished and provoked by these stories, and even wring their hands in sorrow or stare angrily, with tears and mucus flowing down their faces. Only such stories can be called the literature of moral education.
>
> 古人往矣，吾取古事，麗今聲，華袞其賢者，粉墨其慝者，奏之場上，令觀者藉為勸懲興起，甚或扼腕裂眦，涕泗交下而不為已，此方為有關世教文字。[12]

If we can say that Li Zhi's conception of good literature such as *The Story of the Western Wing* promotes individuality and spontaneity, and is oriented toward the writer, then Wang focuses on the relationship between text and reader. Wang brings forward the notion of readerly identification, which becomes a way to stimulate his readers' self-reflection and activate their consciences. His editorial practice exemplifies the idea that the drama can be a morally serious and even reformative genre based on its ability to provoke empathic emotional experiences in readers.

In effect, both Li Zhi and Wang Jide defend *The Story of the Western Wing* as a discourse on human nature, although Li attempts to entrust a sort of political seriousness to the play, whereas Wang seeks to develop a new language of romantic sensibility by participating in the cultural-philosophical discourse of *qing*. By associating drama, and romantic plays in particular, with human feelings, Wang emphasizes the importance of depicting *qing* or love per se in romantic plays: "As for giving vent to human feelings, there should be nothing better than the drama" 快人情者，要毋過於曲也.[13] In a rhymed prose work on *The Story of the Western Wing*, he says, "All principles have boundaries,

---

12 Wang Jide 王驥德, "Za lun" 雜論, in *Qulu* 曲律, Zhongguo gudian xiqu lunzhu jicheng 中國古典戲曲論著集成 (Beijing: Zhongguo xiju chubanshe, 1959), 4.160.

13 Ibid., 159–60.

while feelings are boundless" 凡理有窮，惟情無盡, "If one who has *qing* reads this, he must have sighed over this literature/culture" 倘有情之披覽，當三嘆於斯文.[14] This apparently echoes Tang Xianzu's well-known statement regarding *qing* in the preface to his most notably romantic play, *The Peony Pavilion*, "People only say that this is what cannot be found within the realm of principle, but how do they know that this is definitely the case within the realm of *qing*?" 第云理之所必無，安知情之所必有邪.[15]

Tang Xianzu differentiates *qing* from *xing* 性 in the sense that *qing* materializes *xing* – it is more easily accessible and hence more effectively illuminates *xing*: "Human nature manifests in the secret of heaven, while human feelings are revealed in the material world" 性乎天機，情乎物際.[16] In Tang's view, both *xing* and *qing* are identically heaven-endowed, however, compared with *xing*, *qing* can be universally felt by human beings, and is thereby more effective in representing the defining essence of human nature and in evoking what is common to all people. Therefore, Tang Xianzu sees *qing* more as a public discourse than a private one: "speaking of *xing* without *qing* is a personal point of view, whereas speaking of *xing* combined with *qing* is a public point of view" 離情而言性，一家之私言也，合情而言性，天下之公言也.[17] The act of crossing the boundaries between *qing* and *xing*/*li* 理 demonstrates his attempt to justify desire and to renew moral values with a kind of humanism. In his own words, "Those who have no feelings can be provoked to feel. ... Isn't this to achieve the ultimate happiness of the Confucian moral values through the great opening of human feelings?" 無情者可使有情……豈非以人情之大竇，為名教之至樂也哉.[18] Here, he highlights the emotive power of drama, and its role in spurring people toward a more authentic moral life. The phrase "the great opening of human feelings" evokes the conception of *qing* and *li* 禮 (propriety) in the *Liji* – "[Propriety and righteousness (*li yi* 禮義)] can reach the Way of Heaven because they conform to the great opening of human feelings"

14 Wang Jide, "Qianqiu jueyan fu" 千秋絕豔賦, in *Xin jiaozhu guben Xixiang ji* 新校註古本西廂記, ed. Wang Jide (Beijing: Beijing tushuguan chubanshe, 2004), 6.55a–b.

15 Tang Xianzu 湯顯祖, *Mudan ting* 牡丹亭, ed. Xu Shuofang 徐朔方 and Yang Xiaomei 楊笑梅 (Beijing: Renmin wenxue chubanshe, 1998), 1.

16 Tang Xianzu, "Da Ma Zhongliang" 答馬仲良, in *Tang Xianzu quanji* 湯顯祖全集, ed. Xu Shuofang 徐朔方 (Beijing: Zhonghua shuju, 1999), 3.1516.

17 Quoted from Cheng Yunchang 程允昌, "Nan jiugong shisan diao qupu xu" 南九宫十三調曲譜序. See Han Jingtai 韓經太, *Lixue wenhua yu wenxue sichao* 理學文化輿文學思潮 (Beijing: Zhonghua shuju, 1997), 269.

18 Tang Xianzu, "Yihuang xian xishen qingyuan shi miao ji" 宜黃縣戲神清源師廟記, in *Tang Xianzu quanji*, 2.1221.

所以達天道，順人情之大寳也[19] – which elucidates that true rites are a matter of following the innate desires and feelings of human beings. By rebuilding the relationship between morality and sensuality, Tang advocates a moral life that is in tune with what is deeply felt. He claims that "a person with the mind of the Way must have the character of wisdom; a person with the character of wisdom must have profound feelings" 道心之人，必具智骨；具智骨者，必有深情.[20] To Tang, one's intellectual and moral capabilities correspond to one's sensibilities. That is to say, one can realize the Way ultimately through one's perceptual and sensual experience. In this sense, he proposed the ideal of "the world of *qing*" (*youqing tianxia* 有情天下), when, as a country magistrate of Suichang 遂昌, he followed the teaching of his master, Luo Rufang 羅汝芳 (1515–1588), by sponsoring community covenants (*xiangyue* 鄉約) and delivering lectures to the local people.[21] His ultimate goal was to achieve a common general humanity linked by feelings. This ideal world of ultimate humanity was grounded on the reverence for life (*guisheng* 貴生); indeed, in 1591, when he served as a district warden (*dianshi* 典史) of Xuwen 徐聞, he helped to build an academy to popularize this idea. From Tang's perspective, "the learning of the great man begins with an understanding of life. If one understands life, he will honor the value of his own life, and further value the lives of all people in the world" 大人之学，起于知生. 知生則知自貴，又知天下之生皆當貴重.[22] The ultimate humanity essentially lies in both the realization of individual worth and the feelings of men.

The association of *qing* with morality and sincerity can be also seen in the works of Meng Chengshun. In his preface to Meng's well-known play *Mistress and Maid*, he claims, "For faithful husbands and virtuous wives all over the world, how could they do what they never regret until death only because they take principles for granted? They are sincere in nature, and aroused by *qing*" 天下義夫節婦，所為至死而不悔者，豈以為理所當然而為之邪？篤於其性，發於其情.[23] Meng discusses *qing* as the transcending principle, since *qing* that parallels with sincerity in nature represents the highest good. In this sense, *qing* and virtue directly validate each other, without the medium of principle. In a preface to another play, he says, "If *qing* and *xing* are both based on sincerity, then they are proper wherever they move. … One can see

19 *Liji, juan* 22, in *Shisan jing zhushu*, 11.1101.
20 Tang Xianzu, "Shuian wenji xu" 睡菴文集序, in *Tang Xianzu quanji*, 2.1074.
21 Tang Xianzu, "Qinglian ge ji" 青蓮閣記, in *Tang Xianzu quanji*, 2.1174.
22 Tang Xianzu, "Guisheng shuyuan shuo" 貴生書院說, in *Tang Xianzu quanji*, 2.1225.
23 Meng Chengshun, "Tici" 題詞, in *Jiaohong ji* 嬌紅記 (Shanghai: Shanghai guji chubanshe, 1988), 271.

[the complete sincerity] in minute matters such as the intimate relationship between lovers and in matters of great significance such as what can be seen between heaven above and earth below" 情與性而咸本乎誠，則無適而非正也……細之見於兒女幄房之際，而鉅之形於上下天地之間.[24] To Meng, romantic love exemplifies the ideal of sincerity, and thus moral propriety. In this sense, sincere love itself carries moral goodness.

On the other hand, the ideal of sincerity requires the mutual devotion of lovers, as represented in Wang's preface to *Mistress and Maid*: "The story about Wang Jiao and Scholar Shen seems to resemble what a debauched man and loose woman would do. But I entitled it with [the words] 'virtuousness and righteousness' for they are both faithful to each other to the extent that both of them die and yet never regret" 傳中所載王嬌、申生事，殆有類狂童、淫女所為，而予題之節義，以两人皆從一而終，至於沒身而不悔者也.[25] What is distinguished here is the promotion of mutual loyalty on the part of the lovers, rather than women's unilateral constancy. The protagonists' mutually intense dedication blurs the boundaries between romantic love and virtue. In other words, romantic love becomes the powerful emblem of loyalty and sincerity, which can ultimately justify illicit sex.

This specific concern with loyalty and sincerity is of course associated with the dynastic crisis in the Ming–Qing transition. It is not a coincidence that Meng Chengshun juxtaposes "the sincerity of [Wang Jiao and Scholar Sheng's] erotic sensitivity" 慕色之誠 with Wu Zixu's 伍子胥 (559–484 BCE) and Shen Baoxu's 申包胥 (?–?) loyalty to the country.[26] As a means of enacting a social

24 Meng Chengshun, "'Er Xu ji' tici"《二胥記》題詞, in *Meng Chengshun xiqu ji* 孟稱戲曲集 (Chengdu: Bashu shushe, 2006), 529.

25 Meng, "Tici," 271.

26 Meng, "'Er Xu ji' tici," 529. Wu Zixu and Shen Baoxu were two famous figures from the Spring and Autumn Period. Wu Zixu, a nobleman from the state of Chu 楚, was forced to flee his country after his entire family was executed by King Ping of Chu due to false accusations. Before leaving Chu. Wu Zixu swore to his close friend Shen Baoxu that he would destroy Chu to avenge his father's death. To this, Shen Baoxu solemnly replied, "If you can destroy Chu, I can restore it!" After many hardships, Wu Zixu reached the state of Wu, where he helped Wu grow powerful, and eventually led Wu's army to conquer Chu, fulfilling his oath of vengeance. Meanwhile, to save Chu, Shen Baoxu travelled to the state of Qin to seek help. For seven days and nights, he knelt outside the palace and wept without food or water until the Qin ruler was moved to tears, and dispatched troops to rescue Chu. Qin's intervention forced Wu to withdraw, allowing King Zhao of Chu to return to the capital. Afterwards, Wu Zixu continued to serve the state of Chu with unwavering loyalty. He repeatedly warned the king of Wu, Fuchai 夫差, of the rising threat posed by the state of Yue 越, urging him to eliminate Yue decisively, before it was too late. But slandered by the corrupt minister Bo Pi 伯嚭, Wu Zixu was ordered by the enraged king to commit suicide. Greatly worried and despairing that Wu was doomed to ruin, Wu Zixu issued a prophecy

critique of the state of turmoil, the *qing* represented in the male–female relationship is given prominence as it is made analogous to other human relations. Meng asserts that "since the past, there have not always been loyal subjects and filial sons in the world, but there are often faithful husbands and virtuous wives" 自昔忠臣孝子，世不恆有，而義夫節婦時有之.[27] With the most profound sincerity, the *qing* between man and woman carries morally redemptive power.

In what follows, I begin with a discussion of *The Story of the Western Wing*, widely recognized as the founding text of the *caizi-jiaren* tradition, and examine how the "Story of Yingying" discussed in the previous chapter is adapted and transformed in this romantic play. *The Story of the Western Wing* provides an occasion to explore how new formulas of love and moral values unfold. I then examine *The Peony Pavilion*, a novel entry in the canon of the cult of *qing* that shifts the narrative focus of the *caizi-jiaren* romance to the female protagonist and the affirmation of her subjectivity. Finally, I read Meng Chengshun's *Mistress and Maid*, which delves into the particulars of love and ends with the sublimeness of loyalty, in order to show how this play exemplifies another dimension of the cult of *qing*, the ideal of the unity of sincerity with fidelity.

1 A New Melodrama: *The Story of the Western Wing*

As indicated in the previous chapter, "The Story of Yingying" has made a lasting impact on Chinese literature and culture. It inspired a long list of adaptations, the most renowned of which is *The Story of the Western Wing*. The direct source of this Yuan *zaju* drama is generally considered to be the less well-known twelfth-century *zhugong diao* 諸宮調 (medley) version of the tale. In fact, from the *zhugong diao* version, on through the *zaju* and *chuanqi* dramas of the Yuan and Ming, passion is dealt with in a very different way from the Tang tale. These later adaptations reward passion with marriage, and thus have desire satisfied properly, rather than making passion problematic. Once Wang Shifu's *zaju* drama *The Story of the Western Wing* became popular as both a

before his death, "After I die, cut out my eyes and hang them on the gates of Wu's eastern wall. I will watch Yue's armies bury this kingdom." In the end, Wu was conquered by Yue, as Wu Zixu had warned. The stories of Wu Zixu and Shen Baoxu, who are both remembered as exemplars of loyalty in Chinese history, are recorded in "The Biography of Wu Zixu" 伍子胥列傳 in the *Shiji* 史記 and dramatized by Meng Chengshun in *Er Xu ji* 二胥記 (*The Two Xu Heroes*). See Sima Qian 司馬遷, *Shiji* (Beijing: Zhonghua shuju, 2002), 7.2171–84; Meng, *Er Xu ji*, in *Meng Chengshun xiqu ji*, 265–375.

27 Meng, "Tici," 271.

theatrical performance and as reading literature, Yuan Zhen lost control of his own story: audiences tend to forget the elusive and unsettling plot of the original Tang tale. In fact, *The Story of the Western Wing* is generally acknowledged as having established a new model of the *caizi-jiaren* romance, which informed both contemporary plays and subsequent literature of the late imperial period.[28]

I see *The Story of the Western Wing* as a new model of melodrama in the sense that the play flattens out the gaps and ambivalence that characterize "The Story of Yingying" and instead dramatizes clear-cut conflicts between good and evil.[29] Compared with "The Story of Yingying," *The Story of the Western Wing* pursues a different line of narration and dramatization. Although the play also addresses the protagonists' moral struggles, in particular Yingying's, the tension between romance and propriety is much more easily resolved in the play. We do not see the opposing versions of romance held by the hero and heroine, nor the problem of desire, as in the "The Story of Yingying," but an integrated love story, in spite of digressions and conflicts.

The Story of the Western Wing portrays its protagonists as sincere young lovers caught in the web of passion. The play adds scenes to the original plot of "The Story of Yingying," such as the lovers meeting in the Buddha Hall and their reciting of poems under the moon, which provides the emotional basis for their love. In brief, the play takes place in the Temple of Universal Salvation, which is under siege by the bandit Flying Tiger Sun who seeks to capture Yingying. Yingying and her mother, Madam Cui, agree that Yingying will marry whoever can resolve the crisis. After the hero, Zhang Junrui 張君瑞 or Scholar Zhang, rescues the temple from the siege, however, Madame Cui breaches her promise to accept young couple's marriage, forcing Zhang's to redouble his efforts, the sincerity and intense passion of which deeply touch Yingying all over again. In this way, the further development of their love is made possible.[30] However,

---

28 The popularity of *The Story of the Western Wing* can be seen in the repeated acts of "plagiarism" on the part of other plays of the time, for example, *Dongqiang ji* 東墻記, *Jinhuan ji* 金環記, and *Zhou Meixiang* □梅香, which often copied its plot as well as specific lines; see Zhang, *Yuan zaju zhong de aiqing yu shehui*, 112–13. Its popularity is also demonstrated in vernacular fiction, such as Chapter 23 of *The Dream of the Red Chamber*.

29 I use the term "melodrama" here not with regard to its definition as a genre of drama that flourished in Europe in the nineteenth century, but in the broader sense of sensational stories that focus on exciting events and exaggerated conflicts and emotions.

30 Wang Shifu follows his direct source, Dong Qieyuan's 董解元 *Xixiangji zhugongdiao* 西廂記諸宮調, very closely indeed. Most of Wang's adaptation of the plot of "The Story of Yingying" can already be found in Dong's work. However, Wang considerably tightens up the plot of the story and devotes his play more to dramatic conflicts. For example, Wang has sharpened the characterization of Madam Cui as more status-conscious and

one of the most critical transformations of the play is that Zhang Junrui apparently wants to be married to Yingying from the beginning, which differs from the *chuanqi* tale. In the play, at the first sight of Yingying, Zhang Junrui loses all self-control, dazzled by Yingying's beauty. Soon afterward, when he runs into Yingying's maid, Hongniang, as in "The Story of Yingying," he provides a list of pertinent names and numbers: his personal and courtesy names, his native place, his birth time and age. It is obvious in this context that information concerning one's time of birth and astrological sign are meant as a proposal for marriage. Not least among these is his remark, "I have never been married."[31]

For Zhang in the *chuanqi* tale, passionate desire is separated from social conventions. Therefore, he refuses to turn his romantic heroine into a proper wife, thereby removing the threat of his romance to social morality. By contrast, in the play, Zhang Junrui does not consider romance as a threat to social advancement. In fact, in the opening of the play, Zhang introduces himself as an assiduous scholar, who expresses his "great ambition" to achieve merit and fame.[32] On his way to take the imperial examinations, he goes through Pu Pass to find a friend and catches sight of the running Yellow River. His lyric depiction of the river – "Snowcapped waves beat the long sky, at heaven's edge autumn clouds furl; bamboo hawsers cable together the floating bridge, on the water a steel-blue dragon reclines" 雪浪拍長空，天際秋雲卷；竹索纜浮橋，水上蒼龍偃 – corresponds with his grand ambition, as "a recumbent dragon" symbolizes a hidden talent.[33] Zhang also laments, "A precious sword of price-

devious. In Dong's *Xixiangji zhugongdiao*, Madam Cui only promises to treat Zhang Junrui as a relative at the beginning, which Zhang takes as a promise of marriage to Yingying; whereas in Wang's *The Story of the Western Wing*, Madam Cui promises Yinging to Zhang if he can lift the siege, but goes back on her words due to her concern about Zhang's poverty and low status. It can be said that the conflicts in *Xixiangji zhugongdiao* primarily derive from misunderstandings or mistakes, while Wang's play expresses a stronger moral sense. Moreover, toward the end of *Xixiangji zhugongdiao*, Zhang Junrui and Yingying happily celebrate their marriage with the help of Du Que, who helps to lift the siege and has been promoted to the position of governor. Madam Cui is not mentioned at all. Nevertheless, it is Madam Cui who holds the wedding ceremony for the lovers in Wang's play. Hence, although the *zhugongdiao* version of Yingying's tale has initiated the compromise between passion and marriage, Wang's play proffers a more lucid view on the relations between love and morality in the period under discussion. For the plot of *Xixiangji zhugongdiao*, see "Dong Jieyuan Xixiang ji" 董解元西廂記, in Wang Shifu 王實甫, *Xixiang ji* 西廂記, ed. Zhang Yanjin 張燕瑾 (Beijing: Renmin wenxue chubanshe, 2007), 269–374.

31 Wang, *Xixiang ji*, 29–30.

32 Ibid., 7–8.

33 Ibid., 7; translation by Stephen West and Wilt Idema, in *The Moon and the Zither: The Story of the Western Wing* (Berkeley: University of California Press, 1991), 174.

less value hidden in autumn waters; spring sorrows lade my horse and press upon the embroidered saddle" 萬金寶劍藏秋水，滿馬春愁壓綉鞍.[34] Here, there may be an allusion to Du Fu's line, "In the rising mist is the sword with the star pattern, deep and blue the cloud-rain pond" 鬱鬱星辰劍，蒼蒼雲雨池. The images of both the hidden dragon and sword are associated with the ambitions of a frustrated literatus.[35]

However, the romantic aspect is also suggested in the next few lines of Zhang's aria, "Just as if the Silver River dropped from the nine heavens. … And once it floated a raft to the edge of sun and moon" 只疑似銀河落九天……也曾浮槎到日月邊, which suggests the association drawn between the Silver River (the Milky Way) and the Yellow River.[36] This is an allusion to a story in *Bowu zhi* 博物誌 (*Record of Wide Learning*), in which a man who boards a raft floating on the Yellow River finally arrives at the Milky Way, and there encounters two faithful lovers, the Herdboy and the Weaving Girl. These lines denote a natural confluence of the two realms: the Yellow River and the Silver River, or social ambition and romance. In later times the man floating on the river in this story was said to be Zhang Qian 張騫, who was sent by Emperor Wu of the Han dynasty to make alliance with countries in Central Asia, in order to attack the Xiongnu 匈奴, a nomadic tribe that had caused trouble on the Chinese frontier.[37] Zhang Qian finally won recognition and fame by traveling extensively in Central Asia, and making achievements with lasting impact on the Han relations with foreign countries. Such an association with Zhang Qian further suggests Zhang Junrui's great ambition. Although it seems that Zhang Junrui sets aside his ambition to succeed in the examinations after seeing Yingying, his literary ability is on full display when he writes the first erotic poem to Yingying. Also, at that time, Hongniang cautions him not to forget his career and ambitions.[38] Thus, although it is not Zhang who wants to leave and take part in the examinations in the latter part of the play, Zhang is already prepared when Madam Cui demands that he pass the examinations to secure her consent to marriage. In this respect, love does not conflict with social norms, but facilitates the hero's social advancement.

In fact, the story of Zhuo Wenjun and Sima Xiangru provides the model for the love between Zhang Junrui and Yingying in *The Story of the Western*

---

34 Wang, *Xixiang ji*, 7.

35 Qiu Zhaoao 仇兆鰲, *Du shi xiang zhu* 杜詩詳註 (Beijing: Zhonghua shuju, 1979), 1544.

36 Wang, *Xixiang ji*, 8; West and Idema, *Moon and the Zither*, 174, 82.

37 See Zhang Hua 張華, *Bowu zhi* 博物誌, Sibu beiyao 四部備要. The story of the raft is referred to in *juan* 3, p. 12; the association with Zhang Qian is found in *juan* 1, p. 3.

38 Wang, *Xixiang ji*, 128.

Wing. When he steals into the garden and peeps at Yingying who burns incense and prays for a good marriage, Zhang immediately evokes the story of Sima Xiangru and Zhuo Wenjun.[39] The story was first written down by Sima Qian 司马迁 (145–90? BCE) in his *Records of the Grand Historian* (*Shiji* 史記), in which Sima Xiangru seduces Zhuo Wenjun by his *qin* 琴 (zither) playing, and they elope. In the end, Sima Xiangru wins recognition at court as a famous poet and man of letters, while their marriage is accepted by Zhuo Wenjun's father. Similarly, Zhang is confident of the eventual recognition of his literary talents by the emperor, and he does succeed in the examinations. He also attempts to seduce Yingying by playing the zither, and afterward sings a song that is heavily indebted to the zither songs attributed to Sima Xiangru in *New Songs from a Jade Terrace* (*Yutai xinyong* 玉臺新詠).[40] More importantly, the love between Xiangru and Wenjun is rewarded with marriage, which provides the play with the structure that ends with the hero and heroine's reunion.

However, in the late Han miscellany *Miscellaneous Records of the Western Capital* (*Xijing zaji* 西京雜記), there is an addition to the original story of Sima Xiangru and Zhuo Wenjun: Sima Xiangru intends to take a concubine after he retires to Maoling 茂陵 together with Zhuo Wenjun.[41] Thereupon, Zhuo Wenjun writes a poem, "Baitou yin" 白頭吟 (Lament on White Hair), to express her sadness about being abandoned, so Xiangru desists. By referring to this poem, Yingying conveys her own worries about possible rejection. She tells Zhang after giving herself to him: "My body and my life I entrust to you forever. May you never disdain me in the future and make me lament my white hair" 此身皆托於足下，勿以他日見棄，使妾有白頭之嘆.[42] Although in the *chuanqi* tale Yingying also expresses her longing for a proper marriage and a lasting relationship, the heroine of the play gets a more positive response from Zhang, who not only solemnly avows his love, but also fulfills it at the end of the play. The play does not locate passion somewhere outside real life and its responsibilities, as "The Story of Yingying" does. In act 1 of book 5, Zhang sends Yingying a letter to reiterate his promise after he passes the examinations in the highest category. This is another reversal of "The Story of Yingying," in which Yingying sends a letter to Zhang and makes her last effort to persuade Zhang to marry her. In the play, Zhang takes the initiative in both playing the zither and sending the letter. In this way, Zhang is characterized as a sincere

39 Wang, *Xixiang ji*, 46.

40 This is different from "The Story of Yingying," which portrays Yingying as an expert zither player.

41 Ge Hong 葛洪, *Xijing zaji* 西京雜記, Sibu congkan chubian 四部叢刊初編, *juan* 3, p. 10.

42 Wang, *Xixiang ji*, 173; West and Idema, *Moon and the Zither*, 334.

and responsible lover. In his letter, he intimates that "one who esteems fortune and fame over love is guilty of shortsighted greed" 重功名而薄恩爱者，誠有淺見貪饕之罪.[43] In contrast to the dubious attitude toward private desire in "The Story of Yingying," love has its own moral meaning in the play.

At the same time, Yingying is not rendered an elusive goddess who visits a mortal man and then departs after their sexual union, as in "The Story of Yingying." In the play, the major allusion drawn on for comparison to Yingying is that of Zhuo Wenjun, who elopes to become the wife of Sima Xiangru. Although Yingying is frequently referred to in relation to divine beauty in the play – for instance, the goddess of Wu Mountain, the goddesses of the Xiang River, and Chang'e, the goddess of the moon – these otherworldly images are primarily used to strengthen her worldly physical beauty, rather than denote the elusive nature of love and the lovers' ultimate separation. Furthermore, these vague images are overshadowed by Zhang's lengthy and concrete description of Yingying's physical beauty.[44] In the play, Yingying's representation is based more on earthly experience rather than mythic construction. The play does not aim to evoke dreamlike events, as "The Story of Yingying" does, but brings the story of love to life by focusing on lived experience. Indeed, the *chuanqi* tale and the play deal with sex much differently as well. In the tale, the sexual experience tends to be encapsulated in verse, and the experience itself is ambiguous and elusive, whereas the play concerns the easy satisfaction of passion.

Furthermore, although Yingying's intention is implied in her few words and the letter in the *chuanqi* tale, the play more often alludes to her psychological state and her relationships with other characters. First of all, although her outward actions may indicate hesitation, Yingying has consistent, true feeling for Zhang Junrui. When she first sees him and hears him chant his poem in the garden, she clearly expresses that she falls in love with him to such an extent that she can barely to eat or drink.[45] Also, when Madam Cui promises Yingying to Zhang if he can lift the siege, she is excited about it. Later, when Madam Cui goes back on her promise, Yingying is worried about Zhang's being unable to bear this. After she learns that Zhang is tormented and bedridden, she is so touched that she ultimately commits herself to Zhang.[46] Finally, Madam Cui demands that Zhang pass the examinations before marrying Yingying. Yingying has to bear the pain of the separation and send him off. The famous

43 Wang, *Xixiang ji*, 210–11; West and Idema, *Moon and the Zither*, 373.
44 Wang, *Xixiang ji*, 9–10.
45 Wang, *Xixiang ji*, 76.
46 Ibid., 124–31.

parting scene in act 3 of book 4 gives full expression to Yingying's love for Zhang and her agony of separation. She is represented as a perfect romantic heroine, who values love over fame and fortune, saying "Empty fame on the horns of a snail and profit as tiny as a fly's head tear the mandarin ducks apart" 蝸角虛名，蠅頭微利，拆鴛鴦在兩下裏.[47] Here love is displayed as intense and sincere, rather than ambiguous and elusive, as in "The Story of Yingying." In this respect, *The Story of the Western Wing* makes use of passion instead of making it problematic.

Still, Yingying's outward actions seem like ambivalence toward Zhang, to the extent that she is charged with insincerity by Zhang, and with lying by her maidservant Hongniang. The play makes it clear, however, that Yingying's vacillation derives from her struggle to make a choice between observing social propriety and succumbing to her private desire. In fact, the play assigns the maid Hongniang to take on the singing part to reveal what happens in the heroine's heart. In act 2 of book 3, when Yingying insists on asking Hongniang to take her poem to Zhang, claiming to tell him not to act in an improper manner again, Hongniang points out that Yingying is too deceitful, in that she always has clever words and flowery speeches in front of others to disguise her true feelings toward Zhang. Hongniang readily sees through to the true nature of Yingying's feelings, her love and desire, knowing that Yingying refuses to acknowledge her feelings because she is attempting to keep her love a secret from her mother.[48]

Yingying's relationship to her mother is one of the great developments of the original story in *The Story of the Western Wing*. In "The Story of Yingying," Madam Cui does not come on stage after she introduces Yingying to Zhang. The primary problem in "The Story of Yingying" stems from the hero's and the heroine's different perspectives on romance and its relation to social propriety. Nevertheless, the principal conflict of the story is transformed into that between the lovers and Madam Cui in *The Story of the Western Wing*. "The Story of Yingying" is characterized by its ambivalence and complexity, while *The Story of the Western Wing* is grounded in clarifying confrontation and resolution. The play is adversarial, demonstrating how love triumphs over ill-advised power symbolized by Madam Cui. From the start, Yingying is represented as being sincerely engaged with her lover, whereas the mother is characterized as untrustworthy. When Flying Tiger Sun seals off the temple in which Yingying and her mother are staying with his five thousand troops, Yingying proposes the plan that if anyone drives away the traitorous troops then she will marry

47 Ibid., 195; West and Idema, *Moon and the Zither*, 351–53.

48 Wang, *Xixiang ji*, 293–96.

him. And Madam Cui accepts it. After Zhang Junrui asks his friend, Du Que 杜确, to help lift the siege, Madam Cui sets out a small banquet for Zhang. When Yingying learns of this, she thinks that the small banquet is held for repaying Zhang and simultaneously arranging their marriage. She complains to Hongniang, "She's [Madam Cui] afraid that I'm just goods to be sold at a loss; but when it's two for the price of one, then the deal is on" 他怕我是賠錢貨，兩當一便成合.[49] However, Madam Cui does not arrange their marriage but goes back on her word, due to her concern about Zhang's poverty and low status. Thereupon Yingying decries the fact that her mother's deceit is "as big as heaven."[50] Madam Cui is criticized for her duplicity and placement of profits over what is right. In Yingying's eyes, her mother simply considers her a commodity that can be traded and withdrawn.

In fact, the marriage promise provides legitimacy to the couple's love in the play. Thus, the generational conflicts stem more from the struggle between good and bad than from that between romance and morality. The struggle between virtue and evil is further shown in the appearance of the villain, Zheng Heng 鄭恒, who almost ruins the lovers' marriage by spreading a lie that Zhang had been married to the daughter of the prime minister. Zheng is characterized as a dandy who merely relies on the wealth and reputation of his family and shows his contempt for the poor student Zhang. As Hongniang points out, "Junrui is a gentleman, one of the pure poor; Zheng Heng is a small man, one of the murky crowd" 君瑞是君子清賢，鄭恒是小人濁民.[51] Here we see an unmitigated contrast between a learned scholar who lives a life of frugal obscurity and the man of wealth who abuses power and bullies people, and between trust and dishonesty. The figures of the play are lined up as evil villains and innocent victims. Whereas in "The Story of Yingying," the protagonists are first of all victims of a generally dubious attitude toward romance, they are portrayed in *The Story of the Western Wing* as very much the victims of other figures in the play. Such a melodramatic conception of the subject matter shifts focus from the problem of passion to the problem of virtue. It offers us "a morally legible universe," in which love is used to consolidate the good. As discussed earlier, Li Zhi endorsed *The Story of the Western Wing* as a kind of literature with "childlike mind" or "sincere heart." This is true in the sense that both hero and heroine are characterized as sincere lovers, and that their desire is rehabilitated to a natural impulse. The sincerity and spontaneity of the protagonists' passions are antithetical to Madam Cui's rational calculation and

49 Ibid., 101; West and Idema, *Moon and the Zither*, 258.

50 Wang, *Xixiang ji*, 103; West and Idema, *Moon and the Zither*, 262.

51 Wang, *Xixiang ji*, 229; West and Idema, *Moon and the Zither*, 391.

hypocrisy, and to Zheng Heng's deception. In this respect, love is endowed with the power to reform human nature. *The Story of the Western Wing* exemplifies a new formula of romantic narratives, pitting good against evil in an effort to arouse a strong emotional preference for attachment over social norms and divisions, as well as correct moral judgment.

Thus *The Story of the Western Wing* gives less prominence to the conflict between romance and morality, but rather demonstrates that spontaneous yet socially responsible love can be moral as well. The victory of love is represented as the triumph of righteousness over viciousness. However, the compromise between the lovers and parental authority in *The Story of the Western Wing* does not stem directly from the power of love itself, but depends on the mother's concerns. Only when threatened by Hongniang with public disclosure of the lovers' affair does Madam Cui relent and consent to the engagement, in order to save face publicly. Nevertheless, in an equally famous play, *The Peony Pavilion*, one can see how *qing* itself both realizes and reshapes the ritual. Moreover, while Yingying is somewhat passive in her pursuit of love, the heroine of *The Peony Pavilion*, Du Liniang 杜麗娘, shows strong will and self-awareness. What makes *The Peony Pavilion* unusual is its placement of the heroine in the subject position and its exploration of the possibility of self.

2 The Construction of Interiority: *The Peony Pavilion*

Immediately after its first appearance in 1598, *The Peony Pavilion* by Tang Xianzu made a splash in literary circles and quickly became a legend. According to one of Tang Xianzu's readers, there was no man of letters or scholar without a copy on his desk.[52] *The Peony Pavilion* tells of a girl who dreams of a lover, pines for the love and dies, but ultimately returns to life by her lover's resurrection. With its romantic plot, refined sensibility, and successful characterization of the heroine, Du Liniang, *The Peony Pavilion* achieved unprecedented popularity among Ming-Qing readers. One of the most critical aspects of its popularity has to do with the play's unusual exploration of the heroine's selfhood and existential dilemmas.[53] The messages *The Peony Pavilion* conveys are by no means limited to the theme of frustration and fulfillment of love so common to

52 Lin Yining 林以寧, "Huanhun ji tixu" 還魂記題序, in *Tang Xianzu yanjiu ziliao huibian* 湯顯祖研究資料彙編, ed. Mao Xiaotong 毛校同 (Shanghai: Shanghai guji chubanshe, 1986), 889.

53 See Dorothy Ko, *Teachers of the Inner Chambers: Women and Culture in Seventeenth-Century China* (Stanford, CA: Stanford University Press, 1994), 68–112.

caizi-jiaren stories. The story is not so much about romantic relationship and the intricacies of courtship as it is about contemplation of self and desire.[54]

In scene 10, "The Interrupted Dream," Liniang's dream begins with her discovery of beauty, both her own and that of nature:

> [Zui fu gui:] See now how vivid shows my madder skirt,
> how brilliant gleam these combs all set with gems
> you see, it has been always in my nature to love fine things.
> And yet, this bloom of springtime no eye has seen.
> What if my beauty should amaze the birds
> and out of shame for the comparison
> "cause fish to sink, wild geese to fall to earth,
> petals to close, the moon to hide her face"
> while all the flowers tremble?

> 【醉扶歸】你道翠生生出落的裙衫兒茜，豔晶晶花簪八寶瑱，可知我常一生兒愛好是天然。恰三春好處無人見。不隄防沉魚落雁鳥驚諠，則怕的羞花閉月花愁顫。

> [Zao luo pao:] See how deepest purple, brightest scarlet
> open their beauty only to dry wells crumbling.
> "Bright the morn, lovely the scene,"
> listless and lost the heart
> – where is the garden "gay with joyous cries"?
> Streaking the dawn, close-curled at dusk,
> rosy clouds frame emerald pavilion;
> fine threads of rain, petals borne on breeze,
> gilded pleasure boat in waves of mist:
> glories of spring but little treasured
> by screen-secluded maid.

> 【皂羅袍】原來姹紫嫣紅開遍，似這般都付與斷井頹垣。良辰美景奈何天，賞心樂事誰家院！朝飛暮捲，雲霞翠軒；雨絲風片，煙波畫船——錦屏人忒看的這韶光賤！

---

54 Many scholars have demonstrated that *The Peony Pavilion* reflects the intense debate on *qing* and *li* among late-Ming thinkers, one of whose preoccupations was the placement of self and emotion in the scheme of values. See Zou Zizhen 鄒自振, *Tang Xianzu zonglun* 湯顯祖綜論 (Chengdu: Bashu shushe, 2001), 185–205; Lou Yulie 樓宇烈, "Tang Xianzu zhexue sixiang chutan" 湯顯祖哲學思想初探," in *Tang Xianzu yanjiu lunwen ji* 湯顯祖研究論文集 (Beijing: Zhongguo xiju chubanshe, 1984), 152–73.

[Hao jie jie:] The green hillside
bleeds with the cuckoo's tears of red azalea,
shreds of mist lazy as wine fumes thread the sweetbriar.
However fine the peony,
how can she rank as queen
coming to bloom when spring has said farewell!
Idle gaze resting
there where the voice of swallow shears the air
and liquid flows the trill of oriole.

【好姐姐】遍青山啼紅了杜鵑，荼蘼外煙絲醉軟。牡丹雖好，他春歸怎占的先！閒凝眄，生生燕語明如翦，嚦嚦鶯歌溜的圓。[55]

Du Liniang's self-observation bespeaks a certain measure of self-absorption. We recall that it is her own image in the mirror that makes her spellbound in a moment of enchantment. But when she sighs that "this bloom of springtime no eye has seen," we sense her desire to display her beauty and her feeling of lack. Yet, this sense of lack does not loom large until she visits the garden, when her strong emotions are further aroused by the external stimuli of the scenery, which eventually leads to the dream. She is profoundly touched by the burgeoning beauty of the garden, a symbol of vitality and vigor. The surging of life forces can be seen everywhere in the garden – "deepest purple, brightest scarlet" (*chazi yanhong* 奼紫嫣紅), "the green hillside bleeds with the cuckoo's tears of red azalea, shreds of mist lazy as wine fumes thread the sweetbriar" 遍青山啼紅了杜鵑, "the voice of swallow shears the air and liquid flows the trill of orioles" 嚦嚦鶯歌溜的圓 – all of the imagery suggests the procreative forces of nature, in which she rediscovers her own beauty, her desire, and the self. Seeing the sharp contrast between the blooming of spring and the ruined garden, she becomes anxious about how to deal with her own youthful beauty and the hidden forces at play in her life. In her lament, the "screen-secluded maid" always ignores her own vitality, as well as that of the glorious spring. She now situates herself in the passage of time, and begins to contemplate the loss of her beauty. Her anxiety is born both out of self-pity for her wasted youth, and the fear that her beauty, or her value, will not be known by others, just as the "deepest purple, brightest scarlet / open their beauty only to dry wells crumbling" 奼紫嫣紅開遍，都付與斷井頹垣. Here, nature draws her, because it is in some way attuned to her inner world, reflecting and intensifying her

55 Tang, *Mudan ting*, 53–54; translation by Cyril Birch, in *The Peony Pavilion* (Bloomington: Indiana University Press, 2002), 44–45.

dormant feelings. Thus nature becomes the resonance, or the expression, of a subject. As a result, Du Liniang's anxiety leads to a self-conscious passion, the intensity of which results in the dream, makes Liniang die and come back to life, and provides power for her to quest for her love.

Two scenes later, Liniang returns to the garden, searching for the memory of her dream. Here, the dream serves to establish a subjectivity that can be separated from her body, but that cannot be trapped in her chamber. Wai-yee Li has insightfully observed regarding Liniang that "to fall in love with and die pining for a figure one dreams up is then to endow subjectivity with potential infinitude and willful autonomy."[56] The dream is conceived of as a kind of freedom, a place where people can be anyone, anywhere; the self is liberated and self-worth is realized to the degree that "just as we please ourselves which flower or herb we most love, ah, could we only live or die at will, then who would moan for bitter pain" 這般花花草草由人戀，生生死死隨人愿，便酸酸楚楚無人怨.[57] Dreaming grants the heroine multiple possibilities, and the garden is rightfully a place of dreams.

In "The Interrupted Dream" and scene 12, "Pursuing the Dream," Du Liniang begins her love adventure and pursuit of selfhood. The verse lines of these scenes are extremely subtle and expressive, seeking to articulate the heroine's inner depths which are beyond clear expression. After waking up from the dream, Du Liniang's longing for the love and the figure in the dream makes her fall more deeply into anxiety and self-pity. Before she dies, she paints her self-portrait, out of fear of her beauty being stifled, and with the hope of preserving her beauty forever:

> [Wei fan xu:] Pleasure yields to pain:
> pleasure in the bright vision elegantly demure
> as fairy pendants away;
> pain to predict, as the years deepen
> the fading of tint from eye and lip
> of this Ajiao, locked up in golden chamber.
> Vain labor
> when to no lover's eye this lovely image
> unrolled will bring a tear,

56 Wai-yee Li, *Enchantment and Disenchantment: Love and Illusion in Chinese Literature* (Princeton, NJ: Princeton University Press, 1993), 52. C.T. Hsia also discusses the transcendent state in which one experiences the dream, see Hsia, "Time and the Human Condition in the Plays of T'ang Hsien-tsu," in de Bary, *Self and Society in Ming Thought*, 249–79.

57 Tang, *Mudan ting*, 67; Birch, *The Peony Pavilion*, 61.

when there is none to call
the living Zhenzhen from the painted scroll.
O melancholy fate
that this most imminent presence must stay hid
for latter days to witness.

【尾犯序】心喜轉心焦。喜的明妝儼雅，仙珮飄颻。則怕呵，把俺年深色淺，當了箇金屋藏嬌。虛勞，寄春容教誰淚落，做真真無人喚叫。堪愁夭，精神出現留與後人標。[58]

While the element of self-portrait can be readily seen as a convention of southern drama, Tang Xianzu's treatment of the theme is delicate and original.[59] More importantly, the use of the self-portrait in *The Peony Pavilion* gives rise to such significant issues as a woman's self-understanding, self-fulfillment, and creativity. Du Liniang hopes to preserve her perfect beauty in the world through painting a self-portrait. What is noteworthy here is that she depicts herself as she looked in her dream, not as she looks when she paints the portrait during her illness.[60] In the process of painting, she implies the importance of transmitting the spirit: "The spirit is left behind for later people to appreciate" 精神出現留於後人標. Because this is a portrait that speaks for both its painter and the painted beyond the grave, it thus represents the painter's true essence more than her current state. That is why Liniang's act of painting herself is called "portraying the trueness" (*xiezhen* 寫真). For Liniang, the dreamed self is the authentic embodiment of her spirit, or of what is essential about herself. As Catherine C. Swatek has pointed out, "At the moment of the portrait's creation, Liniang describes her act of self-portrayal as the conveying of her person into the painting."[61]

Of equal importance for the painting is that Liniang paints her self-portrait not only as the demonstration of the essence of her beauty, but also as an encoded record of her dream. In the portrait, Liniang carries in hand a green sprig from a plum tree, which evokes her lover, Liu Mengmei 柳夢梅. Catherine Swatek has convincingly interpreted that the plum tree becomes

58 Tang, *Mudan ting*, 78; Birch, *The Peony Pavilion*, 71.

59 Catherine C. Swatek presents an elaborate discussion on this question in *Peony Pavilion Onstage: Four Centuries in the Career of a Chinese Drama* (Ann Arbor: Center for Chinese Studies, University of Michigan, 2002), 68–98.

60 See Tina Lu, *Persons, Roles, and Mind: Identity in Peony Pavilion and Peach Blossom Fans* (Stanford, CA: Stanford University Press, 2001), 28–62.

61 Swatek, *Peony Pavilion Onstage*, 86.

identified in Liniang's mind with her dream lover.[62] Furthermore, the poem Liniang writes on the portrait – "Union in some year to come / with the 'courtier of the moon' / will be beneath the branches / either of willow or apricot" 他年得傍蟾宮客，不在梅邊在柳邊 – suggests her lover's name and their final union.[63] Through both the image and poem, Liniang makes known her desire in a clever way. She hopes that the portrait might encounter an admirer someday, and that someone will understand the code. As she sings at the moment of her death in scene 20, "That portrait and those brush strokes, telling my heart's desire, may reach someday someone who understands" 有心靈翰墨春容，倘直那人知重.[64] In this sense, the self-portrait functions as the exteriorization of otherwise invisible desires.

Du Liniang's desire to preserve her incomparable beauty inviolate is also a desire for recognition, or a wish for self-validation. Her deepest anxiety lies in the fact that if she does not make a portrait of herself to leave to the world, no one will ever learn of her beauty once she dies.[65] Here her "*qing*" bears the signs of "*zhi*" 志 (ambition), that is, the ambition to leave something for posterity that represents her spirit. When she waits to be brought to life by a lover, what's important here is not the lover himself, but the power of her *qing*, or her desire for self-fulfillment. In fact, as Tang Xianzu has maintained in his preface to the play, "Love is of source unknown, yet it grows ever deeper" 情不知所起，一往而情深.[66] Liniang's *qing* does not come from the object of her love, but from her desire, the subject itself; her *qing* emerges prior to the appearance of Liu Mengmei. This is further demonstrated in the scene of her resurrection, when she cannot actually recognize Liu Mengmei, but only remembers her dream and laments for her youth.[67] Swatek also perceptively notes that the plum is identified with Liniang herself, as well as Liu Mengmei, her mysterious dream lover.[68] Through this image, she and her lover are mysteriously interrelated: Liu is part of her dream self, the creation of her desire, and hence her love for Liu, to some degree, is a kind of self-love; her yearning for the dream lover is a desire for self-affirmation. As a result, in *The Peony Pavilion*, Liu Mengmei is only a conventional and relatively pale figure, so much so that this

62 Ibid., 71–72.
63 Tang, *Mudan ting*, 78; Birch, *The Peony Pavilion*, 70.
64 Tang, *Mudan ting*, 111; Birch, *The Peony Pavilion*, 102.
65 Tang, *Mudan ting*, 76.
66 Tang, *Mudan ting*, 1 (translation from Birch's preface to the second edition of *The Peony Pavilion*).
67 Ibid., 201–203.
68 Swatek, *Peony Pavilion Onstage*, 68–98.

play seems a one-role play: whether or not Liu can rise to the occasion, Liniang will bravely search for love.

As we know, Liniang's desire is so strong that even after she dies she returns as a ghost to the land of the living, and continues her search for a lover. In this lonely and uncertain, but spirit-determined journey, she is often introspective as she contemplates her own state.[69] At this point, she breaks out of the old identity that her social status as a gentry woman has fixed upon her, and seeks to reconstruct a new self, which is associated with the power of *qing*. In fact, having been resurrected by her lover, she calls her return to life the "reopening of her dream realm" (*mengjing chongkai* 夢境重開).[70] Here, Liniang equates *qing*, life, and dreams. In her wandering as a ghost, her passion is not only concerned with the search for a lover, but more and more with the yearning for life, which establishes a special relationship between love and life.[71] *Qing* is regarded as a kind of ability, which can transcend both the constraints of the passing of time and corporeal death.

The end of Liniang's journey has given rise to a lot of interpretive controversy. At the end of the story, Liu Mengmei takes first place in the examinations, and Liniang congratulates herself for finding a husband with far greater official success than any young man her parents could have chosen for her. When she sees Liu off to take the examination she demonstrates how highly she values "rank" and "fame."[72] Many critics think that the latter part of the play becomes a more conventional romantic comedy, in the sense that it ends with the happy union, and both the hero and the heroine are finally rewarded with status and wealth. For example, C.T. Hsia claims that "the romantic passion initially seen as a fierce assertion of life in the stifling environment of a deadened Confucian society is changed beyond recognition as the lovers afflicted with that passion pass beyond the phase of love to seek reconcilement with society."[73] However, this is only partially correct, and it overstates the sharpness of the discontinuity between the former and latter parts of the play. It is all the more questionable that Du Liniang, in the end, becomes another person totally different from the one in the dream, as Tina Lu asserts.[74] Although Du

69 Tang, *Mudan ting*, Scenes 27, 28, and 32.

70 Ibid., 205.

71 C.T. Hsia, in his thought-provoking article "Time and the Human Condition in the Plays of T'ang Hsien-tsu," also discusses the relationship between "*sheng* (life)" and "*qing* (love)" in *The Peony Pavilion* and late-Ming philosophical thought. See Hsia, "Time and the Human Condition in the Plays of T'ang Hsien-tsu," 249–79.

72 Tang, *Mudan ting*, 217–18.

73 Hsia, "Time and the Human Condition in the Plays of T'ang Hsien-tsu," 279.

74 See Lu, *Persons, Roles, and Mind*, 28–62.

Liniang ends in seeking her goal in a way that the social morality allows for, her character and actions do not lack consistency in the sense of self-fulfillment. From Du Liniang's point of view, she makes her incomparable beauty known through *qing* in the dreamworld, and furthermore, she is recognized by society, thereby fulfilling her own worth in the real world (according to social values) by becoming the wife of a *zhuangyuan* 狀元 (person ranking first in the imperial examination).[75] In this way, "the otherworld (the realm of dreams and death) complements rather than contravenes mundane reality."[76]

Hence, Du Liniang's story reveals more about her own subjectivity than anything else. Her courage and strong will render her different from her precursor, Cui Yingying, who hesitates between her own feelings and abiding by her mother's wishes. While Du Liniang is very conscious of her beauty and self-worth, Yingying is almost unconscious of her own beauty – her beauty is instead discovered first by the hero, Zhang Junrui. Yingying's lovesickness is precisely stirred by the appearance of Zhang. By contrast, Du Liniang's *qing* is neither elicited nor determined by Liu Mengmei. In *The Peony Pavilion*, *qing* is innate, and impinges upon the self. It is endowed with a depth, which engenders an inwardness. Du Liniang rediscovers her desire and self in nature, which is resonant with the emotions within her. In other words, the depth of nature lies in that of self. Here, there is a subtle correspondence between nature and human nature, or between personalized nature and naturalized human beings. It is nature that awakens the sentiments within her and draws her in, because nature is in some way attuned to her feelings, so that it reflects and intensifies what she feels. As Liniang asserts, "it has been always in my nature to love fine things" 我一生兒愛好是天然 – the pursuit of beautiful things, or a better self, is heaven-endowed nature, which serves as a starting point of her life journey to self-fulfillment.[77]

Before she dies, she "portrays her trueness"; it is the hero Liu Mengmei's "examining the trueness" (*wanzhen* 玩真) and crying for Zhenzhen 真真 that ultimately lead to her resurrection.[78] When true inner feelings and desires, which come from humans' innate nature, are aroused, people realize their

75 In this sense, Liniang is much more ambitious than the heroine of *The Story of the Western Wing*, Cui Yingying, who decries that "tiny profit" and "empty fame" bring her and her lover apart, and bring about the suffering of parting. What Yingying cares about is the couple's reunion, not official rank and fame.

76 Wai-yee Li presents a detailed discussion on this question in *Enchantment and Disenchantment*, 6.

77 Tang, *Mudan ting*, 53; Birch, *The Peony Pavilion*, 44.

78 Here, Tang Xianzu appropriates the Tang story of Zhenzhen 真真, a girl on a painting who magically comes to life. For Zhenzhen's story, see Du Xunhe 杜荀鶴 (ca. 846–906),

ability to be substantial, conscious, intentional creators of life. As Tang Xianzu claims, "One's body and looks are heaven-endowed nature" 形色即是天性, so one has to cherish them; "As for the nature of heaven and earth, it values human beings" 天地之性人為貴.[79] Therefore, Tang honors the individual worth of men as well as lives all over the world, in response to Luo Rufang's conception of "ceaseless inner vitality" (*shengsheng* 生生), which Luo sees as being embedded in human nature, and finding its expression in the outpouring of *qing*.[80] In this sense, *qing* proffers the subject with the richness and the depth of interiority, as well as the infinitude of action fostered through innate emotional sensitivities, which is expounded by the heroine's dream, death, and rebirth.

It can be said that in *The Peony Pavilion qing* becomes an icon of subjectivity, viewed as a meaningful end per se. The play attempts to construct a new self through the power of *qing*, to the extent that intensity and sincerity go together – the more intense *qing* is, the more likely it is to be natural and good. However, the ultimate self-fulfillment is achieved in the process of socialization in *The Peony Pavilion*, which ends with the reintegration of the self into a larger social whole. At the same time, the members of the family are united by feelings, and thus rites serve to realize *qing*. In the climactic moment of the final scene, in which Du Liniang faints, her father Du Bao is overcome at last by affection or *qing*, exclaiming "My daughter!" It is *qing* that reshapes the father–daughter relationship and, to a certain degree, transcends the sternness of the patriarchal family. This is an endeavor to, in Tang's own words, "achieve the ultimate happiness of the Confucian moral values through the great opening of human feelings." In other words, rites are in actuality a matter of following the innate desires and feelings of human beings. Hence, Tang rebuilds the relationship between the self and society, and between sensuality and morality, thereby realizing the ideal of "the world of *qing*." In this sense, attachment is not just a matter of distinctive particularities; rather, it is also a matter of general properties.

In *The Peony Pavilion*, the love between the hero and the heroine seldom contravenes the social order in a real sense, in that their love is destined and thus affirmed by the providential order, and the lovers are reintegrated into society in the end. However, we cannot fail to note the play's innovations, which concern which aspects of life are marked as worthy and significant.

Songchuang zalu 松窗雜錄, in *Shuofu sanzhong* 說郛三種 (Shanghai: Shanghai guji chubanshe, 1988), vol. 1, *juan* 4, pp. 82–83.

79 Tang, "Guisheng shuyuan shuo," 3.1643.

80 Ibid.; Luo Rufang 羅汝芳, *Mingdao lu* 明道錄 (Taibei: Kuangwen shuju, 1987), 6.5a–b.

The play eulogizes the conjugal relationship as a bond of passion, seeking to compromise the centrality of the father–son/daughter relationship. At the end of the story, the fact that the members of the family are united by feelings not only promotes the male–female relationship, but also shifts its narrative focus onto the female character. Another aspect that distinguishes *The Peony Pavilion* is its placement of the heroine in a subject position and its creation of a subjective space for her. Furthermore, the love represented in the play is an extremely profound emotion from within, to the extent that "the living may die of it, by its power the dead live again" 生者可以死，死者可以生 – a new understanding of passionate love that naturally goes along with further individualization and internalization, as well as subjective power to go beyond both life and death.

If we can say that Tang Xianzu valorizes the individual and subjectivity, and further represents love as a force for realizing and reshaping social morality, then in contrast Meng Chengshun explores the mutuality of the passion between lovers in *Mistress and Maid*, in which passions create a kind of affinity between lovers in which there is no longer a singular self. Meng's point of view differs from Tang's in placing an emphasis on the intersubjectivity of relationships based on *qing* rather than on the celebration of subjectivity, as I will show in the final section of this chapter.

3 *Qing* as the Source of Morality: *Mistress and Maid*

The influence of Tang Xianzu's masterpiece, *The Peony Pavilion*, is made clear in the establishment of *qing* as a supreme value in *Mistress and Maid*. However, *Mistress and Maid* suggests a new direction regarding the understanding of the depth of feeling. The deep love in *The Peony Pavilion* demonstrates a kind of life force, which transcends the rigid boundaries between life and death, between the real and the unreal, and between feeling and ritual. The power of love is primarily reflected in the dichotomy *qing* and *li*, and the ultimate reconciliation between *qing* and *li*, which constitutes an important part of *The Peony Pavilion*. Nevertheless, the depth of feeling is manifested in the profound sincerity and fidelity of the lovers in *Mistress and Maid*, in which the conflicts between *qing* and *li* are downplayed. Although the villain is an immediate cause of the love tragedy, the focus of the play is not on the struggle between evil and the lovers, but on the moving manifesto of faith and the sanctity of love. This is also demonstrated by Meng Chengshun's best-known *zaju* play, *Peach Blossom and Winsome Face* (*Taohua renmian* 桃花人面), in which there are no complications such as parental opposition or a rival suitor, simply a pure presentation of innocent, faithful love.[81] It can be said that Meng's romantic plays delve into the particulars of love and the lovers' intimacy, thereby shaping a different kind of sentimentalism.

In fact, *Mistress and Maid* is a retelling of a love story told in the form of a *chuanqi* tale by Song Yuan 宋遠 (fl. ca. 1280) in the Yuan period. The major plot and characters of the play are already present in the original tale. It tells of young cousins, the student Shen Chun 申純 and the beautiful maiden Wang Jiaoniang 王嬌娘, who fall passionately in love at first sight and pledge to marry. After some twists and turns, Jiaoniang's father finally consents to their marriage. However, Jiaoniang's father later backs out and betroths her to a powerful dandy, Shuai 帥. Learning of this, Jiaoniang starves herself to death and Shen Chun commits suicide as well in order to follow his lover to the grave. The play dramatizes the tale not only in the development of the plot but also in the sensitive elaboration of the interplay between the two young lovers.

As is typical in the *caizi-jiaren* romance, the exchanging of poetry, which suggests comparable talent and companionate love, is a symbolic action that facilitates the development of the story. This is also true in *Mistress and Maid*. However, it also develops new scenes and details that deepen the representation of love. For example, in scene 9, "Sharing the Lampblack," after the protagonists exchange verses with matching rhymes and amorous undertones, Shen Chun visits Jiaoniang under the pretext of thanking her for her poem. She has been collecting lampblack to paint her eyebrows. Here, Meng Chengshun shows his poetic originality by assigning to Shen Chun an aria envying the lampblack:

> Lucky lampblack, I am not so fortunate; it has
> [Hong na'ao]: Served at your dressing table to grace mascara'd brows
> Entered bed curtains, gazed on tiny phoenix slippers
> Smiled as it made lamp flare in happy omen
> Left its trace on pillow by rouge of cheek.
> Your own little hand has scraped it free
> Gathering it here on purpose
> The work of a beautiful girl over many days –
> "Though candle turn to ash, its tears do not dry!"

81 The play is based on a famous poem by the Tang poet Cui Hu 崔護. Its heroine, who falls in love with a young stranger, pines in his absence and is saved from death by his return to claim her hand.

（生）好燈花也，小生到不如他呵！

【紅納襖】他曾傍妝臺畫出螺黛巧，他曾入鴛幃照見雙鳳小，他也曾陪笑靨特地把繁花爆，他也曾照朱顏閑將繡枕描。你親手兒常自調，用意兒收的好。是佳人積久方成也，可不道蠟炬成灰淚未消。[82]

These suggestive lines express the hero's sweet and heartfelt longings in a gentle, touching way. He then requests a portion of the lampblack to make ink. Jiaoniang assents, singing:

This lampblack
[Same tune]: Fit companion for Duan Creek inkstone,
to moisten Jade Rabbit brush hairs
For drafting phoenix-winged characters on Sichuan luan-bird paper
For transcribing "Phoenix Woos Bride" to strum on jasper zither
For composing new lyrics to perform on flute of jade.

這燈花呵，

【前腔】正宜伴端溪蘸將玉兔毫，正宜傳鸞箋寫出丹鳳稿，正宜賦求凰配上那瑤琴操，正宜譜新詞吹入在碧玉簫。[83]

Jiaoniang's lines evidently respond to Shen Chun's suggestive description of the lampblack, conveying her yearnings. Shen Chun laments that he is not so lucky as the lampblack, which always accompanies his lover; Jiaoniang expresses her hope of being an intellectual and affectionate companion to her cousin, just like the lampblack. The use of the same tune pattern for both characters' lines strengthens the symmetry and unity. The lampblack, with which Jiaoniang paints her eyebrows and with which Shen Chun expresses his literary talent and emotional sensibility, symbolizes the association of poetry, feminine beauty, and romance. Moreover, the song "Phoenix Woos Bride" (*Feng qiu huang* 鳳求凰) alludes to the romantic story of Sima Xiangru and Zhuo Wenjun, as well as *The Story of the Western Wing*, in which Zhang plays this song for Yingying, and thus the two lovers understand each other's intentions.

Having promised to give Shen Chun half of the lampblack, Jiaoniang soils her fingers as she divides the lampblack into two piles. She then dusts her hands off on Shen's sleeve. Shen laughs, "I shall cherish these stains as love-tokens."

82 Meng, *Jiaohong ji*, 45; translation by Cyril Birch, in *Mistress and Maid* (New York: Columbia University Press, 2001), 57–58.

83 Meng, *Jiaohong ji*, 45; Birch, *Mistress and Maid*, 58.

But Jiaoniang right away repulses Shen for his explicit teasing. Here, the act of leaving fingerprints on Shen's sleeve prefigures their further intimacy in the scene "Cutting the Sleeve," in which their love is consummated. However, the progression of their romance is full of ups and downs: we see yearnings and rejection, scoldings and kneeling for forgiveness. Such scenes conveying desires and mutual misunderstandings might well have provided a model for similar episodes in *The Dream of the Red Chamber*, as scholars have noted.[84] Such naughty flirtation and quarrels contrast with the tender, sincere confessions of love in the scene that follows, "Hugging the Stove."

In "Hugging the Stove," the young cousins affirm their cherished wish to be together and pledge enduring affection. When Shen Chun sees Jiaoniang sit in the warmth by the stove, he enters, holding a spray of blossoms in hand. He arouses her attention by throwing down the flowers. After they delicately sound each other out, Jiaoniang invites her cousin to sit by the stove with her.[85] It is at this time that the two lovers frankly and passionately profess their feelings and take a vow of eternal love. Here, the action of "hugging the stove" symbolizes their shared feelings, bodies, and fates. It conjures up associations with the story of Zhuo Wenjun and Sima Xiangru, who elope and keep a wine shop to ward off poverty before the court recognizes Sima Xiangru's talent. "Hugging the stove" alludes to the stove on which Sima Xiangru heats the wine for Zhuo Wenjun to serve to their customers. If the original story of Sima Xiangru and Zhuo Wenjun stresses the idea of recognition – that is to say, Zhuo Wenjun recognizes Sima Xiangru's talent, and the couple is happy to remain obscure before Sima Xiangru is ultimately recognized by the court – then *Mistress and Maid* alludes to this symbolic action in the sense that it promotes the concept of the ideal companion, who shares joys, sorrows, and hardships. This is expressed in the hero's and the heroine's chorus:

> [Mao'er zhui tonghua]: Facing each other here by the stove
> We two have told hearts' deepest longings
> Of one too weary to make her toilet in shaded boudoir
> Of one with tear-soaked sleeve by Chu's far stream
> One solitary drinker, gate closed against the blossoms
> One sadly plying her needle as the chill deepens.

84 See Birch, "Introduction," in *Mistress and Maid*, xv.

85 Meng, *Jiaohong ji*, 45.

【貓兒墜桐花】擁爐相對，訴盡兩心愁。一個懶整新妝上翠樓，一個青衫濕盡楚江頭。一個門掩梨花倦對酒，一個寒添錦袖慵挑繡。

[Same tune]: Deepest desires of each
Alike beset by spring sadness
Night after night, dawn after dawn without cease
In life, in death, when will it ever end?
Now today
Maid's mind, man's heart both emptied out:
May it be Heaven's will
Heaven's will to fulfill our match.

【前腔】兩人心事，一樣害春愁。夜夜朝朝無盡頭，生生死死幾時休。今日呵，妾意郎心兩洩漏，願天公有意、有意把姻緣就。[86]

Indeed, the outstanding quality of *Mistress and Maid* lies in its lyrically passionate representation of the mutual devotion between the two protagonists. The harmony this mutuality brings out is both aesthetic and ethical. Qi Biaojia 祁彪佳 (1603–1645) points out that Meng Chengshun's plays are "the poetry of the ancient times; not only the poetry, but also the music."[87] This association with "the poetry of the ancient times" reminds us of the "Great Preface" (*Da xu* 大序) to the *Book of Poetry*, which reads poems as a process of moral education. Qi suggests that Meng's plays, like the poems of ancient times (probably referring to the *Book of Poetry*), give form to human feeling, and cause people to internalize the good. In this regard, Meng's plays approach music, which was seen as the guideline of a medial harmony in traditional literary theory. As is indicated in the *Record of Music* (*Yueji* 樂記), music communicates human affections and natural principles; when someone understands music, he understands rites as well. This attempt to build the relationship between human feeling and principle/ritual can be found in Meng's plays.

In Meng's mind, "The two [Shen Chun and Jiaoniang] look improper at the beginning, and yet end with the proper" 二人始若不正，卒歸於正.[88] In other words, even though people's desire is stirred, the proper can be attained through

86 Meng, *Jiaohong ji*, 53; Birch, *Mistress and Maid*, 69.
87 Qi Biaojia, "Preface to the Five Plays of Meng Chengshun" 孟子塞五种曲序, in *Zhongguo gudian xiqu xuba huibian* 中國古典戲曲序跋彙編, ed. Cai Yi 蔡毅 (Jinan: Qilu shushe, 1989), 4.2745.
88 Meng, "Tici," 271.

mutual devotion that is based on innate sincerity. Meng attempts to make feeling and principle, or desire and rites, merge at the point of sincerity. In fact, after the two lovers reveal their intentions to each other, Shen Chun wishes immediately to fulfill his passion, as Zhang does in the "The Story of Yingying." However, while Yingying keeps silent, Jiaoniang responds to Shen's request: "Surely you understand that when a man and a woman marry it is a matter for long-term planning. Since you have this love for me you should return home to inform your parents and have them send a matchmaker to arrange our union" 豈不知男女婚姻，當圖長久。兄既有情，當歸告尊親，遣媒說合，安得聊為目前苟且之計; "All we need is firmness of purpose on both our parts, and we are bound to succeed in the end. If it is hopeless, I shall recompense you with my death!" 只要兩下心堅，事終有濟。若事不濟，妾當以死相謝.[89] According to this logic, the rite does not hinder the fulfillment of passion, but maintains the purity of love. At the same time, Jiaoniang is obviously assertive in selecting her own partner and bestowing herself on him. Furthermore, notwithstanding her suggestion about the arrangement of marriage, she finally gives herself to her lover in advance of any marital negotiations on the part of her parents. This poses a strong challenge to the rite and underlying morality of arranged marriage. Nevertheless, Meng still believes that the two lovers' behavior can be seen as proper due to their inner sincerity and fidelity. In other words, the focus is on interiority rather than on exteriority. Meng instructs his reader to discover spiritual truth beneath the surface of romance.

Deeply involved with the psychology of his lovers, Meng interiorizes the progress of this ill-fated love, in which the repetitious cycles of parting and pining contribute to the accumulation of tragic force. As one contemporary scholar perceived, "There are people in the world who are deeply involved with feeling; yet, other than Meng Chengshun, who else can present the subtlety and profundity of deep feeling as if he were actually on the scene?" 深於情者，世有之矣，能道深情委折微奧一一若身涉之，顧安得再一子塞乎.[90] *Mistress and Maid* endows the *caizi-jiaren* romance with a new kind of sentimentalism, which is based on the delicacy of the lovers' interactions and their profoundly mutual loyalty. In response to Jiaoniang's solemn promise that she will repay him with her death if their union cannot be fulfilled, Shen Chun swears that in life they will share one pillow, in death one tomb. Jiaoniang's resistance to a mediocre marriage is paralleled by Shen Chun's willing sacrifice of his career, and ultimately of life itself, in loyal fulfillment of his commitment

---

89 Meng, *Jiaohong ji*, 52–53; Birch, *Mistress and Maid*, 68.

90 See Ma Quanqi 馬權奇, "'Yuanyang zhong' tici"《鴛鴦冢》題詞, in Meng, *Jiaohong ji*, 267.

to his lover. What distinguishes Shen Chun from the conventional hero in the *caizi-jiaren* romance is that he is a more devoted suitor. He prizes *qing* above the achievement of rank and fame, "I fear no loss of fame and fortune, only the failure of our marriage hopes" 我不怕功名兩字無，只怕姻緣一世虛.[91] Furthermore, he is resolute in following his love into the shades below, regardless of his parents' grief.[92] Thus *qing* is securely given a value transcendent of other social bonds and social status in defining one's identity.

To Meng, however, what his protagonists' love represents is the utmost sincerity, and thus moral propriety. That is why he entitles the play with the words "virtuousness and righteousness" (*jieyi* 節義). Through conversion to the protagonists' sentimentality, people can internalize the depth of their feeling, which derives from sincerity and loyalty. Indeed, Meng intimates that "the sincerity of Wang Jiao and Shen Chun's erotic sensitivity equals Wu Zixu's and Shen Baoxu's loyalty to the country, and therefore their death is repaid with a mandarin-duck tomb" 申生嬌娘两人慕色之誠，與二胥報仇复國之誠等，故死而致鴛鴦冢之應.[93] Meng associates the moral goodness represented by sincere love with virtues in other human relations such as "Xiao Ji's filiality, Wei Sheng's faith, and Yu Rang's loyalty" 孝己之孝，尾生之信，豫讓之烈.[94]

In Neo-Confucian discourse, *cheng*, or sincerity, means to be true to the mind's intimation of the good, which emphasizes the fundamental importance of the innate coherence of the mind and the myriad things to which it responds. The Neo-Confucian Wang Yangming suggested that the sage "extended his humanity which makes him form one body with Heaven, Earth, and all things, to teach the world, so as to enable the people to overcome their selfishness, remove their obstructions, and recover that which is common to the substance of the minds of all men."[95] Wang highlights that the sense of being one with all things is natural to the human mind, thereby making the sense of unity the foundation for the mind. The goal of learning is to enable people to recover this unity and further realize it in human society. It is the maintenance of sincerity that secures the restoration of the original substance of the mind and confirms the principle of unity between self and human society. Apparently, Meng too believes in the essential unity of all virtues, as is made clear in his aforementioned articulation, "If *qing* and *xing* are both based on sincerity, then they are proper wherever they move. … One can see

---

91 Meng, *Jiaohong ji*, 172; Birch, *Mistress and Maid*, 226.

92 Meng, *Jiaohong ji*, 244–45.

93 Meng, "'Er Xu ji' tici," 529.

94 Meng, "Tici," 271.

95 Chan, *Instructions for Practical Living*, 118–19.

[the complete sincerity] in minute matters such as the intimate relationship between lovers and in huge matters such as what can be seen between heaven above and earth below." Nevertheless, he promotes the ideal of sincerity as a state in which *qing* is fully consonant with the innate coherence of *xing*, and gives prominence to the *qing* represented in the male–female relationship relative to that of other social bonds. He puts it this way:

> Since the past, there have not always been loyal subjects and filial sons in the world, but there are often faithful husbands and virtuous wives. Even faithful husbands are still rare, but there must be a virtuous wife in a village of ten households. Why is this? The most profound feelings in the world lie in the male–female bond. Without resort to the literature of the classics, women have no self-consciousness of where their feelings move toward, so that their feelings can go as far as this.
>
> 自昔忠臣孝子，世不恒有，而義夫節婦時有之。即義夫猶不多見，而所稱節婦則十室之邑必有之。何者？性情所鍾，莫深於男女，而女子之情，則更無籍詩書禮義之文以諷喻之，而不自知其所至，故所至者如此。[96]

It seems that to Meng the affection between men and women represents the most profound sincerity and thus moral superiority, and that the feminine, in the form of pure intuition, is a surer guide to moral truth than the masculine. Thus, romantic love is seen as the source of virtue, and the feminine is idealized as the perfect combination of sensuality and virtue. This view is further developed in the early Qing *caizi-jiaren* fiction, which I will discuss in the next chapter.

As this chapter has discussed, the late Ming elite were more inclined to make use of passion for social harmony rather than to address the problems of passion. In nature, *The Story of the Western Wing* is an urban comedy, which often paints an unsentimental, earthy, and humorous picture of romance. Yet, through critical and editorial practice, late Ming literati invested the play with a new seriousness, elevating it to a cultural ideal. The protagonists' sincere love in *The Story of the Western Wing* is fulfilled and promoted. If this kind of "sincere love" refers to a natural impulse in *The Story of the Western Wing*, then the sincerity of love is thematized and moralized in *Mistress and Maid*. Compared with these two plays, which pay more attention to the conflicts of group division or social hierarchies, *The Peony Pavilion* highlights the individuating quality of attachment. While the deep love in *The Peony Pavilion* demonstrates a

96 Meng, "Tici," 271.

kind of life force, which is naturalized and ultimately integrated into social morality, romantic love is represented as the source of morality itself in *Mistress and Maid*. In this new discourse of love in the late Ming, the protagonists' happy union – in the case of *Mistress and Maid*, the union is realized in the realm of otherworldliness – demonstrates not a fact, but an optimistic vision of ethics – that is, the unity of sensibility and morality – and the natural sentiments as the ground for a happier social order. This point is particularly striking because it applies not only to egocentric but also to empathic emotions. At the same time, the female is constituted as a symbol of spontaneous love and free will, and thus a form of resistance during the historical period under discussion. But after that moment has passed, the female voice tends to flatten into the stereotypical and pure ideology of *qing*. Hence, we will see how the representation of female desire, as well as the *caizi-jiaren* pattern, is modified and parodied in later romantic discourse.

CHAPTER 4

Talent, Identity, and Sociality: the Early Qing *Caizi-jiaren* Novels

Although the *caizi-jiaren* theme had become an enduring subject in various literary genres since the Tang *chuanqi* tales, a new fictional genre dealing exclusively with this subject matter came into being in the early Qing dynasty (1640–1735), only declining around the beginning of the Yongzheng 雍正 reign (1723–1735).[1] It can be defined as a novel of around ten to twenty chapters about romantic love between a young scholar and a young woman, who are equally attractive and talented. Generally speaking, the narrative paradigm of scholar-beauty novels consists of three phases: (1) the talented man and woman meet by chance and get to know each other, often through literary exchange or competition; (2) the hero struggles with antagonists, who often assume his identity and try to steal the woman away; (3) the hero ultimately passes the imperial examination and marries the heroine. Considering the number of titles and number of times they were printed, scholar-beauty novels probably constitute the major type of fiction produced during the early Qing period.[2] Hence, it is important to ask why so many similar novels figured in this period, what was

1 Since many of the works do not have precise dates of composition, this chapter may also explore works written during the Yongzheng reign, regarded as a period of transition from the early to High Qing. As Zhou Jianyu 周建渝 has shown, scholar-beauty novels developed into a different phase from the Qianlong period onward as the social and cultural environment was gradually transformed. See Zhou Jianyu, *Caizi jiaren xiaoshuo yanjiu* 才子佳人小說研究 (Taibei: Wenshizhe chubanshe, 1998), 165–200. For a definition and history of the genre, see also Richard Hessney, "Beautiful, Talented, and Brave: Seventeenth-Century Chinese Scholar-Beauty Romances" (PhD diss., Columbia University, 1979), 29–38; Wang, "The Commercial Production of the Early Qing Scholar-Beauty Romance," 17–20; McMahon, *Misers, Shrews, and Polygamists*, 103–105; Lin Chen 林辰, *Mingmo Qingchu xiaoshuo shulu* 明末清初小說述錄 (Shenyang: Chunfeng wenyi chubanshe, 1988), 55–84.

2 See Wang, "The Commercial Production of the Early Qing Scholar-Beauty Romance," 42–53; Wen Gehong 文革紅, *Qingdai qianqi tongsu xiaoshuo kanke kaolun* 清代前期通俗小說刊刻考論 (Nanchang: Jiangxi renmin chubanshe, 2008), 36–38; Zhu Yixuan 朱一玄, Ning Jiayu 寧稼雨, and Chen Guisheng 陳桂聲, eds., *Zhongguo gudai xiaoshuo zongmu tiyao* 中國古代小說總目提要 (Beijing: Renmin wenxue chubanshe, 2005); Shi Changyu 石昌渝, ed., *Zhongguo gudai xiaoshuo zongmu* 中國古代小說總目 (Taiyuan: Shanxi jiaoyu chubanshe, 2004); Sun Kaidi 孫楷第, *Zhongguo tongsu xiaoshuo shumu* 中國通俗小說書目 (Beijing: Zuojia chubanshe, 1957). The boom of this type of fiction attracted the attention of contemporary critics such as Liu Tingji 劉廷璣 (1654–?), who commented on it in his *Zaiyuan zazhi*

HTTPS://DOI.ORG/10.1163/9789004693357-006

reflected in the love between the scholar and beauty stereotypes, and what the archetypal narrative present in these texts hints at regarding the sociocultural contexts in which they were produced and used.

In discussing the major features of this type of fiction, some scholars have taken the prominence of talented women in the narratives as a celebration of women's self-determination and a neutralization of sexual differences.[3] Others, by contrast, have contended that these works strive to desexualize *qing* 情 through the assertion of chastity, and thus demonstrate a conservative transition during the early Qing.[4] The elevation of the hero's poetic talent also strikes researchers because this talent ends up producing a self-contained lyric world, thus departing from the Confucian model of literati life.[5] However, setting aside such a dichotomous framework of progressive and conservative aspects in the understanding of women's role, or of the private and public realms in the definition of the literate elite's identity, may yield a more nuanced and complex understanding of literary production and cultural identity during the early Qing period.

Therefore, my aim in this chapter is to see how romantic discourse in this transitional period evokes the sense of self and demonstrates a new interest in resocialization immediately after the dynastic transition. Scholar-beauty novels reflect on the late Ming notion of *qing* and attempt to convey a sense of self with a new frankness through shifting the emphasis from passion (*qing*) to talent (*cai* 才), or by basing passion on talent. By so doing, these novels set the stage for the elaboration of the new ideals of emotional expression, in which friendship and sexuality are linked, and conventional moral norms are set aside in favor of a more open and egalitarian manner. At the same time, they employ romance to express a sense of male sociality built on the recognition and exhibition of talent within communities of like-minded literary men.[6]

在園雜志; see Huang Lin 黃霖 and Han Tongwen 韓同文, eds., *Zhongguo lidai xiaoshuo lunzhu xuan* 中國歷代小說論著選 (Nanchang: Jiangxi renmin chubanshe, 1990), 390.

3 See McMahon, *Misers, Shrews, and Polygamists*, 99–125; Lin, *Mingmo Qingchu xiaoshuo shulu*, 74–98; Zhao Xingqin 趙興勤, "Cai yu mei – Mingmo Qingchu xiaoshuo chutan" 才與美——明末清初小說初探, in *Ming Qing xiaoshuo luncong* 明清小說論叢 (Shenyang: Chunfeng wenyi chubanshe, 1986), 4.14–23; Ma Xiaoguang 馬曉光, "Tianhuazang zhuren de 'caiqing hunyinguan' ji qi wenhua tezheng" 天花藏主人的'才情婚姻觀'及其文化特征, *Zhongguo renmin daxue xuebao* 14, no. 2 (1989): 98–105.

4 See Huang, *Desire and Fictional Narrative*, 206–35.

5 See Chi Xiao, *The Chinese Garden as Lyric Enclave: A Generic Study* of *The Story of the Stone* (Ann Arbor: Center for Chinese Studies Publications, University of Michigan, 2001), 4–14.

6 By sociality, I mean the sense of union that arises within a certain social group or a community, and the ensuing process of socialization. "Sociality" here is used in a general sense, although I draw on Margaret Gilbert's discussion of the concept in relation to plural subject

Thus, innate talent worked as a new avenue by which the literate elite could claim distinction and a sense of collective identity. Both the affectionate marriage and a new kind of intense friendship, which are extensively grounded in talent, emerged, in turn, as new forms of emotional refuge that spread immediately after the dynastic transition.

Furthermore, the intellectual turn in the early Qing, a period of cultural disruption and social transition, reflected the Han Chinese elite's profound anxiety about their identity and cultural continuity as they sought to reinvent their own relation with the new political and social order. As scholars have shown, they adapted themselves to the new regime through various kinds of social and literary activities, and to some extent shaped the cultural agenda of the court.[7] Early Qing scholar-beauty novels can be seen as part of the same cultural project, in other words, from the viewpoint of resocialization and stabilization immediately after the fall of the Ming. As we shall see, these works suggest a double-edged agenda, in the sense that the literary construction of a communal ideal based on talent made possible both a renewal of cultural identity and an accommodation with the new order. Scholar-beauty novels provide us with an insight into the intricacies of private and public, of social identity and empire-building, within the cultural framework of the early Qing period.

In scholar-beauty novels, the talented woman is given a certain form of power or agency, rather than being merely the product of the male literatus's self-projection. In these works, a form of subjectivity comes into being along with a new female ideal that particularly emphasizes the heroine's intellectual superiority, inner qualities, and literary activities.[8] However, rather than reading the glorification of female talent as simply representing a progressive perspective on culture, I see it, again, as an aspect of the larger cultural project of

---

theory. See Gilbert, *Sociality and Responsibility: New Essays in Plural Subject Theory* (Lanham, MD: Rowman & Littlefield, 2000).

7 For example, Tobie Meyer-Fong's study of the anthologies of early Qing poetry demonstrates the Han elite's effort to reconstitute elite communities and friendship networks and accommodate itself to the new Manchu regime. See Meyer-Fong, "Packaging the Men of Our Times: Literary Anthologies, Friendship Networks, and Political Accommodation in the Early Qing," *Harvard Journal of Asiatic Studies* 64, no. 1 (2004): 5–56.

8 Recent developments in the field of women's writing culture in the Qing have demonstrated how the talented women of this era appropriated the normative women's virtues and literary/cultural ideal for self-empowerment. See, for example, Yang Binbin's study on women's self-authored exemplary life stories, *Heroines of the Qing: Exemplary Women Tell Their Stories* (Seattle: Washington University Press, 2016), and Chengjuan Sun's examination of three reputed women authors, *Women as Writing Subjects in High Qing China: Reconfiguring the Poetics of Feminine Propriety* (Seattle: Washington University Press, 2024).

the early Qing Han elite's self-fashioning in reaction to the Manchu conquest; that is, as a reassertion of cultural identity in the form of talent that at first informs women's autonomy, and eventually can apply to men as well. A careful reading of these texts helps understand how power is given to women and exercised through them, and how at the same time the kind of subjectivity represented in scholar-beauty fiction assumes a form of female power that ultimately leads to submission to the normative social structure. Scholar-beauty novels made it possible for their male authors not only to promote a project of self-construction through the use of female agency, but also to define what a self-conscious woman desires. In this sense, this type of fiction cannot be read as the demonstration of either a framework of repression or a form of liberation, nor as concerning male powerlessness.

Given that scholar-beauty novels as a category feature similar themes and structures, I shall examine a few examples that can be used as models for other romances and which typify the fictional motifs explored in this chapter, in particular the celebration of female talent as exemplified in *The Two Talented Beauties* (*Ping shan leng yan* 平山冷燕), and the theme of male sociality as highlighted in *The Affinity of a Map* (*Huatu yuan* 畫圖緣) and *The Phoenix Pool* (*Fenghuang chi* 鳳凰池).[9] Although my focus is mainly on examples of chaste romance, which enjoy numerical superiority and better embody the fantasized idealism that characterizes this kind of fiction in the early Qing, I also examine some erotic romances, such as *Awakened from a Love Dream* (*Qingmeng tuo* 情夢柝), *The Butterfly Go-between* (*Hudie mei* 蝴蝶媒), *Omen of the Illustrated Screen* (*Xiuping yuan* 綉屏緣), and others.[10] Whether chaste or unchaste, scholar-beauty romances foreground the fantasized ideal of self-definition and social formation through an emphasis on the overriding importance of talent and of a sense of community.

In what follows, I begin with an analysis of various prefaces in order to discuss the philosophical principles of *qing* and *cai* embedded therein, and then

---

9 None of the scholar-beauty novels have identifiable authors. We only know that most authors were likely from the lower stratum of the literary elite and active in the Jiangnan region. They formed a circle of writer-friends unknown to the public. Regarding their background, see Hessney, *Beautiful, Talented, and Brave*, 4–29; Zhou, *Caizi jiaren xiaoshuo yanjiu*, 30–44; Nienhauser, *Indiana Companion to Traditional Chinese Literature*, 785.

10 Keith McMahon's study has shown that the genre encompasses both the chaste romance and its erotic counterpart, but he also recognizes the connection between the two types of writing. In McMahon's view, even a highly erotic scholar-beauty romance adheres to the same basic narrative formulae as a chaste romance. See McMahon, *Misers, Shrews, and Polygamists*, 99–149. *Qingmeng tuo*, *Hudie mei*, and *Xiuping yuan* are among the five early-Qing works discussed by McMahon as typical examples of the erotic romance. For the novels' titles, I adopt McMahon's translation.

turn to the texts proper to show the operation of the cultural logic that celebrated the talented woman while also explaining the role of male sociality and its relevance to the particular historical and cultural moment of the early Qing.

1 From Passion to Talent: a New Sense of Self

The preface to the edition of *The Two Cousins* (*Yu jiao li* 玉嬌梨), one of the earliest scholar-beauty novels, preserved in the Tokyo Cabinet Library contains a statement that contrasts *The Two Cousins* with *Jin Ping Mei* by claiming that the former emphasizes a "desire for beauty from a true heart" (*haose zhenxin* 好色真心) and a "sophisticated and urbane sensibility" (*yunji fenliu* 蘊藉風流).[11] *The Two Cousins* seems to take aim at a competing authority on novel writing by invoking a quintessentially authentic love and a refined sensibility. Even in the more erotic scholar-beauty novels we find marked rhetorical similarities. The preface to *Omen of the Illustrated Screen*, for example, asserts that "both the love of talent and the desire for beauty naturally bear authenticity" 怜才好色，自有其真.[12] *Qing* is expressed as a manifestation of genuineness or purity, and is thus capable of maintaining a stable inner self, precluding superficial or unrestrained sex. The narrator of *Omen of the Illustrated Screen* further differentiates that novel from classical erotic novels such as *Rou putuan* by intimating that it is concerned with sincere love rather than with an overflowing of sensual desire resulting in a dispersal of the self.[13] Both *Jin Ping Mei* and *Rou putuan* actually end in a situation in which the hero is exhausted by sexual lust, and thus in a renunciation of passion on a note of self-dissolution. In contrast, scholar-beauty novels, including the erotic type, bear a strong sense of self-construction. For instance, the hero of *The Two Cousins* passes the examination as *zhuangyuan*, marries, and lives happily ever after, while the protagonist of *Omen of the Illustrated Screen* marries five women, retires from official life, and lives happily too. Both heroes build their reputation of talent and genuineness locally as well as in the capital.

11 See "Yu jiao li xu" 玉嬌梨序, in *Yu jiao li* (Beijing: Zhonghua shuju, 2000), 173. For the dating of *Yu jiao li*, see Qiu Jiangning 邱江寧, *Qingchu caizi jiaren xiaoshuo xushi moshi yanjiu* 清初才子佳人小說敘事模式研究 (Shanghai: Sanlian shudian, 2005), 9–22; based on an examination of various editions of the work, Hessney also concludes that *Yu jiao li* dates back to at least the Shunzhi period (1644–1661), although its authorship remains uncertain. See Hessney, *Beautiful, Talented, and Brave*, 5–11.

12 *Xiuping yuan*, Guben xiaoshuo jicheng (Shanghai: Shanghai guji chubanshe, 1994), 48.3.

13 Ibid., 6.14b, 20.8a (Guben xiaoshuo jicheng edition, vol. 48, 118, 367).

In *A Story of Loyal Love* (*Dingqing ren* 定情人), the hero, Shuang Xing 雙星, claims:

> The proper relations between ruler and subject and between father and son are based on nature (*xing* 性), and thus one's nature can be exhausted entirely by loyalty and filial piety. As for a harmonious relationship between husband and wife, it involves nature (*xing*) and, at the same time, feelings (*qing* 情). Once nature and feelings are both involved, feelings may emerge and disappear, they may be shallow or deep – everything may happen, and no one can decide for himself. Only when a man encounters a woman who overwhelms and intoxicates his heart, and thereby fulfills his wishes, will he be stable and not change any more.[14]
>
> 君臣父子之倫，出乎性者也，性中祇一忠孝盡之矣。若夫妻和合，則性而兼情者也。性一兼情，則情生情滅，情淺情深，無所不至，而人皆不能自主。必遇魂銷心醉之人，滿其所望，方一定而不移。

Such a statement suggests a renewed association of *qing* with morality and self. *Qing* is taken as a natural and inevitable source of moral cultivation and self-fulfillment. This way of thinking was expressed by numerous literati in late Ming Neo-Confucian discourse. Of interest here, however, is the issue of self-mastery (*zizhu* 自主). According to this statement, one can keep the initiative in one's own hands only in a state in which *qing* is neither excessive nor insufficient. Desires and feelings can become positive forces when they are properly juxtaposed with nature. As Tianhua zang zhuren 天花藏主人 (The Master of the Heavenly Flower Sutra), who was widely acknowledged as an important author and editor of a dozen scholar-beauty novels, states in his preface to *A Story of Loyal Love*, "If one wants to control his heart and correct his nature, he has to stabilize his feelings first" 慾收心正性，又不得不先定其情.[15] Yet the way to stabilize one's feelings is to let oneself be, and remain, deeply in love (*hunxiao xinzui* 魂銷心醉) with a woman who can fulfill one's desires. However, whether a woman is a worthy lover can only be "measured by our subjective feelings" (*ping wu qing yiwei hengliang* 凴吾情以爲衡量).[16] Thus, the author reformulates the idea of *qing* as being maintained by both subjective and moral feelings.

---

14 *Dingqing ren* (Shenyang: Chunfeng wenyi chubanshe, 1983), 1.5.

15 See "Dingqing ren xu" 定情人序, in *Zhongguo lidai xiaoshuo xuba ji* 中國歷代小說序跋集, ed. Ding Xigen 丁錫根 (Beijing: Renmin wenxue chubanshe, 1996), 1258.

16 *Dingqing ren*, 1.5.

In other words, he seeks to develop the concept of *qing* into that of *dingqing*, which eventually leads to self-mastery (*zizhu*). In *A Story of Loyal Love*, chastity is highlighted in the sense that it accords the lovers self-sufficiency and makes them impervious to the desire for outsiders. The novel is particularly interesting in that both protagonists have their chastity tested. The hero Shuang Xing and the heroine Jiang Ruizhu 江蕊珠 always maintain a sense of decorum. They never have physical contact, nor do they see each other alone. Shuang Xing also declines a marriage proposal until after he has gained top honors in the examinations. Even though he later marries the maid Caiyun 彩雲 to fulfill the wishes of Ruizhu, he insists on abstaining from any physical intimacy with her, thereby remaining faithful to Ruizhu. After Caiyun assures him that she will never pressure him, he thanks her for allowing him to preserve his reputation for chastity. In this story, the hero's insistence on guarding his chastity stands for a kind of *zizhu*.

The erotic romance also makes explicit the kind of self-mastery usually represented in the chaste romance. In *Awakened from a Love Dream*, a work popular from the early Qing on, the heroine is portrayed as both gifted and attractive, but above all as having such a dignified manner that she never abuses her literary talent to drop any sexual hint. This is because "her feelings arise from her appreciation for [the hero's] talent, and therefore cannot be surmised in terms of personal designs" 因憐才處，生出這種情來，不可以私意測之.[17] *Awakened from a Love Dream* further has the hero, Hu Chuqing 胡楚卿, suggest that it is proper for a man to have only one wife in his lifetime, unless he has no son: otherwise he will not be a man of integrity (*junzi* 君子).[18] As in *A Story of Loyal Love*, maintaining one's moral purity, exemplified in *Awakened from a Love Dream* in the male and female protagonists' avoidance of premarital sex, is expressed as a means of gaining the gentlemanly identity of a true *junzi*. Indeed, the unchaste aspects of *Awakened from a Love Dream* only concern peripheral and villainous characters in a side plot that serves as a negative foil to the chaste love of the protagonists.

At the same time, scholar-beauty novels attempt to build a dialectic relationship between self-determination and the providential order (*tianxin* 天心), as illustrated in *A Story of Loyal Love*, where the hero Shuang Xing argues with his mother about whether a marriage is prescribed by heaven:

> However, the mind of heaven is dim, and thus hard to follow; whereas in human affairs there are both beauty and ugliness, vivaciously manifesting themselves

---

17 *Qingmeng tuo*, 5.4a (Guben xiaoshuo jicheng edition, vol. 91, 75).

18 Ibid., 6.6a (vol. 91, 79).

> before one's eyes. One cannot simply follow the mind of heaven, and not be the master of oneself. However, if one masters oneself, this may precisely be a manifestation of the mind of heaven. Therefore, I want to do whatever I like, so as to accord with the mind of heaven.[19]
>
> 但天心茫昧，無所適從，而人事卻有妍有媸，活潑潑在前，亦不能盡聽天心而自不做主。然自之做主，或正是天心之有在也。故孩兒欲任性所為，以合天心。

The argument here is still concerned with the question of *zizhu*. But the convergence between man and heaven is emphasized in the sense that only the fulfillment of people's natural desires and sentiments allows them to reach self-mastery, and this is also what heaven has designed for people. As was made clear by prominent early Qing thinkers, the Heavenly Principle is designed to maintain the universality and sociality of self-interest.[20] The message here is that self-interest and public order are not opposed to, but compatible with, each other. This view is also highlighted in Tianhua zang zhuren's preface to *The Affinity of a Map*:

> Providential chance is bestowed indifferently by heaven, and people unknowingly receive it. Though there seems to be no cause, suddenly branches and leaves appear, and then flowers and fruit, and they combine to form a tree. It is also like single threads or single strands: there is a reason for which they do not get in a tangle. This is why it is marvelous, why it is subtle. We cannot but call it providential chance and ascribe it to heaven. ... It is because love stirs men, generosity moves men, and talent and beauty affect men that one dreams about them and winds toward them, almost without caring about life or death. How would one ask about fate? Only because one does not ask about fate is fate subtle and heaven intriguing.

---

19 *Dingqing ren*, 1.3.

20 Wang Fuzhi is representative in this regard. Conceding that desire is the essence of human nature, he insists that "the public value of human desire is the ultimate heavenly principle" 人慾之大公即天理之至矣. See *Sishu xunyi* 四書訓義, *juan* 3, in *Chuanshan quanshu* 7.137. In other words, the heavenly principle accommodates rather than excludes human desire. This kind of sociality of self-interest is found as well in Gu Yanwu's statement that "when the private desires all over the world are harmonized, they become the public interest all over the world" 合天下之私以成天下之公. See "Yan siqizong", in *Rizhi lu jishi* 1.59.

緣者，天漠然而付，人漠然而受者也。雖若無因，而忽生枝生葉，生花生果，湊合成樹；又若一絲一縷，有因而不亂者，此其所以為奇，所以為妙，不得不謂之緣，而歸之天也 …… 惟情動人，恩感人，才美關人，故夢牽菟引，婉轉將迎，幾不知性命死生，又安問緣？惟不問緣，而緣之所以為妙，天之所以為奇。[21]

According to Tianhua zang zhuren, fate (*yuan* 緣) seems to function spontaneously, like the growth of a seed into a tree, but there is also a reason for it and an order to it. That fate, as the manifestation of heaven's will or mind, governs all creation has been a traditional view, yet the emphasis shifts to the spontaneity of human participation and its coincidence with the providential will: in other words, while a cosmic moral order is there to guide passion, passion provides the motive force. People can pursue their happiness in accordance with the moral order thanks to the reconciliation between the fundamental goodness of heaven and the moral autonomy of human beings. A similar conception of *yuan* is found in numerous other novels, such as *Two Marriages* (*Liang jiaohun* 兩交婚) and *Omen of the Illustrated Screen*: "Although a lucky chance is bestowed by heaven, it is man who fulfills this chance" 機緣雖主於天，而所以為此機緣則人也; "Although this is a heavenly opportunity, it is also human effort that makes it so" 這雖是天緣湊合，也由人力使然.[22] This emphasis on human agency means that following the providential order should not lead to the presumption that people have no will of their own, or, on the contrary, that somehow they are purely in charge. Instead, people either exert an influence on fate or unknowingly fulfill it through their own endeavors: this is how scholar-beauty fiction perceives the relation between self and the order.

As such, the appropriation of the aesthetics of *qing* is evident in various discursive comments of scholar-beauty novels. Yet, underneath the surface of the revival and continuation of *qing* aesthetics lay the fashioning of a new sense of self, one more focused on the intrinsic moral mind and spiritual purity signaled by chastity. In contrast to the late Ming trend in which *qing* was conceptualized as a form of radical subjectivity, scholar-beauty novels make an attempt to channel sexual relations into newly responsible ends by subtly reinterpreting the meaning of *qing* and expressing a sense of self-responsibility.[23] Still, this reinterpretation does not simply involve the demonstration of moral

---

21 See Ding, *Zhongguo lidai xiaoshuo xuba ji*, 1256–1257.

22 *Liang jiaohun*, 5.59a–b (Guben xiaoshuo congkan 古本小說叢刊 edition [Beijing: Zhonghua shuju, 1987–1991], vol. 23, 1127); *Xiuping yuan*, 16.7b (Guben xiaoshuo jicheng edition, vol. 48, 306).

23 On the late Ming formation of *qing* as an expression of radical subjectivity, see Ko, *Teachers of the Inner Chambers*, 68–114; Wm. Theodore de Bary, "Individualism and Humanitarianism in Late Ming Thought," in de Bary, *Self and Society in Ming Thought*, 163.

excellence and self-control, it also, and more significantly, incorporates a new preoccupation with talent.

As mentioned above, the concept of *dingqing* replaces that of *qing* and leads to the question of how to maintain the constancy of *qing* and of self-mastery. Accordingly, the focus of *qing* gradually shifts from self-indulgent passion to morally secured talent.[24] Talent stabilizes desire in the sense that, to rephrase an idea prevalent in the scholar-beauty novels of the period, a rare beauty draws her very beauty from a rare genius, and that beauty lasts only as long as the literary gift endures. The relationships between *qing*, *se* 色 (beauty), and *cai* are conceptualized as follows: "Love comes from beauty, and beauty depends on talent" 情生於色，色因其才 and "When one's talent is awesome, one's brilliance in appearance always causes fish to sink out of sight and flying cranes to drop down" 才既驚人，則容貌之光華，未有不沉魚落雁者也.[25] In other words, beauty connotes both appearance and talent, and above all, intelligence and literary talent are the decisive elements. In fact, the confluence of love, beauty, and talent is apparent in the images of the heroines in both Ming and Qing narratives. However, in the late Ming cult of *qing* we see feelings, or love, promoted as the main virtue, whereas talent occupies a more conspicuous position in scholar-beauty fiction.[26] Some authors of scholar-beauty novels even claim that their main purpose is "to exhort people to show concern for the talented and warn them from desiring mere sensual pleasure" 憐才為勸，好色為戒, or to have the chaste heroine indicate that "she merely admires talent and by no means longs for a handsome appearance" 不過是憐才，並非慕色.[27] Beauty and love cannot be separated from virtues such as chastity in scholar-beauty novels, but literary talent is far more emphasized as an expression of inner qualities.

---

24 Although talent is common and significant in the entire scholar-beauty discourse, beginning with the stories of Sima Xiangru 司馬相如 and Zhuo Wenjun 卓文君, the importance of literary talent never attains such heights as in early Qing scholar-beauty novels. For a general exploration of how elite masculinity is constructed through *cai* in the scholar-beauty model, see Geng Song, *Fragile Scholar: Power and Masculinity in Chinese Culture* (Hong Kong: Hong Kong University Press, 2004), 69–86. From another perspective, Zhou Jianyu points out that the emphasis on talent exempted scholar-beauty novels from being banned during the literary inquisitions that became increasingly intense during the Qing dynasty. See Zhou, *Caizi jiaren xiaoshuo yanjiu*, 210–211.

25 See "Chun liuying xu" 春柳鶯序, in Ding, *Zhongguo lidai xiaoshuo xuba ji*, 1268; *Yu zhiji* 玉支璣 (Shenyang: Chunfeng wenyi chubanshe, 1983), 14.135.

26 For the passion/beauty/talent triangle in the new ideal of femininity in the late Ming, see Ko, *Teachers of the Inner Chambers*, 68–114, 143–178. Ko discusses the primacy of *qing* as a new attribute of late Ming womanhood.

27 See "Chun liuying xu," 1267; *Jinxiang ting* (Zhengzhou: Zhongzhou guji chubanshe, 1994), 2.20.

As is made clear by Tianhua zang zhuren, who straightforwardly describes scholar-beauty novels as "books about [possibly 'for' or 'by'] talented men" (*caizi shu* 才子書), the question of talent is central to them. His "Preface to the Combined Edition of the Book of Seven Talents" 合刻七才子書序 ("seven talents" referring to the four protagonists of *The Two Talented Beauties* and the three of *The Two Cousins*) reads as follows:

> Heaven endows people with nature. Even though people may be wise or ignorant, everyone possesses potential virtues such as filial piety and loyalty, or chastity and fidelity. It is only when it comes to literary talent and feelings that some people attain them, while others do not. Therefore, every type of moral character and behavior can be fostered by the average person, whereas the talent that embroiders tigers and carves dragons is found only seldom in a thousand years. … Since I cannot devote myself to a person [able to recognize my talent] and am not able to bear the feelings of discouragement, I have no alternative but to give vent to my Golden Millet Dream of achievement by means of fictitious characters. … All that is pleasant and surprising on the page is what I want to sing and cry out from my heart. … Moreover, this book is not obscure but clear. Above, it can assist Zou Yan's high-sounding talk, below, it can supplement Su Shi's literary sketches, and in between it may also perform along with Emperor Xuan's Pear Garden. Why should one want to wait for later generations to appreciate it? We will see that, once this book comes out, people all over the world will be like Yang Xiong [in their appreciation]. If people all over the world are like Yang Xiong, then it can be known that the author deserves to be called a Yang Xiong. If so, won't heaven and earth's will to generate talent and people's inclination to cherish talent find some comfort? Alas! Although [this romance] won't inflame people's hearts in the same way as filial piety and loyalty, or chastity and fidelity, still, the nature and emotions granted by heaven can be said to play their part in its achievement!
>
> 天賦人以性，雖賢愚不一，而忠孝節義莫不皆備，獨才情則有得有不得焉。故一品一行，隨人可立，而綉虎雕龍，千秋無幾。…… 欲人致其身而既不能，欲自短其气而又不忍，計无所之，不得已而借烏有先生以發洩其黃粱事業。…… 凡紙上之可喜可可惊，皆胸中之欲歌欲哭。…… 矧此書白而不玄，上可佐鄒衍之談天，下可補東坡之說鬼，中亦不妨與玄皇之梨園雜奏。豈必俟之後世？將見一出而天下皆子雲矣。天下皆子雲，則著書不愧子雲可知矣。若然，則天地生才之意，與古今愛才之心，不少慰乎？嗟，嗟！雖不如忠孝節義之赫烈人心，而所受于天之性情，亦云有所致矣。[28]

28 See Ding, *Zhongguo lidai xiaoshuo xuba ji*, 1241.

Through the display of the intricate relationships between nature (*xing*), feelings (*qing*), and talent (*cai*), Tianhua zang zhuren obviously elevates the role of talent in defining one's self. He points out that people have nature in common, while talent and feelings, which are grounded on one's individuality, differ from person to person. By combining *cai* with *qing*, he effectively connects the question of talent to the presumably rejected late Ming aestheticism. But talent takes on new importance as a mark of distinction. Again, in his preface to *The Story of One Gentleman and Two Sisters* (*Jin Yun Qiao zhuan* 金雲翹傳), Tianhua zang zhuren argues that everyone's nature is the same, but that each individual has his or her own feelings: "Why do people have different emotions and an infinity of responses? Considering all that one's nature can be exhausted, one knows right away that it is something general. But happiness, anger, sorrow, and pleasure, which exist in one's nature, are expressing subtler feelings" 何感者亦異，而應者亦萬端？又若夫其性之所能盡者，始知性其大端也。而性中之喜怒哀樂，又妙有其情也.[29] In other words, he contends that, although *xing*, or common nature, carries a variety of feelings, it cannot fully explain the functioning of *qing*, an ineffable attribute that provokes the individual's sense of agency. This comment betrays an idiosyncratic perspective and an ultimately self-aggrandizing voice, and yet it also makes it clear that both *xing* and *qing* consist of one's essence. In saying this, he attempts to bridge the private and the public through the compatibility of *xing* and *qing*. In this regard, *cai*, and, in particular, literary talent, serves as a convenient medium that links personal feelings and a common nature: this is because it derives from one's *xing*, while elucidating one's *qing*. As one of the female protagonists in *The Two Talented Beauties* says, "The main concern of your question is the genius of a literary scholar and a poet. This type of genius is said to spring from man's nature. Genius is indeed included in human nature, but nature cannot adequately define its capacity."[30] An innate *cai* is introduced here as both a distinctly sophisticated sensibility and part of the common nature of human beings.

At the end of the preface, by comparing both the author and readers to the famous writer and scholar Yang Xiong 揚雄 (53 BCE–58 CE), Tianhua zang zhuren further sees the prospect of identification between author and reader and the talented protagonists, thereby invoking the concept of talent and recognition among like-minded men, a diverse rather than exclusive group of

---

29 Ibid., 1252. Martin Huang also translates part of this preface when he discusses the containment of *qing* in the early Qing. See Huang, *Desire and Fictional Narrative*, 49–50.

30 *Ping shan leng yan* 平山冷燕 (Beijing: Renmin wenxue chubanshe, 1987), 8.94; translation from Hessney, *Beautiful, Talented, and Brave*, 161.

people bound together by an interest in scholar-beauty fiction. According to Tianhua zang zhuren, novel writing, as a form of exhibition of talent, not only gives vent to the author's various feelings but also evokes empathy among his readers. In this sense, both our common nature and the special functions of feelings – the kind of *xingqing* 性情 that heaven has conferred on us – are fulfilled in the form of talent. This is a way for Tianhua zang zhuren to define scholar-beauty fiction as an efficient medium to project one's self-definition and cultivate one's public profile. This may explain why he calls romances "books of talented men" (*caizi shu*), a term also used by Jin Shengtan 金聖嘆 (1610–1661) to characterize the books he edited. This type of *caizi shu* proved to be a great commercial success in the early Qing, suggesting that by that time the image of talented men had captured the attention of a large number of authors and readers.

2 Celebration of Female Talent and the Civilizing Project

The prefaces discussed above elucidate the concept of *cai*, a perfect fusion of *xing* and *qing*, as a morally secure means of forging an individual's sense of self. Let me at present focus on one of the best-known scholar-beauty novels, *The Two Talented Beauties*, which is typical in its celebration of talent, and in particular, of female talent. We will see the implication of the discourse of talent in shaping scholar-beauty novels, and how the novel helped produce a subject who understands himself, or herself, in terms of talent.

The plot of *The Two Talented Beauties* begins with the emperor's search for gifted students throughout the empire. The talented heroine Shan Dai 山黛 impresses the emperor with her poems on white swallows, and then successfully passes his personal test. After more testing, Shan Dai bests all officials and skeptics, and everyone sends her gifts, hoping to get a poem from her hand. Her father decides to find some female secretaries to help his daughter in answering the huge number of requests for samples of her writing. Leng Jiangxue 冷绛雪, a brilliant and beautiful girl from Yangzhou, responds to Shan's call for two reasons: first, she wants to meet a scholar in the capital to marry, and second, she believes there is no one more brilliant than she in the whole empire and wants to test her abilities against those of the famous Shan Dai. On her way to the capital, she visits many historical sites and writes a poem on the wall of a temple dedicated to Confucius's disciple Minzi 閔子. Ping Ruheng 平如衡, a handsome young scholar, stops for a rest at the temple on his way to visit his uncle. He writes a poem in reply, which is both in praise of her verse and a challenge for her to compete with him. Leng finally finds Ping's answer and regards him as the one who has recognized her self (*zhiji* 知己), but here specifically her talent.

After Leng arrives in the capital, both she and Shan Dai are amazed at each other's ability and decide that their relationship will be that of friends on a "host–guest" basis. However, the emperor orders a censor, Wang Gun, to expand the search for men of talent. Wang goes to Songjiang to supervise the local examinations and discovers a real talent, Yan Baihan 燕白頷, whom he grades the highest. Yan learns from a friend about Ping, who is now living with his uncle in Songjiang. At a gathering, Ping and Yan become good friends out of their mutual admiration for their genius. Hearing about Shan Dai's success in the capital, they consider that if Shan Dai and Leng Jiangxue are really poetic geniuses, then they should have the girls as their wives. So they change their names and travel to the capital to investigate Shan Dai. After arriving, the young scholar-poets exchange verses with the girls, and they all admire each other's talent. Ping also finds out that Shan Dai's secretary is the girl who wrote the poem on the temple wall. In the end, Yan becomes the *zhuangyuan* in the palace examination, while Ping ranks as *tanhua* (number three). The emperor awards Wang Gun a promotion and orders him to act as go-between in the marriage of Yan to Shan Dai and Ping to Leng Jiangxue.

As this summary suggests, romance is actually of relative unimportance in the novel. The text mostly recounts the prodigious literary talents of the protagonists, quoting fifty-four poems composed by the heroes and heroines, most of them conveying personal ambition or dealing with occasions such as examinations and banquets. In a sense, the novel is more concerned with the homosocial mode of literary companionship and competition than with heterosexual romance. Other chaste or unchaste romances are largely similar in this regard. For example, *The Phoenix Pool*, also entitled *Sequel to the Book of Four Talents* (*Xu si caizi shu* 續四才子書), contains around thirty poems, while *The Affinity of a Map* has more than forty. The erotic romance *The Butterfly Go-between* features as many as forty-eight poems, which, besides exchanges of love poetry, include a variety of pieces expressing aspirations, "chanting on objects" (*yongwu shi* 詠物詩), or written on other social occasions. One of the heroines of *The Butterfly Go-between*, a gifted poet on a par with the hero, considers that if she were a man and they had a poetic competition, she would match or even excel him.[31]

As is suggested at above, a close look at *The Two Talented Beauties* shows that it takes as its focus not so much the protagonists' manifestations of love as their literary talents. We are told that the story is set in the "prosperous times

---

31 *Hudie mei* 蝴蝶媒, 4.38a–b (Guben xiaoshuo jicheng edition, vol. 92, 75).

of the preceding dynasty" (*xianchao longsheng zhi shi* 先朝隆盛之時), when a wise emperor ordered a search for "real talents living in seclusion" (*yinyi zhencai* 隱逸真才).[32] A variety of Ming literary masters are listed as hallmarks of this glorious age in the culture of letters: "As for those who were famous for prose writing, there were the four masters Wang [Shizhen] 王[世貞], Tang [Shunzhi] 唐[順之], Qu [Jingchun] 瞿[景淳], and Xue [Yingqi] 薛[應旂]. Regarding leading experts on poetry and rhapsody, there were the so-called 'former seven talents' and 'latter seven talents.' Truly their poetic writing, drinking, talent, and reputation soared above the Northern Dipper, their intimacy and enthusiasm were admired by the world" 文章名公，有王、唐、瞿、薛四大家之名；詞賦鉅卿，有前七才子、後七才子之號。真詩酒才名高於北斗，相知意氣傾于天下. The novel thus offers a nostalgic retrospection on Ming literary culture. The explicit reference to historical figures of the Ming dynasty is not devoid of political and historical significance. In fact, most scholar-beauty novels are set during the Ming. Furthermore, at the subsequent banquet held by the emperor to thank the officials for supporting his order, the appearance of a pair of white swallows again evokes a remembrance of two historical literati officials of the early Ming, Shi Daben 時大本 and Yuan Kai 袁凱, both renowned for their "white swallow" poems. The emperor orders his ministers to emulate the masterpieces of the two poets, but no one is able to answer the call. Ironically, only ten-year-old Shan Dai, the daughter of Grand Secretary Shan Xianren, presents a poem responding to, and actually surpassing, the previous pieces. The brilliance of her talent is therefore regarded as a manifestation of "civilization scattering through the four corners of the country" 文明之化所散見於于四方者也.[33] Later, Shan Dai goes to court in a composed and self-contained manner, and ultimately her gift is confirmed in the face of all kinds of tests delivered by the emperor and his officials.

While the novel is seemingly devoted to an unrealistic fancy about the marvels of female talent, a particular idea of cultural superiority and personhood is steadily cultivated. From the very beginning, Shan Dai is represented as "self-composed in her deportment, just as if she were a scholar of humble origin" 舉止悠閑，宛如一寒素書生.[34] She takes no interest in such external ornaments as "brocaded and embroidered clothes, pearls and emeralds" (*jinxiu cuizhu* 錦繡翠珠), but instead "wears light make-up and unostentatious clothes, sits quietly in her loft chamber, burns incense and sips tea, reads

32 *Ping shan leng yan*, 5.50.

33 Ibid., 1.11.

34 Ibid., 2.15.

books and writes compositions to divert herself" 淡妝素服，靜坐高樓，焚香啜茗，讀書作文，以自娛樂.[35] Such ideal femininity underscores an inner purity and intellectual loftiness paralleling the "gentlemanly manners of a scholar-official" (*shidafu zhi qi* 士大夫之氣).[36] As indicated in the preface to *Spring Trochilus* (*Chun liuying* 春柳鶯), "One who knows of the proper way of appreciating talent and beauty can attain the truth in choosing lovers and selecting scholars. [The author] has told me that since antiquity wise men have risen from matted doors and narrow alleys, and virtuous women have been found in coarse clothes and thornwood hairpins. As for brocades and delicacies, and ornamented pillars and carved beams, they are all just the surface" 知憐才好色之正，得用情取士之真。嘗謂余言，古來賢士出於席門陋巷，德婦見之裙布荊釵，如錦衣玉食，繡柱雕樑，俱屬外焉者.[37]

Such statements do not stake out new territory by drawing parallels between the desire for talent and that for beauty, or between wise men and virtuous women. But it is noticeable that what they have in common is to speak of something that resides within and that is genuine, something beyond the "surface" (*wai* 外). That is to say, by conceptualizing a kind of identity that focuses on a woman's inner qualities, the notion of talent is connected to that of beauty. Shai Dai's feminine charm emerges out of her innate talent. As previously cited, "Love comes from beauty, and beauty depends on talent" 情生於色，色因其才. One of the heroes in *Spring Trochilus* also uses pure, unadorned womanly beauty as a metaphor for his inner self in a poem praising the chrysanthemum: "When did she ever apply thick powder and oily paint, eliciting the envy of young girls? At all places her deportment is the graceful attire of the recluse" 何曾粉膩青娥妒，到處風流逸士妝.[38] The reader is directed to discover the truth – of both the story and the beauty – beneath the surface, as beauty is valued only when it is the manifestation of one's true self and innate talent. As Ping Ruheng tells Yan Baihan, a woman's beauty fades with time, while her "air of poetry and learning" 詩書之氣 will always remain with her.[39] The enduring values of purity and genuineness that link talent to self require one to look inward.

We also find a similar expression in Shan Dai's "white swallow" poem:

---

35 Ibid.

36 Ibid.

37 Ding, *Zhongguo lidai xiaoshuo xuba ji*, 1267.

38 *Chunliu ying*, 6.7b, Guben xiaoshuo jicheng edition (Shanghai: Shanghai guji chubanshe, 1992), vol. 88, 230.

39 *Ping shan leng yan*, 14.173.

夕陽門巷素心稀，	As the sun sets in the alleys, pure hearts are rare,
遁入梨花無是非。	Yet the white swallow escapes among pear flowers, not involving herself in gossip.
淡額羞從鴉借色，	Her light forehead disdains to borrow colors from crows,
瘦襟止許雪添肥。	Her tight garment merely allows getting fat from snow.
飛回夜黑還留影，	Flying back from dark night, she leaves her shadow,
銜盡春紅不浣衣。	Carrying all spring flowers, she does not change the colors of her clothes.
多少艳魂迷画栋，	How many pretty souls get lost among ornamented buildings,
卷帘唯我洁身归。	Only I furl curtains and return with my pure body.[40]

The poem stresses the heroine's persistence in retaining her true colors and her snow-like purity like the "white swallow." By maintaining her true self she is independent of outer circumstances or social situations, and further differentiates herself from the "pretty souls" who lose themselves underneath the "surface" of the "ornamented pillars and carved beams" mentioned in the preface to *Spring Trochilus*. As an expression of her self as well as a presentation of her poetic talent to the emperor, this poem suggests that the heroine's identity depends not only on the purity of her body but also on her literary talent, as demonstrated by her exquisite and fresh poetic style. When the hero Yan Baihan reads the poem, he highly praises the second couplet, impressed as he is by the heroine's superior skills in making apt poetic lines.[41] This kind of poetic language, with its novel diction and unconventional syntax, repeatedly appears in scholar-beauty novels. As a matter of fact, a so-called *Ping shan leng yan* style 平山冷燕体 became popular in the early Qing.[42] In this sense, poetry, as the most convenient way to exhibit one's literary talent and inner self, is deployed in the pursuit of distinction and interiority.

In *The Two Talented Beauties*, the poems written on the occasion of the hero and heroine's first encounter also focus on personal aspiration more than on sentiments of love. When the other heroine, Leng Jiangxue, passes a temple to Minzi on her way to the capital, she quotes the words of Yan Yuan 顏淵, another renowned disciple of Confucius: "What kind of man was Shun? What

40 Ibid., 1.10.

41 Ibid., 11.132.

42 He Zhuo 何焯 (1661–1722), who was a scholar and calligrapher in the Kangxi period and studied under Li Guangdi 李光地 (1642–1718), mentions this in a letter to a friend. See "Yu mou shu" 與某書, in *Yimen xiansheng ji* 義門先生集, *juan* 7, Xuxiu siku quanshu 續修四庫全書 (Shanghai: Shanghai guji chubanshe, 1995–2002), 1420.216.

kind of man am I? He who exerts himself will also become such as he was" 舜何人！予何人！有爲者，亦若是.[43] By reciting these words, Leng asserts that everyone can cultivate his or her moral autonomy through persistent effort. Subsequently, she writes a poem on the wall of the temple:

千古權門貴善辭，	Since antiquity, powerful clans have favored flattering eulogies,
蛾眉何事反趨之。	How have the "curly eyebrows" hastened into their service?
只因深信尼山語，	Only because I deeply believe in what Confucius said,
磨不磷兮涅不緇。	That a hard object cannot be made thin when ground, that a white object cannot be made black when steeped in a dark fluid.[44]

In this poem, Leng Jiangxiu cites the *Analects* to justify her employment by a powerful man as a way of maintaining her independence and integrity while serving him. She only comes from a rich family in a village, a lower origin than the well-born Shan Dai. When Song Xin 宋信, who has lost the literary contest with her and is henceforth bearing a grudge, recommends that she serve Shan Dai as a maid, her father is somewhat apprehensive that she might be trapped into slavery. Yet Leng Jiangxue believes that her talent will surely protect her from bringing disgrace on herself and her family. In fact, she is confident about her own talent to the extent of looking down upon such "latter seven masters" as Wang Shizhen and Li Panlong 李攀龍, who are said to be Song Xin's literary friends. She believes that even the emperor will not treat her without proper respect. Her way of thinking is reminiscent of Shan Dai's idea right before her visit to the imperial court: "When men of letters in ancient times were facing the emperor, it is only because they exhibited such talent and such spirit and were called men of genius that they felt no confusion" 古文人在天子前，有如此之才，有如此之气，谓之才子，方不有愧.[45] In their view, talent transcends classifications of social status and bestows power and autonomy. In the end, Leng Jiangxue makes good her declaration by becoming a friend of Shan Dai on a "host–guest" basis.

---

43 *Ping shan leng yan*, 7.84–85; *Mengzi zhushu* 孟子注疏, *juan* 5, *shang*, in *Shisan jing zhushu* 十三經注疏 (Taibei: Xin wenfeng chuban gongsi, 2001), vol. 20, 214; see Legge's translation in James Legge, *The Works of Mencius* (New York: Dover Publications, 2011), 235.

44 *Ping shan leng yan*, 7.85.

45 Ibid., 2.15.

Thus, talent becomes an essential quality that not only transcends the limits of social identity but also maintains moral agency. The last line of the poem, which alludes to Confucius, further confirms the assertion that talent and moral nature can converge. When Zilu 子路 asked Confucius why he condescended to serve a mutinous minister, Confucius replied, "Is it not said, that, if a thing be really hard, it may be ground without being made thin? Is it not said, that, if a thing be really white, it may be steeped in a dark fluid without being made black?" 不曰堅乎？磨而不磷；不曰白乎？涅而不緇.[46] Only with such unbending spirit can a literary man deserve the title "man of genius" to which Shan Dai refers. In this sense, talent embodies purity and transcendence and enables her to act decisively and disregard social constraints. By appropriating the Confucian ideal of harmonizing personal ambition and moral purity, the author endows his talented heroine with a sense of herself as innately upstanding and independent, and the type of female subjectivity thus engendered in turn works as a form of cultural ideal. Given the special historical and cultural moment of the early Qing, it is not beyond possibility that this kind of self-justification was associated with a reflection on the part of Han literary men on how to deal with the political and moral challenges posed by the Manchu conquest. The transcending quality of talent would facilitate both their autonomy and their social and cultural integration into the new regime.

Talent here can therefore be understood as a concept defining how literary elites conceived of themselves as subjects and perceived the relationship between the self and the social world. To be sure, in the scholar-beauty novels this kind of subjectivity works first through a form of female talent and agency and through a romantic discourse. One of the heroes, Ping Ruheng, who is attracted by the talent and the spirit displayed in Leng Jiangxue's poem, composes a companion poem using the same rhyme scheme:

又見千秋絕妙辭，	Once again, I see the most exquisite writing in a thousand years,
憐才真性孰無之。	Who does not have the true nature to appreciate talent?
倘容秣馬明吾好，	If you allow me to express my desire by "feeding my horses,"
願得人間衣盡緇。	I wish that all robes in the world were blackened.[47]

The hero intimates that it is the marvelous talent of the heroine who has inscribed her writing on the wall that entices him. However, "*liancai*" 憐才 (the

46 *Lunyu yizhu* 論語譯註, ed. Yang Bojun 楊伯峻 (Beijing: Zhonghua shuju, 1980), 17.183; Legge, *Confucian Analects*, 321.

47 *Ping shan leng yan*, 7.86.

appreciation of talent) can be construed as the hero's appreciation of the heroine's talent and vice versa. An innate *cai*, or a tendency toward appreciating *cai*, derives from the true nature of a human being. Again, *cai* works here in a continuum with *xing* and *qing*. "Feeding horses" refers to the marital ceremony, thereby articulating the hero's wish to marry Leng. The last line alludes to the poem "Ziyi" 緇衣 (Black Robe) in the *Book of Poetry*, in which a wife makes a black robe for her husband, an official.[48] According to Zheng Xuan's 鄭玄 note, the black robe symbolizes a wise man (*xianzhe* 賢者). If so, the image of *ziyi* has a double meaning here: it is associated with conjugal harmony and moral purity, with private feelings and a public career. And *cai* is precisely the medium that bridges personal feelings and common nature, or the private and the public. This responding poem elucidates the heroine's spiritual value as a partner in marriage, and at the same time represents the hero's self-definition as a man of virtue and talent destined for public service.

The poetic voices of the protagonists are obviously oriented toward a strong sense of self-assertion. In actuality, the novel as a whole is animated by a cultural project of fashioning oneself into someone capable of both personal autonomy and success in the public arena. As soon as the emperor comes across the two talented heroines and appoints them, he increases his efforts to search for men of talent throughout the empire. The logic is that "if such literary geniuses can emerge from the boudoir, how could there be no admirable scholars among the men?" 女子中尚能有才人，豈男人中反無佳士.[49] Likewise, if a young girl can claim possession of autonomy, then a literary man must similarly have a self to withhold. Indeed, both heroes refuse Censor Wang Gun's recommendation for public service and take the metropolitan examination on their own. When they finally pass the examination, the emperor extols them in the following terms: "You two do not depend on anything, and thus your will to establish yourselves on your own can be said to have in the end been achieved" 汝二人不依不附，卓立之志，可謂竟成矣.[50] This sort of will corresponds to the heroines' autonomy and moral purity. In other words, the narrative that aims at producing the talented and self-conscious woman offers a model of subjectivity that can apply to the hero just as much as to the heroine. Ultimately, the theme of female agency provides a common ideal for individuals. The basic qualities of individual identity are supposed to develop through the example of the heroine's talent and self-determination. In this

---

48 See "Zhengfeng. ziyi" 鄭風．緇衣, in *Shijing zhuxi* 詩經注析, ed. Cheng Junying 程俊英 (Beijing: Zhonghua shuju, 1999), 219–20.

49 *Ping shan leng yan*, 11.130.

50 Ibid., 20.250.

respect, the appearance of the talented heroines serves as a rehearsal of, or prelude to, the discovery of the heroes in the examination during the search for unknown persons of talent. Yet this does not mean that the recognition of the true genius of an obscure woman is simply a metaphor for the imperial recognition of the male protagonist's talent: rather, it needs to be considered under the larger cultural project of early Qing self-fashioning in reaction to the Manchu conquest.

Admittedly, the emphasis on women is probably a response to several factors at the same time. Consider, for instance, the long-standing tradition of analogy between sexual relations and political situations, going back to the *Songs of Chu*, in which the male literatus's anxiety about his marginalized status impels him to identify with equally marginalized women.[51] Viewed in the political context of the early Qing, the appropriation of agency from women also allowed a cultural identity to be claimed without evident subversive echoes. Yet the development of the ideal of a female self in scholar-beauty fiction does not only imply the hero's (or male author's) own, projected self, it also embodies a positive force in its own right. The novels make female protagonists visible and award them both literary reputation and imperial patronage, allowing them to exercise agency on their own, or as partners of men. The well-developed interiority present in the role of the heroines further shapes their sense of themselves as individuals. It is especially revealing to consider how, in Chapter 2 of *The Two Talented Beauties*, the emperor awards Shan Dai a jade ruler, a symbol of her own achievements that also comprises the legal authorization to measure others' talents on the emperor's behalf. The emperor also gives her a gold scepter to defend herself, when choosing a husband, against any vulgar man who would try to take her by force. With these imperial authorizations, Shan Dai is granted authority and allowed to preserve a self that no man will be able to possess by virtue of his wealth and rank: only his talent will do it. The trope of female power in this case situates the heroine as the subject of romance as well as the object of male desire. By doing so, the novel fantasizes the woman as an active agent within literary culture, giving her access to new literary identities and social roles.

51 See, for example, Martin Huang, *Literati and Self-Re/Presentation: Autobiographical Sensibility in the Eighteenth-Century Chinese Novel* (Stanford, CA: Stanford University Press, 1995), 88–97; Martin Huang, *Negotiating Masculinities in Late Imperial China* (Honolulu: University of Hawai'i Press, 2006), 33–52; Li Zhihong 李志宏, *Mingmo Qingchu caizi jiaren xiaoshuo xushi yanjiu* 明末清初才子佳人小説敘事研究 (Taibei: Da'an chubanshe, 2008), 197–255.

The new veneration of female superiority in scholar-beauty fiction both echoed and encouraged women's writing culture in the society of the time. The newly active women writers and readers whom Dorothy Ko and Susan Mann have studied are projected onto the competent female characters in works like *The Two Talented Beauties*.[52] It may be due to this increased literary activity among women and to their obvious talents that male authors were provoked to reconsider the representation of women in their novels. Given the motif of female excellence and the increasingly widespread literacy among women in the seventeenth and eighteenth centuries, we can safely assume the presence of a female readership for scholar-beauty novels. In fact, the interlineal commentator in *The Two Talented Beauties* is probably intended to be read as a woman, since she calls herself *qie* 妾 in the commentary to Chapter 12.[53] One also thinks of Judith Zeitlin's research on the commentary edition of *The Peony Pavilion* by Wu Wushan's 吳吳山 (1658–?) three wives, which vividly demonstrates how the act of reading gave shape to women readers' self-perceptions, made it easier for them to cross the boundary between fiction and reality, and thus helped them construct their world as they pleased.[54] It is easy to imagine that scholar-beauty fiction evoked in the same way a profound identification between women readers and women characters, thereby creating a kind of "feminine sensibility" capable of drawing in women readers. Such stories about female superiority suggested to women an alternative to conventional feminine virtue and a degree of independence, as can be seen in some dramatic and *tanci* works written by and for women.[55] We need not assume, therefore, that the works discussed here were experienced solely as models for male personhood: reading this sort of fictional works had a subjective meaning for women as well as men.

---

52 Dorothy Ko and Susan Mann have examined how the spread of women's education redefined both the woman's sphere and womanhood in seventeenth- and eighteenth-century China. See Ko, *Teachers of the Inner Chambers*, 116–176; Susan Mann, *Precious Records: Women in China's Long Eighteenth Century* (Stanford, CA: Stanford University Press, 1997), 76–120.

53 *Ping shan leng yan*, 12.141. Traditional Chinese commentaries on fictional works often take the form of a commentator providing comments or explanations on the text between lines in a manuscript or printed edition.

54 See Judith T. Zeitlin, "Shared Dreams: The Story of the Three Wives' Commentary on *The Peony Pavilion*," *Harvard Journal of Asiatic Studies* 54, no. 1 (1994): 127–79.

55 See Hua Wei, *Ming Qing funü zhi xiqu chuangzuo yu piping* 明清婦女之戲曲創作與批評 (Taibei: Zhongyang yanjiuyuan Zhongguo wenzhe yanjiusuo, 2003); Siao-chen Hu 胡曉真, *Cainü cheye weimian – jindai Zhongguo nüxing xushi wenxue de xingqi* 才女徹夜未眠 ——近代中國女性敘事文學的興起 (Beijing: Beijing daxue chubanshe, 2008).

In other words, scholar-beauty novels provided role models for the self-construction and socialization of men *and* women in the sociocultural atmosphere of the early Qing. They conveyed the notion that innate talent has its own transcendency and therefore is a significant factor in individual identity. In a way, this ideal of self could reach beyond region, faction, and even gender, making it possible for diverse individuals to coexist within Han civilizing culture. For the Han literary elite of the early Qing, attempting as they did to adapt themselves to the consolidation of Qing rule, and yet being faced with a cultural and moral predicament, the use of talent to claim cultural authority and autonomy functioned as an effective way of developing a new sense of identity, and eventually achieving social integration. In this sense, scholar-beauty fiction provides an insight into the early Qing Han elite's project of fashioning themselves through a reaffirmation of cultural superiority by way of talent – wherein talent informs, and to a certain degree supersedes, moral excellence. This project of self-fashioning coincided, in a circuitous way, with the imperial enterprise of civilizing, from which Manchu rulers derived legitimacy as they planned to build a unified empire out of diverse local and ethnic cultures. Susan Mann has shown how elite women became an emblem of this civilizing project, and also that this virtually predates the High Qing era.[56] The idealization of a female self is essentially part of this larger cultural project. Women emerge in scholar-beauty fiction as heroines of civilization – as cultural heroes – possessing and expressing a cultural refinement displayed in their literary talent, and thus as guardians of Chinese literary culture and public morality through their literary voice. Endowed with subjective qualities, their voices become everyone's.

To be sure, such meanings attributed to talented women did not lead to a radical reevaluation of social and moral norms. Scholar-beauty novels stage and manipulate women's agency by domesticating the powerful image of the talented woman, and by bringing her under control as a result. As can be seen in *The Two Talented Beauties*, the gold scepter empowers Shan Dai to choose, but only within the framework of the familial order. It points to something that can be acquired only through her consent and his talent, and henceforth defines what a self-conscious woman ultimately desires, to wit, a good match for her talent. Although they are initially empowered, the talented women merely end in perfect union with the scholars and thus keep in line with patriarchal standards. In fact, the talented husbands the heroines choose for themselves often happen to be the ones their parent(s) choose for them. Accordingly, the theme of female talent and gender fluidity in the novel is not meant to dismantle the

56 See Mann, *Precious Records*, 19–44, 76–120.

gender hierarchy, but to undertake a larger cultural project of self-fashioning that at first assumes a form of female subjectivity, only to extend it to men, who were believed to be even more qualified for that kind of autonomy. Such a representation of female talent helps us to understand women's status as both the agent and the product of the cultural project that shapes the novel.

3 The Poetics of Community and Male Sociality

As we have just seen, scholar-beauty novels first endow talented women with the inner depth and subjective values nurtured by literary talent, and then develop these into a discourse of subjectivity applied to men as well as women. It is equally important to look at how they delineate a socioliterary world marked by parallels between both the same and the opposite sexes. At first, scholars and beauties are drawn to each other on account of their mutual possession of idealized traits. As seen in *The Two Talented Beauties*, both Shan Dai and Leng Jiangxue exhibit a typical predilection for refined manners as well as for literature, just like the scholar-poets for whom they are meant. The narrator specifically compares them to poor scholars in terms of their elegant and self-respecting manner, and in the way they establish their fame through literary composition and poetic exchange.

Likeness in scholar-beauty novels works as a principle of affinity not only between lovers, but also between the same sexes, creating a form of identificatory friendship. In *The Two Talented Beauties*, for example, as soon as Shan Dai and Leng Jiangxue meet, they see in each other their own mirror image: elegant, beautiful, and talented. In Chapter 8, rejecting her father's suggestion that the two girls swear sisterhood, Shan Dai elevates friendship over sisterhood: Leng's outstanding talent will simply shine more brilliantly in her identity as an independent friend than as Shan's sister. In the latter case, instead, her talent would only be made manifest through relying on the eminent position of the Shan family. Their friendship resembles that of the heroes, which is predicated upon their inner identification, and in particular upon their literary talent, with no regard for their disparate social backgrounds. Yan Baihan and Ping Ruheng quickly become friends because both possess superior literary talent and inner purity. At their first meeting, they not only exchange poems but also compose a poem together: the way the young men associate with each other parallels the lovers' pledging mutual affection.

Such parallels establish both love and friendship as shared spaces of community. The male and female protagonists in scholar-beauty fiction act in the service of communal ideals as well as for their own ends. The heroines going through parallel marriages, such as Leng Jiangxue and Shan Dai, befriend each other because of their enthusiasm for each other's talent. The women in a polygamous marriage have each other as close friends as well, and are glad to stay together with the hero for literary companionship, as illustrated in *The Two Wives Well Met* (*Wan ru yue* 宛如約) (Chapter 10), *The Two Cousins* (Chapter 16), *Awakened from a Love Dream* (Chapter 20), and *The Butterfly Go-between* (Chapter 15). In some instances, for example in *The Affinity of a Map* (Chapter 8), *The Phoenix Pool* (Chapter 4), and *Happiness in the World* (*Renjian le* 人間樂) (Chapter 2), women impersonate men, become friends with the hero, and socialize with him in a poetry exchange or in some other situation. In the case of *Awakened from a Love Dream*, one of the heroines disguises herself as the hero, meets the other heroine, also in male disguise, and then exchanges poetry with him/her (Chapter 15). The two women in male attire call each other "brother," a form of address usual among male friends. Likewise, in *The Two Talented Beauties* the heroines, disguising themselves as men, trade their literary works with the heroes through an interesting crosswise exchange between Shan Dai and Ping Ruheng, Leng Jiangxue and Yan Baihan. All of these occasions, in which women are connected to each other or to the heroes by means of the friendship and talent characteristic of the links between men, highlight the overriding importance of communal ties.

Of more complexity is the male sociality solidified in the world of romance, in which male characters also share companionship with and emulate each other through common literary and social pursuits. They possess like abilities in the exchange of matched poetry, and even alternate opinions and situations when it comes to their experiences in seeking beauties and rising from anonymity through literary contests and examinations. *The Affinity of a Map* provides one of the best examples of the kind of male sociality I am describing here. The novel starts with a spring outing at Mount Tiantai, where the hero, Hua Tianhe 花天荷, a scholar from Wenzhou, runs into an immortal who gives him some secret maps. Using them, Hua discovers a wonderful garden and immediately becomes intimate friends with its owner, Liu Qingyun 柳青雲. When Hua and Liu meet, Hua admits that he desires a wife that would be as beautiful and talented as Liu.[57] Responding that he will act as a go-between for him, Liu then plans to have his twin sister Lanyu 藍玉 marry Hua. Thereafter most of the narrative of *The Affinity of a Map* consists of the identificatory friendship between the two young men. Hua accepts Liu's mother's request to stay with them for a while, and the two heroes spend their days drinking wine and writing poetry. Hua also acts as Liu's tutor to help him

57 *Huatu yuan* 畫圖緣 (Shenyang: Chunfeng wenyi chubanshe, 1985), 7.80.

prepare for the local examinations, in which Liu does very well. Moreover, Hua settles Liu's marriage with Zhao Hongrui 趙紅瑞, who mistakes Hua for Liu. Later, Liu convinces Hua to accompany him to the imperial examinations in the capital, but as they are about to depart Hua is appointed commander in chief of the Liang-Guang area. Liu succeeds in persuading him to accept the post as a means of fulfilling his ambition. At the end, Hua is made a marquis because he has rendered outstanding service in subduing a serious rebellion. As this summary suggests, the aim of the story is not so much to narrate a heterosexual love story as it is to explore the sense of male sociality and community based upon intimate friendship and literary gatherings. In a sense, Liu Qingyun's arranging a match between Hua Tianhe and his twin sister, who is as beautiful and talented as him, ensures enduring intimacy between Hua and himself. Zhao Hongrui's mistaking Hua for Liu Qingyun also demonstrates the interchangeability between the heroes. One might say that the talented heroines play a part in cementing the heroes' friendship and reinforcing their sense of community in a romantic way.[58]

Such identificatory friendship between young men finds an even more direct expression in *The Phoenix Pool*. This scholar-beauty novel recounts how one of the heroes, Yun Jian 雲劍, befriends an expert in military arts, Wan Renwei 萬人唯, and how Yun leaves home, where he has been entrapped by a villain, Bai Ben 白賁, for Suzhou to begin his adventures with the help of Wan. Later, Yun and another hero, Shui Mei 水湄, become sworn brothers, being deeply attached to each other (*liangge zhenzheng rujiaosiqi, jinlan jieyi* 兩個真正如膠似漆，金蘭結誼) because they are perfectly matched in talent. At last, both Yun and Shui achieve great success in the imperial examinations and, as officials, go on a punitive expedition to exterminate a rebellion in Sichuan. Just before their first meeting, when Shui Mei learns from his uncle about Yun Jian's literary genius, he longs for Yun's poems to quench his passion. When he says, "Right now I am so frustrated, I want to meet the shadow of a genius and in the end it is impossible!" 於今如此坎坷，要見一個才子的影兒，竟不能夠, Shui cries his heart out and swears to find Yun – otherwise he will never return home.[59] In response, when Yun Jian learns of Shui's story, he laments,

58 My emphasis on women's role in the cementing of male friendship and community is not meant to deny the agency of women's talents in the formation of their own literary groups. Instead, it reminds us of the emergence of the women's writing culture and literary communities studied by Dorothy Ko. See Ko, *Teachers of the Inner Chambers*, 116–76.

59 *Fenghuang chi* 鳳凰池, 3.11a (Guben xiaoshuo jicheng edition, vol. 94, 93).

> I have not seen his genius, but I have seen his passion first; since I have seen his passion, that is enough for me to perceive his genius! His genius derives from his passion, and his passion stems from his genius. I have never known someone with such passion. If I fail his passion, I will also fail his genius!
>
> 小弟未見伊人之才，而已先見伊人之情，既見伊人之情，足以悉見伊人之才矣！伊人之才，才生於情也，伊人之情，情生於才也。有如此之情，而我竟未知，我負伊人之情，即負伊人之才了。[60]

This configuration of passion (*qing*) and genius (*cai*), or feelings and talent, which can be readily seen in descriptions of the relationship between a scholar and a beauty, applies here to a heightened version of friendship between two men. Friendship between males in a sexual relationship is possible, and is actually depicted, in Ming-Qing fiction, but in the case of scholar-beauty novels male friendship and homosocial relations, widely present in both chaste and erotic romances, substantially differ from the homosexual; the latter only occurs in erotic stories such as *The Cross-Dressed Scholar's Three Wives* (*Yu lou chun* 玉樓春) as a side plot involving lower-class characters like actors, and thus is strictly hierarchical.[61] In scholar-beauty novels, the exchangeability between *qing* and *cai* highlights a certain kind of attribute that is innate and spontaneous, and furthermore a desire for the recognition of this attribute.

As discussed above, the interpretation of *qing* in light of *cai* in these romances represents an effort to extricate the notion of *qing* from the taint of overwhelming desire, and thus to reshape a sense of self based on talent and inner purity. With the emphasis on *qing* between the heroes, however, the sense of self is more concerned with structuring an identity by means of friendship and communal life than with speaking of the subject's private world. As seen in *The Phoenix Pool*, the discourse on friendship, which refers to *qing* as something that can be appreciated and articulated only through the authentication of *cai*, is elevated as a vital means of life consolation and self-fulfillment.

---

60 Ibid., 6.10a (vol. 94, 175).

61 The late Ming cult of *qing* provides the possible fluidity between homosocial bonds and homosexual relationships; yet the homosocial and the homosexual were not fully conflated categories in premodern Chinese culture and its literary representations. For a discussion on this issue, see Joseph McDermott, "Friendship and Its Friends in the Late Ming," in *Jinshi jiazu yu zhengzhi bijiao lishi lunwen ji* 近世家族與政治比較歷史論文集 (Taibei: Zhongyang yanjiu yuan jindai yanjiusuo, 1992), 67–96; Joseph S.C. Lam, "Music and Male Bonding in Ming China," *Nan Nü* 9, no. 2 (2007): 70–100; Song, *Fragile Scholar*, 125–156; Giovanni Vitiello, *The Libertine's Friend: Homosexuality and Masculinity in Late Imperial China* (Chicago: University of Chicago Press, 2011), 53–92.

To be known (*zhi* 知) is to have one's person recognized in the ideal community of the talented. In this, the novel explores a notion of identity shared with like-minded men and based as much in relationships as in autonomy. The friendship significantly produces a sense of collective identity, thereby nullifying the social risks of the overweening self that early Qing thinkers generally criticized when they reflected on it.[62] The emphasis on male friendship signifies that emotions are still used as positive drives to live a moral life, but can be completely fulfilled only in a social context. Parallels and companionship invoke one of the scholar-beauty novel's generic attributes as an antidote to the overflowing of self-interest. This aspect of personhood, shaped in a sense of belonging to a collectivity, becomes the paramount concern within the world of scholar-beauty fiction.

Accordingly, scholar-beauty novels devote a large amount of space to the depiction of the male protagonists' social activities, with a focus on their literary gatherings and ultimate success in the imperial examinations. As Aying 阿英 has pointed out in his comments on *The History of Love in the Tower of Dreaming the Moon* (*Mengyue lou qingshi* 夢月樓情史), an early Qing scholar-beauty novel that has so many missing pages that the complete story cannot be reconstructed, the faithful detailing of the life history of the hero and his friends in his literary coterie is a predilection that runs through such novels in general.[63] Indeed, substantial parts of the heroes' lives are spent in socializing, from local gatherings to sojourns in the capital away from their hometowns. Numerous scholar-beauty novels begin with a scene of "*jiaoyou*" 交游, in which people socialize and make friends through traveling, sightseeing, and poetry writing. For example, *The Butterfly Go-between* stages in its opening the hero and his two friends sharing a bed, chatting, and traveling together in eastern Zhejiang. *Omen of the Illustrated Screen* starts with a visit to West Lake and a poetic gathering there involving the hero and his friends. Both *The Two Cousins* and *Spring Trochilus* portray male characters enjoying plum blossoms outside the city wall. In these works, communicating through poetry becomes the instantiation of sociability by expressing the shared friendship of a select circle of talented men and reinforcing their social networks. Scenic sites and gardens offer platforms for social gatherings at which the hero and his friends

---

62 See, for example, Wang Fuzhi, *Chuanshan quanshu*, vol. 7, 137; vol. 12, 9–13, 557–70, 640–42; Huang Zongxi 黄宗羲, *Huang Zongxi quanji* 黄宗羲全集 (Hangzhou: Zhejiang guji chubanshe, 1993), vol. 10, 470. For a discussion of the relationship between their thought and early Qing literature, see Wai-yee Li, "Introduction," in *Trauma and Transcendence in Early Qing Literature*, ed. Wilt L. Idema, Wai-yee Li, and Ellen Widmer (Cambridge: Harvard University Asia Center, 2006), 1–70; Huang, *Desire and Fictional Narrative*, 53–56.

63 See Sun, *Zhongguo tongsu xiaoshuo zongmu tiyao*, 384.

can demonstrate their literary talent and locate themselves within the matrix of local culture and society.[64] In most cases, the heroes in scholar-beauty novels hail from the culturally prestigious Jiangnan area, or are mainly active in that district.[65] The emphasis on the heroes' socializing in Jiangnan suggests the authors' attempt to promote their cultural identity and autonomy by establishing a local community as the locus of personal interactions and a stage for cultural and social practices. Many of these works further strengthen and authenticate this utopian community by having the child of one of the members of the community marry the child of another member.

Male sociality is further consolidated when the heroes study together in preparation for the examinations, or take and pass the examinations together. Though anchored in a communal space built on friendship and literary companionship, the male protagonists in the novels always look toward the capital and the court. Civil service is still the foremost pursuit for almost all of them, and *jiaoyou* is among the most important parts of their career path. A narrative paradigm of scholar-beauty novels is that the hero, together with his literary associates, generally travels to the capital, exhibits remarkable poetic ability at court or among the coterie of the metropolitan elite, and eventually passes the imperial examinations. The trip from the local community to the capital and the activities that this involves enlarge the social world of the male protagonists, and in this way generate a cultural identity that both builds on the local level and strengthens the political and cultural cohesion of the country as a whole. Correspondingly, the formation of community networks

---

64 For its historical counterpart, Tobie Meyer-Fong's study of early Qing Yangzhou demonstrates that social gatherings at scenic sites and gardens facilitated the promotion of a shared cultural identity on the part of the literati of that time. See Tobie Meyer-Fong, *Building Culture in Early Qing Yangzhou* (Stanford: Stanford University Press, 2003), 35.

65 For the most part, the settings of the novels are in the Jiangnan region. The authors of scholar-beauty novels hailed primarily from Jiangnan, and thus wrote from the same cultural place. Various poetry societies were also active in Jiangnan, combining literary and political endeavours and surviving the Ming-Qing transition. See He Zongmei 何宗美, *Mingmo Qingchu wenren jieshe yanjiu* 明末清初文人結社研究 (Tianjin: Nankai daxue chubanshe, 2003); Xie Guozhen 謝國楨, *Ming Qing zhiji dangshe yundong kao* 明清之際党社運動考 (Shanghai: Shanghai shudian chubanshe, 2005); Xie Zhengguang 謝正光, *Qingchu shiwen yu shiren jiaoyou kao* 清初詩文與士人交遊考 (Nanjing: Nanjing daxue chubanshe, 2001); Li, "Introduction," 15–16; Meyer-Fong, "Packaging the Men of Our Times," 5–56. Although the literary construction in scholar-beauty novels does not necessarily reflect an actual state of being, it served as a field of discourse reflecting the same trend. Despite the lack of detailed historical materials, it is possible that the novels were connected to the major trend of restoration and reintegration in Jiangnan under the new Manchu rule. Of course, they also focus attention on Jiangnan because of the dynamics of the publishing industry and of the reading public in this area.

betokens a process of integration into the imperial state and at the same time the assertion of a certain national importance. In this sense, the role of male friendship is dedicated to the combination of community solace with an interest in self-advancement and to the resulting expression of a dynamic tension between the relative autonomy of the elite community and the incorporation of its members into the state.

As the hero makes his way along the path to the court, the talented woman he encounters also manifests a double persona: she is both the facilitator of an inner circle and the embodiment of imperial recognition. While the heroes often begin their adventures in the pursuit of beauties, they genuinely accept the social truth that one reaps the greatest reward for oneself and one's family by being successful in the examinations, and that a scholar cannot truly win a beauty's heart until he passes them. As Yun Jian says in *The Phoenix Pool*, "Public fame and official rank are the key to marriage. If we don't find a way to success and fame, even though there are renowned beauties in the chambers and fairy maidens in the jade towers, they will not let poor scholars get close to their talk and smiles!" 功名乃婚姻關頭，假使功名無路，雖深閨有艷質名姝，瓊樓有仙姿淑媛，終不容青氈寒士，得親其笑語耳.[66] In some cases, the heroes appear unflinching in their pursuit of this goal right from the beginning. In other cases, although they initially do not intend to take the examinations, they become convinced to do so by their parents, their friends, or indeed by the beauties they are in love with.[67] In novels such as *The Two Talented Beauties*, the heroines have already earned a literary reputation in the capital, so that the heroes' journey in pursuit of a beauty is also one in search of connections to the court and beyond. Ultimately, to be a good match for the talented woman means to be approved by the imperial authority: the talented man is what a woman desires and what the emperor chooses. Talented women not only serve as the cement of friendship and community, they are also a form of cultural capital among the social networks that will advance the heroes' careers. Scholar-beauty fiction thus connects conjugal harmony with political power, letting its heroines assume a pivotal and symbolic role at the crossroads where the community meets the state and where private and public intersect.

As such, the sense of community strikes a complex balance between the maintenance of cultural autonomy and the accommodative impulses

66 *Fenghuang chi*, 8.22b–23a (Guben xiaoshuo jicheng edition, vol. 94, 226–27).

67 *Ping shan leng yan*, *Lin'er bao* 麟兒報, *Feihua yanxiang* 飛花艷想, *Haoqiu zhuan* 好逑傳, *Wan Ru Yue* 宛如約, *Fenghuang chi*, *Qiao lianzhu* 巧聯珠, etc., belong to the former case, while *Liang jiaohun*, *Dingqing ren*, *Huatu yuan*, *Chun liuying*, *Mengzhong yuan* 夢中緣, *Shenghua meng* 生花夢, and others, belong to the latter case.

demanded by the times. In fact, this double-edged agenda is further symbolized by the rivalry between the heroes and the impostors, another stereotype that characterizes the heroes' path to the court in scholar-beauty narratives. As mentioned previously, the romances usually involve many scenes of social meetings, of poetic gatherings in particular, where the heroes strike mutual friendships predicated on their equal literary capabilities and on their common pursuit of the talented beauty. But they have to differentiate themselves from the "fake literary geniuses" (*jia mingshi* 假名士) who all too often appropriate the hero's identity and try to steal the woman away. For instance, *Spring Trochilus* offers an account of how the hero Shi Chizhai 石池齋 and his friend Huai Yiren 懷伊人 reciprocate each other by writing poems, and how they compete with an untalented and ugly villain, Tian Youxuan 田又玄, who later will attempt to become the private tutor of the heroine Mei Lingchun's 梅淩春 brother by assuming Shi's name. This narrative substratum reveals the process by which the protagonists define themselves through both identification and differentiation.

In *The Two Talented Beauties*, as in *Spring Trochilus*, the ugly and untalented antagonists, motivated by either lust or revenge, seek to displace the hero and capture the beauty. They usually accomplish this by stealing the hero's poems and appropriating his identity. Zhang Yin 張寅 is a good example of such an antagonist. Zhang's father, the head of the Ministry of Personnel, attempts to have his son placed at the top of the list of successful candidates in the local Songjiang examination, but the real talent, Yan Baihan, is discovered by Censor Wang Gun, as we have seen, and scores the highest. The situation leaves Wang no choice but to grade Zhang Yin second. Thereupon Zhang Yin seeks revenge on Yan by plotting to marry Shan Dai. By passing off Ping's and Yan's poems as his own, he nearly succeeds in tricking the girls into believing he is a genuine scholar, but his artifices are ended by the emperor's personal investigation and order that Yan marry Shan Dai and Ping marry Leng Jiangxue.

To some extent, antagonists such as Zhang Yin are comparable to the villains found among the dramatic figures in Yuan and Ming drama, from whom they probably derive. Yet they differ in the manner in which the struggle between antagonists and protagonists is dealt with. In Yuan and Ming drama, the conflict, which is primarily one between good (*shan* 善) and evil (*e* 惡), is so intense that it often ends with the destruction of either the protagonist or the antagonist. Thus, Zheng Heng 鄭恒, the villain in *The Story of the Western Wing*, commits suicide by throwing himself from a tree, while both the hero and heroine of *Mistress and Maid* die for their love when they are persecuted by the powerful villain featured in that play (see Chapter 3). In contrast, the encounters of antagonists and protagonists in scholar-beauty novels take the form of an opposition between authentic (*zhen* 真) and spurious (*jia* 假), and by no means develop into an irreconcilable confrontation. The negative figures in these novels are usually characterized as impostors rather than powerful dandies, so that they often (though not always) end up at some point in the narrative regretting their bad deeds and mending their ways, and are eventually forgiven by the protagonists or by the emperor. At the conclusion of *The Two Talented Beauties*, the emperor reprimands Minister Zhang and his son for their fraud and violent revenge, yet pardons them because of Minister Zhang's diligent service (*nianqing qianwu qinlao, gu mianjiu* 念卿銓務勤勞，姑免究).[68] For their part, Yan and Ping forget about past grudges, make friends with Zhang Yin, and treat him with great courtesy (*bunian jiu'e, rengren zuo xiangzhe, youli xiangdai* 不念舊惡，仍認作相知，優禮相待).[69] In *Chun liuying*, similarly, the impostor Tian Youxuan escapes punishment at the end and continues to be employed by the hero Shi as an administrator of agriculture in his government; while in *The Affinity of a Map*, the hero Hua even entrusts the former villain, Bachelor Lai, with cutting off the head of the bandit leader, whereupon all the rebels surrender.

In other words, even though the gifted heroes define the self in opposition to untalented, deceitful, and obsequious characters, the narratives seem to downplay a form of competition intense enough to lead to the annihilation of one or the other of the parties, thus pointing toward an ultimate social cohesiveness. On the one hand, the novels make the communal quality of literary talent a vital part of their heroes' identity; on the other, they conceive of a harmonized social world and political order as part of the early Qing restorative process. Whereas the Yuan and Ming romantic plays are formulated as adversarial, offering us a morally legible universe by displaying how love and the good triumph over ill-advised power, the early Qing romances rewrite the political or historical complications by shifting the focus to tension *and* reconciliation between the self and the other, or the authentic and the spurious, providing a solution that legitimates and celebrates social integration. They dramatize an optimistic formula for the empire's ultimate return to a state of peace and social solidarity.

Scholar-beauty novels foreground a process of reconciliation and restoration relevant to their unique historical circumstance. It is only against this backdrop that friendship, literary community, and affectionate marriage can be understood as forms of emotional refuge. By elevating talent as an intrinsic attribute that is able to transcend the classifications of social identity, status,

---

68 *Ping shan leng yan*, 20.249–50.
69 Ibid.

and even gender, the novels provide a site for imagining how people of diverse backgrounds can unite in relation to an ideal of selfhood and community. The overall emphasis on harmony – in concrete terms, the reconciliation between the protagonists and the antagonists – also meets the new regime's need to suppress or neutralize opposition. Furthermore, the heroes' ultimate success in the examinations, which is the climax of the stories, provides an imaginary solace to the unforgotten social aspirations of the authors by invoking a common goal for all educated men in traditional China.[70]

When it comes to the matter of audience, the genre's broad appeal also facilitated the formation of an open horizon wherein new cultural identities could begin to take shape and integrate reading communities. Scholar-beauty novels provided a large market for the printing industry, reaching readers of various social levels, including males and females, the literary elite, and the educated urban masses.[71] With their depiction of idealized love and characters and of shared cultural pursuits and political interests, they evidently aimed to entice common readers eager to join this select group and share in its cultural prominence to purchase and read the books. Despite actual class differences among their characters, scholar-beauty novels promoted a shared cultural idea that elided and hid them. The imagined community they portrayed encouraged hopes to claim one's identity and attain security in an increasingly stratified and competitive society; in the same way, the wide circulation of scholar-beauty novels made possible a cultural space bringing readers together, regardless of their social and economic status, thereby contributing to social integration as part of the restorative process of the early Qing.

70 Benjamin A. Elman has studied the way the imperial examination system contributed to a partnership between government and the elite through the establishment of a commonly shared cultural ideal. See Benjamin A. Elman, *A Cultural History of Civil Examinations in Late Imperial China* (Berkeley: University of California Press, 2000).

71 We have seen for example that scholars such as He Zhuo and Liu Tingji commented on scholar-beauty novels in their writings. Some versions of scholar-beauty fiction feature interlinear notes aimed at less well-educated readers. The interlinear commentator of *Ping shan leng yan* is probably a woman, as we have also seen. Moreover, the printing quality of the books ranged from good to poor. Xia Jingqu 夏敬渠 mentions three "exquisite books": *Huizhen ji* 會真記, *Mistress and Maid*, and *Haoqiu zhuan*, which according to him were printed neatly on white paper, with illustrations at the beginning; see Xia Jingqu, *Yesou puyan* 野叟曝言 (Beijing: Renmin wenxue chubanshe, 1985), chap. 31. Some of the novels were reprinted as miniature books, called *jinxiang ben* 巾箱本 (portable or pocket editions), which were designed for travelers or women. For a detailed examination, see Wang, "The Commercial Production of the Early Qing Scholar-Beauty Romance," 61–67, 92, 171–75. For a general study of printing, the book trade, and audience in late imperial China, see Cynthia J. Brokaw, "On the History of the Book in China," in *Printing and Book Culture in Late Imperial China*, ed. Cynthia J. Brokaw and Kai-wing Chow (Berkeley: University of California Press, 2005), 3–54.

The rise of scholar-beauty novels did not simply produce a new subgenre among the protean literary corpus of Chinese fiction, but a type of new emotional style of sentimentalism. It also demonstrated the exploration of new sociocultural possibilities in the dynastic transition, in which emotional and moral norms were relaxed and simultaneously rebuilt. The creation of the novels can be viewed as part of the larger constellation of activities through which early Qing men, in the face of the political and moral challenges posed by the conquest, reinvented their own identity, promoted their communal ideals, and eventually adapted themselves to the new political order. For the Han literary men of the early Qing, in particular, who sensed the loss of cultural glory and felt a need for continuity with a hallowed past, the veneration of literary talent and companionship suggested a reclaiming of Han cultural superiority and autonomy. I have stressed the importance of the Jiangnan region in this respect.[72]

Once the new dynasty was solidly established by the end of the Kangxi reign, this process of recovery and reintegration could be seen as basically complete, and coincidentally, scholar-beauty novels also started declining. The apex of the process of imperial reintegration coincided with the zenith in their production. Hence, the novels symbolize a kind of initiative in (re)creating the authority of literary culture and making that culture the basis for accommodation with the new rule. The reestablishment of cultural authority via imperial examinations was exactly in accord with the new regime's need to legitimize itself through "civilizing" (*wenmin zhihua* 文明之化), as stated in *The Two Talented Beauties*.[73] The new Manchu rulers did search out the Han literati's cooperation through imperially sponsored projects such as the *boxue hongci* 博學鴻詞 (extensive learning and great language) examination of 1679 and the editing projects organized by the court.[74] Yet the realization of their civilizing project also lay in the Han literary men's own act of redefining their cultural identity and recreating their community in relation to the new political center, as represented, purposefully or inadvertently, in the scholar-beauty novels. In this sense, the literary men were both the agent and the product of the civilizing project; and in the novels this was also the case of their female counterparts.

72 See note 65 in this chapter.

73 Regarding the relationship between Qing state building and examinations, and in particular the Jiangnan elite's involvement in the civilizing project, see John Williams, "Heroes within Bowshot: Examination Administration, the Lower Yangzi Delta, and the Qing Consolidation of Empire," *Late Imperial China* 30, no. 1 (2009): 48–84.

74 For the Kangxi emperor's co-optation and at the same time subjugation of the literary elite during his rule, see Harry Miller, *State versus Gentry in Early Qing Dynasty China, 1644–1699* (New York: Palgrave Macmillan, 2013).

CHAPTER 5

The Diversification of Desire in *The Dream of the Red Chamber*

At the outset of *The Dream of the Red Chamber* (also known as *Shitou ji* 石頭記, *The Story of the Stone*), the author, Cao Xueqin, speaking through one of his characters, criticizes the stream of scholar-beauty novels of the early Qing for their clichéd and simplified characterizations, and refers to them as "a thousand novels with the same tone, and thousands of people with the same face" 千部一腔，千人一面.[1] In explaining the origins of the book in the opening chapter, the Voiding-the-Void Taoist (Kongkong daoren 空空道人), who is in search of immortality, chances to be passing by the foot of Green Ridge Peak when he catches sight of a large stone with a long story inscribed on it. In the subsequent exchange between the Stone and the Voiding-the-Void Taoist, the Stone responds to his reader's charges that his story is ahistorical and amoral by asserting originality. He emphasizes how his story is distinguished by situating it within the repertoire of narratives available in the literary tradition, including licentious "unofficial histories," "erotic novels," and "scholar-beauty romances." Indeed, in *The Dream of the Red Chamber* not only are the literary stereotypes represented in these novels put into question but also the kind of sentimentalism typified by both late Ming scholar-beauty plays and early Qing scholar-beauty novels, as well as their utopian hopes for self-fashioning and social order, which gradually came to be seen as false or ill-founded in the intellectual discourse of the eighteenth century.

Seen from another perspective, however, *The Dream of the Red Chamber* can itself be construed as a culmination of the same scholar-beauty paradigm, even though the ethos of the masterwork has moved well beyond that of preceding scholar-beauty novels.[2] That is to say, the late Ming sentimentalist

1 See Cao Xueqin, *The Story of the Stone*, trans. David Hawkes and John Minford (London: Penguin, 1973–1986, abbreviated as SS hereafter and followed by volume and page numbers), 1.49–50; Cao Xueqin, *Chongjiao bajia pingpi Honglou meng* 重校八家評批紅樓夢, ed. Feng Qiyong 馮其庸 (Nanchang: Jiangxi jiaoyu chubanshe, 2000), 1. 4–5. This version is mostly based on the *Chengjia* 程甲 edition. Except when otherwise indicated, all translations of the novel come from Hawkes and Minford's translation.

2 I-Hsien Wu discusses how the novel responds to erotic literature, as well as scholar-beauty drama and fiction, paying special attention to the way that the novel's reshaping of their generic conventions and narrative functions plays a part in the identity formation of its

HTTPS://DOI.ORG/10.1163/9789004693357-007

discourse continues to shape the core issues of emotion in *The Dream of the Red Chamber*, although the novel explores in depth the new possibilities of emotional expression, in an effort at both reflecting on the conception of sentimentalism itself and developing new sensibilities distinct from those of the previous era. That is to say, what scholar-beauty fiction brings forward continues to exist in *The Dream of the Red Chamber*. For example, poetic sensibility, as well as the resulting interiority expressed in poetry, constitutes a stable feature of *The Dream of the Red Chamber*. The question of truth and falsity, the very core of the conflicts in scholar-beauty fiction, remains the basic concern of the later masterwork in the manner in which the real and the feigned are opposed yet inextricably intertwined. Moreover, the dialectical relationships between the self, community, and social order are profoundly probed and queried in *The Dream of the Red Chamber*.

As a highly creative reworking of its influences, *The Dream of the Red Chamber* testifies to the complexity and magnitude of all of these issues. One of the most important aspects in which this masterpiece transcends its predecessors, however, is in the elevation of the sense of individuality. In comparison with scholar-beauty novels, *The Dream of the Red Chamber* is far more alive to the use of poetry as a vehicle of individuality than its predecessors, by means of offering a fuller and more convincing presentation of the inner lives of its characters in the form of poetry and talent. Especially with regard to its fascination with women characters, *The Dream of the Red Chamber* may be seen as a compensation for an earlier deficiency: the tendency for women characters to be talented and learned, yet devoid of individuality and richness.[3] The characterization of women in this great novel resists reductive typology to the extent that their images no longer just index collective ideals, but rather illustrate the diversity of desire. Through the representation of diverse positions and desires, *The Dream of the Red Chamber* evinces a process of construction that simultaneously fabricates and demystifies individuality. If scholar-beauty novels strive to draw a clear line between false and true based on poetic talents that create and sustain interiority, authenticity, and a collective identity, then the later masterwork further develops this inner quality into an aesthetic sensibility that is individualized, and at the same time transcends the dichotomy

---

protagonists; see *Eroticism and Other Literary Conventions in Chinese Literature: Intertextuality in "The Story of the Stone"* (Amherst, NY: Cambria Press, 2017).

3 Ellen Widmer has pointed out the part *The Dream of the Red Chamber* played in nurturing the type of "feminine sensibility" and the "interiority" that developed in its women readers who both identified with and resisted the plight of the female characters in the novel. See Widmer, *The Beauty and the Book: Women and Fiction in Nineteenth-Century China* (Cambridge, MA: Harvard University Asia Center, 2006), 281–91.

by turning it into an object of philosophical contemplation, as reflected in the couplet "Truth becomes fiction when the fiction's true; real becomes not-real where the unreal's real" 假作真時真亦假，無為有處有還無.[4] The indeterminacy involved in the novel's tendency to undercut the very ideals of *qing* and self-construction that it seems to embrace, together with the ambiguous emotional experiences that self-reflection brings out, produces the individual complexity and richness.

Moreover, the construction of the poetic community in the garden assumes an equally, if not more, important role in enacting self-construction and claiming a cultural identity in *The Dream of the Red Chamber*. However, the masterwork is not trying to integrate community into the regime, or to assert and promote the centrality of the examination system – a move that is fundamental to the scholar-beauty novels – but to call into question the relationship of communal society with public order. In this chapter, I look at how emotional sensitivities and memories foster the formation of the subject, or constitute part of the subject itself, in the novel. Through a textual comparison between various versions of the novel, I discuss how the author develops an intriguingly personal tone and a distinctive mode of affective expression in the making of the self and establishes identity that is extended into memory. I also demonstrate how the central questions of the scholar-beauty novels – the theme of true and false, the representation of desire, the issue of interiority, and the tropes of female talent and poetic gatherings – are kept alive in *The Dream of the Red Chamber*, yet with a focus on emotion-relevant nuances of expression and action.

1 The Diversification of Female Desire

As many scholars have noted, *The Dream of the Red Chamber* consistently represents its characters, as well as other themes, by means of complementary opposites and balanced juxtapositions. Andrew Plaks examines the overall structural and thematic patterns of complementary bipolarity present in

4 SS, 1.55; Cao Xueqin, *Zhiyanzhai pingpi Honglou meng* 脂硯齋評批紅樓夢, ed. Huang Lin 黃霖 (Jinan: Qilu shushe, 1994), 1.12. With the exception of the "fanli" 凡例 and the first chapter, which are added from the *Jiaxu* 甲戌 manuscript, the first eighty chapters of this edition are primarily based on the *Gengchen* 庚辰 text. The later forty chapters, as well as the missing sixty-fourth and sixty-seventh chapters, are based on the *Chengjia* edition as the primary source.

the construction of one of the novel's primary settings, Prospect Garden.[5] Martin W. Huang focuses our attention on the endless tension between *qing* and *yu* 慾 (desire) in *The Dream of the Red Chamber*.[6] Maram Epstein further explores the dialectics between the "aesthetics of authenticity" and orthodoxy – two competing discursive constructions of desire.[7] However, I seek to go beyond these dualistic approaches, and to elucidate the multiplicity of desires and self-fashioning in terms of the novel's strategic maneuvering of female desire in the labyrinth of social relations and systems.

Although critics often discuss the two principal female characters in the novel, Lin Daiyu 林黛玉 and Xue Baochai 薛寶釵, in relation to the competition between private desire and public order, I reflect on female desire in a more dynamic context, not merely centering on private passion, but also on desire in a more general sense. Thus, besides Lin Daiyu and Xue Baochai, a third major female character, Wang Xifeng 王熙鳳, who is seldom juxtaposed with the two pure, unmarried girls, needs to be included in the discussion. In fact, as Zhang Xinzhi 張新之 (1820?–1850?) comments regarding Chapter 20 of *The Dream of the Red Chamber*, "Money and sex are both the character '*qing*'" 財色都是"情"字.[8] The resulting juxtaposition of two kinds of jealousy – one caused by money and power, between married women; the other aroused by love, between unmarried women – are both motivated by desire, suggesting that the common presence of female desire subverts the pure/polluted and *qing*/*yu* dichotomy that exists on the surface of novelistic representation.

The reference to female desire pervades the narrative in the form of women's illness. We are told that Xue Baochai, who is considered a "cold beauty" due to her grace and self-control, instead suffers from "a congenital tendency toward overheatedness (*redu* 熱毒)." Indeed, an extratextual comment in the *Jiaxu* 甲戌 edition explicitly connects this condition to the question of desire, stating, "Her desire bursts into flames so that all the bad fire attacks her" 凡心偶熾，是以孽火齊攻.[9] This mysterious illness that points to her inborn desire can be suppressed only by "Cold Fragrance Pills," a strange medication with a persistent reference to the number twelve.[10] Since "all the references to the

5 See Andrew Plaks, *Archetype and Allegory in the Dream of the Red Chamber* (Princeton, NJ: Princeton University Press, 1976), 178–211.

6 See Huang, *Desire and Fictional Narrative*.

7 Epstein, *Competing Discourses*, 13–119.

8 Cao, *Chongjiao bajia pingpi Honglou meng*, 20. 426.

9 Cao, *Zhiyanzhai pingpi Honglou meng*, 131.

10 Cao, *Zhiyanzhai pingpi Honglou meng*, 7.131–32; SS, 1.168. When Baochai says that she is unaware where the monk gets the medication, the commentator remarks, "I deeply know that this is collected from the Mountain of Spring Awakening, and mixed with water

number twelve should be read as symbolic of the twelve beauties" 凡用十二字樣，皆照應十二釵 as is indicated by the early commentator on the novel Zhiyanzhai 脂硯齋 (Red Inkstone), it follows that the symbolic implications of this illness do not merely apply to Xue Baochai, but can be extended to all of the female characters in the novel.[11] Likewise, Daiyu's tragic death is implied to have been caused by her unfulfilled passion or desire, while Wang Xifeng's symptoms of chronic menstrual bleeding are brought on by an excessive concern about the household, or more accurately, by her desire for power (Chapter 61). Therefore, the major difference between these three characters does not lie in the existence of desire, but in the ways in which they channel their particular desires.

One can readily perceive that Lin Daiyu, Xue Baochai, and Wang Xifeng represent three female character types that often appear in Ming-Qing narratives: the talented beauty, the exemplary woman, and the shrew, respectively.[12] While the talented beauty and the virtuous woman are often heroines of the scholar-beauty romance, shrews more commonly appear in pornographic novels. However, that *The Dream of the Red Chamber* incorporates all of these stereotypes in its fictional world demonstrates its ambitious inclusivity, in which all these models are repeatedly questioned, reversed, and complicated, and sometimes even subjected to the reshaping force of parody. Consequently, the novel's juxtaposition of Wang Xifeng with the other two beauties calls into question the uniform idealization of women figures, thus diversifying female desire: Lin Daiyu lyricizes her desire in the name of *qing*; Xue Baochai moralizes her desire in the form of *zhi* 志 (ambition); Wang Xifeng realizes her desire through the manipulation of power and money. These various forms of desire work as complicated dialogues with the public realm and social order. As a result, the characterization in the novel, through the delicate depiction of how the characters vent their desires, contributes to fashioning individuals

---

in the Sea of Sadness, … and made up in the Hall of Intangible located in the Land of Illusion" 余則深知是從放春山采來，以灌愁海水和成 …… 在太虛幻境空靈殿上炮製配合者也. The novel's male protagonist, Jia Baoyu 賈寶玉, Baochai, and all the other girls are thus linked together in that the cure of Baochai's illness resonates with Baoyu's visit to the Land of Illusion.

11 Cao, *Zhiyanzhai pingpi Honglou meng*, 131. For a discussion on the metaphorical meaning of the illness, see Huang, *Desire and Fictional Narrative*, 311–12.

12 Keith McMahon studies this issue in *Misers, Shrews, and Polygamists*. Yenna Wu provides a detailed discussion on the type of the virago, or shrew, and the socio-psychological foundations of the characterization of this stereotype; see *The Chinese Virago: A Literary Theme* (Cambridge, MA: Council on East Asian Studies, Harvard University, 1995), 19–50.

that both exist in relation to other individuals and social realms, and which are on display in a personal way.

Scholars have pointed out the difficulty with which the novel's protagonists, Jia Baoyu and Lin Daiyu, express their feelings (or "adult" desire) to each other, and how they rely on *The Story of the Western Wing* and *The Peony Pavilion* to communicate their passion.[13] In fact, the predestined affinity between the hero and heroine affords them a special intimacy from the beginning. This special feeling also generates endless quarrels between them, but they never try, or are able, to name it. Not until she reads *The Story of the Western Wing* and hears *The Peony Pavilion* does Lin Daiyu acquire a new understanding of this unnamable feeling. Although it is usually thought that these two romantic plays awaken the lovers' passion, I would argue that it is aroused more by the poetic lines than by the romantic stories themselves.

In Chapter 23, Jia Baoyu is overcome by a vague and undefined boredom. To cheer him up, his servant, Tealeaf (Mingyan 茗煙), goes out and buys books "of a kind Jia Baoyu had never heard about," including biographies of famous beauties and *The Story of the Western Wing*. Lin Daiyu's reactions to the drama evince the degree to which she has been taken captive by the verbal and rhetorical traces of the text, as well as the content of this famous drama: "She felt the power of the words and their lingering fragrance. Long after she had finished reading, when she had laid down the book and was sitting there rapt and silent, the lines continued to ring on in her head" 自覺詞藻警人，餘香滿口。雖看完了書，卻只管出神，心內還默默記誦.[14]

Furthermore, Jia Baoyu and Lin Daiyu immediately appropriate the lines from the drama to tease each other, that is, to place themselves into the literary texts. Later in the same chapter, after Lin Daiyu is separated from Jia Baoyu, she hears actresses singing the arias from *The Peony Pavilion*, and is entranced once again by the evocative text of the play:

> Although she was paying no particular attention to the singing, a snatch of it chanced suddenly to fall with very great clarity on her ear, so that she was able to make out quite distinctly the words of two whole lines of the aria being sung: "Here multiflorate splendor blooms forlorn / Midst broken fountains, mouldering walls –" They moved her strangely, and she stopped to listen. The voice went on: "And the bright air, the brilliant morn / Feed my despair / Joy and gladness have withdrawn / To other gardens, other halls –" At this point the listener unconsciously nodded her head and sighed. "It's true," she thought, "there is

---

13 See Yu, *Rereading the Stone*, 234–46; Huang, *Desire and Fictional Narrative*, 294–98.

14 Cao, *Zhiyanzhai pingpi Honglou meng*, 23. 400; SS, 1.464.

good poetry even in plays. What a pity most people think of them only as entertainment. A lot of the real beauty in them must go unappreciated." She suddenly became aware that her mind was wandering and regretted that her inattention had caused her to miss some of the singing. She listened again. This time it was another voice: "Because for you, my flowerlike fair / The swift years like the waters flow –" The words moved to her to the depth of her being. "I have sought you everywhere / And at last I find you here / In a dark room full of woe –" It was like intoxication, a sort of delirium. Her legs would no longer support her. She collapsed on to a near-by rockery and crouched there, the words turning over and over in her mind. Suddenly she thought of a line from an old poem she had read quite recently: "Relentlessly the waters flow, the flowers fade." From that her mind turned to those famous lines written in his captivity by the tragic poet-emperor of Later Tang: "The blossoms fall, the water flows / The glory of the spring is gone / In nature's world as in the human one." And to some lines form *The Western Chamber* which she had just been reading: "As flowers fall and the flowing stream runs red / A thousand sickly fancies crowd the mind." All these different lines and verses combined into a single overpowering impression, riving her soul with a pang of such keen anguish that the tears started from her eyes.

偶然兩句吹到耳內，明明白白，一字不落，唱道是："原來奼紫嫣紅開遍，似這般都付與斷井頹垣。"林黛玉聽了，倒也十分感慨纏綿，便止住步側耳細聽，又聽唱道是："良辰美景奈何天，賞心樂事誰家院。"聽了這兩句，不覺點頭自歎，心下自思道："原來戲上也有好文章。可惜世人只知看戲，未必能領略這其中的趣味。"想畢，又後悔不該胡想，耽誤了聽曲子。又側耳時，只聽唱道："則為你如花美眷，似水流年……"林黛玉聽了這兩句，不覺心動神搖。又聽道："你在幽閨自怜"等句，亦發如醉如痴，站立不住，便一蹲身坐在一塊山子石上，細嚼"如花美眷，似水流年"八個字的滋味。忽又想起前日見古人詩中有"水流花謝兩無情"之句，再又有詞中有"流水落花春去也，天上人間"之句，又兼方才所見《西廂記》中"花落水流紅，閒愁萬种"之句，都一時想起來，湊聚在一處。仔細忖度，不覺心痛神痴，眼中落淚。[15]

Here, readers cannot overlook the repeated references to Lin Daiyu's state of "being moved strangely," "being moved to the depth of her being," "being intoxicated," and so on. In this way, the heroine steps into the labyrinth of desire by situating herself in an intertextual lyric context, much more so than in the

15 Cao, *Zhiyanzhai pingpi Honglou meng*, 23. 401–2; SS, 1.465–67.

romantic plot;[16] as such, language (more precisely, poetic language) itself creates desire. Apparently, what Daiyu really savors in her listening is "the words of the lines of the aria," instead of the music or the story proper. Although she hears the music first, she pays no attention to the singing until she identifies the lines of the aria. "'It's true,' she thought, 'there is good poetry even in plays. What a pity most people think of them only as entertainment. A lot of the real beauty in them must go unappreciated.'" Here, Hawkes' translation of *hao wenzhang* 好文章 as "good poetry" is a very nice interpretation of the term in the narrative. Lin Daiyu's thought about the lyric diction of the play actually echoes Jia Baoyu's. The overheard lines from the drama further trigger her recollection of other literary texts, both other poetry and poetic lines from the play itself.[17] For example, Lin Daiyu associates what she hears from *The Peony Pavilion* with "a line from an old poem" and Li Yu's famous lines, and then further relates them to *The Story of the Western Wing*. What is going on here is obviously textual association, with poetry at the center.

The Story of the Western Wing and *The Peony Pavilion* are two of the most renowned Chinese "poetic dramas," with a strong lyric quality. It is not surprising, then, that the plays excite Lin Daiyu's lyric imagination: she constructs a world of fallen petals and flowing water, in which the fundamental theme – the transience of life and youth – is implied and emphasized. While such images are common in traditional poetry, the lines from *The Peony Pavilion* which arrest Lin Daiyu's attention particularly stress the image of the female persona in the poetic scene. When Lin Daiyu is deeply drawn to the poetic scene, she is also obsessed with her own image that already becomes one with the image in that lyric scene. This scene unmistakably evokes the fear of mortality and impermanence, a motif that runs throughout the history of Chinese poetry, and thus Lin Daiyu's hearing of the lines, and her recollection of other related poems, quickly thrust her into this fear. The rendered phenomenon of humans and flowers both inevitably fading elicits her anxiety about the self. Just as Du Liniang obtains a sense of self in encountering the seasonal scenery, Lin Daiyu starts her self-dramatization and self-pity by lyricizing her being.

From this point on, she often uses such poetic lines from romances to interpret her own emotional life. For example, in Chapter 35, Lin Daiyu again associates lines from *The Story of the Western Wing* with her own residence. Seeing the shadows of the bamboos and the dew-pearled moss, she thinks of two lines she had read in *The Story of the Western Wing*: "A place remote, where footsteps

---

16 See Chi Xiao's discussion in his illuminating article "Lyric Archi-Occasion: Coexistence of 'Now' and Then," *Chinese Literature, Essays, Articles, Reviews* 15 (Dec. 1993): 17–35.

17 For a detailed discussion on the lyrical contextuality, see ibid.

seldom pass / And dew still glistens on the untrodden grass." This causes her to reflect on the heroine of that play, as she laments that "Ying-ying may have been unfortunate, but at least she had a widowed mother and a little brother. I have no one."[18] Here, by using the poetic expression of the dramatic text, she lyricizes the world in which she lives, and further lyricizes her own condition as the extension of her physical location. It is important to look at how her act of lyricizing is closely related to both the rising and channeling of her secret desire. As a matter of fact, the quotation is the opening of the poem that Yingying sends to Zhang to invite him to the rendezvous where they will make love. Lin Daiyu's words expressing her recognition that a beautiful woman has an unfortunate fate echo a phrase in the very next scene of the play, when Yingying is lamenting her mother's change of heart about her marriage. By identifying her own environment with the poetic world, she has inserted herself into the poetic scene and has meditated on and expressed her secret emotion according to the modes of the poetic language of the play.

Lin Daiyu is moved by two dramatic texts in Chinese literary history, *The Story of the Western Wing* and *The Peony Pavilion*, both of which are not only highly daring in their glorification of love, but also forceful in their enchanting diction. It can be said that Lin Daiyu's experience of reading *The Story of the Western Wing* and *The Peony Pavilion* is first of all enabled by a peculiar mode of reading poetry. As she "make[s] out the words distinctly," and "recite[s] the text in her heart," she internalizes the images and the emotion that the poetic lines provide, and at the same time channels her unnamable feeling. To be more precise, what the lines of the two plays arouse is not merely sentimentality, a way of channeling desire through lyricizing, but also the generation of a new desire. *The Story of the Western Wing*, *The Peony Pavilion*, the old poems related to the lines from these two plays, and probably the heroine herself and her view of life, all have become the "good poetry" in Lin Daiyu's act of lyricizing.

Not only does Lin Daiyu begin to quote lines from her reading to explain and to shape her real life, she also creates a psychological reality through her own writing of poetry. Her two lengthy monologues on the vicissitude of the seasons, "The Song for Burying Blossoms" and "The Flower of the Peach," correspond to her reading of the lines regarding fallen petals. "Autumn Window: A Night of Wind and Rain," another well-known poem from the novel, is also a work modeled on such poems as "Woman's Sorrow in the Autumn" (*Qiugui yuan* 秋閨怨) and "The Grief of Parting" (*Bieli yuan* 別離怨), which she is shown reading by lamplight. "Moved by what she read, she was inevitably drawn to give outlet to

18 Cao, *Zhiyanzhai pingpi Honglou meng*, 35. 578; SS, 2.174.

her feelings in composition and had soon completed a 'song of separation' of her own."[19] She feels compelled to represent her act of desiring only once her desire is aroused through the reading of the representation of others' desires. Yet any process of representing desire is itself a process of experiencing desire, and triggering desire.

Lin Daiyu lyricizes her desire through reading and writing poetry (or reading the poetic lines from dramatic texts). It is often said in Chinese poetic theory that through poetic writing "what is intently on the mind" is articulated (*shi yan zhi* 詩言志).[20] This formula shows that the Chinese poetic tradition both values inner experience and suggests the role of poetry in fostering communality with others. First of all, Lin Daiyu's poetic writing is described as involving interiorization and self-reflection. In Chapter 34, when Jia Baoyu sends Lin Daiyu two used silk handkerchiefs as a token of his love, she perceives his intention and slips into a turmoil of emotions. She feels so happy that Baoyu has been able to grasp the cause of her troubles, while at the same time sad because she does not know how her trouble will be resolved; she then feels ashamed that she is always crying and quarrelling with him. As such, she reflects on her own desires and situation, and then pours out her feelings in three spontaneous poems, which she writes on the handkerchiefs. Yet writing not only expresses desire, but further creates it, as her subsequent act of mirroring suggests:

> [She] was preparing to write another quatrain, when she became aware that her whole body was burning hot all over and her cheeks were afire. Going over to the dressing-table, she removed the brocade cover from the mirror and peered into it.
>
> "Hmm! 'Brighter than the peach-flower's hue,'" she murmured complacently to the flushed face that stared out at her from the glass, and, little imagining that what she had been witnessing was the first symptom of a serious illness, went back to bed, her mind full of handkerchiefs.
>
> 林黛玉還要往下寫時，覺得渾身火熱，面上作燒，走至鏡臺揭起錦袱一照，只見腮上通紅，自羨壓倒桃花，卻不知病由此萌。一時方上床睡去，猶拿著那帕子思索，不在話下。[21]

19 Cao, *Zhiyanzhai pingpi Honglou meng*, 45. 731; SS, 2.400.

20 Although in a narrow sense "*zhi*" means political or ethical inspiration, it can be understood more broadly as "what is intently on the mind," an extended psychological definition. For a discussion of this definition, see Stephen Owen, *Readings in Chinese Literary Thought* (Cambridge, MA: Harvard University Press, 1992), 40–41.

21 Cao, *Zhiyanzhai pingpi Honglou meng*, 34. 573; SS, 2.168.

This act reminds us of her predecessor from *The Peony Pavilion*, Du Liniang, who takes a look at herself in the mirror and immediately comes to self-love and self-pity. The act of mirroring suggests the attempt to look at oneself as others might. For Lin Daiyu, she is at this moment both the reflection and the gazer, both the one who desires and the object of desire. In this case, to desire is also to be desired.

On the other hand, this episode is a more profound manifestation of the tacit mutual understanding of the lovers than ever before. When she receives the handkerchiefs, Lin Daiyu sighs, "In his painstaking efforts, he has been able to perceive my pains" 寶玉這番苦心，能領會我這番苦意.[22] Indeed, she uses the word *zhiji* 知己 (recognize the self) to gauge her relationship with Jia Baoyu in Chapter 32, in which Jia Baoyu demonstrates to Shi Xiangyun 史湘雲 and Aroma (Xiren 襲人) that his deepest attachment to Lin Daiyu stems from the fact that Lin Daiyu has never tried to persuade him "to establish himself and acquire a name." The term *zhiji* means not only an intimate friend with amorous overtones but also one who recognizes and appreciates the friend's hidden ability and true worth. She sees Baoyu as the only person who can recognize her true value and essence, that is, she deeply approves of Baoyu's values and lyricized lifestyle symbolized by the life in the garden.[23] Just like Jia Baoyu, Lin Daiyu takes "good poetry" (*hao wenzhang* 好文章) as the focus of her appreciation of literary texts, and of her understanding of life.

In fact, a deep longing for recognition is not only a significant dimension of Daiyu's relationship with Baoyu, but also embedded in her behavior on other occasions. When Yuanchun 元春 visits the newly constructed garden and asks Baoyu and her cousins to compose poems in Chapter 18, Daiyu confidently seeks to display herself by expressing her poetic talent. This kind of desire for public recognition is also illustrated by her histrionic demonstration of the superiority of her poetic skills in other poetic contests held among the girls and Jia Baoyu (Chapters 37 and 38).[24] Undeniably, the self's longing to be known and to be validated can be seen everywhere in Lin Daiyu's behavior and thoughts. Her three poems on the chrysanthemum composed on the gathering of their poetry club (Chapter 38) – "I write my constant grief, filling the page with self-pity, who understands the brief words of my heart recounting the

22 Cao, *Zhiyanzhai pingpi Honglou meng*, 572. My translation.

23 For Baoyu's tendency toward a lyricized life, see Xiao, *The Chinese Garden as Lyric Enclave*, 75–92.

24 Anthony Yu points to these examples to show that Lin Daiyu's behavior betrays a consistent streak of competitiveness and a deep need for recognition. See Yu, *Rereading the Stone*, 233–34.

autumn" 滿紙自憐題素怨，片言誰解訴秋心; "Do not say there are no people you can talk with, why not converse with me for a moment since I understand you" 休言舉世無談者，解語何妨片語時; "Whom I tell about my solitude and sorrow when I wake up, fading grass and chilly mists are full of deep feelings" 醒時幽怨同誰訴，衰草寒煙無限情 – also exhibit her self-assertion and call for one who can converse with her on a spiritual level, that is to say, one who can know and recognize her essence and uniqueness.[25] As can be seen in her poetic lines and her act of self-display, the search for unique, personal value as a lover, as a family member, and as a poet, is an important aspect of her desires.

At the same time, however, her yearning for companionship or communion is persistent in her sentiments and her frequent agonizing, although such a need for identification is always displayed in the form of differentiation. She often compares herself with Xue Baochai, and finds out that Baochai's situation is much better than hers since Baochai at least has the company of a mother and an elder brother of considerable wealth; when Jia Baoyu, Shi Xiangyun, or other family members praise or show intimacy toward Xue Baochai, she reacts in a sarcastic manner and exhibits the self-assertive intention to compete with Baochai. Lin Daiyu's sensitivity and excessive reactions to the slightest teasing or criticism of her peers or family members demonstrate her anxiety about whether she is truly and sincerely accepted by the Jia family. However, her relationship with Xue Baochai is gradually reconciled after Baochai lectures to her about proper reading (Chapter 42) and sends her bird's nest syrup (Chapter 45), and later she also builds a sisterly friendship with Shi Xiangyun and Xue Baoqin 薛寶琴. In this sense, identification as well as differentiation constitutes a dimension of Lin Daiyu's claim for self-identity.

This characterization of Lin Daiyu is reminiscent of the heroines in *caizi-jiaren* drama and fiction. Although conventional heroines usually possess poetic talent and exchange poetry with the hero, Lin Daiyu internalizes the lyric tradition and lyricizes the reality.[26] In *The Dream of the Red Chamber*, poetry assumes a role in the construction of the protagonists' interiority and individuality, rather than serving as a mere medium through which to convey their mutual attraction. Lin Daiyu's profound, secret communion with Jia Baoyu is based on their common yearning for the lyricized life.

---

25 Cao, *Zhiyanzhai pingpi Honglou meng*, 38. 632–33. My translation.

26 Chi Xiao has aptly pointed out the "lyricized style of living" of Chinese literati, in which poetry and the garden play an important role. Xiao argues that they see lyric aesthetic values as an existential meaning, obsessed with a kind of sensuous existence of nature. Xiao, *The Chinese Garden as Lyric Enclave*, 61–99.

In many regards, *The Dream of the Red Chamber* is a text that both exploits and parodies the scholar-beauty tradition. Lin Daiyu is without doubt a talented beauty. Nevertheless, she is unlike the heroines of romantic plays such as *The Story of the Western Wing* and *The Peony Pavilion*, who immediately fulfill their passion or sexual desire once they fall in love with the hero, and in the end manage to return to the familial order; nor is she like the talented beauties of the seventeenth-century scholar-beauty romances, who keep *qing* within the boundaries of *li*. However, *The Dream of the Red Chamber* is profoundly involved in the workings of desire in Lin Daiyu's case. As indicated through Jia Baoyu's own words, it is because she "cannot quell her heart" (*bu fangxin* 不放心) that Lin Daiyu has made herself ill.[27] Read allegorically, this inability to "quell one's heart" refers to the obsession with desire, which is the central issue in the characterization of Lin Daiyu.[28] In this way, the novel differentiates itself from its antecedents by fashioning a female protagonist who is unable to fulfill her desire, and instead lyricizes her life as a way of channeling and sustaining her frustrated desire.

Like Lin Daiyu, Xue Baochai is also one of the talented, beautiful girls in the garden. On the other hand, however, she tends to be characterized as a virtuous woman. In fact, in the early Qing *caizi-jiaren* novel, the talented beauty is often represented as virtuous, keeping her private passion within the boundaries of ritual. Unlike these virtuous beauties, however, Xue Baochai never intimates her desires in the name of *qing* (even though this *qing* is regulated by *li*). She is depicted as following a prescribed order of womanly behavior in various regards, not merely in terms of chastity. She is chaste, self-sacrificing, self-restrained, and makes efforts to discipline her husband after she gets married in the last part of the narrative. Nevertheless, a fuller development of her hidden motives and desires renders Xue Baochai a more interesting character than conventional virtuous woman in *caizi-jiaren* fiction and other domestic novels.[29]

---

27 Cao, *Zhiyanzhai pingpi Honglou meng*, 32. 546.

28 Anthony Yu has analyzed how Lin Daiyu is held captive by her emotions and desires to the very end, which causes her tragic experiences and makes her the most memorable and moving character of the narrative. See Yu, *Rereading the Stone*, 219–55.

29 The exemplary woman also recurs in domestic novels. For example, Yan Mengqing 燕夢卿, the heroine of *Lin Lan Xiang* 林蘭香, a novel considered by some to have in many ways anticipated *The Dream of the Red Chamber*, is the very model of a virtuous daughter and wife, who follows the instructions on womanly behavior rigidly, and thus is too perfect to be interesting. Martin Huang attempts to explore the issue of lesbian relationships in this novel (see Huang, *Desire and Fictional Narrative*, 184–205), but even though lesbian relationships are subtly hinted in the narrative, they are not profoundly developed and explored with regards to the ramifications of desire. As for the possible

Indeed, Xue Baochai is an excellent example of a woman who tries to comply with the prescriptions of Confucian moral codes. Given the surging waves of her desire lurking in the narrative, however, Xue Baochai is not as simple a model of wifely virtue that she may at first appear to be. A case in point is a small detail in Chapter 45, in which the narrator tells us that Xue Baochai is reminded by "the first nip in the air that the hours of darkness were gradually lengthening."[30] One of the commentators in the *Gengchen* edition sees this mention of lengthening darkness as a euphemistic reference to her irrepressible desires, and calls it *chunqiu zifa* 春秋字法.[31] The commentator tells us that the narrator seldom presents us with a clear view of Xue Baochai's desire, leaving it to the reader to figure out her psychological state. Martin Huang has perceptively discussed Xue Baochai's "improper adult desire with regard to Jia Baoyu."[32] As mentioned earlier, as a cold beauty, Xue Baochai is also described as suffering from "a congenital tendency toward overheatedness." That is to say, despite her cold appearance, she can be very hot inside, motivated by desires. It is such subtle hints at her innate desire that often make her virtuous or chaste behavior suspicious.

An example that shows such interesting dialectics between desire and virtue/chastity is the ambiguous but meaningful scene of Jia Baoyu's visit to Xue Baochai in Chapter 8. As the commentator Yao Xie 姚燮 (1805–1864) points out, "This is the first time the meeting of Jia Baoyu and Xue Baochai is described in the novel" 書中寫寶玉與寶釵見面，此尚第一次也.[33] It is significant that the first detail which catches Jia Baoyu's and the reader's eye is Xue Baochai sewing on her bed. Zhang Xinzhi, another of the novel's commentators, notes that "this needlework is woven extremely fine and closely" 此針線甚密.[34] Here, Zhang may see "needlework" (*zhenxian* 針線) as symbolic in its close relation to the working of desire, for in the narration that follows, he continuously makes comments on Baochai's secret desire as well as Jia Baoyu's desire for

---

link between *Lin Lan Xiang* and *The Dream of the Red Chamber*, see Yu Zhiyuan 于植元, "Lin Lan Xiang lun" 林蘭香論, in *Ming Qing xiaoshuo luncong* 明清小說論叢, vol. 1 (Shenyang: Chunfeng wenyi chubanshe, 1984), 190–213; Zhang Jun 張俊, "Lun Lin Lan Xiang yu Honglou meng jiantan lianjie Jin Ping Mei yu Honglou meng de lianhuan" 論林蘭香與紅樓夢兼談連接金瓶梅與紅樓夢的連環, in *Ming-Qing xiaoshuo luncong* 明清小說論叢, vol. 5 (Shenyang: Chunfeng wenyi chubanshe, 1987), 63–84.

30 Cao, *Zhiyanzhai pingpi Honglou meng*, 45. 728; SS, 2.395.

31 See Cao, *Zhiyanzhai pingpi Honglou meng*, 45. 728. *Chunqiu zifa* euphemistically refers to a critical approach in historical narrative and other writings, said to have been adopted by Confucius in compiling *The Analects*.

32 See Huang, *Desire and Fictional Narrative*, 298–312.

33 *Cao, Chongjiao bajia pingpi Honglou meng*, 8. 180.

34 Ibid.

her. Immediately after the reference to the needlework, Xue Baochai's appearance is depicted from Jia Baoyu's point of view. In fact, Xue Baochai's well-worn clothing without any hint of luxury or show – proper appearance that demonstrates her purity/chastity – instead highlights her beauty ("without rouge, her lips are red; without brush, her eyebrows are blue-black" 唇不點而紅，眉不畫而黛), and thus increases her sensuality with which Jia Baoyu is fascinated. Thus, despite the obvious simplicity Xue Baochai displays, something contrary lurks beyond the grasp of the casual eye.

Later in this scene, Jia Baoyu inquires about Baochai's health. It is then that Xue Baochai puts down her needlework, lifts up her head, and talks to Baoyu. Zhang Xinzhi comments, "Is it true that she did not lift up her head until now?" 至此始"抬頭"，信乎.[35] This implies that doing needlework is actually a way in which Xue Baochai hides her interest in Jia Baoyu. After a close look at each other, Xue Baochai asks to see Jia Baoyu's jade piece (with which he was born, held in his mouth); and subsequently, through the mouthpiece of Xue Baochai's maid, Oriole (Ying'er 鶯兒), Jia Baoyu is informed of the fact that Xue Baochai has a golden locket which perfectly matches his jade piece. Zhang Xinzhi has claimed that this is Baochai's deliberate strategy to remind Jia Baoyu of their destined marriage. He also indicates that Xue Baochai's golden locket is a metaphor of her "trap" for Jia Baoyu – a trap made of her "needlework."[36] In this way, needlework can be seen as a symbol of the working of desire on the part of Xue Baochai, a way of fulfilling as well as hiding her desire. As the "womanly work" required by Confucian instruction for women, needlework both conceals her desire and gives her a position secured by tradition and convention, suggesting a complicated relationship between Xue Baochai's desire and her virtuous behavior.

Another frequently quoted and discussed scene implying Xue Baochai's "improper" desires is also associated with needlework. In that scene, in Chapter 36, Xue Baochai sits beside the thinly clothed, sleeping Jia Baoyu, sewing, with a fly-whisk in readiness at her side.

> Aroma sat at his bedside sewing, a white horse-hair fly-whisk with a handle of white rhinoceros-horn at her side. Baochai entered the "cabinet" and laughed softly at Aroma.
>
> "Aren't you being rather over-cautious?" she whispered. "What's the fly-whisk for? Surely no flies or mosquitoes can get in here?"

---

35 Ibid.

36 See Zhang Xinzhi's interlineal comments in *Cao, Chongjiao bajia pingpi Honglou meng*, 8.182–83.

"Oh, it's Miss Bao! I wasn't expecting you," she whispered. "You gave me a shock – no, we don't get any flies or mosquitoes in here, but there's a little tiny insect that finds its way through the holes in the netting …"

"That's not surprising," said Baochai. "… This kind of insect breeds in the inside of flowers and is attracted toward anything fragrant. That's why you get them inside the house."

While she was speaking, her eyes fell on the sewing that Aroma had just put down. It was a pinafore of the kind children wear, with bib and apron in one (*doudu*). It was of white satin lined with red silk, and the pattern Aroma was embroidering on it was mandarin ducks disporting themselves in a background of lotuses. …

So intent was Baochai on the embroidery that she sank down almost without realizing what she was doing into the place Aroma had just vacated. It really was a most beautiful piece of work; in fact, she found it irresistible, and taking up the needle, began sewing it where Aroma left off.

襲人坐在身旁，手里做針線，旁邊放著一柄白犀麈。寶釵走近前來，悄悄的笑道："你也過于小心了，這個屋里那里還有蒼蠅蚊子，還拿蠅帚子赶什麼？"襲人不防，猛抬頭見寶釵，忙放下針線，起身悄悄笑道："姑娘來了，我倒也不防，唬了一跳。姑娘不知道，雖然沒有蒼蠅蚊子，誰知有一种小虫子，從這紗眼里鑽進來，人也看不見，只睡著了，咬一口，就象螞蟻夾的。"寶釵道："怨不得。這屋子後頭又近水，又都是香花兒，這屋子里頭又香。這种虫子都是花心里長的，聞香就扑。"說著，一面又瞧他手里的針線，原來是個白綾紅里的兜肚，上面扎著鴛鴦戲蓮的花樣，紅蓮綠葉，五色鴛鴦。寶釵道："噯喲，好鮮亮活計！這是誰的，也值的費這麼大工夫？"襲人向床上努嘴兒。寶釵笑道："這麼大了，還帶這個？"襲人笑道："他原是不帶，所以特特的做的好了，叫他看見由不得不帶。如今天氣熱，睡覺都不留神，哄他帶上了，便是夜里縱蓋不嚴些兒，也就不怕了。你說這一個就用了工夫，還沒看見他身上現帶的那一個呢。"寶釵笑道："也虧你奈煩。"襲人道："今兒做的工夫大了，脖子低的怪酸的。"又笑道："好姑娘，你略坐一坐，我出去走走就來。"說著便走了。寶釵只顧看著活計，便不留心，一蹲身，剛剛的也坐在襲人方才坐的所在，因又見那活計實在可愛，不由的拿起針來，替他代刺。[37]

Both traditional commentators and modern scholars have noticed the strong references to sexual desire in this passage, such as white rhinoceros-horn and

37 Cao, *Zhiyanzhai pingpi Honglou meng*, 36. 598; SS, 2.201–203.

the image of insects breeding in the insides of flowers.[38] However, the most evident indication of the uncontrollable desire burning inside Xue Baochai might be the image of the pinafore that Aroma is embroidering. "Mandarin ducks disporting themselves against a background of lotuses" (*yuanyang xilian* 鴛鴦戲蓮) is traditionally regarded as a symbol of affectionate coupling and physical union. Yet the design works not only as a sexual symbol, but also as an image of the celebration of fecundity. That is why this pattern often appears on the pinafores of children. Through the use of such an image sexual desire is made safe and framed in a mode of legitimate procreation, a discourse sanctioned by patriarchy. Furthermore, Jia Baoyu is apparently too old to wear this sort of pinafore. By infantilizing Jia Baoyu, both Aroma and Xue Baochai transform and "purify" their desire for him.

Since Aroma is Xue Baochai's shadow self in the novel, her needlework reflects Xue Baochai's unconsciousness. When Xue Baochai takes up the needle and begins sewing the pinafore with the image of the mandarin ducks, she creates a scene of domestic felicity, as well as an extension of Jia Baoyu's initial view of her sewing on her bed. But what is more meaningful is the needlework's irresistible attraction for Xue Baochai: "So intent was Baochai on the embroidery," and "it really was a most beautiful piece of work; in fact, she found it irresistible, and taking up the needle, began sewing it where Aroma left off." The needlework powerfully elicits Xue Baochai's internal desire, which, in turn, inspires her to produce needlework. Here, more significant than the pattern itself is the actual medium of needlework. In contrast to Lin Daiyu's poetry, although the needlework is also a way of arousing and channeling desire for Xue Baochai, it is expressed in a way which is celebrated by Confucian morality. In these two different types of artifice, we can perceive two visions with regard to desire: lyricizing and moralizing.

In Xue Baochai's case, marriage works as a means of further venting her desire into something moral and appropriate. In Chapter 8, Xue Baochai not only informs Jia Baoyu of their destined marriage, but also tactfully proposes the "marriage of gold and jade" (*jinyu liangyin* 金玉良姻). According to Hong Qiufan's 洪秋藩 (fl. ca. 1911) commentary, Xue Baochai intends to present her golden locket and her suggestion of the "marriage of gold and jade" not only to Jia Baoyu but, more importantly, also to Grandmother Jia and Madam Wang, Baoyu's grandmother and mother, respectively.[39] "The marriage of gold and jade" is a statement of ideal marriage, and of a perfect match in social status,

38 See Huang, *Desire and Fictional Narrative*, 305–307; Cao, *Zhiyanzhai pingpi Honglou meng*, 36. 598.

39 *Cao, Chongjiao bajia pingpi Honglou meng*, 8.196.

which never conflicts with the orthodox view of marriage approved by the social order and family order, that is, *mendang hudui* 門當戶對 (to be well matched for marriage, socially and economically).

Of course, the meaning of marriage cherished by Confucian values is not confined to this match in social status. Although Lin Daiyu realizes this point, she neglects the other aspect, which may be even more important. For Lin Daiyu, marriage is something that sustains private passion and a lyricized life. This idea eventually leads her to despair, and ultimately to death. By contrast, Xue Baochai sees marriage as a means of moralizing desire, which is crucial to the Confucian interpretation of marriage. What is really dangerous here is not sexual desire itself, but the lyricized life that excludes the familial duty and order. In fact, the elders of the family connive in allowing the physical relationship between Aroma and Jia Baoyu. Madam Wang and the family accept Aroma precisely because of her attempt to prevent Jia Baoyu from developing his own lyric world. In this regard, Aroma shadows Xue Baochai again. Xue Baochai says at one point, "Since we are husband and wife, I should be able to look to you for lifelong support. Our life together should be based on something more than the passion of a moment."[40] As demonstrated by all the previous examples, Xue Baochai is actually bothered by her own innermost desires, her attraction to Jia Baoyu, which cannot be unrelated to sexual desire. However, she transforms it through an insistence on virtue into the Confucian master narrative. Likewise, her love for Jia Baoyu is not shown through spontaneous passion – the so-called *rouqing siyi* 柔情私意 (Chapter 115) – but in her constant attempt to persuade Jia Baoyu to pursue "merit and fame" (*gongming* 功名). This attempt climaxes in her final debate with Jia Baoyu in Chapter 118, which ends with her plea that he take at least one degree to repay "heaven's favor and our ancestor's virtue." All of these demonstrate that Xue Baochai accepts the conventional role of women in a Confucian family, and holds the belief that it is a husband's duty to establish his fame through taking the imperial examination and living in the world of officialdom. This is the way her desire for Jia Baoyu works. In actuality, despite her irrepressible desire for Jia Baoyu, she attempts to treat him either as a child (through infantilizing him) or as a Confucian husband, thereby securing her desire.

Throughout the narrative, Xue Baochai plays an active role in pursuing Confucian goals, thereby achieving her own self-fulfillment in some approximation of the "sagehood" that is championed by Neo-Confucian philosophers. Chapter 56 even portrays her as a learned reader of Zhu Xi (see Chapter 1). It can be said that in molding herself into the accepted pattern of virtue, she

40 *Cao, Chongjiao bajia pingpi Honglou meng*, 115. 2610; SS, 5.329.

internalizes and sincerely embraces the Confucian values, rather than sacrificing, or suppressing, her personal desires for the larger collective interest of the group, as some scholars believe.[41] In fact, the pursuit of self-fulfillment in the Confucian sense is also, essentially, a desire. It happens, though, that Xue Baochai's desire is merely a "correct" one, a desire to be a perfectly virtuous woman who upholds the priorities of the family, its structures and values, and can put in order and unite a family. On the other hand, however consciously and deeply she moralizes her desire, what actually makes a character such as Xue Baochai vivid and interesting is not her unmistakable virtue, but her inborn desire that sometimes surfaces in the narrative, her desire for recognition as a virtuous woman, and the way in which she channels that desire, all of which contribute to a more complex interpretation of an exemplary woman.

In opposition to the girls in the garden, Wang Xifeng is not a person of literary grace but a clever and capable woman who has a ready tongue – in this respect, she is often compared with Lin Daiyu in the narrative. Moreover, she actually provides the economic support for the poetry club in the garden. Hence, she is subtly intertwined with the discourse about talented beauties and the narratives of the "otherworld" of the garden. Like the two other female characters discussed earlier, therefore, Wang Xifeng cannot simply be categorized into a certain character type, such as the shrew or *pofu* 潑婦 (literally, "scattering woman"). In several fundamental ways, certainly, she is in line with the definition of the *pofu* in Keith McMahon's sense.[42] Although the representation of excessive sexual desire is a conventional way to characterize the shrew, such representation is not truly a primary concern of *The Dream of the Red Chamber*.[43] Instead, her characterization focuses more on her manipulating politics and business.

It is undeniable that Wang Xifeng's desires, especially her sexual desires, are narrated more boldly and directly than those of Lin and Xue. Nevertheless, she is not characterized as indulging her sexual desire as much as Pan Jinlian 潘金蓮 in *Jin Ping Mei*; here, the focus shifts to her manipulation of money

41 See Yu, *Rereading the Stone*, 239; Huang, *Desire and Fictional Narrative*, 298.

42 See McMahon, *Misers, Shrews, and Polygamists*, 55–81.

43 As for the discursive construction of the category "wanton women," or "*yinfu*" 淫婦, as well as the ambiguity and the instability of the term's connotations, see Wu, *The Chinese Virago*; Mark Stevenson and Wu Cuncun, eds., *Wanton Women in Late-Imperial Chinese Literature: Models, Genres, Subversions and Traditions* (Leiden: Brill, 2017). The extensive examination of the *yinfu* theme shows how the images of transgressive women are prevalently circulated in Chinese traditional texts – both didactic and literary texts – and how this theme locates transformations, repetitions, and exceptions in the patriarchal order, and thus requires an unremitting rereading.

and power. If we say that *Jin Ping Mei* bases Pan Jinlian's shrewish nature on her desire for *jing* 精 (semen), then Wang Xifeng's desire for *jin* 金 (money) is highlighted in *The Dream of the Red Chamber*. Although there are implicit associations between *jing* and *jin* (at least in terms of their similar pronunciation), while a shrew such as Pan Jinlian obtains money and even a sense of control only through the use of sex as a weapon, Wang Xifeng is described as directly acknowledging her desire for money and power. Moreover, the fulfillment of her sexual desire and her dominance over men, to some extent, are based on her power and money.

More often than not, traditional commentators associate the desire for money with Wang Xifeng's destiny in the story. As mentioned earlier, Zhang Xinzhi's commentary on Chapter 20 observes that "Money and sex are both the character '*qing*.'" Apparently, Zhang regards the longing for money, like that for love, as one aspect of *qing* (or desire). In this chapter, Jia Huan 賈環, Jia Baoyu's half-brother by his father's concubine, Aunt Zhao 趙姨娘, is playing a game of checkers with the maids for money. But when he loses the game, he does not want to pay the money. At this time, Jia Baoyu comes and gives his half brother a scolding and sends him away. After Jia Huan returns to his mother's room and gives his version of the incident, Aunt Zhao complains that people are prejudiced against them. It happens that Wang Xifeng is passing by outside at this moment and hears what Aunt Zhao says, and she shouts back at Aunt Zhao and castigates her for her jealous attitude. In the end, Wang Xifeng gives Jia Huan money to appease him. As Zhang Xinzhi points out, "when it comes to the character 'money,' this is the main theme" 歸到錢字，乃是主意.[44] He also notes, "'To castigate a jealous attitude' foreshadows her suffering from money [in the end], which is the main story of Wang Xifeng" "彈妒意" 為因財受害伏根株也，乃鳳姐傳.[45]

In fact, there are many accounts of Wang Xifeng's transactions and deals. For example, her exploitation of family connections for personal gain begins as she complies with the request of an old nun at the Water-moon Priory to relieve the troubles of her former employers, the Zhang family, and ultimately procures a profit of three thousand taels of silver.[46] This happens immediately after she comes into power in the Ningguo 寧國 Mansion, helping Jia Zhen 賈珍 with the management of the household. Here, the quest for money and power are intimately connected. Making profit from family connections is rendered a means of enjoying the kind of satisfaction that power brings

44 Cao, *Chongjiao bajia pingpi Honglou meng*, 20.421.
45 Cao, *Chongjiao bajia pingpi Honglou meng*, 20.426.
46 Cao, *Zhiyanzhai pingpi Honglou meng*, 14. 251–53; SS, 1.271–79.

her – “Secure in her authority, respected and obeyed by all, Xifeng contemplated her achievement with a certain amount of satisfaction.”[47] It is noticeable that Wang Xifeng further engages in usury, which signifies her insatiable desire. By this means, her desire is materialized, and henceforth, through materializing her desire, she aspires to sustain her desire forever.

Wang Xifeng’s dominance over men is accordingly based on her control of money and use of power. For example, the presentation of her ambiguous relationship with Jia Rong 賈蓉, the son of her husband’s cousin, is situated in the context of Jia Rong’s borrowing a glass screen for a *kang* 炕 (a heated bed) from Wang Xifeng. This situation makes Wang Xifeng’s superior status conspicuous. In this way, her dominance over Jia Rong has more to do with power and money than with sex. Even her relationship with her husband Jia Lian implies her relentless drive for the manipulation of money and power. Consider, for instance, Chapter 44, in which Wang Xifeng catches Jia Lian committing adultery with a female servant, Bao Er’s 鮑二 wife, causing a great disturbance in the Jia household. Through dramatizing herself as a mistreated wife, she wins Grandmother Jia’s sympathy, so that Jia Lian eventually apologizes to her for his adultery, compelled by Grandmother Jia’s prestige. As a result, Bao Er’s wife hangs herself. Jia Lian wants to give the family of the woman some money to pacify them, but Wang Xifeng refuses to do so. As a result, Jia Lian has to charge the amount he secretly gives them to “miscellaneous expenses” of the household.

Another case is Wang’s entrapment of You Erjie 尤二姐, whom Jia Lian secretly marries as his concubine. When Wang Xifeng discovers that her husband has taken You Erjie as a mistress, she devises an intricate strategy to eliminate the concubine without arousing suspicion. One critical plot Wang Xifeng exploits is to lure You Erjie’s former fiancé, Zhang Hua 張華, with money, and cajoles Zhang Hua into suing Jia Lian, thereby exerting pressure on Jia Lian and the family. She later goes to the Ningguo Mansion and there makes a terrible scene, since You Erjie, a relative of the mistress of the Ningguo Mansion, was introduced to Jia Lian by the master of the Ningguo Mansion. Wang Xifeng threatens to tell the Jia family matriarch (Grandmother Jia) what they have done in leading Jia Lian into committing criminal adultery, and thus extorts five hundred taels of silver from them. In the end, capitalizing on the influence of both the Jia and Wang families, she bribes the courts and ends the case. Eventually, she overpowers all her rivals and secures her own position in the

47 Cao, *Zhiyanzhai pingpi Honglou meng*, 14. 234; SS, 1.274, slightly modified.

family (in the sense that, if Erjie had had a son, then she would have profoundly threatened Wang Xifeng's power and status in the family). Furthermore, Wang Xifeng refuses to give Jia Lian money to arrange a proper funeral for You Erjie, leaving him speechless with resentment (Chapter 68). This incident marks the high point of Wang Xifeng's avarice and abuse of power, as well her dominance over her husband and other men through her manipulation of money and power.

In the two cases above, one can see that a crucial characteristic of a shrew, jealous rage, is also prominent in Wang Xifeng's relationship to her husband. However, it is noteworthy that, in both cases, she not only exhibits her violent temper to frighten her husband into submission, but skillfully takes advantage of various kinds of relationships in the family to restrain and control her husband, demonstrating her slyness and political stratagems. Wang Xifeng's jealous rage is not only represented by her act of "scattering," but more importantly, takes the form of playing family politics. In effect, besides her managerial skills which make her stand out among her peers, she also has a quick wit and ready tongue, with which she manipulates other people's perceptions and ingratiates herself with Grandmother Jia to win her unconditional trust. In order to realize her personal aspirations, she appears to observe the rituals of the family as a virtuous wife in front of the elders, thereby winning their favor and ensuring her power.

Although the characterization of Wang Xifeng is built on the shrew stereotype of characters such as Pan Jinlian, who is primarily described as a sexual vampire, how Wang Xifeng's desire interacts with the social and familial order at the level of materiality is further explored. Besides, other aspects of her individuality are displayed in the narrative. For example, she is a witty interlocutor at family gatherings and shows touching motherly love to her daughter. In contrast to Pan Jinlian's suffocating depravity in *Jin Ping Mei*, we find in Wang Xifeng the existence of a more authentic humanity: partly demonic, yet partly kind. Another instance of her kindness is her sincere sympathy for Qin Keqing 秦可卿 (her friend as well as her niece by marriage). These depictions enrich and complicate her representation of the character type of the shrew.

In essence, Wang Xifeng's manipulation of power and money, and the extension of her power to society beyond the family in particular, defy the orthodox division between passive, inner woman and dominant, outer man. Nevertheless, she subverts norms and conventions through a seeming conformity to them. Like Xue Baochai, she vents her desire around and through social norms, but her excessive self-interest, as well as the hierarchy of the family system, leads to her ultimate tragedy. At the same time, the search of the garden – which is triggered by the discovery of a love purse, and results in the expelling of some of the girls from the garden, as well as Wang Xifeng's falling under suspicion[48] – not only leads to the collapse of the idyllic world of poetry that is shared by both Lin Daiyu and Jia Baoyu, but also signifies Wang Xifeng's fall from power. In fact, although the three women vent their desires in different ways, they share a common, interlinked destiny – they all fail to escape their tragic fates, which are already foretold in the verses from the official register that Jia Baoyu reads in his dream journey in Chapter 5. That the fates of the three beauties are interrelated demonstrates the diversity of desires which both shapes the subject in relation to social norms and morality and underlies the conflicts with the unified social and moral order.

Through the Stone/narrator's critique, the author of *The Dream of the Red Chamber* exhibits his ambition to write against stereotypes. Lin Daiyu, Xue Baochai, and Wang Xifeng, as constructed subjects, all resist reductive typology. They are more profoundly explored than the antecedents of their character types, especially in terms of the workings of desire. They differ from each other in the ways in which they deal with desire: lyricizing, moralizing, and materializing. The juxtaposition of these three different modes of channeling desire provides the novel with a chorus of multiple perspectives. Despite the competing views of various characters, however, the narrative still creates an underlying tension that unifies and enlivens an otherwise static plot through the mediation of desire, which not only brings into question a single social and cultural ideal, but transgresses the boundaries between various dichotomous categories, such as *qing*/*yu*, true/false, and private/public.

---

48 In Chapter 73, a half-witted maid called "Simple" picks up a beautifully embroidered purse, the design on which consists of a pair of naked human figures locked together in an embrace. The appearance of the purse suggested that the garden is polluted, in that the moral order in the garden has been endangered, and thus Lady Wang authorizes a search of the garden for other "dirty" things. As a result, a few girls, who are thought of as corrupting Baoyu, are expelled from the garden, and Lady Wang also moves Baoyu out soon afterwards. That is to say, the love purse causes a problem in terms of breaking the boundaries of purity and pollution in the garden. For an extensive discussion on the significance of the spatial transgression in legitimate desire, see Louise Edwards, "Painting Boundaries of Sex Segregation in Qing China: Representing the Family in *The Red Chamber Dream*," in *The Family Model in Chinese Art and Culture*, ed. Jerome Silbergeld and Dora C.Y. Ching (Princeton, NJ: Princeton University Press and P.Y. and Kinmay W. Tang Center for East Asian Art, 2013), 339–72.

2 Nostalgia as a Dual Strategy of Self-Fashioning and Self-Reflection

As we have seen in the preceding discussion, *The Dream of the Red Chamber* is less about the discovery of the very existence of human desire, or its repression or liberation, than it is about the exploration of how it is created and channeled. The process of weaving the web of desire, the accommodation of the diversity and heterogeneity of various characters' desires and interests in particular, offers a venue through which an array of individuals is fashioned. Its sense of the individual contains an unequivocal gesture of opposition to the propensity to generalization and universalism characteristic of scholar-beauty novels. Curiously enough, on the other hand, the highlighting of the pluralization and the juxtaposition of the forms of human desire brings to the work a heightened awareness of the limits of any individual's uniqueness, and thus a self-reflexive nature.

In terms of characterization in *The Dream of the Red Chamber*, there is little doubt about the significance of desire and emotion (*yu*/*qing*) in the construction of self and subjectivity. Furthermore, desire and emotion often lurk behind language, or are created by language or discourse. Although the three women characters discussed above are constituted through a series of distinguished discourses, literary talent pervasively takes on a central role as the mark of distinction and the means for the revelation of interiority. Even though Wang Xifeng seldom writes poetry in the narrative, the only poetic line she produces in the game of linking verses in Snowy Rushes Retreat – "Last night the north wind blew the whole night through" (Chapter 50) – is deemed a skillful beginning of a poem (albeit unpolished), which makes clear her potential talent and personal style. More apparently, Xue Baochai's intention and her personal ambition are conveyed through her poetic writing on various occasions. Indeed, for the girls in Prospect Garden, their poems do not simply concern the display of the poet's craftsmanship but also the representation of their individuality or interiority. The novel's skillful use of poetry elaborates the characters' inner self, thereby avoiding the flatness of scholar-beauty romances. In comparison with scholar-beauty novels, *The Dream of the Red Chamber* offers a fuller and more convincing presentation of the inner lives of its characters in the form of poetry, and this in turn provokes a more profound identification between the reader and the characters. In Daiyu's case in particular, her emotions and inner mind are approached primarily through poetic language characteristic of her reading and writing. Her act of lyricizing does not express an already existent true self but brings the self into being. As indicated before, both Baoyu and

Daiyu institute an inner self and make their "true nature" manifest by means of poetry writing. Through the medium of poetry, *The Dream of the Red Chamber* is given a subjective and inward valence, making possible the recognition of how characters sense themselves as individuals.

By locating his characters in the realm of personal nostalgia, moreover, Cao Xueqin intimates a profound emotional bond to them, through which he renders his narrative remarkable in its process of constructing individuality and interiority. In Chapter 1, Cao Xueqin ventures to criticize scholar-beauty novels for their undistinguished characters represented via a mechanical framework, while he stresses that his work differs from them in the subtlety and originality with which it describes its characters as individuals. Through the mouth of the Stone, he asserts that he has contemplated the actions and motives of the numerous women whom he has spent half a lifetime studying with his own eyes and ears. The Stone insists, "All that my story narrates, the meetings and partings, the joys and sorrows, the ups and downs of future, are recorded exactly as they happened so as not to serve merely for reader's eyes (interest) and instead lose the authenticity of the story" 至若離合悲歡，興衰際遇，則又追蹤攝跡，不敢稍加穿鑿，徒為供人之目而反失其真傳者.[49] The term "authentic story" (*zhenchuan* 真傳) that Cao uses here highlights the authenticity of a person's being in the narrative in which a self emerges. Indeed, the passionately nostalgic tone persistent in the narrative deepens and internalizes the sense of authenticity. Since the girls are whom the Stone/narrator spends half a lifetime witnessing and living with, their stories constitute part of his own past, in which his being can reside. By claiming the authenticity of the girls' stories, the narrator demonstrates that his past takes on the solidity of corroborated experience as well, thereby inviting us to wander into his experience. As such, the novel itself becomes the site of memory.

From the beginning, the Stone of the supernatural realm alludes to the mechanisms of nostalgia. The Stone's recounting of his earthly journey sets up the framing of memory in its focus on "all of those girls at that time" 忽念及當日所有之女子, by means of which the author expresses his desire to create individual existences out of memory.[50] As is known, the Stone assumes the role of the narrator in the novel, but it has a symbolic double in the jade piece that Baoyu wears around his neck. According to the *Jiaxu* (1754) and *Gengchen* 庚辰 (1760) manuscript editions of the novel, the Stone is incarnated not as

49 Cao, *Zhiyanzhai pingpi Honglou meng*, 1.5–6; SS, 1.50.

50 Cao, *Zhiyanzhai pingpi Honglou meng*, 2.

the man, but as the piece of jade that Baoyu is born with.[51] Thus, it is the Stone, rather than the Divine Luminescent Stone-in-Waiting, or Baoyu, that "returns to the source" (*fanben huanyuan* 返本還原). The first print editions of the novel (previously the novel had been circulated in handwritten manuscripts), published in 1791 and 1792, known as the *ChengGao* 程高 editions, by contrast, describe how the fairy Disenchantment (Jinghuan xiangu 警幻仙姑) transforms the Stone into the Divine Luminescent Stone-in-Waiting, who is reborn as Baoyu and takes part in the illusion of human life. Accordingly, the Cheng–Gao editions end in Baoyu's final enlightenment as a moral lesson of retribution and the ideal of enclosure by repeatedly emphasizing that the Stone's "substance had returned to the Great Unity" (*xingzhi gui yi* 行質歸一) and "man and stone become once more a single whole" 兩番人作一番人, thus invoking the moral order that "prosperity comes with virtue, and calamity with evil" 福善禍淫，古今定理.[52]

The most critical divergence between the two versions – the original manuscripts and the Cheng–Gao editions – however, lies equally, if not more so, in the narrative tone and the mode of emotional expression as in the conception of the development of the story. In the preface (*fanli* 凡例) of the *Jiaxu* edition, an intensely personal tone unfolds before us, through a gesture of recollection. Although the author refers to the past as "a series of dreams and illusions" (*yifan menghuan* 一番夢幻) and exploits a moving confessional tone in recalling it, he exhibits a strong desire to "weave and record all of these, and tell the world about them" 編述一記，以告普天下人,[53] to the extent that he intensely

51 Both Wai-yee Li and Qiancheng Li point out the distinction between the Stone and Jia Baoyu, and the role of the Stone in claiming the wisdom of hindsight as a detached observer. See Li, *Enchantment and Disenchantment*, 212; Qiancheng Li, *Fictions of Enlightenment: "Journey of the West," "Tower of Myriad Mirrors," and "Dream of the Red Chamber"* (Honolulu: University of Hawai'i Press, 2004), 115–18.

52 See Cao, *Chongjiao bajia pingpi Honglou meng*, 120. 2765, 2762–63. The contrast between the varied systems of editions is also displayed in their different descriptions of the dream vision. Along with the transformation of the Illusory Realm of Great Void into the Paradise of Truth, the profound paradox suggested by the couplet "Fiction becomes true when truth is fiction; where the unreal is real, real becomes the unreal" 假作真時真亦假,無為有處有還無 is replaced by the confident assertion that "When fiction departs and truth appears, truth prevails; though not-real was once real, the real is never unreal" 假去真來真胜假，無原有是有非無 (Cao, *Chongjiao bajia pingpi Honglou meng*, 116.2625; SS, 5.285). Wai-yee Li aptly remarks on how a vision of aesthetic plentitude gives way to a specifically moral dimension here. See Li, *Enchantment and Disenchantment*, 249.

53 Cao, *Zhiyanzhai pingpi Honglou meng*, 2. Except for the *Menggao* 夢稿 edition, all other commentary manuscripts exploit this syntactical structure, despite small variations.

claims a kind of subjectivity that resides in his "aspirations and writings" (*jinhuai bimo* 襟懷筆墨):

> Even my present poverty – the thatched beams and wicker lattices, tiled stove and string bed – [relieved as it is by] the morning breeze and evening moon, willows by the doorsteps and flowers in the garden, does not impede the breadth of my aspirations and my writing.
>
> 雖今日之茆椽蓬牖，瓦灶繩床，其風晨月夕，階柳庭花，亦未有傷于我之襟懷筆墨者。[54]

In this sentence, what possibly impedes the author's emotional expressions are "the thatched beams and wicker lattices, tiled stove and string bed," whereas "the morning breeze and evening moon, willows by the doorsteps and flowers in the garden" assist in maintaining his literary aspiration. In broadly juxtaposing these contrasting phrases, however, the author passionately conveys that neither his aspirations nor his writings are impaired, with a focus on a flowing expression of emotions. In contrast to such a personal and passionate tone, both the *Chengjia* and *Chengyi* editions rephrase this sentence into the following:

> Therefore, confronted with the thatched beams and wicker lattices, tiled stove and string bed, my aspirations are not impeded; moreover, facing the morning breeze and evening moon, willows by the doorsteps and flowers in the garden, I feel that my writings are touched up.
>
> 故當此蓬牖茆椽，繩床瓦灶，未足妨我襟懷；況對著晨風夕月，階柳庭花，更覺潤人筆墨。[55]

Admittedly, this editing skillfully corrects the grammatical disorder of the original manuscripts, but at the same time it dispenses with the strong emotion and personally stylistic expression, and thus also with a kind of interiority, making the narrative tone frank, neat, and impersonal. The perfectly paralleled phrasing of the *ChengGao* editions tends to revert to the style of traditional storytelling: a seemingly calm and objective, yet more static and moralistic, tone.

---

54 Ibid.

55 Cao, *Chongjiao bajia pingpi Honglou meng*, 2. Here, the *Menggao* edition is the same as the *ChengGao* 程高 editions.

In this aspect, the beginning of the first chapter serves as another example. The *Jiaxu* edition begins, "Speaking of the origin of the book, although it borders on the absurd, it is full of interest if you reflect on it closely" 說起根由，雖近荒唐，細諳則深有趣味.[56] In the *ChengGao* editions, it is adjusted to a parallel style typically present in storytelling – "Though the answer to this question may at first seem to border on the absurd, reflection will show that there is a good deal more in it than meets the eye" 說來雖近荒唐，細玩頗有趣味.[57] The former evokes the sense of process that arouses the experiences of wonder and curiosity, and produces the ceaseless reflective potential of the remembering subject, whereas the latter creates the impression of a fixed origin and enclosed necessity through the use of a formulaic style of expression.

More often than not, the Cheng–Gao editions succeed in changing the overall narrative tone by forming an expressive sentence into an assertive one. As to the motivation for writing this book, according to the Jiaxiu edition, the author himself says,

> As I struggle in this mundane world of dust and grime without accomplishing anything, I suddenly remember those girls of those bygone days. I go over them one by one, examining and comparing them in my mind's eye, and I feel that in action and understanding they were indeed vastly superior to me. How did it come about that a presumably dignified man should compare so unfavorably with all those girls. This is indeed a time of deep shame, useless regret, and helpless frustration!
>
> 今風塵碌碌，一事無成，忽念及當日所有之女子，一一細推了去，覺其行止見識，皆出於我之上。何堂堂之鬚眉，誠不若彼一干裙釵！實愧則有餘，悔又無益之大無可奈何之日也！[58]

The Cheng–Gao editions transform the original tone from a highly emotional projection into an assertive narration, by replacing the rhetorical question – "How did it come about that I, a presumably dignified man, should compare so unfavorably with those girls?" 何堂堂之鬚眉，誠不若彼一干裙釵 – with the statement that "I, a presumably dignified man, compare so unfavorably with

56 Cao, *Zhiyanzhai pingpi Honglou meng*, 1.1. All other commentary manuscripts are same as the *Jiaxu* edition in this passage, but only replace "諳" with "按", with the exception of the Biancang edition 卞藏本, which misses the word "深", and of the Menggao edition – "說起根由，雖近荒唐, 細按頗有趣味."

57 Cao, *Chongjiao bajia pingpi Honglou meng*, 1.2; SS, 1.47.

58 Cao, *Zhiyanzhai pingpi Honglou meng*, 2; See Wai-yee Li's translation in *Enchantment and Disenchantment*, 165.

those girls" 我堂堂鬚眉，誠不若彼裙釵.[59] The following sentences in the Cheng–Gao editions and the manuscripts demonstrate a similar difference. In the manuscripts, the following sentence takes up the previous emotional expressions in a fluid style – "This is indeed a time of deep shame, useless regret, and helpless frustration!" 實愧則有餘，悔則無益之大無可如何之日也; however, in the Cheng–Gao editions this is turned into a narrative statement with the subject "I": "I am indeed in deep shame, with useless regret, and in a time of helpless frustration" 我實愧則有餘，悔又无益，大無可奈何之日也.[60] The narrative tone of the manuscripts highlights the dimension of interiority, process, and struggle, in a dynamic syntactical structure, while the Cheng–Gao versions apparently tend to tell the story in a manner of harmony and enclosure. However, it is the sense of inner struggle that makes the narration more self-reflective, and thus expressive and attractive.

Seen in this light, the original manuscripts and the printed versions reflect two conflicting visions whose intriguing presentation lies more in the narrative discourse than in the plotting itself. They differ, as it were, in their treatments of the novel's relationship with the reader, as well as the flow of memory – it is incumbent on the narrator to decide whether to tell the story in a discourse-oriented way or in a plot-oriented way. What matters here is not simply the forwarding of the plot, but the process of discursive formation. The manuscripts contain a specific undertone of retrospection and seek to transfer those immediate feelings to their readers. At the same time, the author-narrator's emotional distance from his topic makes his tone replete with contemplative uncertainty. Such a narrative effect is strengthened by keeping the Stone and Baoyu distinct, as well as by making the two mystically correlated. Hence, the Stone attains the potential both of being immersed in the interior self of Baoyu and of pondering as a spectator.

For all the overall retrospective tone, the author-narrator lets the Stone function as the third-person narrator, telling the story as if he needed to view himself as a character in a novel in order to write about his subjective experiences. This is the case with Chapter 18, in which Yuanchun 元春 is allowed to be reunited with her family. The manuscripts such as the *Gengchen* edition let the Stone jump out from the account of the splendor of the scene to remind the reader of his memory at the foot of Greensickness Peak, as well as

---

59 The *Gengchen* edition presents a slightly different version: "How did it come about that I, a presumably dignified man, should compare so unfavorably with these girls?" 何我堂堂鬚眉, 誠不若此裙釵哉？

60 Cao, *Zhiyanzhai pingpi Honglou meng*, 2; Cao, *Chongjiao bajia pingpi Honglou meng*, 1.

Yuanchun's special relationship with Baoyu. According to the commentary in the *Gengchen* edition, these seemingly abrupt self-commentaries of the Stone are deliberately inserted here for the purpose of estrangement.[61] This differentiation between the Stone and Baoyu creates ironic distance between the tone of self-redemption of the mythic passages and the sense of self-obsession in the mimetic narrative.

What is equally noteworthy is that, when "the author" speaks of the renamings of the novel, he intimates that Cao Xueqin edited it for ten years and rewrote it five times.[62] Zhiyanzhai comments here:

> If he says that Xueqin simply edits and rewrites it, then who writes this preface? It serves to show that the author's brush is extremely sly. You will see much like this later. This is precisely where the author uses mist and clouds to create a hazy effect just like a painter.[63]
>
> 若雲雪芹批閱增刪，然則開卷至此這一篇楔子又系誰撰？足見作者之筆，狡猾之甚。後文如此者不少。這正是作者用畫家煙雲模糊處。

The distance between Cao Xueqin and the author himself is deliberately created for the effect of self-reflexivity, as is that between Baoyu and the Stone. It is such an ironic distance that facilitates the realization of the wholeness of self-awareness. Both Baoyu's and the Stone/narrator's views are limited and unreliable, and hence this is where the distinction between author and narrator arises.[64] As Zhiyanzhai comments on the deliberate recording of the pattern and words inscribed on the Stone/jade piece in Chapter 8, "[the author] suddenly writes these words to turn the illusory into the real, and to turn the real into the illusory, thus playing with truth and falsity in an unrestrained style" 又忽作此數語，以幻弄成真，以真弄成幻，真真假假，恣意遊戲于筆墨之中.[65] Through the workings of nostalgic memory, the author traverses at once the supernatural realm and the earthly sphere, and

---

61 See Cao, *Zhiyanzhai pingpi Honglou meng*, 18. 302–303. In fact, "casual writings" such as the Stone's personal comments are often omitted in the *ChengGao* editions, probably as they are considered to be irrelevant to the development of the plot. Both Chapters 53 and 78 present such cases, the former being an articulation of "the pattern of Hui" (*Hui wen* 慧紋), and the latter regarding the literary technique for writing an elegy. See Cao, *Zhiyanzhai pingpi Honglou meng*, 53.847, 78.1219.

62 Cao, *Zhiyanzhai pingpi Honglou meng*, 1.7; SS, 1.51.

63 Cao, *Zhiyanzhai pingpi Honglou meng*, 1.7.

64 Wai-yee Li, *Enchantment and Disenchantment*, 210–15.

65 Cao, *Zhiyanzhai pingpi Honglou meng*, 8.153.

thus writes about the past in a minutely detailed but distanced way. His skillful manipulation of the multiple points of view that switch between the author, the Stone, and the hero Baoyu produces a striking complexity in the narrative.

On the one hand, nostalgia serves as a way of keeping the past alive, in which resides a remembered self. The novel is described as "a true record of real events," and yet it does not simply provide us with an accurate or complete picture of the author's past, but rather transforms the past into something approximating what he imagines himself, that is to say, it is the representation of memory rather than an unmediated representation of the past, as the introductory quatrain, which is stated to have been added into the novel by Cao Xueqin, makes clear: "All men call the author fool; / None his secret message hears." 都雲作者癡，誰解其中味[66] The all-significant "*chi*" 痴 plays a critical role in the author's creative remembering, as the site of identity formation and individual refuge. "*Chiyu*" 痴語, a term typically found in traditional Chinese poetics, represents the high individuality of poetic personae. It can be said that Cao Xueqin succeeds in the making of the self by producing a type of "*chiyu*" in the congruent manifestations of elegiac tone and stylistic oddity.

On the other hand, the author frees himself from it by describing his past from a distance in the form of the Stone. Although we cannot judge whether the ultimate unity of the Stone and Baoyu in the Cheng–Gao editions – the Stone attains nirvana and returns to Greensickness Peak after living out the life of Baoyu, which culminates in his eventual awakening and renunciation of the world – is in complete accord with Cao Xueqin's original idea; the Stone can also stand outside of himself (even if we see Baoyu as the incarnation of the Stone) to discern the state of his own being in a self-conscious process of looking back. The way in which the Stone and Baoyu are linked together constitutes a certain complex relationship to the past. As a matter of fact, the Stone's transformation into jade (*yu* 玉) highlights the *yu* desire of Baoyu's being, while the Stone-in-Waiting, as *qing* incarnate, strengthens Baoyu's self-pursuit in the form of *qing*, and further complicates such a relationship. That is, for all the recognition of the illusion of self, the author finds himself unable to stop writing out his vivid memories, and vice versa – the novel, which so desperately seeks to reconstitute a distinct self, fashions in the end a self that has been relentlessly called into question by the structuring of the narrative. It is the novel's distinctive mode of remembrance working through the means of both Baoyu and the Stone that simultaneously displays self-pursuit and self-questioning.

In fact, the nostalgic pattern of thought is ubiquitous in the Chinese intellectual and literary sphere. As Stephen Owen has illustrated, remembrance,

66 Cao, *Zhiyanzhai pingpi Honglou meng*, 1.7; SS, 1.50.

or the meditation upon the past, always demonstrates the dimension of negation, such as impermanence or lack, which serves as the impetus for self-reflection.[67] However, *The Dream of the Red Chamber* further develops a kind of self-scrutiny in the narrative pattern by maneuvering the perspectives of the narrator and characters. Thus, the seeming paradox caused by the transcendental wisdom of the mythic sphere and the intense longing and lamentation in the real life can be construed in the active and dynamic process of acquiring self-knowledge, including both *qing* and *yu*, both self-affirmation and self-questioning. The extended history of the novel's writing and the problematic process of transmission also exemplifies the fact that the profound motivation behind the narrative involves the intertwined relationship between time and desire. Whether as a story to be remembered or as a story to be revised, *The Dream of the Red Chamber* works not just as an artifact, but as an agent that makes both memorial dynamics and continuous self-reflection possible for its author, its commentators, and its readers.

Instead of locking the narrative into a fixed position, the author always approaches his characters and exhibits self-observation from alternative perspectives. In so doing, his nostalgia unfolds in an endlessly open process of critical inquiry inseparable from both skepticism and self-constitution, which subverts and problematizes dualistic classification, such as truth/fiction, self/other, real/unreal, and so on, other than simply a linear or accumulative development of individuality, or a mere transcendental enlightenment inherent in an enclosed and cyclical narrative. There are many examples of pairing, mirroring, and doubling around Jia Baoyu, which highlight a philosophical view of mutability. In this respect, Zhen Baoyu is most apparently matched with Jia Baoyu. Zhen Baoyu is not simply an exact physical replica of Jia Baoyu but corresponds to him in almost every aspect of life and disposition. In Chapter 56, in which representatives of the Zhen family bring gifts to the Jia family, it is revealed that Zhen Baoyu lives with his grandmother, often plays truant, and is thoroughly spoiled, just like Jia Baoyu. According to Jia Yucun's report in Chapter 2, like Jia Baoyu, Zhen Baoyu also insists on having girls with him while doing lessons and on the very purity of girls. Besides, in his dream encounter with Zhen Baoyu in Chapter 56, Jia Baoyu finds out that Zhen family has a mansion with a garden just like his own beloved Prospect Garden.

However, it is a great shock for the novel's protagonist Jia Baoyu to discover that another person, Zhen Baoyu, is exactly like himself. Convinced of his own uniqueness, he remains incredulous when people are talking about there being

67 See Stephen Owen, *Remembrances: The Experience of Past in Classical Chinese Literature* (Cambridge, MA: Harvard University Press, 1985).

another Baoyu. But shortly thereafter Jia Baoyu's confidence is shaken. "Had he a double? When he told himself that he couldn't possibly, he now began to feel that perhaps after all he had."[68] When he drifts into sleep, he finds himself in an exact copy of his own Prospect Garden and meets several maids here like Faithful (Yuanyang 鴛鴦), Aroma, and Patience (Ping'er 平兒). Bewildered by the unaccountable hostility of the maids, he wanders into a courtyard that bears some resemblance to Green Delights, Baoyu's residence, in which he finds Zhen Baoyu is also worried about his cousin's illness (here a mirroring of Daiyu). Interestingly, here Jia Baoyu overhears Zhen Baoyu discussing his dream as well as his disbelief in Jia Baoyu's existence:

> I heard Grandmother say that there is another Bao-yu in the capital who is exactly like me, but I didn't believe her. I've just been having a dream in which I went into a large garden and met some girls there who called me a "nasty creature" and wouldn't have anything to do with me. I managed to find this Bao-yu's room, but he was asleep. What I saw was only an empty shell lying there on the bed. I was wondering where the real person could have got to.
>
> 我聽見老太太說，長安都中也有個寶玉，和我一樣的性情，我只不信。我才作了一個夢，竟夢中到了都中一個花園子裡頭，遇見幾個姐姐，都叫我臭小廝，不理我。好容易找到他房裡頭，偏他睡覺，空有皮囊，真性不知那裡去了。[69]

Aroma shakes Baoyu awake after she hears him calling out his own name in his sleep, and subsequently attributes his dream to seeing his own reflection in the mirror. As is well known, the perception of one's mirror-image is a vital moment in the development of a sense of selfhood and the constitution of a human subject. The reflection image alludes to the recognition of the illusory nature of the self. This perception is directly shown in the image of the empty form left on the bed. By means of witnessing and vicariously participating in Jia Baoyu's suffering and loss, according to the Cheng–Gao editions, the Stone's worldly karma is completed, and its substance returned to the Great Unity. In other words, the Great Unity is mirrored in the unity of the Stone and Baoyu. Their distinction in the manuscripts, however, exhibits an endless process of critical inquiry inseparable from both skepticism and self-constitution, rather than a mere transcendental enlightenment. Likewise, the trope of a dream within a dream in the episode of the interaction between the two Baoyus

---

68 SS, 3.85; Cao, *Zhiyanzhai pingpi Honglou meng*, 56.895.

69 SS, 3.86; Cao, *Zhiyanzhai pingpi Honglou meng*, 56.896.

points to the proposition that "there is the real in the false, and the false in the real," suggesting a relentless self-reflexive trajectory centered in process, a moving towards rather than an arrival. It is the constant self-reflexivity manifested in the intriguing dialogues between the Stone and the two Baoyus that imparts subjectivity to both the author and his characters. As such, the narrative describes the self as constituted based on the deeply intertwined relationship between the author, the narrator, and the characters. Such a dynamic mode of thinking brings the subject into being and turns the narrative into a critical medium that sustains its moral agency through relentless self-inquiry.

The Dream of the Red Chamber exhibits a compelling sense of self-consciousness as it depicts how Jia Baoyu confronts his own limitations as well as contradictions. Jia Baoyu struggles throughout the novel in pondering over the girls' fate and his true identity, thereby cultivating an understanding of the selflessness of the self. As the commentator Erzhi daoren 二知道人 noted on the significance of Zhen Baoyu's representation in the novel, "The reason why Xueqin creates such a character as Zhen Baoyu is out of concern that the reader will misunderstand Jia Baoyu to be unique" 雪芹寫一甄寶玉者，恐閱者誤以為賈寶玉爲絶特也.[70] In fact, we can perceive that Jia Baoyu keeps penetrating the comfortable shell of self-complacency in the progress to adulthood and individuality. In Chapter 30, Baoyu wanders in the garden and by chance sees a young girl named Lingguan 齡官 crouching under a trellis of rambler roses and using a hairpin to scratch the character "*qiang*" 薔 repeatedly on the ground, unaware of the downpour around her. Baoyu is puzzled at her act and does not know that she is actually in love with Jia Qiang 賈薔. When Jia Baoyu realizes the real meaning of her scratching *qiang* on the ground in Chapter 36, he is in a reflective, self-critical mood, and utters: "I'm not surprised that Father tells me I have a 'small capacity but a great self-conceit.' I mean, that stuff about all of you making a river of tears for me when I die: I realize now that it's not possible. I realize now that we each have our own allotted share of tears and must be content with what we've got."[71] This incident has a profound impact on Baoyu, making him realize that love is exclusive and that everyone has their own destined person. From then on, he begins to reflect on his own view of self and love. In Chapter 49, after meeting with Baochai's and Li Wan's cousins, Jia Baoyu sighs with wonder, "Heavenly lord, what a store of beauty you must have at your disposal to be able to produce such paragons! I've been like the frog living at the bottom of the well who

70 Erzhi daoren 二知道人, "Honglou meng shuomeng" 紅樓夢說夢, in Yisu一粟 ed., *Honglou meng ziliao huibian* 紅樓夢資料彙編 (Beijing: Zhonghua shuju, 1964), 99.

71 Cao, *Zhiyanzhai pingpi Honglou meng*, 36.604; SS, 2.210.

thought the world was a little round pool of water. Up to now I've always believed that the girls in this household were without equals anywhere; but now, even without my needing to go outside, here they come, each one more beautiful than the last! Today has been an education for me."[72] Here we see that the protagonist's self is formed in relation to the girls around him, as the commentary in the *Gengchen* edition demonstrates, "the entire case of *qing* must be registered through Brother Stone" 通部情案，皆必從石兄掛號.[73] All the girls associate with Baoyu on an emotional level, in the sense that Baoyu's self-perception is largely obtained through the observation of the girls' fates, and that his own self is constructed over the course of recalling the interactions between him and the girls. Baoyu's awareness of the limits of an individual derives from the recognition of the diversity and complexity of the phenomenal world.

Hence, his self-reflection does not point towards a language of the extinction of self, but an accommodation of the diversity and heterogeneity of feelings and interests, or a justification of the pluralization. The multiplicity of character pairings occurs in the novel to the extent that one character frequently has several matches. Other than Zhen Baoyu, Jia Baoyu is also matched with several like-minded men of feeling and refinement such as his schoolmate Qin Zhong 秦鐘. Likewise, Baochai is paired with Aroma so clearly that the author writes about "Aroma" while ostensibly writing about Baochai. Lin Daiyu and Skybright (Qingwen 晴雯, Baoyu's maid) are also closely paired in that both have sharp tongues and mirror each other's fates. The nun Miaoyu is considered to be a symbolic twin of Daiyu's in terms of their shared exquisite taste and poetic sensibility.[74] The famous commentator Zhang Xinzhi even thinks that Daiyu has five "shadows" (*yingshen* 影身) in the novel: Skybright, Xiangyun 湘云, Crimson (Xiaohong 小紅), Si'er 四兒, and Wu'er 五兒.[75] The use of multiple pairings is so common that the novel is called a "book of reflections" (*yingshu* 影書).[76] Various characters are juxtaposed with or echo one another. Given the author's use of layers of irony and indeterminacy, the singularity of the characters as well as the narrative's meaning becomes problematic.

This continuous trope of doubling thus reflects an extreme manifestation of sympathy and doubt about the self. Many characters in the novel are described

72 Cao, *Zhiyanzhai pingpi Honglou meng*, 49.778; SS, 2.469–70.

73 Cao, *Zhiyanzhai pingpi Honglou meng*, 49.744.

74 Tu Ying 涂瀛, "Honglou meng wenda" 紅樓夢問答, in Yisu ed., *Honglou meng ziliao huibian*, 143.

75 Cao, *Chongjiao bajia pingpi Honglou meng*, 21.437.

76 Sun Qufu 孫渠甫, Shitou ji weiyan "石頭記微言", in Yisu ed., *Honglou meng ziliao huibian*, 266.

as having "inborn deficiency" (*buzu zhi zheng* 不足之症), symbolizing a discontented self that demands development through an active process of recognition and reflection. Since the self is always formed in relation to significant others, nothing is wholly one thing or the other, but rather each participates in each other, much like Baochai and Daiyu – together they are regarded as manifestations of "two-in-one" (*jianmei* 兼美) – and numerous other character pairs in the novel that have both opposing and complementary features. The self that is desperately sought in the novel is thus surpassed by a collective existence based on shared experiences in the nostalgia frame. In memorializing Baoyu's and the girls' past, the author creates a literary community, Prospect Garden, which is not merely formed by the particular emotions, stories, and obsessions of individuals, but also grants all the participants an existence beyond the individual. Ultimately, Cao Xueqin submerges himself and his protagonists in this mutually appreciative aesthetic community.

3 The Community of Prospect Garden: Cultural Nostalgia and Social Criticism

The purpose of nostalgia in *The Dream of the Red Chamber* is to construct an identity in the romantic-aesthetic realm that is conceived of as an alternative sphere of existence. Setting up his story in the individual's memories, Cao Xueqin raises questions on the claims of uniqueness and self-autonomy, and yet refashions the self in a format that belongs to a wider community, a community he constructs in his writings out of his cherished poetry society. We recall that Baoyu has a natural fondness for gatherings, and that Prospect Garden provides him with a main locus for literary gatherings. The garden sustains a world that contains a variety of cultural resources in the Chinese literary tradition, such as poetry, arts, literary entertainment, and above all a lyricized way of life embodied by the much-valued poetry society.[77] All of the poetic moments, sites, images, sensations, and gestures in the garden and their proliferated meanings become a comprehensible sense of identity, which the characters who live there achieve.

Admittedly, the emotional interaction between the two protagonists, Baoyu and Daiyu, imbues them with a sentimental identity. Although they do not address romantic poems to each other, Daiyu writes three quatrains on a pair of old handkerchiefs, which Baoyu sends Skybright over to accept from her (Chapter 34). These stylish poems – they center on highly personalized

77 See Xiao, *The Chinese Garden as Lyric Enclave*, 177–89.

images such as tears, idleness, sleeves, pillows, bamboo, etc., rather than stock phrasing – are indicative of her interiority, the kind of passion triggered by Baoyu's significant gift and his inexpressible attachment to her. The recurrent images of tears obviously allude to their shared destiny in the repayment of a "debt of tears," referring to the mythic frame story of the novel that highlights the dimension of *qing* in Baoyu's earthly experience.

However, such a sentimental identity is largely rooted in the unrestrained atmosphere of Prospect Garden. In fact, the constitution of a personal self within the literary cultural milieu maintained by the garden serves as an equally, if not more, important means of identity building. As discussed in preceding sections, in Daiyu's case, the self's longing to be recognized is exhibited not only in her relationship with Baoyu, but in a wider sense, in the manifestation of her inclination and talent within the community of the poetry club. Baoyu's self-fashioning and his eventual detachment from the world are even more inseparable from the rise and the fall of the garden.

The garden of the novel has been characterized as a profound representation of literati culture in late imperial China.[78] Just like Baoyu's or the Stone's emotional bond to the past, the literary construction of the garden stands out as a means of cultural nostalgia, in which particular sites and gestures become at once material and symbolic, so that an individual identity, through the medium of the community, is achieved. We see in the novel the vivid depiction of the particular feelings and experiences of individuals, and yet equally importantly, these depictions contribute to the sense of place, in that people become part of the cultural landscape of their places of residence. By carrying out their characteristic activities, the people of Prospect Garden become part of what defines the place and the culture it represents. There emerges here a closely woven fabric of collective and individual experiences, public and personal memories, and thus public and personal selves.

Looking back upon life in the garden in the novel gives rise to a moment of self-absorption, with which comes a nostalgic longing for a kind of culture that transcends the limit of time. The author is less interested in giving an account of that life than he is in removing it from time altogether, so that Prospect Garden and the cultural community it sustains are endowed with an enduring nature. They are left as a kind of measureless being beyond duration, a being written in exclusively cultural terms. As the Voiding-the-Void Taoist makes clear in reading the inscription on the Stone in the opening chapter, "it has no discoverable dynastic period, and it contains no examples of moral grandeur among its characters – no statesmanship, no social message of any kind"

78 Ibid.

第一件，無朝代年紀可考；第二件，並無大賢大忠理朝廷治風俗的善政.[79] By means of claiming to erase temporality and only to focus on a number of females who reside in the garden, the narrative, particularly that of life in the garden, is stripped of historical and social-political dimensions. Allowing his memorable moments, sensations, and characters to unfold in a non-dynastic, unofficial, and essentially cultural way, the author escapes time but not their physical, evocative existence.

Memory remakes things, making them different from how they were. On top of that, cultural memory participates in the construction of the personal past.[80] This is also manifested by the narrative's chronological contradictions in relation to the ages of the major characters in the extant manuscript versions. The interlineal comment in Chapter 45 of the *Gengchen* edition significantly reminds us that Daiyu is stated to be only fifteen years old at that time, and yet it is six years after Daiyu first came to the Jia household, at which time she was stated to be thirteen.[81] The reminder here implies that such achronological problems present in *The Dream of the Red Chamber* are probably a deliberate attempt to obscure the narrative's temporal frame. By blurring the flow of time both in the garden and in memory, Cao provides his characters with a cultural identity that surpasses historical and social boundaries, while he submerges himself in the cultural community characteristic of the garden. Through readers, especially commentators such as Zhiyanzhai, this community is further shared, and thus a community of like-minded remembers is created, in which they grant each other some sense of culturally nostalgic being.

In fact, the theme of transmission, or cultural transmission, is ingeniously dramatized in the appearance of Cao Xueqin as a character in the novel, who is defined as a transmitter or transcriber of the fictional/cultural text rather than a creator/writer. This may be construed in the frame of the lasting tradition of "expounding [on writings of one's predecessors] without producing anything new" (*shu er bu zuo* 述而不作), a cultural format that emphasizes the importance and practices of transmission and memorialization. Cao Xueqin as a fictional character is described as "reading and editing [the novel] for ten years, and rewriting it no fewer than five times" 披閱十載，增刪五次, and he is just one editor within the extending chain of textual transmission and circulation.[82]

79 Cao, *Zhiyanzhai pingpi Honglou meng*, 1.4–5; SS, 1.49.

80 See Peter Burke, "Shaping Memories," and Thomas Docherty, "Memento Mori," in *Literature and Cultural Memory*, ed. Mihaela Irimia (Leiden: Brill, 2017), 17–30, and 50–62 respectively.

81 Cao, *Zhiyanzhai pingpi Honglou meng*, 45.729.

82 Cao, *Zhiyanzhai pingpi Honglou meng*, 1.7.

In this sense, *The Dream of the Red Chamber* is not a singular work but a series of texts carrying out cultural transmission and transformation.

As pointed out by his intimate friends – "the old dream of Yangzhou has been awakened for a long time" 揚州舊夢久已覺; "in memory of the wonders of the wind and the moon in the Qinhuai area" 秦淮風月憶繁華 – what Cao Xueqin constantly looks back on in the novel is not merely his own past in the south and that of the Cao family, but also a sense of cultural memory and identity.[83] The cultural environment of the Jiangnan area in the early Qing, in which Ming loyalists and intellectuals gathered and lived, was inextricably interwoven with its late Ming predecessor. Cao Yin 曹寅 (1658–1712) was in contact with Yu Huai 余懷 (1616–1696) – who was associated with many members of the Restoration Society (Fushe 复社), and well known as a writer of a memoir about the late Ming – during his service as Suzhou zhizao 蘇州織造 from the twenty-ninth to the thirty-first year of the Kangxi reign (1691–1693), when they both participated in the literary gatherings of the Jiangnan area. Cao Yin also asked Yu Huai to inscribe a poem on his collection of paintings, and included Yu's works of lyrics (*Yuqinzhai ci* 玉琴齋詞), which was prefaced by Wu Meicun 吳梅村 (1609–1672), in his own collection of books entitled with his style name "Lianting" 楝亭.[84] Such traces of contacts strengthen the possible intertextual relationships between *The Dream of the Red Chamber* and those late Ming resources.

As it is, *The Dream of the Red Chamber*'s association with the late Ming modes of expression is more delicate than is usually recognized. Cao Xueqin consciously refers to seventeenth-century literature and culture. His Prospect Garden identifies with the literary imagination of Ming loyalists during the early decades of the Qing period. The staging and plotting of Baoyu's dream of visiting the Land of Illusion, for instance, evidently allude to Zhang Dai's 張岱 (1597–1689?) "Langhuan fudi" 琅嬛福地 (The Blessed Grounds of Langhuan). When Baoyu steps into Department of the Unfortunate (*Boming si* 薄命司), he sees a dozen or more large cupboards with paper strips pasted on their doors, and cannot help opening them and turning over the registers in them one after another. The mysterious pictures and the inexplicable scripts and lines draw Baoyu into particularly profound contemplation. Similarly, Zhang Dai describes how he dreams of the Blessed Grounds of Langhuan, in which there

83 See Yisu ed., *Honglou meng ziliao huibian*, 7.

84 Zhu Zhiyuan 朱志遠, "Banqiao zaji de zuozhe Yuhuai yu Cao Yin jiaoyou kao"《板橋雜記》的作者余懷與曹寅交遊考，*MingQing xiaoshuo yanjiu* 明清小說研究, 3(2008): 280–88.

are swift and twisting torrents and precious flowers, and where the shelves teem with book collections:

> I open a book and read it. There is a lot of seal script like tadpoles, bird tracks, and thunderbolts. When I read them in my dream, I seem to be able to make sense of their intractability and obscurity. Living at leisure with nothing to do and then at night dreaming of this, after I awake I reflect upon it, and feel a desire to obtain a piece of choice land and make an approximate version of the dream.
>
> 開卷視之，多蝌蚪、鳥跡、霹靂篆文，夢中讀之，似能通其棘澀。閒居無事，夜輒夢之，醒後佇思，欲得一勝地彷彿為之。[85]

It was said that Zhang Hua 張華 (232–300), a statesman of the Western Jin dynasty, ran into a man while traveling through a cave, who led him to a place hidden within a stone gate, with lofty palaces and ancient trees. There was also a secret room full of strange books about events before the Han dynasty, most of which had Zhang never heard of. Zhang Hua asked for the name of the place and was told that is was "The Blessed Grounds of Langhuan," where god of heaven collected and preserved books.[86] Drawing on this tale, Zhang Dai envisions his own garden with the inscription "Blessed Grounds of Langhuan" on its gate as a bibliographic heaven, which manifests the ideal of maintaining the cultural tradition, especially after the collapse of the Ming. Just like Zhang Dai, Cao Xueqin sets his Land of Illusion in his dream, and yet projects the dream into Prospect Garden, which is filled with accumulations of cultural images.

In additional to Zhang Dai's "Langhuan fudi," many literary pieces about similar imaginary gardens were written during the late Ming and early Qing period, such as Liu Shilong's 劉士龍 (fl. *c.*1603) "Record of the Wuyou Garden" (Wuyouyuan ji 烏有園記), Dai Mingshi's 戴名世 (1653–1713) "Record of the Yi Garden" (Yiyuan ji 意園記), Huang Zhouxing's 黃周星 (1611–1680) "Record of the Jiangjiu Garden" (Jiangjiuyuan ji 將就園記), and so on. Such pieces created a potential space that could bring a sense of belonging to literary men of the time, especially for those who had experienced social and cultural dislocations after the fall of the Ming – they attempted to reconstruct a dreamscape that they could inhabit, and through which they could recover a culture

85 Zhang Dai, "Langhuan fudi ji" 瑯嬛福地記, in *Taoan mengyi* 陶庵夢憶 (Shanghai: Shanghai guji chubanshe, 1982), 79; translation, with slight modification, from Philip A. Kafalas, *In Limpid Dream: Nostalgia and Zhang Dai's Reminiscences of the Ming* (Norwalk: East Bridge, 2007), 18.

86 See Yin Shizhen 尹世貞, *Langhuan ji san juan* 瑯嬛記三卷 (Jinan: Qilu shushe, 1995), 3–4.

built of both personality and cultural fantasy. Ellen Widmer has suggested that Huang Zhouxing's imaginary garden can be regarded as a foil to that of *The Dream of the Red Chamber*, although enough evidence has yet to be found to prove a direct influence.[87] However, it is not impossible that Prospect Garden derives from the influences and sources of these imaginary gardens. At the end of Chapter 17, one commentary explicitly notes that the description of the Prospect Garden in this chapter can be read as a literary essay of this kind – "Record of the Prospect Garden" (Daguanyuan ji 大觀園記).[88] This title invites an analogy to the aforementioned works about imaginary gardens in the late Ming and early Qing.

This mode of garden writing serves as a vehicle to express political despair, as well as nostalgia for the late Ming at the beginning of the Qing. The heterogeneous cultural traditions of the late Ming and its subversive contemplation of self, desire, and moral order tended to be repressed or deliberately forgotten by official cultures during the early Qing. The Ming loyalists' anxiety about a forgotten past and their endeavor to transcend the constraints of temporality are encountered in those fantastic gardens. Although Ming loyalism is by no means an issue in *The Dream of the Red Chamber*, Cao Xueqin seeks to recount the occluded counter-cultural memory of the late Ming, nourishing the suppressed traditions of culture and knowledge that run as an undercurrent below the mainstream of the hegemonic views of the early to mid Qing. By reincorporating certain repressed unofficial literary traditions by means of intertextual discourses, the novel makes the occluded or repressed reappear, and compensates for what was lost as a result of cultural constraints.

The supreme authority of the early Qing court, in particular its appropriation and ideologizing of Lixue (see Chapter 1), might also have prompted Cao Xueqin to return to the Xinxue traditions in pursuit of spiritual resources. In view of the references to Xinxue that appear in Baoyu's contemplation and his conversations with the girls, one might suggest that Cao Xueqin carries on the heritage of Xinxue in looking nostalgically back at late Ming culture. A case in point is in Chapter 19, where Aroma exhorts Baoyu to study hard, reporting Baoyu's sarcastic remarks about scholarship – according to Baoyu, "Illumination of Clear Virtue" (Mingmingde 明明德) is the only genuine book

87 Ellen Widmer, "Between Worlds: Huang Zhouxing's Imaginary Garden," in *Trauma and Transcendence in Early Qing Literature*, ed. Wilt Idema, Wai-yee Li, and Ellen Widmer (Cambridge, MA: Harvard University Asian Center, 2006), 277–79.

88 Cao, *Zhiyanzhai pingpi Honglou meng*, 17.295.

ever written, and all the rest are forgeries.[89] Baoyu thinks of "Illumination of Clear Virtue" as the most valuable teaching of Confucius, and the most authentic representation of Confucian thought. Indeed, it was precisely "Illumination of Clear Virtue" that was promoted by Wang Yangming as the key concept of his theoretical exposition – "The task of 'The Great Learning' consists in manifesting the clear character"《大學》工夫即是明明德;[90] "The various steps from the investigation of things and extension of knowledge to the bringing of peace to the world are nothing but manifesting the clear character" 自格物致知至平天下，只是一個明明德.[91]

In interpreting how to seek intuitive knowledge and to manifest one's "clear character" described in *The Great Learning*, Wang highlights the concepts of "humanity" (*ren* 仁) and "sincerity" (*cheng* 誠). He clarifies the clear character as the "character of the mind" – that is, humanity – and further articulates it by quoting a famous saying by Cheng Hao 程顥 (1032–1085): "The man of humanity regards heaven and earth and all things as one body" 仁者以天地萬物為一體.[92] As for the way of illuminating the clear character, Wang thinks that it is "none other than to make the will sincere" 明明德只是個誠意.[93] Seeing sincerity as the original substance of the mind, Wang interprets sincerity as a state of mind, and thus asserts that the attempt to restore this original substance is the work of thinking how to be sincere. Therefore, he believes that "only with ultimate sincerity in the world can one completely develop one's nature and understand the transformation and nurture of heaven and earth" 惟天下至誠，為能盡其性，知天地之化育, quoting *The Doctrine of the Mean*.[94] In this sense, he assents to preserving humanity with "sincerity and seriousness" (*chengjing* 誠敬).[95]

89 Cao, *Zhiyanzhai pingpi Honglou meng*, 19.332; SS, 1.391. "Illumination of clear virtue" is from "The Great Learning" 大學, a Confucian classic, which begins with the line "The Way of Great Learning lies in illuminating the clear virtue, renovating the people, and resting in the highest good" 大學之道在明明德，在親民，在止於至善. "Illumination of clear virtue" encapsulates the core teaching of "The Great Learning."

90 Wang Yangming, *Chuan xi lu zhushu*, 88; Chan, *Instructions for Practical Living*, 91.

91 Wang, *Chuan xi lu zhushu*, 58; Chan, *Instructions for Practical Living*, 56.

92 Wang, *Chuan xi lu zhushu*, 58; Chan, *Instructions for Practical Living*, 56.

93 Wang, *Chuan xi lu zhushu*, 58; Chan, *Instructions for Practical Living*, 56. At another point, he identifies with what his student says: "In recent years I have realized through personal experience that the task of manifesting the clear character consists only in making the will sincere" 近年體驗得明明德功夫只是誠意. See Wang, *Chuan xi lu zhushu*, 179–80; Chan, *Instructions for Practical Living*, 188.

94 Wang, *Chuan xi lu zhushu*, 13; Chan, *Instructions for Practical Living*, 13.

95 Wang, *Chuan xi lu zhushu*, 80; Chan, *Instructions for Practical Living*, 78–79.

As Wang claims that "the human mind and things form the same body" 人心與物同體, Baoyu is said to show deep sympathy even for the insentient or non-feeling – "when he sees a swallow he talks to the swallow, when he sees the stars or the moon, he sighs and groans and mutters away to himself like a crazy thing."[96] In this particular moment of union of subject and object, one can feel the kind of affective power of the subject, which Wang Yangming considers as a transformative and inclusive capacity.

According to Wang, the external world cannot exist independently of thought: namely, the mind is the exclusive locus of realities. In this sense, the whole world is only the one that we ourselves experience – "Not only animals and plants, but heaven and earth also, form the same body with me. Spiritual beings also form the same body with me" 豈但禽獸、草木，雖天地也與我同體的，鬼神也與我同體的.[97] When he is asked what the mind of heaven and earth is, he explains:

> My clear intelligence is the master of heaven and earth and spiritual beings. If heaven is deprived of my clear intelligence, who is going to look into its height? If earth is deprived of my clear intelligence, who is going to look into its depth? … Separated from my clear intelligence, there will be no heaven, earth, spiritual beings, or myriad things, and separated from these, there will not be my clear intelligence. Thus they are all permeated with one material force. How can they be separated?
>
> 我的靈明，便是天地、鬼神的主宰。天沒有我的靈明，誰去仰他高？地沒有我的靈明，誰去俯他深？…… 天地、鬼神、萬物，離卻我的靈明，便沒有天地、鬼神、萬物了；我的靈明，離卻天地、鬼神、萬物，亦沒有我的靈明。如此，便是一氣流通的，如何與他間隔得？[98]

How to restore the individual's original unity with heaven, earth, and all things, and how to sustain a moral life that is spontaneous and unfeigned were central concerns of Wang's thought. It is our instincts of benevolence, the natural empathy for all things, that bring us into harmony with others and all living things, and thus become the key to the illumination of clear virtue. Wang's idea

96 See Wang Yangming 王陽明, *Chuan xi lu lanwaishu* 傳習錄欄外書 (Shanghai: Shanghai guji chubanshe, 2017), 248; Chan, *Instructions for Practical Living*, 257; Cao, *Zhiyanzhai pingpi Honglou meng*, 35.588; SS, 2.189.

97 Wang, *Chuan xi lu lanwaishu*, 248; Chan, *Instructions for Practical Living*, 257.

98 Wang, *Chuan xi lu lanwaishu*, 248; Chan, *Instructions for Practical Living*, 257–58.

of sensibility, sincerity, and benevolence evokes an ethics of sympathy, giving us an insight into the way Baoyu behaves and talks.

In Chapter 35, Baoyu hears that Fu Shi 傅試, one of his father's proteges, has a younger sister called Fu Qiufang 傅秋芳, who is said to be both beautiful and talented. Baoyu has not actually seen her, but he has formed in his imagination a picture of her to the extent that he is completely "serious and sincere" (*chengjing*) in worshiping her from afar. This suggests that Baoyu, who is ultimately sincere, can fully develop his nature and form the same body with the external world, as Wang Yangming emphasizes in illustrating the relationship between sincerity and humanity. Baoyu also directly uses the concept of *chengjing* to justify his effort to compose an elegy for Skybright.[99] In both cases, the thoughts and evaluations of Wang Yangming's treatise, the claim to a moral vision more deeply felt, no doubt provided a source of inspiration for the novel. But at the same time, the narrator's use of the descriptor "*chengjing*" for Baoyu's relations with girls has some degree of sarcasm, suggesting an ironic distance from Wang's theoretical discourses.

Another response Cao makes to the late Ming culture is to replace *qing* with the "lust of the mind" (*yiyin* 意淫). At the outset of the novel, the fairy Disenchantment protests against the saying "love feelings unsullied by any taint of lust" (*qing er buyin* 情而不淫), a cliché of the conventional *caizi-jiaren* story – as an unknown interlineal commentator suggests – but points out that "to experience loving feelings is, even more assuredly, a kind of lust" (*zhiqing geng yin* 知情更淫).[100] Hence, she coins the word "lust of the mind," and articulates the affective power of this original term: "That blind, defenceless love with which nature has filled your being is what we call here 'lust of the mind.' 'Lust of the mind' cannot be explained in words, nor, if it could, would you be able to grasp their meaning. Either you know what it means or you don't."[101] The word *chiqing* 痴情 ("blind, defenceless love" or "obsessive longing") was most often used in the cultural discourse of the late Ming, indicating an innate sensibility and highly subjective feeling. Along with the conventionalization of the scholar-beauty culture, "*qing*," as part of the self-definition of the late Ming literati elite, as well as its reformative power, has become obscured, and thus has become a mere floating signifier, such that Cao engages in the invention of such a special term pointing to a new kind of interiority too ambiguous to define in normative terms.

99 Cao, *Zhiyanzhai pingpi Honglou meng*, 78.1233; SS, 3.575.
100 Cao, *Zhiyanzhai pingpi Honglou meng*, 5.107; SS, 1.145.
101 Cao, *Zhiyanzhai pingpi Honglou meng*, 5.108; SS, 1.146.

As discussed in preceding chapters, the late Ming literati's straightforward claim on sensual desires and their pursuit of moral cultivation led to the gap between the mundane aspects of the true self and inner transcendence. For example, Yuan Hongdao's (see Chapter 1) love of nature is especially tinged with personal and sensual color. In fact, many of his landscape essays are concerned more with records of pleasurable moments than with descriptions of natural scenery. Yuan's obsession with nature is not rooted in the love of natural objects but rather an assertion of sensual desires and subjective experiences, which mark his genuineness. At the same time, however, there is constantly an introspective tone in Yuan's landscape essays. Moreover, in his later writings he showed deep repentance for his earlier claims that the pursuit of sensual pleasure was his primary concern.[102] This kind of self-reflection likewise lies in the process of the celebration of the true self and authentic self-expression, *zhenchuan* 真傳, in *The Dream of the Red Chamber*. For Cao Xueqin, expressing the attributes of *zhen* involves the attempt to fill the gap between worldly desires and self-cultivation in the Xinxue sense, which is thereby realized in the conception of "lust of the mind" as a kind of superior sensibility and inner transcendence. By the ironic distance he simultaneously keeps from the pursuit of *zhen* and *cheng* (or *chengjing*) in the narrative, Cao demonstrates that he is keenly aware of the uncertainties and paradoxes in the quest for inner truth. As such, Cao replaces *qing er buyin* or *chiqing* with his own invention of *yiyin*, which, according to the commentary in the Jiaxia edition, means *titie* 體貼 (consideration or sympathy) alone.[103] As Disenchantment further clarifies, "Because of this 'lust of the mind' women will find you a kind and understanding friend; but in the eyes of the world I am afraid it is going to make you seem unpractical and eccentric."[104] Baoyu's profound sympathy with the girls defines the distinctiveness of his *qing*. Focusing on its inherently inexpressible nature, the concept of *yiyin* names a new type of feeling, suggesting both the depth and the uncertainty of the subject, and thus an attempt to foster an inclination toward sympathy. As a form of empathetic bonding, *yiyin* endows the term *qing* with the feature of humaneness and openness, pointing towards the emotional interests of other people, thereby providing us with nonegoistic imaginations of emotion-rich situations. Cao Xueqin makes clear to us that, like memory and language, emotion is something the self has by virtue of being a self. Such emotional sensitivities form the groundwork for

---

102 See Martin Huang's discussion on "desire, anxiety, and ambivalence during the late Ming," in Huang, *Desire and Fictional Narrative*, 5–22.

103 Cao, *Zhiyanzhai pingpi Honglou meng*, 5.108.

104 Cao, *Zhiyanzhai pingpi Honglou meng*, 5.108; SS, 1.146.

the ethical behavior of the characters in the novel, but the ultimate grounding of its ethics is found in empathy. It is this kind of self-reflection and the sense of sympathy, which are built into the narrative pattern of *The Dream of the Red Chamber*, that produce the conditions that make the agency of the subject/intersubject possible. In this sense, the cultural tradition of *qing* is developed, taking on new meanings for its admirers.

Furthermore, the literary construction of Prospect Garden exhibits a dynamic interaction between personal memory and cultural nostalgia. To a great degree, the making of Baoyu's identity quest consists in the collection of cultural memory, in particular the nostalgia for late Ming culture, which promotes a retrospective stance involving a critical force that points to both individual identity and dominant views. Dissatisfied with the socio-moral order of his time, Wang Yangming engaged himself in revitalizing the moral vision grounded on a doctrine that encompassed the cognitive, the practical, and the affective together. Wang's subjective approach opened up a good many possibilities for both individual development and self-expression in literature. *The Dream of the Red Chamber* explores such a possibility in a critical way. What is equally, if not more, important is that the rising of Xinxue and the later Wang Yangming School evokes political objectives and effects, in that they attempt to cope with the problems of living a proper life amid the social changes induced by economic expansion, the venality of officials, and injustice in general. Such political dimensions and critical forces likewise play an essential role in the narrative of *The Dream of the Red Chamber*, as is shown in the narrator's implicit critique of the supreme authority and the hierarchical order: "It [the novel] does not intend to worry about the current situations of the time, nor to make abusive remarks on the world" 非傷時罵世之旨 and "It has nothing to do with the current events" 毫不干涉時事: though repeatedly underlined in the narrative frame, these denials of political references are particularly marked as "important sentences" (*yaojin ju* 要緊句) in Zhiyanzhai's commentary, and thus instead suggest that political objectives are one of the most critical dimensions in the novel, a kind of absent presence lingering in the narrative.[105] In particular, the deliberate omission of these political references in the Cheng–Gao editions implies that the later versions are far less politically sensitive than the original.

According to Deng Yunxiang's 鄧雲鄉 study, Baoyu's criticism of the setting of Sweet Rice Village (*Daoxiang cun* 稻香村) as not being "natural" explicitly points to the hypocrisy of the monarchy – in that there is always a farmyard situated in the royal garden – with the purpose of elucidating the importance

105 Cao, *Zhiyanzhai pingpi Honglou meng*, 1.6–7.

that the ruler attaches to agriculture by referring to the ritual of *guanjia* 觀稼.[106] It has been suggested elsewhere that the "destiny of the Wood and the Stone" (*mushi zhi meng* 木石之盟) is actually an implicit criticism of the Yongzheng emperor's arbitrariness and dictatorialness, a characteristic satire on the mainstream political discourse of the time.[107] Furthermore, when Baoyu makes an ironic remark on the old saying "a scholar dies admonishing and a soldier dies fighting," he says:

> The court holds its power from Heaven, and it's unthinkable that Heaven should lay the huge responsibility of empire on any but the worthiest shoulders. So you can see that all those death-with-honour characters were thinking only of their own personal fame and glory. They weren't really thinking of the cardinal principles of righteousness.
>
> 那朝廷是受命于天，他不圣不仁，那天地斷不把這萬幾重任與他了。可知那些死的都是沽名，并不知大義。[108]

On the surface, this lengthy comment epitomizes the discourse of loyal duty to the sovereign; however, it subtextually suggests the idea of being loyal to the world for all, rather than the emperor alone. As it was, the late Ming saw the emergence of unconventional ideas that one should take as one's sense of right and wrong not from that of the monarch (*miaotang zhi shifei* 廟堂之是非) but that of the world (*tianxia zhi shifei* 天下之是非).[109] *The Dream of the Red Chamber* in a way echoes this form of humanism in the late Ming, which emphasizes both the pursuit of individuality and that of egalitarian human relationships, thereby facilitating the formulation of critical discourse on autocratic monarchy.

For all the cultural obsession with the garden, therefore, this does not mean that the author renders it a self-contained ideal world that disregards its economic and social grounds. We are told in Chapter 17 that Prospect Garden is constructed on the original site of Huifang 會芳 Garden, whose source of

106 See Deng Yunxiang 鄧雲鄉, *Honglou fengsu tan* 紅樓風俗譚 (Beijing: Zhonghua shuju, 2015), 523–25.

107 See Chen Hong 陳洪, "'Honglou meng' mushi kaolun"《紅樓夢》木石考論, *Wenxue yu wenhua* 文學与文化 3 (2016): 24–35.

108 Cao, *Zhiyanzhai pingpi Honglou meng*, 36.601; SS, 2.205–206, with minor revisions.

109 Gu Xiancheng 顧憲成 (1550–1612), the renowned thinker and leader of the Donglin Party 東林黨, claimed this in his conversation with Prime Minister Wang Xijue 王錫爵 (1534–1611). See Gu Yingtai 谷應泰, *Mingshi jishi benmo* 明史紀事本末 (Shanghai: Shanghai guji chubanshe, 1994), 66.263.

water is located in the degenerate Ningguo Mansion. This fact compromises the garden's status as a purely utopian world. As discussed earlier, through the manipulation of the relationship between the characters, the narrator, and the author, Cao turns the narrative into a critical inquiry that achieves distance and freedom from the kind of literary culture he cherishes and at the same time extends socially critical consciousness from the late Ming onward. By so doing, he maintains the attachment to the physical artifacts and aesthetic effects of the culture, while criticizing the social-political system in which it is rooted. Therefore, although the construction of Prospect Garden seems to erase the distance between the cultural and the historical-social dimensions, it actually codifies that distance, to the extent that a nuanced exploration of the redefinition, or reformation, of literati culture is expressed in the novel.

What is especially meaningful in the novel is the feminization of the garden and the making of a non-hierarchical garden through the use of poetic pseudonyms to put aside conventional modes of address, to the extent that one of its most provoking readers, Chen Tui 陳蛻, refers to *The Dream of the Red Chamber* as having "the aim of Great Harmony" (*datong zhi zhi* 大同之旨).[110] In this, *The Dream of the Red Chamber* poses an indirect but nonetheless profound challenge to the basic premises that had served to define the social-political system on which literati culture was predicated. It implies a view that both acknowledges the plurality and diversity of human beings, and pursues social cohesion, as well as communal ideals that define their cultural identity. All of these ambivalent explorations in the novel evoke the very profound sense of introspection that enables possibilities to occur.

By identifying with the "stone unfit to repair the sky" (*wucai kequ bu cangtian* 無才可去補蒼天), Cao Xueqin alludes to his personal dilemma of failing to enter the public sphere as a literary man. In this sense, cultural memory functions as a paradoxical existence of both aesthetic attachment and a means of political criticism. Public affairs and political discourse are things that seem to be absent, but are always hidden beneath the surface of the personal narrative. The novel strives to form a new basis of humanity and an ethics of sympathy, and simultaneously to seek and regain the path to the public realm for an authentic self. This seemingly paradoxical matrix is of the utmost importance in *The Dream of the Red Chamber*, in that it implies a permanent state of uncertainty about self and an unremitting effort at making changes. It is central to individual identity and, therefore, to community life and to politics.

---

110 Chen Tui 陳蛻, "Lie Shitou ji yu zibushuo" 列石頭記於子部說, in Yisu ed., *Honglou meng ziliao huibian*, 269.

CHAPTER 6

Women's Self-Exploration in *Karmic Bonds of Reincarnation*

Karmic Bonds of Reincarnation was composed in roughly the same period as *The Dream of the Red Chamber*. Like *The Dream of the Red Chamber*, *Karmic Bonds of Reincarnation* calls into question the ideal *caizi-jiaren* romance, yet in quite a different way. It can be said that *Karmic Bonds of Reincarnation* marks a radical departure from the conventional *caizi-jiaren* mode. If *The Dream of the Red Chamber* displays its ambition to explore the diversity and ramifications of female desire, then *Karmic Bonds of Reincarnation* attempts to redefine women's desire and to fashion a new sense of female self. Despite its commitment to telling a touching scholar-beauty story, *Karmic Bonds of Reincarnation* exceeds the limits of the conventional romance not only in its extended elaborations of the heroine's adventure, but also in its vivid representation of the heroine's psychological realities and the plight that the patriarchal system imposes on the desiring woman in both the inner and the outer sphere.

Karmic Bonds of Reincarnation has been long regarded as one of the most distinguished *tanci* works. *Tanci*, a genre of fiction in the form either of alternating prose and verse passages or all in verse, produced a separate literary and cultural domain reserved for female authors in the second half of the eighteenth century and later.[1] While women writers in premodern China rarely tried their hand at prose fiction, they adopted the genre of *tanci* and developed a female narrative voice. In this sense, *tanci* served as a primary means of women's involvement with fiction in late imperial China.[2] *Karmic Bonds of*

1 Scholars have recently provided substantial research on the evolution of this "women's genre." See Siao-chen Hu 胡曉真, *Cainü cheye weimian* 才女徹夜未眠 (Taibei: Maitian chuban, 2003), 3–61, 185–218; Bao Zhenpei 鮑正培, *Qingdai nüzuojia tanci xiaoshuo lungao* 清代女作家彈詞小說論稿, 98–300; Yu Zhang, *Interfamily Tanci Writing in Nineteenth-Century China: Bonds and Boundaries* (Lanham, MD: Lexington Books, 2018); Li Guo, *Women's Tanci Fiction in Late Imperial and Early Modern China* (West Lafayette, IN: Purdue University Press, 2015), 1–32; Li Guo, *Writing Gender in Early Modern Chinese Women's Tanci Fiction* (West Lafayette, IN: Purdue University Press, 2021), 1–36.

2 So far we only know a very limited amount of vernacular novels attributed to women writers, such as Wang Duan's 汪端 (1793–1839) *Yuan Ming yishi* 元明遺史 and Gu Chun's 顧春 (1799–1876?) *Hongloumeng ying* 紅樓夢影. For a study of women's fictional writing, and the vernacular novel in particular, see Widmer, *The Beauty and the Book*, 181–248.

HTTPS://DOI.ORG/10.1163/9789004693357-008

Reincarnation circulated in the form of hand-copied manuscripts until it was edited and published in 1821. But it enjoyed great popularity even while it was still being written.[3] Its author, Chen Duansheng 陳端生 (1751–1796), a native of Hangzhou, came from a scholar-official family. She began to write *Karmic Bonds of Reincarnation* in 1768 in Beijing, where her father held an official position. In 1769, she moved, along with her father, to Dengzhou in Shandong province, where she continued to write and finished sixteen of the work's *juan* (volumes). After she got married, she did not resume her writing until the spring of 1784, when she finished the seventeenth *juan*. But after that she never took up her story again.

Presenting her story as a sequel to another *tanci* work, *The Jade Bracelet* (*Yuchuan yuan* 玉釧緣), Chen Duansheng starts her narrative by having the protagonists from that work reborn as her hero and heroines in order to fulfill their unfulfilled desires and destinies.[4] The story of *Karmic Bonds of Reincarnation* is set during the reign of Emperor Chengzong 成宗 of the Yuan dynasty (r. 1294–1307). The beautiful and talented heroine, Meng Lijun 孟麗君, is the daughter of a high government official, who returns to his hometown of Kunming 昆明 to carry out the prescribed period of mourning for a deceased parent. Both Huangfu Shaohua 皇甫少華, the son of a military commander, and Liu Kuibi 劉奎璧, the emperor's brother-in-law, ask to marry Meng Lijun. Lijun's father finally decides to marry her to Huangfu Shaohua, who wins an archery contest with Liu Kuibi. Su Yingxue 蘇映雪, Lijun's handmaiden and companion, secretly watches the contest and falls in love with Shaohua. Filled with resentment, Liu Kuibi traps Shaohua and tries to burn him to death. But his sister, Liu Yanyu 劉燕玉, helps Shaohua escape from the garden, and after that they become secretly engaged. Liu Kuibi then persuades his father to frame the Huangfu family for treason, and then manages to get the emperor's

3 The earliest extant printed edition is the Baoren tang 寶仁堂 edition of 1822. For more on Chen's biographical accounts and the textual history of *Karmic Bonds of Reincarnation*, see Chen Yinke 陳寅恪, *Lun Zaisheng yuan* 論再生緣 (Hong Kong: Youlian chubanshe, 1959); Toyoko Yoshida Chen, "Women in Confucian Society – a Study of Three T'an-tz'u Narratives" (PhD dissertation, Columbia University, 1974); Marina Hsiu-wen Sung, "The Narrative Art of Tsai-sheng-yuan – a Feminist Vision in Traditional Confucian Society" (PhD dissertation, University of Wisconsin–Madison, 1988). All references to this *tanci* work are from Chen Duansheng 陳端生, *Zaisheng yuan* 再生緣 (Beijing: Huaxia chubanshe, 2000), from which all translations are my own unless otherwise noted. This edition is based on the Sanyi tang 三益堂 edition of 1850, which appears to be a reprint of the Baoren tang edition of 1822.

4 For a summary of the contents of *The Jade Bracelet*, see Tan Zhengbi 譚正璧 and Tan Xun 譚循, *Tanci xulu* 彈詞敘録 (Shanghai: Shanghai guji chubanshe, 1981), 132–34; translated in Wilt L. Idema and Beata Grant, *The Red Brush: Writing Women of Imperial China* (Cambridge, MA: Harvard University Press, 2004), 735–37.

approval of his marriage to Meng Lijun. The unwilling Lijun dresses herself as a man and flees. To avoid imperial punishment, Yingxue agrees to marry Liu Kuibi in Lijun's place, but on the wedding night, she attempts to kill Liu Kuibi and ends up trying to commit suicide by jumping into the Kunming Lake. Fortunately, she is saved by Prime Minister Liang Jian 梁堅 and his wife, who adopt her as their daughter and bring her along to the capital. At the same time, Meng Lijun, under the name of Li Junyu 酈君玉, goes to the capital, passes all examinations at the head of the list, and marries the prime minister's adopted daughter, who turns out to be none other than her former servant Su Yingxue. Afterwards, Lijun quickly attains the highest rank in the bureaucracy, and is ordered to supervise the military examinations, in which Huangfu Shaohua wins first place. In a few battles against Korean invaders, Shaohua achieves great feats and restores the fame and power of the Huangfu family. But Meng Lijun still tries her best to maintain her male identity, until Huangfu Zhanghua 皇甫長華, on behalf of her younger brother Shaohua, devises a plot to get Lijun drunk and take off her shoes so that her bound "lotus" feet are revealed. Once the Yuan emperor discovers this fact, he visits Lijun on a stormy day, and says that he will forgive her only if she becomes a royal consort. Meng Lijun refuses him, and falls into profound despair, spitting up blood.[5]

Chen Duansheng's story stops here. She wrote the first seventeen *juan*, but it was left to another woman writer, Liang Desheng 梁德繩 (1771–1847), to finish the work with a conventional conclusion: the empress dowager issues an edict pardoning Lijun and adopting her as a daughter, and orders Lijun and Shaohua to consummate their marriage; Yingxue is married to Shaohua as well. Liang shifts the focus of the narrative from the heroine's self-questing and internal process to the importance of chastity, filial piety, and patriarchal lineage, although she tries to "put herself in Chen's shoes" (*sheshen chushi* 設身處世) and lets Meng Lijun continue to express her regret (over her return to a female identity).[6] Chen stopped writing in 1784, twelve years before her death in 1796. She therefore had enough time to complete her work, yet, intriguingly, she suspended her ambitions as a writer, even as her readers pushed her to update and conclude the story. Some scholars suspect that the reason why Chen Duansheng did not succeed in finishing her work is that she could find

5 For a detailed plot summary of *Karmic Bonds of Reincarnation*, see Tan and Tan, *Tanci xulu*, 154–55; translated in Idema and Grant, *The Red Brush*, 737–39.

6 At the beginning of *juan* 18, Liang Desheng intimates that "[You] should know that it is a difficult matter to place oneself in the other's shoes; I tentatively continue the book to join in the fun" 須要知，設身處世為難事；我姑且，逢場作戲續餘音. See Chen, *Zaisheng yuan*, 1069.

no final resolution for her heroine or chose to intentionally leave her work open-ended.[7] Although, according to the available historical materials, it is hard to determine whether the inconclusive ending of Chen's work is intentional, there is a discontinuity between Meng Lijun's will and the possible ending Liang added, in which the cross-dressed heroine remains complicit with conventional norms of femininity.

As can be seen in the synopsis above, *Karmic Bonds of Reincarnation* seems to follow the basic plot design of the scholar-beauty romance, and yet it revises conventional romances through its elaborations of its heroine's pursuit of a public career. Women in male disguise are also common in scholar-beauty romances. However, this topos is neither psychologically elaborated, nor does it constitute the main plot.[8] In these male-authored stories, women usually cross-dress in order to meet the hero and test his literary talent, with a view to marrying him; or one of the heroines disguises herself as the hero, meets the other heroine, and in the end both heroines marry the hero.[9] Although the heroine's cross-dressing gives her a certain agency, her primary purpose is to obtain an ideal marriage. The cross-dressed heroine in these narratives comfortably accepts her return to the role of wife, without further display of the complications that gender transformation causes. By contrast, *Karmic Bonds of Reincarnation* allows the heroine to constantly defer, or refuse, the resumption her female identity, and thereby gradually shapes a woman's inner self in the process of narrative, by means of fantasy. At the same time, it delicately displays the heroine's internal process when she is forced to enter marriage and give up her public career. In this chapter, therefore, I will examine how Chen Duansheng presents the interiority of the cross-dressed Meng Lijun by revising the conventional tropes of romantic discourse, and how Meng Lijun and other women involved in the cross-dressing episodes both act upon their agency through social norms and encounter profound predicaments in the patriarchal society.

---

7 See Guo Moruo's comments and conjectures, in his article "Zaisheng yuan qian shiqi juan he ta de zuozhe Chen Duansheng" 〈再生緣〉前十七卷和它的作者陳端生, in *Guo Moruo gudian wenxue lunwen ji* 郭沫若古典文學論文集 (Shanghai: Shanghai guji chubanshe, 1985), 862–73; see also Qian Ma, *Feminist Utopian Discourse in Eighteenth-Century Chinese and English Fiction: A Cross-Cultural Comparison* (Burlington, VT: Ashgate, 2004), 51–52.

8 Siao-chen Hu discusses this issue in *Cainü cheye weimian*, 163.

9 The former case can be found in *Huatu yuan* 畫圖緣 (*The Affinity of a Map*) and *Baigui zhi* 白圭志 (*The Tale of the White Jade Tablet*); for the latter, see *Fenghuang chi* 鳳凰池 (*The Phoenix Pool*), *Lin'er bao* 麟兒報 (*The Son of Good Fortune*), and *Chun liuying* 春柳鶯 (*Spring Trochilus*).

1 The Tropes of Gardens and Self-Portraiture

During the Ming-Qing period garden culture gained real momentum, both in the practice of garden-building and the aesthetic construction of gardens.[10] In the Ming-Qing imaginary, gardens took shape around the dualities between inner and outer, containment and freedom, and possibilities and limitations. The garden is both connected to the house and self-sustained, and thus can become the "locus of privacy" through which to develop a certain freedom (from domestic decorum).[11] At the same time, the garden provides the potential for access to the outside, the space beyond the wall.[12] As previously discussed, the trope of the garden figured strongly in scholar-beauty drama and fiction, with *The Peony Pavilion* being the most prominent case. In these romantic stories, the garden functions either as a setting of courtly love, or as a site of social gatherings, in which literary men seem to create a fluid border region that traverses the private and public realms. Women's gardens in their *tanci* works also provide them with a space to free themselves from womanly duties and social disorder, and to construct a "locus of privacy," which suggests the possibility of liberation through its marginality.[13] In *Karmic Bonds of Reincarnation*, however, the garden not only serves as a metaphor for passionate love or transcendental possibilities, but more distinctively as the exit toward the public sphere, through which the heroine begins her journey of escape from her marriage and pursuit of a public career. While the Ming-Qing *caizi-jiaren* romances center on the progress toward the goal of a happy marriage, the role of the garden and its relationship with marriage is far more complicated in women's *tanci* works such as *Karmic Bonds of Reincarnation*.

---

10 See Craig Clunas, *Fruitful Sites: Garden Culture in Ming Dynasty China* (Durham, NC: Duke University Press, 1996), 91–103; Joanna F. Handlin Smith, "Gardens in Ch'i Piao-chia's Social World: Wealth and Values in Late Ming Kiangnan," *Journal of Asian Studies* 51 (1992): 55–81.

11 See Francesca Bray, "Decorum and Desire: An Archetectonics of Domestic Space in Late Imperial China," in Xiong Bingzhen 熊秉真 and Lü Miaofen 吕妙芬, eds., *Lijiao yu qingyu: Qian jindai Zhongguo wenhua zhong de hou/xiandianxing* 禮教与情慾：前近代中國文化中的後/現代性 (Taibei: Zhongyang yanjiuyuan jindaishi yanjiusuo, 1999), 21.

12 Andrew Plaks raises the concept of "bipolar complementarity" in describing the Chinese literary garden, see Plaks, *Archetype and Allegory*, 146–77; Keith McMahon further explores the cultural significance of garden and wall as the continuum of containment and openness, see McMahon, *Causality and Containment in Seventeenth-Century Chinese Fiction* (Leiden: Brill, 1988).

13 See Siao-chen Hu's analysis of two women's *tanci*, *Bi sheng hua* 筆生花 (*Flowers from a Brush*) and *Jinyu yuan* 金魚緣 (*Golden Fish Affinity*), in her insightful monograph *Cainü cheye bumian*, 193–203.

In *Karmic Bonds of Reincarnation*, Chen describes several unusual engagements that occur in the garden. One of them is the result of the archery contest between Shaohua and Kuibi, which is held in the garden of the Meng household. The heroine, Meng Lijun, is to be betrothed to the winner, Shaohua. Her engagement to Shaohua, won through a contest of military skill, is an unusual departure from love and marriages represented in conventional romances, which are based on displays of literary talent.[14] Yet, of more interest in this episode is that Su Yingxue falls in love with Shaohua after she watches the two young men competing from behind a curtain. That night, she has a love dream in which she is engaged to Shaohua. Referring to Du Liniang in *The Peony Pavilion* – "Apparently tonight the daughter of the Sus, again appears like Du Liniang" 分明今夕蘇家女，又似當年杜麗娘 – this scene is an obvious imitation of the "Interrupted Dream" scene of *The Peony Pavilion* (see Chapter 3).[15] Similarly, the dream demonstrates the power of desire. Although the amorous garden of *The Peony Pavilion* has been de-sexualized here – unlike Du Liniang, Su Yingxue does not have a sexual liaison with her lover in her dream – it also involves the secret meeting of lovers and Yingxue's determination to pursue her ideal man in the dream. In fact, just before that dream, she argues with her mother about her future marriage: "Who wants to marry a wealthy man, if [by doing so] they are fated to marry a stupid and vulgar man?" 誰人要嫁豪華子，哪個該婚愚俗男.[16] These lines make clear her fear of the "phoenix and crow" marriage arranged by her mother, and the fact that she would prefer her own choice to a bad arrangement.

Another engagement, which is made between Shaohua and Liu Yanyu, occurs by means of a dream as well, and happens in the garden. Yanyu dreams of her dead mother who tells her of Kuibi's scheme and orders her to save Shaohua who is trapped in the garden so that she can eventually marry him. She does exactly what her mother "tells" her to do and proposes herself to Shaohua. In the name of obedience to her late mother, she is engaged to her "dream" man, without the permission of her father. In this sense, this is a marriage of self-choice too. In fact, a later writer, Qiu Xinru 邱心如 (who lived in the first half of the nineteenth century), the author of *Flowers from a Brush* (*Bi sheng hua* 筆生花), aptly notes the subversive nature of this marriage when

---

14 This aspect of the plot possibly indicates that Chen Duansheng values military valor more than literary talent, and thus attributes remarkable military abilities to the hero and many other characters. But it is equally possible that she attempts to reserve literary talent, to which she might attach more importance, for her heroine, who passes all of the imperial examinations at the head of the list.

15 Chen, *Zaisheng yuan*, 30.

16 Ibid., 28.

she criticizes the idea behind this episode: "Liu Yanyu makes a private engagement against the three obediences, so why is the title of Chaste and Filial Lady conferred upon her? ... Moreover, can she be called virtuous when she marries without an arrangement?" 劉燕玉，終身似訂三從失，怎加封，節孝夫人褒美焉？…… 何況這，無媒而嫁豈稱賢?[17] Of course, behind this private engagement lies a more practical agenda: since she is the daughter of a concubine, the indifference of her legal mother (and probably her father, as well) propels her to worry all the more about her own future, that is, her marriage. The dream is, therefore, the transformation of her own desire and anxiety into form.

Insofar as these garden scenes point toward the attainment of true love and a happy marriage, their significance is not distinguishable from those in conventional romances. However, Chen Duansheng's concerns go beyond the affirmation of the respectability of love and the sanctity of marriage. Her use of the garden at times diverts from the goal of matrimony as she chooses other, more liberated ways to pursue the self than the conventional form of marriage. In this sense, *Karmic Bonds of Reincarnation* is actually an "anti-romance" fiction.

Karmic Bonds of Reincarnation's "anti-romantic" nature is represented by the author's rewriting of the garden from a place of trysts to a gate to the outer world, in which the heroine fulfills herself in ways that circumvent conventional norms. Refusing to obey the imperial order and her father's commands to marry Liu Kuibi, Lijun disguises herself as a man and runs away. The night before the wedding, she flees through the door of the garden for the capital, to take the imperial examinations.[18] It is from the garden that the heroine begins her journey of escape from her destiny of marriage and begins her search for self-fulfillment in the public sphere. The garden serves as an inner–outer continuum, a transitional sphere, through which she can step out of the domestic sphere in which she is fixed; it represents an imaginary exit to an alternative world and a free self. In fact, Du Liniang in *The Peony Pavilion* also experiences a process of entering the garden and then stepping out of it. When she discovers the garden and enters it, she rediscovers her self and begins to explore the limitations and possibilities of the self in highly dense language and melancholic gestures; when she steps out of the garden, she begins her journey of pursuing her dream through death and resurrection. As discussed earlier, her journey is also that of pursuing her life's ambition, to make her beauty and her self known to others. In this regard, Lijun's pursuit of self is a similar case; however,

17 Qiu Xinru, *Bi sheng hua*, 1.

18 See Chen, *Zaisheng yuan*, chap. 11. Moreover, it is also through the door of the garden that Liu Yanyu flees away from the marriage arranged by her legal mother.

while Liniang fulfills herself by obtaining a man worthy her beauty and talent, Lijun seeks to realize her talent in official life. Although both Liniang and Lijun are more interested in themselves than in the man, Lijun becomes a female subject, not through the fulfillment of romantic love, but through overcoming her desire for romantic love.

What is more noteworthy is that Meng Lijun paints a self-portrait before leaving home in disguise to sit for the imperial examination. Although she says the self-portrait is left to comfort her parents in the absence of their beloved daughter, we as readers can see beyond this to appreciate Meng Lijun's portrait as a powerful metaphor for female selfhood. A major theme in the rhetoric of Chinese portrait painting is that the portraitist should aim to capture the "true inner spirit" of the subject, as well as his or her physical likeness. Indeed, "transmitting the spirit" is a common term for portraiture. In Meng Lijun's case, this idea is fully dramatized in her creation of three different paintings before coming up with a sufficiently animated portrait of herself. While painting, Meng Lijun examines her own image in the mirror, disturbed by the idea that her "unequalled, unique beauty is so difficult to render." Her thoughts are expressed in the following lines:

仔细再观明镜内，	Carefully, I look into the bright mirror again.
真正是，无双绝世一多姣。	Indeed, I am a peerless, a unique beauty.
芳心不觉如刀绞，	My heart cannot help feeling like it's being cut by a knife –
欲写真容怎样描?	How should I paint my portrait?[19]

Although one could explain the painter's consternation as springing from dismay over the imminent separation from her parents, Meng Lijun's self-pity makes the situation more ambiguous. While finishing the second portrait, she sighs, "Meng Lijun, you have such a beautiful face, but why are you so ill-fated?" 咳，孟麗君呀孟麗君，我看如此容貌，何故這般薄命.[20] This immediately calls to mind the sentimental clichés of yearning for love. Yet, it also seems to suggest a more general, deeper sense of lack or absence. This is further illustrated by Meng Lijun's irritation at the portrait's failure to capture her character. Unable to find an appropriate way to represent her uniqueness, she asks herself repeatedly, "How can I portray myself?" She feels ambivalence and uncertainty as she struggles to achieve an intelligible and authentic form of self-representation. When the third portrait is finally produced, it

19 Chen, *Zaisheng yuan*, 150.
20 Chen, *Zaisheng yuan*, 151.

seems perfect – but perhaps too perfect for her to accept. Again, she doubts the painting's authenticity, and gains more confidence in it only upon receiving her maidservant's note of approval. The difference between the painting and its subject is repeatedly expressed. Moreover, she inscribes a poem on the portrait to record her resolution to adopt male attire. This scene, too, alludes to *The Peony Pavilion*, in which Du Liniang also draws three self-portraits and inscribes a poem on the last and best one.[21] For Du Liniang, the poem and the image together constitute a statement about attaining a husband worthy of her beauty. Yet in Meng Lijun's self-portrait, the poem is in fact a *negation* of the image: "I wish to replace the shell-shaped coil with black gauze hat" 愿教螺髻換烏紗.[22] It expresses the desire to achieve social accomplishments that can be accessed only through a male identity, rather than marriage to a worthy husband. This scene thus challenges the conventions established in *The Peony Pavilion*, particularly with regard to the standards by which the heroine desires to be recognized. By juxtaposing feminine beauty and its negation (through the desire for a male identity), Meng Lijun's portrait displays not only the desire for recognition, but also for transformation. It illustrates the gap between the social expectations placed on the heroine and what she wishes to be, thereby complicating gender roles. Du Liniang paints portraits to preserve her own feminine beauty, whereas for Meng Lijun, the portrait is a tender farewell to her feminine beauty and a representation of the ambiguity of her self-image and identity; Du's portrait still presents her as an object to be desired so that she is ultimately resurrected by her lover, while Meng's portrait, just like a commemorative portrait, merely laments and commemorates what no longer is.[23] In other words, Meng's image is at once a hindrance to her

---

21 In fact, *Karmic Bonds of Reincarnation* is part of a series of *tanci* works related to *The Peony Pavilion*. In *The Jade Bracelet*, some characters are closely related to those found in yet another piece, *Xiao jinqian* 小金錢 (*Little Gold Coins*). The heroine of *Xiao jinqian*, Liu Qingyun, is said to be a descendant of Liu Mengmei and Du Liniang, the hero and heroine of *The Peony Pavilion*. More significantly, there is a direct reference to Liu Qingyun in *Karmic Bonds of Reincarnation*. It is the examples of Liu Qingyun and Xie Yujuan (a female character in *The Jade Bracelet*), who disguise themselves as men, that inspires Meng Lijun to flee from home, also disguised as a man. See Tan Zhengbi 譚正璧, and Tan Xun 譚尋, "Tanci xiaoshuo suoshou Zaishengyuan de yingxiang" 彈詞小說所受再生緣的影響, in *Pingtan tongkao* 評彈通考 (Beijing: Zhongguo quyi chubanshe, 1985), 206–207.

22 Chen, *Zaisheng yuan*, 153.

23 Judith T. Zeitlin compares the different functions of "auto-effigy" (which, for example, Du Liniang paints) and "commemorative effigy." See Zeitlin, "Making the Invisible Visible: Portraits of Desire and Constructions of Death in Sixteenth and Seventeenth-Century

self-fulfillment and part of her self. In this sense, Meng Lijun both identifies with, and refuses to identify with, her female body.

Later, when Lijun's portrait falls into the hands of Shaohua and is hung in his study, he immediately becomes obsessed with it, talking to it aloud when no one else is present, expressing his longing for the lovely young woman. A similar scene can be found in *The Peony Pavilion* in a scene entitled "The Portrait Examined," in which the hero, Liu Mengmei, succeeds in summoning Du Liniang by continuously calling to her. However, in Shaohua's case the result of his amorous calling is mere frustration. Whereas Du Liniang (or at least her ghost) quickly responds to Liu Mengmei's summons and subsequently enters into a sexual liaison with him, Meng Lijun, in contrast, refuses to return to the domestic sphere and fulfill the romantic relationship. Furthermore, while Meng Lijun is pursuing her career as prime minister in the male world outside, Shaohua sits in his room longing for love. With this, the traditional image of an abandoned woman longing for a man in her chamber is turned upside down: Meng Lijun now takes the role of the one always absent (conventionally that of the man), and Shaohua takes on the role of the woman left behind to languish and sigh in her (now *his*) chamber. In this respect, the author clearly challenges those gender stereotypes that portrayed women as weaker and more easily overcome by emotion.

In fact, as in *The Peony Pavilion*, Meng Lijun's self-portrait can be seen as a means to externalize the unfulfilled desires harbored within the female body. Du Liniang's portrait functions to preserve her youthful beauty and repressed desire, such that she ultimately comes to life in response to male desire.[24] Nevertheless, Meng Lijun's portrait does not reply to male desire, but conveys the ambiguity of her desire, as well as the uncertainty of the gender roles she performs – "a mode of passage between genders," to use Judith Butler's term.[25] Meng Lijun's portrait demonstrates that neither desire nor the self can be fully regulated by social and gender norms. In Lijun's portrayal of her own self-image, the act of cross-dressing disrupts the primacy of the body as the locus of identity and transcends the prevailing notions of masculine and feminine. This is further illustrated by the fact that *Karmic Bonds of Reincarnation* evokes a kind of eroticism in which gender is rendered a floating performance.

At various points in *Karmic Bonds of Reincarnation*, the act of cross-dressing accompanies sexually equivocal scenes and transgressions of propriety. Meng

---

China," in *Crossing Boundaries, Attending to Early Modern Women*, ed. Jane Donawerth and Adele Seeff (Newark: University of Delaware Press, 2000), 57–60.

24 Ibid., 48–79.

25 Butler, *Undoing Gender*, 43.

Lijun's simultaneously masculine and feminine features win her admiration from both genders. The very ambiguity of these scenes, with both a seemingly innocuous side and a more transgressive side, creates room for the author to manipulate the question of propriety. Because the disguise is apparent to the reader, the cross-dressed heroine's flirtations with her/his "lovers" can be disavowed as unrealistic. Hence, the text's light treatment of sexual innuendoes and other transgressions of propriety are saved from being offensive. Beyond what the reader sees, however, is what the characters do and how the author portrays their perceptions of each other. In this context the challenge to social morality seems more fraught.

After all, the cross-dressed Meng Lijun is loved by both a woman and a man. Disguised as a man, Meng Lijun sets off to take the imperial examinations. On her way to the capital, she meets an old man at an inn. The old man, named Kang, likes her very much and adopts her as his foster son. In a later scene, Kang's concubines, Rouniang 柔娘 and Dejie 德姐, who fall in love with the cross-dressed Meng Lijun at first sight, try to seduce Lijun. By referring to the story of Hongfu 紅拂 and Li Jing 李靖, in which a courtesan discerns a young man's talent and elopes with him, Dejie suggests the possibility of adultery:[26]

贱妾痴心慕相公，	Foolishly, I am infatuated with you;
可怜思念梦魂中。	Alas, I yearn and long for you in my dreams.
[...]	
倘若郎君心不弃，	Perhaps you will not reject me,
可图良会一宵中。	We can plan a rendezvous one night.
虽然不敢私奔想，	Although I dare not hope for marriage,
片刻相亲也遂胸。	A single moment of intimacy would satisfy me.[27]

Although Meng Lijun refuses her (and Rouniang) in a mild and polite way, she seems to sympathize with their romantic feelings:

柔娘德姐两佳人，	Rouniang and Dejie, two beautiful ladies,
如此多情有我心。	Treat me with such affection.
几度流连真爱慕，	With no thought of leaving, they truly admire me,
十分关切果相亲。	Care for me and love me.
奴家若是真男子，	If I really were a man,
未必其间不动心。	I might not remain unmoved.

26 The story of Hongfu and Li Jing is told in the Tang tale "Qiuran ke zhuan" 虬髯客傳 (The Story of a Man with Curly Whiskers), in Lu, *Tang Song chuanqi ji*, 264–74.

27 Chen, *Zaisheng yuan*, 195.

见我几时情已乱，	They've only just met me, their feelings are confused:
风流阵里欲消魂。	In the array of romance their souls are almost dissolved.
可怜辜负佳人意，	Alas, I must disappoint these beauties,
好叫我，要作情时难作情。	They put me in a situation where even if I want to be kind, I cannot be kind.[28]

Here, both the cross-dressed heroine and her female admirers transgress social norms. While the original tale of Hongfu and Li Jing focuses on a courtesan's recognition of a young man's talent and the hero's subsequent achievements, the story is employed here for amorous dialogue. The female admirer makes her desire shamelessly explicit, and thus openly violates codes of feminine behavior. It seems that the author does not insist on chastity in all cases, although the heroine's chastity is actually the motivation for her disguise. The two concubines behave in a much bolder manner than what would be allowed by social propriety if the woman they loved were actually male. Yet these passions are experienced by the female characters as real within the context of the story, and could also be experienced as such by the reader.

Moreover, the relationship between the heroine and her female admirer makes the story even more transgressive, because the heroine is her female admirer's foster "son." Yet this major transgression, the symbolic incest, is treated very lightly. While the "shameless" conduct of the female admirer openly violates the dictates of familial hierarchies and conventional morality, this kind of conduct seems understandable to the heroine as well as the author. Chen Duansheng describes these shameless women in a comic, but not negative, way. This very light treatment of what would be a major contravention of the marital and familial order distorts hierarchical norms in a safe, but provocative way.[29]

Chapters 51 and 52 feature a romantic flirtation between the heroine and her male admirer, the emperor. Again, Chen Duansheng treats conventional eroticism playfully and lightly. In these two chapters, because Meng Lijun's fiancé,

28 Ibid., 195–96.

29 Andrew Plaks discusses how the problems of conjugal and filial relations, which abound in some Ming-Qing novels, such as *Jin Ping Mei* and *Xingshi yinyuan zhuan* 醒世姻緣傳 (*Marriage as Retribution Awakening the World*), break down Confucian familial hierarchies, and further how this disarray of human relations at the family level links to the corresponding collapse of the entire macrocosm. See Plaks, "After the Fall: Hsing-Shih Yin-Yüan Chuan and the Seventeenth-Century Chinese Novel," *Harvard Journal of Asiatic Studies* 45, no. 2: 543–80.

Huangfu Shaohua, has reported her real identity to the court, the emperor begins to suspect that his prime minister is a woman, although he defends Lijun in front of other officials. Later, the emperor invites Lijun to visit the imperial garden. There he flirts with her, spilling dew from the willow branches onto her lotus-flower-like face while she is passing beneath the trees. During their visit in the garden, the emperor and his minister exchange poetry, suggesting comparable talent and companionate love. Their poems contain many sexual references, including several alluding to stories of Concubine Yang and Emperor Ming of the Tang dynasty.[30] In the narrative, the heroine does not express her sexual or romantic desires too explicitly – and in this respect she plays by the rules of female propriety. By contrast, these poems illuminate the heroine's subjective experience of romance with great frankness, and without any anxiety about maintaining her moral purity. Such adoption of erotic allusions and sexual frankness not only grants the heroine a certain degree of agency, but also demonstrates the woman author's power to disrupt literary conventions.

More interestingly, these highly flirtatious scenes do not happen between the heroine and her fiancé, but rather between Lijun and a potential lover. As a result, Lijun's social identity as loyal wife, which should have become fixed as a result of her engagement to Shaohua, is rendered unstable and fluid. In addition, because Lijun insists on being a man and the emperor does not openly challenge him/her, the romantic banter is possibly homoerotic as well.[31] Here, desire is not fully determined. As Butler has observed, sexuality "emerges precisely as an improvisational possibility within a field of constraints."[32]

In the end, Lijun refuses the emperor's erotic request. Thus, the classical romantic story of Concubine Yang and Emperor Ming is revised and negated. This love scene is doomed to end in failure on two counts. First of all, the chaste heroine of *tanci* works has to shun premarital sex, particularly with a man other than her fiancé. Usually, in such a case, suicide would be the only dignified way for a heroine to extricate herself from this situation. Yet Lijun chooses a more ingenious escape: "Anyone else would not be able to escape this right now. The pure and virtuous could not but decide to commit suicide;

30 Chen, *Zaisheng yuan*, 784.

31 This issue is rendered even more manifest in the Yue theater version of this story. *Karmic Bonds of Reincarnation* constitutes a significant piece in the Yue opera repertoire. In Yue opera, women play all roles. Because the emperor is thus played by a woman, his desire for Lijun may be seen as same-sex as well as opposite-sex staging. See Jin Jiang, *Women Playing Men: Yue Opera and Social Change in Twentieth-Century Shanghai* (Seattle: University of Washington Press), 100–102.

32 Butler, *Undoing Gender*, 15.

the fickle and lascivious would merely give in to the emperor and accept his favors. As for me, I still have a plan to extricate myself, and so I am unlikely to be reduced to the helplessness of either type" 若是別個呢，此刻是脫不過的了，無非玉潔冰清者執意尋死，楊花水性者侍御承恩。至於我酈明堂是還有個脫身之計，不致到這等無能.[33] Here, the heroine resists two major patriarchal discourses about women (suicide and submission), and attempts to find a third way instead, a way to survive in a male society as a man despite being a woman. He/she sternly criticizes the emperor's frivolous attitude toward his prime minister and threatens resignation. He/she claims that, if he/she "shares the bed with him in the imperial garden tonight, people will definitely say that he/she must have obtained all of his/her prestige and power by coquettish charms" 今宵禁御同床榻，一定說，貴顯都從狐媚來.[34] In other words, her need to refuse the emperor is compounded by her desire to protect her female identity from being revealed, and to secure her fame as prime minister. Thus, her seemingly virtuous act of maintaining her chastity illuminates the tension between being physically female and socially male. Indeed, her "masculine" speech and behavior further confuses the emperor: "Wait! Judging from her/his words and facial expression, he/she does not seem a woman."[35] The emperor assumes he can master her sexually, yet she refuses his sexual advances because she wants to be treated as a competent prime minister above all. This conflict is reinforced in the moment when she finally reveals her "true identity." When the emperor finally ascertains that his prime minister is in fact a woman in Chapter 65, he schemes to make her his consort, but Lijun again refuses him. Her refusal demonstrates her desire for independence. In this way, Chen Duansheng rewrites the story of a woman's destiny.

Through the creation of erotic scenes that transcend the binary of masculine and feminine, *Karmic Bonds of Reincarnation* opens up new possibilities. The female can be readily signified by what is both masculine and feminine, as can the male. Although the heroine of *Karmic Bonds of Reincarnation* initially claims that she has taken on a male identity in defense of her betrothal to Shaohua, the story at times infringes upon sexual taboos, and highlights the heroine's refusal to wed. The discourse of chastity is employed in *Karmic Bonds of Reincarnation* as a means of rejecting authority (orders from the emperor or parents, for example) and of acquiring independence from men. Moreover, Meng Lijun's romantic dialogue with both Dejie and the emperor complicates her claim of chastity and her lawful marriage (with Shaohua), here symbolizing

33 Chen, *Zaisheng yuan*, 785.

34 Ibid., 787.

35 Ibid., 787.

stable (feminine) gender identity within the conventional familial order. In a playful mode, these "unfeminine" scenes problematize the familial order and gender hierarchy.

2 Interiority: the Long-Delayed Moment of Disclosure

Most male-authored texts featuring cross-dressed heroines, such as scholar-beauty novels, greet the revelation of the heroine's true identity with shock and wonder. In these texts, the heroine passes from one certainty to another (male to female), without presenting her inner reflections while disguised or upon the return to her female identity. By contrast, women authors tend to give voice to their heroines' inner thoughts. Gender reversal provides a convenient vehicle for expressing their social ambitions and desire for male privilege, which can ultimately lead to involvement in the political realm. In *Karmic Bonds of Reincarnation*, the act of cross-dressing not only helps to illuminate, but also to construct, the interior being of its female characters. After Meng Lijun adopts male attire, the act of cross-dressing gradually alters and affects her mind to the extent that she is reluctant to go back to her female identity. Before the narrative reaches the moment of disclosure, Lijun experiences a process of identity crisis. It is represented not an easy switch from one certainty to another – from male to female, or from outer (*wai*) to inner (*nei*) – but in terms of a chronicle of her fluctuating attitudes and emotions, the dramatization of her identity crisis, and the shaping of her sense of self.

At first, Meng Lijun justifies her cross-dressing as a means of maintaining her chastity while helping Huangfu Shaohua restore his family's reputation. While she constantly defers revealing her female identity, she also repeatedly employs the rhetoric of female virtue and wifely duty, and suggests that Su Yingxue, her fake wife, marry Shaohua, too. However, after Lijun is made Minister of War, she gradually questions her destiny of marrying Shaohua and resuming the conventional role of woman. She says to herself:

今朝复任尚書位，	Today, I have also been made President of the Board,
也算得，	Thus,
世上裙钗第一人。	I can be counted as Number One of all the women in the world.
何須洞房花燭夜，	What need do I have for a night of wedding candles in a bridal chamber?
安心且做幾年官。	At ease, I will serve as an official for a couple of years.

九重丹陛皇恩重，	On the red steps of the palace, I have received imperial favor,
做一個，	So, I will be a
赤膽忠心保國臣。	Loyal guardian of the state.[36]

Here, Lijun reforms her wifely duties into official duties, even though she qualifies it with a claim that this move will be "temporary." When she gets more involved in her new role, she expresses her wish to remain male even more emphatically, as is shown in a private conversation with her "wife," Su Yingxue: "If you ask about my intentions, I somehow do not want to marry into the Huangfu family" 若言我意如何樣，卻有些，不欲于歸皇甫門.[37]

When Meng Lijun becomes prime minister, she is more determined than ever to keep the male role, enjoying the freedom from the restrictions placed on women. In Chapter 43, Lijun expresses her social ambitions, and argues that she has a capacity to perform this (male) social role and to support herself. In this chapter, Lijun's brother runs into her maidservant, Ronglan, in her residence (the residence of the prime minister), and he begins to cast doubts on Lijun's true identity. By asking Lijun to go to the Meng house and see Mrs. Meng who has fallen ill out of longing for her daughter, he schemes to force Lijun to reveal her identity at home. Indeed, when Mrs. Meng pretends to pass out, Lijun is so worried that she reveals her identity to her mother and other family members. When she does so, however, she asks them to keep this matter a secret, and argues:

為什麼，	So why insist
定要复姓配皇甫？	On my taking back my surname and marrying Huangfu Shaohua?
麗君雖則是裙釵，	I may be a girl in skirts, her hair fastened down with pins,
現在而今立赤階。	But at this moment I stand before the steps of the throne!
[...]	
何須必要歸夫婿，	Why should it be so urgent that I marry a husband?
就是這，	Why should I care
正室王妃豈我懷？	For the title and rank of a prince's main wife, a royal consort?
況有那，	what is more,

36 Chen, *Zaisheng yuan*, 302.
37 Ibid., 343.

宰臣官俸嵬嵬在，	The official salary of a prime minister is as high as the sky,
自身可養自身來。	I am fully capable of taking care of myself![38]

Lijun does not consider the position of official wife as the most valuable – she refuses to be recognized in this way, and instead pursues her ambitions for a more independent role, thereby demonstrating the autonomous existence that her *wai* identity grants to her. Her social position becomes primary, and hence she would rather not marry, since marriage would require a complete retreat to the domestic sphere. At this point, she brings forth the issue of self-support. Her argument suggests that employment and financial independence are important means to individual autonomy. Rather than agreeing that it is a woman's nature and incapacity that determine her subordinate position, she calls attention to the economic reasons for this condition, and thus exposes the injustice that the patriarchal society does to women by making them financially subordinate to men. This is unusual as the theme of self-support is rarely put forward in literary accounts of cross-dressing from the Ming-Qing period. Wider issues of freedom and social privilege seem more important to Chen Duansheng and her heroine Meng Lijun.[39]

Karmic Bonds of Reincarnation offers an extensive account of Meng Lijun's struggle over whether to reveal her true identity, or whether to retreat from the realm of *wai* and return to the *nei* sphere. During this process, Lijun is torn by the conflicts produced by her various identities and the *nei/wai* distinction, and between her private desires and public ambition. Later on, although Lijun urges her family to keep her identity secret, her mother is so happy that she tells the truth to Lijun's wet-nurse, who now resides in the Huangfu household. The news eventually passes to the Huangfu family, and Shaohua then reports the prime minister's true identity to the emperor. But Lijun denies these reports at court by telling the emperor that she disguised herself as Meng Lijun in the Meng house merely to console Lijun's mother who is terribly ill. When Lijun's parents are summoned to the court, she denounces them for asserting that she is their daughter. Moreover, she expresses her "anger" to the emperor by threatening to resign, causing the emperor to scold and punish Lijun's parents. After being reprimanded by the emperor for identifying the prime minister (known publicly as Li Junyu) as her real daughter, Meng Lijun's

38 Ibid., 664; translated in Idema and Grant, *The Red Brush*, 747–48.

39 Economic self-sufficiency becomes a major issue in the writings of the feminist Qiu Jin 秋瑾 (1875–1907), some of which is translated into English in Idema and Grant, *The Red Brush*, 767–808.

mother's already poor health worsens. Although Meng Lijun uses her power as prime minister to prevent her parents from questioning her identity, she does not escape a guilty conscience over this. She thinks to herself, "Li Junyu, shame on you – smart, talented person that you are, but look what an unfilial daughter you've become" 酈明堂啊酈明堂，可嗔爾聰明蓋世的才人，倒做了世間的逆女 and "Others repay their parents for their kindness, I alone do not do so with all my heart" 別人多報劬勞德，惟有我，未盡心來未盡腸.[40]

Moreover, Shaohua falls ill too, out of distress over the emperor's order that he marry an impostor, Xiang Nanjin, within three months. Still suspecting that the prime minister is actually Meng Lijun in disguise, he asks the prime minister to visit him with the ulterior motive of revealing her true identity. When Lijun arrives to find him in such a state of poor health and fatigue, she is moved by his strong affection for her and suddenly feels very sad: "Like the floods of autumn, her tears are about to flow forth. Like the spring mountain full of tenderness and love, she is heartbroken. Pale of countenance and sad of mind, even she, this hard-hearted person, is deeply touched" 秋水盈盈將淚下，春山脈脈已心傷。容慘淡，意凄惶，感到情疏鐵石腸.[41] In fact, Lijun experiences a real inner struggle over whether or not she should marry Shaohua. She thinks to herself, "Besides, Zhitian [the courtesy name of Shaohua] is neither heartless nor faithless. ... It is fine to acknowledge my relationship to him. However, how could a teacher marry a student?" 芝田況且非無義 …… 要認也可將就認，然而我，老師怎樣嫁門生.[42] Since Meng Lijun served as the chief examiner for the examination in which Huangfu Shaohua passed, she repeatedly mentions the impossibility of combining two contradictory hierarchical relations: that of teacher/student and husband/wife. Here, we see Lijun taking advantage of her identity as a teacher to refuse her identity as a wife, just as she uses her status as prime minister to refuse her role as a daughter. She cleverly uses these conflicting hierarchical relationships to defend her act of maintaining the male role. In the meantime, however, her deeply felt dilemma is also embodied in the contradiction between these identities. She can be either a teacher or a wife, either the prime minister or a daughter; she cannot be both at the same time. As Butler has perceptively pointed out, an identity is "neither fatally determined nor fully artificial and arbitrary."[43] On the one hand, Lijun

40 Chen, *Zaisheng yuan*, 829–30.

41 Ibid., 883.

42 Ibid., 829.

43 See Butler, *Gender Trouble*, 187. Butler's criticism of established identity categories primarily concerns the construction of heterosexual desire. However, in imperial China, family serves as a more important site of gender production than heterosexuality. In this

sincerely feels apologetic as a daughter and sympathetic toward Shaohua; on the other, her social aspirations propel her desire for an expansion of her gender roles into the *wai* sphere. However, the segregation of the sexes deprives her of a legitimate access to full personhood in both the *nei* and *wai* spheres, both the familial as well as the political realm. Hence, she has to adopt a *wai* identity and give up her old female roles of daughter and wife. The gender distinction and other social hierarchies determine that Lijun cannot be a person who is both filial and proper while also fulfilling her social aspirations.[44] So, although barely managing to restrain herself, she is, in the end, determined to retain her male identity, particularly after she discovers that both her parents and her fiancé have attempted to reveal her true identity. Here, the display of Lijun's inner conflict reflects the tension that exists between her actions and her feelings, and between female selfhood and social conventions, indicating the "category crisis," to use Marjorie Garber's term.[45]

This conflict of *nei/wai* identities culminates in the ultimate revelation of the heroine's disguise. Towards the end of the story, Meng Lijun's shoes are removed while she is drunk, and her secret is revealed. Upon awakening to find one of her shoes gone, she is so mortified that she spits up blood. Here, we find one of the most moving passages in the entire work, representing her inner state:

錦邊綾襪一拉開，	Once her silk socks with brocade edges are taken off,
腳帶紛紛散下來。	Cloths for foot-binding fall down in profusion.
拉盡白綾觀仔細，	Pulling down the white cloth and looking carefully,
只剩下,	She finds out that what is left is
一雙睡鞋實实奇哉	only a pair of sleep shoes – how strange.
[...]	
癡呆呆，	Becoming dull,
一体四肢如土木；	Her body and limbs are like earth and wood;
渺茫茫，	Remote and indistinct,

respect, see Tani E. Barlow, "Theorizing 'Women,'" in *The Question of Women in Chinese Feminism* (Durham, NC: Duke University Press, 2004), 253–89.

44 Rosenlee also points out this kind of predicament embedded in the *nei/wai* distinction when she discusses the problematic nature of female literacy and its effect on learned women in traditional China. See Li-Hsiang Lisa Rosenlee, *Confucianism and Women: A Philosophical Interpretation* (New York: SUNY Press, 2006), 110–17.

45 Marjorie Garber, *Vested Interests: Cross-Dressing and Cultural Anxiety* (London: Routledge, 2002), 16.

三魂七魄赴泉臺。	Her soul goes to the underworld.[46]
真個是，	Indeed,
如癡如醉亂了懷。	Her mind is in disarray, as if drunk.
叠着脚，	Putting one foot on top of the other,
錦襪烏靴都撇下；	She takes off the silk stockings and black boot;
低着頭，	Hanging her head,
明眸秋水不能檯。	She cannot raise her bright eyes, which are like autumn water.
恨一聲，	She curses –
無言無語情愈急；	Silent, she is more worried;
嘆口氣，	She sighs –
含怒含愁意轉哀。	Angry and anxious, she becomes sad.
頃刻間，	Instantly,
繚亂千端無可理；	She cannot compel the ten thousand strands of ideas into order.
纏縈萬緒力難排。	Her mind is in a tangle of a thousand strands;
心神一動傷心血，	Her mind and heart have been hit, and bleeding.
櫻口中，	From her cherry lips,
幾點鮮血噴出來。	A few drops of blood spill out.
[...]	
只見那，	[Su Yingxue] only sees
白綾脚帶散床前，	The white silk for foot-binding scatter in front of the bed,
上沾着，	And on them
滴滴鮮紅一口血。	the scattered drops of a mouthful of red blood.[47]

Meng Lijun's bound feet turn out to be the ultimate obstacle to the maintenance of her disguise, and eventually serve to disclose her true identity. In this sense, her bound feet become alien to her, a dichotomy highlighted in the striking contrast between the white silk and red blood.[48] In male-authored cross-dressing

46 This line does not mean that she literally dies, but rather depicts her state of being in a daze.

47 Chen, *Zaisheng yuan*, 1035–36.

48 Chen Duansheng's attitude toward bound feet is ambiguous. When she describes the empress's attendants' discovery of Lijun's bound feet, the bound feet are eulogized with an exclamation of wonder. Based on this, some scholars claim that Chen Duansheng identifies with men's erotic objectification of women and internalizes the virtues expected of a woman; see Zhao Yongbing 趙永冰, "Daizhe jiaoliao de shengming zhi wu – cong 'Zaisheng yuan' kan chuantong Zhongguo nüxing xiezuo de kunjing" 戴著腳鐐的生命之舞——從《再生緣》看傳統中國女性寫作的困境, 244–56. Admittedly, it is hard

texts the revelation of the heroine's true identity usually produces a variety of comic effects. In many scholar-beauty romances, the heroine's identity is revealed as part of a wedding scene. But here, the moment of revelation seems like the act of deflowering, an act of violence to the heroine's inner self as well as to her body. The frequent use of initial three-syllable phrases here – such as "*chi dai dai*" (becoming dull), "*miao mang mang*" (remote and indistinct), "*zhen ge shi*" (indeed), etc. – also creates a tense tempo, reflecting Lijun's agitated state of mind.[49] Moreover, because of the uncertainty of personal pronouns in Chinese lyrics, this passage can be read either as a third-person narration, or as a more powerful first-person expression of Lijun's anger and despair.

Meng Lijun is so obsessed with her public achievements and her social position that she curses Shaohua for his insistence on marrying her. In more conventional male-authored texts, love and marriage serve to reinstate gender distinctions and demonstrate the woman's ultimate subordination as she gives up the privileges of male identity for the sequestered life of a wife. But Meng Lijun, who makes every effort to maintain her/his agency and autonomy, and to control her/his own fate, curses the hero for his love: "Pushing me so hard, you let me have no choice but expose my original identity" 終日逼生和逼死，逼得我，今朝務欲現原身.[50] This denunciation points not only towards her husband-to-be, but also the wider social forces that have driven her to despair. This vivid expression of her sense of coercion endows the work with the force of tragedy.

In the Chinese medical imagination, vomiting of blood derives from the disorders of emotional influence, an etiology of stasis that is identified with anger and congestion.[51] Thus, the destabilization of blood in the revelation scene above is simultaneously a bodily manifestation of all the restless

---

to judge Chen's actual attitude. To some extent, there is possibly an internalization of the social values imposed on bound feet present in the text. But of particular importance is that, from the perspective of the narrative, the admiration of the bound feet is presented from the attendants' point of view, while Meng Lijun's own observation of her bound feet, which causes the final discovery of her female identity, conveys a sense of sorrow and despair.

49 It is hard to convey the use of three-syllable phrases in English translation.

50 Chen, *Zaisheng yuan*, 1039.

51 According to Charlotte Furth, traditional Chinese *fuke* 婦科 deemed blood the leading factor that led to women's internal illnesses, and developed the thought that fire and emotion played a critical role in congested *yin* 陰 blood. She cites the comments of Zhang Gao 張杲, a Song medical thinker, on women's illness, "In treating the disorders of women, if you can both treat their longings and desires and ease their worries, not one will fail to be healed." See Charlotte Furth, *A Flourishing Yin: Gender in China's Medical History, 960–1665* (Berkeley: University of California Press, 1999), 88.

cravings of the heroine's desiring self. The tragedy represented in *Karmic Bonds of Reincarnation* lies in the fact that the heroine's inner reality established in the process of cross-dressing conflicts with social reality; she pursues a more autonomous identity than society has allowed her. If we say that the female-to-male transvestitism produces the resulting vision of bodily androgyny and thus secured the balancing of blood within the body, then the "gender reveal" resulting from the exposure of her bound feet signifies a disorder marked by blood expulsion, leading to a body out of balance. As such, Lijun's body becomes a site where conflicting ideas of identity are contested – her inner self is based on a malleable androgyny and claim for a common humanity while her social gender is predicated on fixed hierarchy.

Such a conflict is further reflected in the heroine's encounter with the emperor. When the emperor, who is already aware of Lijun's true identity and has kept this secret, comes to see Meng Lijun during a storm, he offers the only way to save Lijun's life – that is, to make her his concubine. Furthermore, he warns her that, as an imperial concubine, she can no longer behave independently, as if she were still the prime minister. He also orders Suhua/Yingxue to marry him along with Lijun, which makes Lijun even more disappointed. The emperor's solution suggests a total retreat to the domestic sphere and conformity to the patriarchal hierarchy. Thus, stating her willingness to die, Lijun refuses the emperor calmly and resolutely, thereby demonstrating her resistance to the violence of power (both male power and imperial power). If we assume that Lijun had romantic feelings for the emperor in the imperial park, and thus he is a potential lover to her, then at this moment the lovers' encounter becomes a contest between two radically different ideologies – the heroine's pursuit of an autonomous personhood and the treatment of the heroine as a desired object – which ends in Lijun's wrath and despair, as well as their estrangement.

The thoughtful exploration of the heroine's psychological life in *Karmic Bonds of Reincarnation* exposes the internal contradiction that exists among her multiple identities as official, teacher (of Shaohua), and woman (lover, wife, and daughter). For Meng Lijun, these three roles are in conflict with one another, since they belong to the different spheres of *nei* and *wai*. The inner and outer spheres establish the boundaries of gender by shaping the divisions of space and labor as the foundation of social life, thereby denoting the gendered moral precepts and hegemonic social norms. In deciding to maintain her male role, therefore, Lijun transgresses the moral framework of the conventional cross-dressing narrative's fictional world. In *Karmic Bonds of Reincarnation*, the practice of cross-dressing actually enables the heroine to fashion her sense of self, and to identify with her *wai* identity. Instead of recognizing her male role as artificial and imposed, she seeks to adopt it permanently as her own, since the concealment with a male persona is the only means of legitimizing her desire for agency. Although Lijun takes the male disguise, however, she does not adopt a completely male stance, and therefore retains a female selfhood that interacts with and reflects on the *nei/wai* distinction and the conflicts between public ambition and domestic concerns. *Karmic Bonds of Reincarnation* thereby exposes the tragic plight of a woman within the patriarchal system. As expressed in Chapter 67, when Lijun's female identity is revealed, she feels that "from all directions, the dark clouds surge up layer upon layer" 四面的，層層陰雲湧起來.[52] The "darkness" contained in the work lies in the heroine's repeated introspection, and her quest for self-fulfillment. In this sense, the moment of spitting blood not only expresses anger, shock, disappointment, and hurt concerning the disclosure of her gender, but also exhibits the heroine's forceful longings for a plurality of identity grounded on an androgynous mind, and functions as a symbol of the complex agency of women. As a language of power in Chinese medicine and ritual, blood speaks of women's bodily stigma and thus the gendered relations of hierarchy in the body.[53] For Meng Lijun, however, the spitting of blood is instead presented as the power of pollution and a vehement claim for transmutation.

3 A Collective Fantasy Centered on Process

By providing a window into the inner thoughts of the cross-dressed heroine, *Karmic Bonds of Reincarnation* rewrites the ideological meaning, as well as the narrative conventions, associated with cross-dressing in Ming-Qing fiction and drama. For women *tanci* authors such as Chen Duansheng, the act of cross-dressing serves as wish-fulfillment, in that the heroine justifies her cross-dressing in order to keep her chastity, but she chooses to keep her male role even after the moral aim is fulfilled. In comparison with the mediums of drama or poetry that also attracted numerous women writers' attention, the generic characteristics of *tanci* allowed authors like Chen Duansheng greater flexibility and new directions, in the sense that the variable length of *tanci* makes possible a longer process of transformation. *Karmic Bonds of Reincarnation* can therefore be seen as a narrative centered on process. This

52 Chen, *Zaisheng yuan*, 1046.

53 For example, religious beliefs about the pollution of blood in childbirth essentialize the female as unclean. For an extensive discussion on the discourse of blood in the construction of gender, see Furth, *A Flourishing Yin*, 305–309.

process generates a self open to being changed and reshaped, whose identification with the masculine or feminine shifts fluidly. Of course, the vernacular novel (*zhanghui xiaoshuo* 章回小說) also provides this convenience because it allows for a narrative of great length. However, women writers seldom wrote novels. Also, significantly, the prosimetrical form gives the *tanci* genre a more convenient way of creating interiority. Yet, whereas the vernacular novel is deeply influenced by the objectivity of historical writing, and therefore rarely concerns itself with the characters' thoughts, verse works better for the presentation of the characters' psychological state and their self-expression. The ambiguity of personal pronouns in verse also facilitates the author's ability to shift from third-person narration to first-person expression, as in the moving passage in which the heroine of *Karmic Bonds of Reincarnation* is revealed to be a woman.

Moreover, the relatively loose structure of the *tanci* genre allows the narrative to include numerous mini-episodes of mistaken identity, thereby infinitely deferring narrative resolution. In *Karmic Bonds of Reincarnation*, besides the heroine's act of cross-dressing, there are other scenes of mistaken identity, and other characters' expression of desires and confusion prompted by other disguises. These episodes complicate the story's general narrative flow, and make *Karmic Bonds of Reincarnation* something of a collective fantasy.[54] For example, Wei Yong'e, the cross-dressed bandit leader, is a *wu* 武 (military) foil to Meng Lijun's *wen* 文 (literary) role. Yong'e's father, a general under the command of Huangfu Shaohua's father, is framed and imprisoned, just like Shaohua's father. Disguising herself as a man, Yong'e escapes, but is held up by a group of bandits on her way. She kills the bandit leader and becomes the new leader of the bandits. In that sense, Yong'e's adventure is a parallel to Lijun's. Both women venture into the world of men and attain power and prominence. While Lijun achieves public recognition with her literary and medical skills, Yong'e exhibits her strength in martial arts. Of course, compared with Lijun, Yong'e is a more conventional cross-dressed woman in that she is one who is far more willing to return to her female identity and marriage, although she is presented as somewhat disappointed about her marriage, since she loves Shaohua more than her husband-to-be, Xiong Hao. Still, the parallel between Lijun and Yong'e contributes to a vision of totality.

In addition, the appearance of an impostor who aims to usurp the identity of the "real" Meng Lijun adds further interest to the plot. Xiang Nanjin is

54 By fantasy, I primarily mean wish-fulfillment, or the idealization of the act of cross-dressing, rather than its illusory aspect. Of course, women authors at times see their wild fantasy in the *tanci* writing as a daydream, as I will discuss later in this chapter.

the daughter of a merchant in Yunnan. It happens that she has a maid who previously worked for the Meng family and who tells her about Meng Lijun. Nanjin is deeply moved by Meng Lijun's story, identifying with her chaste character and the act of disguising herself in male attire, to the extent that she considers Meng Lijun as the one who recognizes her self (*zhiji*). This emotional identification with Meng Lijun results in a kind of interiority. Meng Lijun thus becomes a model and inspiration for Nanjin, who finds a new sense of self in Lijun's story. Therefore, when Nanjin learns that her father is plotting to have her marry Shaohua, she is immediately taken with the idea. Nanjin desires to improve upon her status as a member of the merchant class by masquerading as Meng Lijun. Yet even more than this, she is fascinated by the idea of taking on a disguise, and by the dramatic transformation of self that this disguise might bring about. When she does disguise herself as Meng Lijun, she looks in the mirror as Meng Lijun had done while painting her self-portrait. Nanjin is pleasantly surprised by the new self-image she encounters: "This is truly strange. How have I come to look exactly like Miss Meng?" 真正怪事，奴怎麼像起孟小姐来.[55] The image of Meng Lijun's likeness in the mirror is suggestive of the formation of a new interior reality and new opportunities for Nanjin. Nanjin's self-observation illuminates a blurring of the boundaries between fantasy and reality. This resulting interiority reminds us of the female protagonist in Wu Zao's 吳藻 (1799–1863) play *The Disguised Image* (*Qiaoying* 喬影), in which the heroine, dressed as a male scholar, drinks wine while reading Qu Yuan's 屈原 (340–278 BCE) poem "Encountering Sorrow" (*Lisao* 離騷) and examining her self-portrait in male disguise. She vents her resentment about having no recognized outlets for her talents through a long monologue. By identifying with the renowned frustrated male poet Qu Yuan, the heroine reveals her wish to be drawn into the historical and literary mainstream, and to be remembered in the realm of culture.[56] Likewise, the heroine's intense sense of self is also expressed in the play based on her aspirations to be recognized by the world.

Excited about her disguise and the new possibilities it produces, Nanjin travels to the capital. On the way, she reads books, adding her own notes and comments, and composes poems about her travels. In late imperial China, it

---

55 Chen, *Zaisheng yuan*, 694.

56 For a detailed discussion of Wu Zao's play, see Hua Wei, *Ming Qing funü zhi xiqu chuangzuo yu piping*, 119–27. There are also English translations of *Qiaoying* available, see Idema and Grant, *The Red Brush*, 687–93; Susan Mann and Yu-yin Cheng, eds., *Under Confucian Eyes: Writings on Gender in Chinese History*, 239–50; Shu-chu Wei, "*Qiaoying* (The Image in Disguise), by Wu Zao," *CHINOPERL Papers* 26 (2005): 171–80.

was quite common for women to travel with their husbands and fathers to their official posts and to compose poems along the way.[57] This must have happened to Chen Duansheng when her father went from Beijing to Dengzhou to assume his post. Moreover, the sub-plot featuring Nanjin's journey may derive from Chen Duansheng's mother's account of a trip from Beijing to Yunnan.[58] Chen Duansheng's projection of her own experience onto the character Nanjin reinforces their identification as talented women. In this sense, they are really "soulmates," regardless of who is real and who is fictional. This blurring of the real and the fake or fictional is a recurring theme in *Karmic Bonds of Reincarnation*. When Xiang Nanjin is brought to court, she, with a quick-witted mind, answers all the questions posed by Lijun's father and brother. Consequently, the emperor, all the courtiers, and even her father and Shaohua believe her to be the real Meng Lijun. In the end, when Lijun's mother is called in and reveals Lijun's true identity, Lijun tries her best, and manages to maintain her false identity for a little while longer. The titles of Chapters 53 and 54, in which the above takes place, are "The False Lady Always Speaks the Seemingly Real" and "The Real Daughter at Times Pretends," respectively. These ironic titles suggest the profound fluidity between the real and the false. "True or not true" reflects the uncertainty of identity, as "like or not like" captures the fundamental ambivalence embodied in a portrait. If Xiang Nanjin is "false" in that she plays the role of Meng Lijun, then Meng Lijun is not "real" either, since she, in turn, plays the role of Li Junyu (her false name). However, both women take delight in their miraculous transformations into someone they desire to be.

The self, then, is not to be fully realized in one's ordinary identity prescribed by society, but rather by moving into a completely new persona. This is "a desire for transformation itself, a pursuit of identity as a transformative exercise, an example of desire itself as a transformative activity," in Kate Bornstein's words.[59] The characters' movements between various identities problematize the notion of essence and stability regarding both class and gender. As Xiang Nanjin is fascinated with claiming Meng Lijun's identity, Meng Lijun is obsessed with taking a male role. Both the disguise of the impostor, who desires upward mobility and identifies with the heroine, and the cross-dressing of the

57 Grace Fong examines travel records and poems by women who accompanied husbands and fathers to official postings. See Grace S. Fong, *Herself an Author: Gender, Agency, and Writing in Late Imperial China* (Honolulu: University of Hawai'i Press, 2008), 85–120.

58 For Chen Duansheng's and her mother's travel experiences, see Chen Yinke, *Lun Zaisheng yuan*, 56–60, 103.

59 Butler quotes Kate Bornstein in *Undoing Gender*, 8.

heroine, who longs for male power, are kinds of fictionalization. These acts of fictionalization change the characters' subject positions and gender identities. Indeed, we can see in the cross-dressed heroine a figure of the woman writer herself, someone who also takes pleasure in the act of fictionalization, and whose writing can be seen as a form of mental cross-dressing. In this way, the association between disguise, fictionalization, and ecstasy are thematized in *Karmic Bonds of Reincarnation*.

In fact, the authorial self-expression in the opening and closing passages of each *juan* (or chapter) can be seen as a generic feature of women's *tanci* works. In these passages, the author talks to the reader about her personal life, her literary composition, her happiness and suffering. Siao-chen Hu has argued that these passages derive from an autobiographical impulse common to women *tanci* writers.[60] In fact, such authorial self-description works as a reflexive act, just like the self-portrait of Meng Lijun, calling her identity into question. On the other hand, within the story proper, the cross-dressed heroine exists as an extension of the author, who brings an alternative self into being through fictionalization. In this way, women *tanci* writers project not only an idealized self but also a multiplicity of possibilities through which they can establish their interior reality and construct their fictional world as they please. This illuminates what Seán Burke calls "the creation of an aesthetic identity which seeks to transcend or negate the biographical subject."[61]

At the same time, Chen Duansheng situates her heroine within a sequence of interrelated fictional narratives. For example, it is the models of Liu Qingyun 柳青云 and Xie Yujuan 谢玉娟 – the heroine of another *tanci* work, *Little Gold Coins* (*Xiao jinqian* 小金钱), and a female character in another piece, *The Jade Bracelet* – who disguise themselves as men, that inspire Meng Lijun to flee from home, also disguised as a man. The representation in these narratives provides the inner truth, while the reality becomes its mirror in these works. It can be said that Meng Lijun's adventure is precisely the continuation of her textual precursors' stories. By referring to a series of previous *tanci* works, Chen Duansheng indicates that she belongs to a particular tradition of fictionalization. She makes no attempt at closure in her fiction. The interpretation and continuation of her tale are left in the hands of her audience and readers. In that vein, Siao-chen Hu suggests the formation of a "reading community" among women who wrote and read *tanci*, and a special "textual relationship"

---

60 Hu, *Cainü cheye weimian*, 62–99. For a translation of one such long autobiographical passage, see Idema and Grant, *The Red Brush*, 749–52.

61 Seán Burke, "Writing the Self," in *Authorship: From Plato to the Postmodern: A Reader* (Edinburgh: Edinburgh University Press, 1995), 303.

among these women. She also examines the "intertextuality" between *Karmic Bonds of Reincarnation* and a series of other *tanci* works.[62] In this sense, *tanci* can be seen as a genre centered on process, in which the act of cross-dressing provides women authors with "a space of possibility structuring and confounding culture."[63] This "space of possibility" is maintained as a collective, unending fantasy by women writers who participate in a lineage of interlinked narratives.

Of course, this does not mean that women *tanci* authors were not conscious about the gulf between objective reality and their cross-dressing fictions.[64] In *Karmic Bonds of Reincarnation*, many authorial passages begin with the description of seasonal scenery outside the window, and end with a reference to the author's fictional writing. For example, at the end of Chapter 16, the author says,

春風融和雲路闊，	The spring wind is warm and genial, and the cloud-roads are broad;
夜廊寂靜竹窗深。	The corridor at night is quiet, and the bamboo window is deeply hidden.
朝朝敷衍興亡事，	Morning after morning, I make up this story of rise and fall,
日日追求幻化情。	Day after day, I pursue the pleasure of literary fantasy.[65]

The recurrent image of the seasonal scenery through the window provides the setting for the author's writing, and at the same time, the image of a window suggests the boundary between *nei* and *wai*. The expanding world outside prominently contrasts with the deep, enclosed space of *nei*, in which she only "pursue[s] the pleasure of literary fantasy day after day." Here, one feels not only her enthusiasm for fiction, but also her sense of dissatisfaction at her inability to cross the boundary between reality and fiction, between *nei* and *wai*.

---

62 See Hu, *Cainü cheye weimian*, 3–61.

63 Garber, *Vested Interests*, 17.

64 In her discussion on the double-meaning of the garden trope, Siao-chen Hu shows the paradoxical relationship the author feels between the real world and the fictional one. The creation of a fictional world provides a space of imagination and a dialogue with reality, but, at the same time, the fictional nature of the literary world demonstrates the limitation she feels in reality, and the impossibility of literally escaping from it. See Hu, *Cainü cheye weimian*, 163.

65 Chen, *Zaisheng yuan*, 234.

Women's *tanci* works exhibit a complicated range of ideological meanings represented in the practice of cross-dressing. Generally speaking, these texts comply with conventional notions of feminine virtue. They address readers from a specifically feminine point of view. In these regards, these works represent the type of "feminine authority" proposed by Nancy Armstrong: as writing for, by, and about women.[66] In Chen Duansheng's words, "I am not willing to send my manuscripts for vulgar eyes [publication]; I only preserve them for women in the chambers" 不願付刊經俗，惟將存稿見閨儀.[67] Yet these fanciful adventure stories base their plots on the act of cross-dressing – in actuality a way of resisting their femininity – and in this way they encounter and play with the "limitations of feminine authority."[68] Through the theme of cross-dressing, they, intentionally or unintentionally, transgress a variety of social norms and gender stereotypes. A careful investigation of the narrative resolution of these *tanci* works by women suggests that it is a mistake to take the motivations offered for a character's cross-dressing at face value. In this regard, *Karmic Bonds of Reincarnation* serves as a good example.

As scholars have claimed, *Karmic Bonds of Reincarnation* is not a feminist work in the modern sense of the word.[69] It does not have the kinds of explicit political connotations required by modern feminism. Chen Duansheng does not go so far as to destabilize binary thinking about gender, in Butler's and Garber's sense. Neither does she seem to be advocating for real social change, or aiming at fundamentally overthrowing the social system. Indeed, Chen Duansheng generally identifies with the basic values of Confucian society – for example, loyalty, filiality, and chastity. Although she embraces these values, she also makes her cross-dressed heroine dangerously subversive. Chastity – a symbol of women's segregation from men, and bodily loyalty to one man – is repeatedly utilized to reject authority, and ultimately to turn feminine submission into its very opposite, a degree of independence from men. This raises the question of agency by revealing that the subversion of gender norms is located in their constructions, that is to say, agency or possibility is enabled by the participation in the constitution of norms.[70]

---

66 Nancy Armstrong "Postface: Chinese women in a Comparative Perspective: A Response," in Ellen Widmer and Kang-I Sun Chang eds., *Writing Women in Late Imperial China* (Stanford: Stanford University Press, 1997), 402; Widmer, *The Beauty and the Book*, 286.

67 Chen, *Zaisheng yuan*, 122.

68 Armstrong, "Postface," 402.

69 See Idema and Grant, *The Red Brush*, 739; Zhao, "Daizhe jiaoliao de shengming zhi wu," 244–56.

70 See Butler, *Gender Trouble*, 181–90.

More importantly, *Karmic Bonds of Reincarnation* evokes a powerful sense of female subjectivity, particularly surrounding their place in patriarchal society. The practice of cross-dressing helps to shape the heroine's inner self. We can perceive, in this process, a female subject developing by way of conflicts, emotions, and aspirations. Although Meng Lijun, like other (more conventional) cross-dressed heroines, can only acquire agency as a man, her male role is progressively internalized and intensified. At the same time, the heroine's adoption of male attire does not mean that she stops thinking as a woman faced with the particular dilemmas caused by the *nei/wai* distinction. In this sense, *Karmic Bonds of Reincarnation* is not simply a one-dimensional fantasy, but a profound tragedy that raises particularly problematic questions about individual psychology, personal fulfillment, and gender identity. It creates a collection of female selves that cannot be defined by, or encompassed within, romantic discourse, but which are molded and altered by seeking a peculiar way of emotion expression, engaging in meaningful struggles, and taking significant actions. Its sense of open-endedness signifies the kind of unpredictability and particularity constituted by the constant revision and renewal of the cross-dressing theme in the community of women *tanci* authors, as well as a process of ongoing negotiation and the pursuit of the open-endedness of the self.

Conclusion: the Role of Emotion and Community – Negotiating Private and Public

In this book I have embarked on a journey through romantic discourse represented by the *caizi-jiaren* narrative type, tracing the contours of the images of women and the literati in conjunction with their intimate feelings that are nonetheless deeply shaped by social and cultural practices. My chapters do not comprise a conventional literary history of romantic narratives, but rather function as new avenues for exploring these texts within their larger cultural and historical frameworks. Indeed, these narratives present somewhat similar experiences of love to those in the Renaissance and Romantic texts in the west. As Paolo Santangelo has persuasively argued, however, the basic drive behind them is completely different, and reflects a multiplicity of complex aspects constructed by different cultures.[1] Thus, I situate *caizi-jiaren* stories in issues such as changing moral evaluations and the historical conditions that sustained them, in terms of which I refer more to overall historical situations than specific historical events. Throughout this book, ideas about gender, identity, and above all agency are primarily discussed, along with the central issues of intellectual discourses, especially the transformation of Confucianism, in which we see the shifts of moral authority from the political system to the individual, from the reliance on the external to a focus on the internal – whether that be the innate moral mind or the spontaneity of *qing* – with a new conception of the self as grounds for morality. This forms a trajectory of dynamics between private and public, and of the interactions between the literati elite and particular historical situations. Doing so profoundly reflects the way literati understood the changing world around them and made choices about how to respond to that world.

As a mode of writing, *caizi-jiaren* narratives offered literati authors a forum in which to address their concerns for self-cultivation and social accommodation within their particular historical and cultural milieus. It is through a perpetual re-examination of the conceptions of the self and its agency that these narratives chart new dimensions in the shaping of the literate elite's identity, as well as a form of subjectivity that is grounded in both self-construction and self-questioning. They also shape a sense of self and cultural distinction by means of various communal ties. The unremitting revision of the concept of

1 Santangelo and Boros, *The Culture of Love in China and Europe*, 439, 802.

 | HTTPS://DOI.ORG/10.1163/9789004693357-009

qing and the expression of collective identity point to the goal of containing the threat of excessive self-interest.

As Giddens points out, identity is a mode of thinking about ourselves, and thus our creation. He describes identity as a project, something always in process.[2] In this process of becoming, identities are seen as a question both of agency and of social determination, or discursive construction.[3] The discussion of *Karmic Bonds of Reincarnation* in Chapter 6 leverages this understanding of subjectivity as an ongoing construction to examine how social structures and discourses are not only constraining but also enabling, and how gendered subjectivity enables the heroine to act in specifically gendered ways. So too in *The Dream of the Red Chamber* (Chapter 5), both the narrator and the characters become the authors' interlocutors, and their voices thus represent different versions of a self and render in between the positions of subject and object. Both texts are self-reflexive, to some degree, in framing the narratives around the dialects of truth and fiction. Both are open-ended works in search of the open-endedness of selves. Such a capacity for self-scrutiny enables agency to occur, and inscribes the moral power in subjective experience. In fact, both increasing internalization and the pattern of self-reflection run through the *caizi-jiaren* narratives discussed here. Many of these narratives demonstrate a distinctive mode of writing the self and an ethical imperative to experiment with voice, positing a new construction of subjectivity. They unfold through a dynamic process of self-constitution and socialization, thereby envisaging individuals whose emotions are culturally constructed and who are still capable of making changes, engaging in social criticism, or reflecting upon cultural traditions.

This paradoxical mode of thinking produces the conditions that make a subject or agency possible, rather than pointing to only revalidation of orthodoxy or the ultimate self-disillusionment.[4] Paolo Santangelo has keenly pointed out that the various and contradictory conceptualizations of *qing* that were emphasized in the literary works of late imperial China and through whose presentation of a conflict of values – the inconsistency between dominant Confucian morality and individual genuine feelings in particular – was posed the question of whether the legitimation of passions should be deemed a mere return

2 Anthony Giddens, *Modernity and Self-identity: Self and Society in the Late Modern Age* (Cambridge: Polity Press, 1991), 1–10.

3 Anthony Giddens, *The Constitution of Society: Outline of the Theory of Structuration* (Cambridge: Polity Press, 1984), 30–40.

4 See Santangelo and Boros, *The Culture of Love in China and Europe*, 800–802.

to traditional values or an exploration of a new self.[5] Understanding the competition between and evolution of different representations of *qing* as being grounded in a dynamic process of self-reflection and intellectual inquiry deepens our perception and understanding of the ways in which emotions evolve with the times and the innovative implications of its negotiation with orthodox currents and social rules. This process brought about a variety of emotional experiences, certain negative feelings in particular, such as anxiety, perplexity, and hesitation, which could not be named or defined by existing knowledge or language but which gave rise to the possibility of crossing boundaries and grasping the freedom that results from the transformation of one's life course, in which numerous contradictions and unmeasurable elements occur. In this process, we see a self that can never entirely be circumscribed by dominant discourses, but which is to a significant degree altered by its own struggling to find a better way, or to create personal variation on prevailing rules, although it did not formulate explicit political protest, or promote a unique ideology. The integration that the self achieves, always provisional, builds on the intention of modification, the attempts at exploration, and the concept of intersubjectivity. It is in this process of becoming that agency is manifested and lived; it is also in the probing of the cultural contexts in which the various literary modes of *qing* were circulated that literature can teach us more about emotions and selfhood.

The questioning of a unified self also results in an approach to subjectivity that is based upon group identity and community identity rather than individuality. As can be seen in early Qing scholar-beauty novels, community stands within the individual–state continuum, aiming at the rebuilding of the ideological and moral grounds of the imperial state and the role of literati in it. *The Dream of the Red Chamber*, *Karmic Bonds of Reincarnation*, and other texts discussed in this book participate in the formation of an imagined community as well – whether it purports to justify pluralization, to maintain a cultural autonomy, or to fashion the literati identity or gender consciousness of the time – making possible a space of endless self-renewal in which the relationships between self and other, and between private and social, are unremittingly interacted with and adjusted. More often than not, people socialized and communicated in the imagined community in the form of poetry, through which they shared the identity of members of a select circle of talented men/women. Indeed, the use of poetry as a vehicle of sociability as well as individuality can

---

5 See ibid., 439–50.

be traced to an old format of the cultural discourse – that "poetry may serve to commune" (*shi keyi qun* 詩可以群).[6]

In the ongoing projects of both self-fashioning and community building, the heroine embodies talent and purity, qualities that at first endow her with an inner depth and an ability to act on her own, and further help the heroes work out their own autonomy of self and community. In all of this she plays both subjective and objective roles. We need not assume, at the same time, that the works discussed here were experienced solely as models for male personhood. All of them were popular with both women and men, and this dissemination of a female ideal also defined both what a literary woman desired and how she represented a female self in her own writing. Women authors as well as men accepted the coding of the heroine as initially bestowed subjectivity and self-determination but ultimately kept in line with the normative social structure – otherwise she would end in an inevitable tragedy like Lin Daiyu in *The Dream of the Red Chamber*. As such, women authors had to manage the difficult task of simultaneously subverting and conforming to patriarchal standards. Stories about female superiority, as in some drama and *tanci* works written by and for women, suggested to women readers an alternative to marriage and strengthened their independent aspirations. Just like the process of cross-dressing, the act of writing fashions a female subject who both internalizes the form of power she is given and understands the particular dilemmas she encounters. In seeing the female as part of big cultural projects, I reveal the gender logic in its formation, as well as women's status as both products and agents of hegemony.

The term *qing* idealizes authenticity and individual expression. When the individual's own *qing* becomes his or her source of correct judgment, love and moral power converge. Most of the *caizi-jiaren* narratives discussed in this book are characterized by a moralizing zeal and a cultural process of subject and identity formation. The transformation of the means of moral evaluation always reflects a certain degree of identifying with the changing social and historical circumstances, and at the same time a critical component. Within the Confucian context, neither *qing* nor *li* is a static conception, their historical meanings are changing and the underlying motivation for these changes is the dynamic process of negotiations between *shi* 勢 – state power or the specific

6 According to Zhu Xi's annotation, "*qun*" 群 here means "harmony without following others" (*he er bu liu* 和而不流). See Zhu Xi, ed. and annot., *Sishu zhangju jizhu* 四書章句集註 (Shanghai: Shanghai guji chubanshe, 2006), 232.

historical conditions – and the *shi* 士.[7] The works discussed here come from various time periods and bespeak a variety of social and identity crises, give a logic and a coherence to the curve of emotion history, and to some extent serve as vehicles for the expression of social criticism. *Qing*, as a kind of idealized passion, became the source of virtue in late Ming culture with the purpose of reforming human nature and thus social relationships. In the case of *The Story of the Western Wing*, the power of *qing* leads to the defeat of evil, while *The Peony Pavilion* both denounces social realities such as the corruption of the bureaucracy and reshapes ritual to realize the ideal of the "world of *qing*." The focus on *qing* virtually implies a focus on a kind of personhood that coexists with the network of social relationships and cultural tradition. *The Peony Pavilion* looks inward and portrays its heroine as committed to an ideal of passion and self, but at the same time finishes with her sense of self-fulfillment in the process of socialization. Kong Shangren's 孔尚任 (1648–1718) *Peach Blossom Fan* (*Taohua shan* 桃花扇), on the other hand, problematizes the sentimental self-indulgence of its main protagonists, and puts in question the value of *qing* and the culture in which it is rooted.

The *caizi-jiaren* modes across their generic and historical variations represent new articulations and formations of character and relationship in formation, and thus of subversion in the emergent sense, although they are frequently marked by the inclusion of essential conventions. But when they become, in their turn, models of reproduction, there can be a new alternative to dominant hegemonic modes, a creation of latent and newly possible consciousness.[8] In the earlier period, passion is written as something that is incompatible with, and thus challenges, marriage, an institution shaped by lineage and political considerations. However, late Ming drama's revision of *chuanqi* tales establishes a new model of interiority and fashions its own morality that is foreign to any previous notions of psychological depth and individual identity. Love within marriage develops to take on the status of an ideal in scholar-beauty novels from the seventeenth to the eighteenth centuries, in which marriage and intense friendship based on talent and mutual appreciation formed new models of emotional refuge. However, over time this ideal gradually came to be reincorporated into the existing regimes of emotion and lost its destabilizing thrust. In its critical reflection on the conventions of scholar-beauty novels, *The Dream of the Red Chamber* expresses the need to conceive of a new

---

7 For a detailed discussion on this issue, see Wang Hui 汪暉, *Xiandai Zhongguo sixiang de xingqi* 現代中國思想的興起 (Beijing: Sanlian shudian, 2004).

8 See Raymond Williams, *Marxism and Literature* (Oxford: Oxford University Press, 1977), 206–12.

emotional relationship unrecognized by existing literary codes, as the sentimental self, part of the self-definition of the literati elite, progressively loses its critical tension with social reality. A novel that has not been approached within the limited space of this book, Wen Kang's 文康 (ca. 1821–1875) *A Tale of Heroic Lovers* (*Ernü yingxiong zhuan* 兒女英雄傳), written around a century after *The Dream of the Red Chamber*, reformulates the masterpiece for a new cultural and moral ideal, replacing its preference for uncertainty and diversity with a narrative and moral authority. Through the reaffirmation of the value of filiality, *A Tale of Heroic Lovers* merges scholar-beauty romance and chivalric fiction into a mixed genre, making it possible for the heroine to launch a new mode of social and moral existence.[9] The *caizi-jiaren* mode of writing is therefore significant in the sense that it shows us the dynamic dimensions of Chinese intellectual and cultural tradition and its possibilities for historical change, as well as a special way in which literature participates in ongoing affective discourse. The conception of "*qing*" creates a space of indeterminacy, migrating between private and public, body and mind, reality and illusion, and subject and non-subject, and thus provides us with a key to ponder the ways that personal emotions enter the public realm and the history of Chinese society's transition to modernity. In this sense, *The Dream of the Red Chamber* works precisely as an allegory of emotion history, in which emotion claims are neither true nor false but rather are the imprints of life in transformation and attempts to explore, which involve a perpetual state of uncertainty and struggle.

9 See Epstein, *Orthodox Passions*, 27–31.

Bibliography

Abu-Lughod, Lila. *Veiled Sentiments: Honor and Poetry in a Bedouin Society*. Berkeley: University of California Press, 1986.

Abu-Lughod, Lila, and Catherine A. Lutz, eds. *Language and the Politics of Emotion*. Cambridge: Cambridge University Press, 1990.

Allen, Joseph R. "Dressing and Undressing the Chinese Woman Warrior." *Positions* 4, no. 2 (1996): 343–79.

Allen, Sarah M. *Shifting Stories: History, Gossip, and Lore in Narratives from Tang Dynasty China*. Cambridge, MA: Harvard University Asia Center, 2014.

Ames, Roger T. and Henry Rosemont, Jr., trans., *The Analects of Confucius: A Philosophical Translation*. New York: Random House, 2010.

Armstrong, Nancy. *Desire and Domestic Fiction: A Political History of the Novel*. New York and Oxford: Oxford University Press, 1987.

Armstrong, Nancy. "Postface: Chinese women in a Comparative Perspective: A Response," in Ellen Widmer and Kang-I Sun Chang eds., *Writing Women in Late Imperial China* (Stanford: Stanford University Press, 1997), 402.

Bao Zhenpei 鮑震培. *Qingdai nü zuojia tanci xiaoshuo lungao* 清代女作家彈詞小說論稿. Tianjin: Tianjin shehui kexueyuan chubanshe, 2001.

Barrett, T.H. *Li Ao: Buddhist, Taoist, or Neo-Confucian*. New York: Oxford University Press, 1992.

Bian Xiaoxuan 卞孝萱. *Tangren xiaoshuo yu zhengzhi* 唐人小說与政治. Xiamen: Lujiang chubanshe, 2003.

Bian Xiaoxuan 卞孝萱 and Zhang Qinghua 張清華. *Han Yu pingzhuan* 韓愈評傳. Nanjing: Nanjing daxue chubanshe, 1998.

Birch, Cyril, trans. *Mistress and Maid*. New York: Columbia University Press, 2001.

Birch, Cyril, trans. *The Peony Pavilion*. Bloomington: Indiana University Press, 2002.

Bol, Peter K. *"This Culture of Ours": Intellectual Transitions in T'ang and Sung China*. Stanford, CA: Stanford University Press, 1992.

Bray, Francesca. "Decorum and Desire: An Archetectonics of Domestic Space in Late Imperial China." In *Lijiao yu qingyu: Qian jindai Zhongguo wenhua zhong de hou/xiandianxing* 禮教与情慾：前近代中國文化中的後/現代性, edited by Xiong Bingzhen 熊秉真 and Lü Miaofen 呂妙芬, 7–72. Taibei: Zhongyang yanjiuyuan jindaishi yanjiusuo, 1999.

Brokaw, Cynthia J. "Tai Chen and Learning in the Confucian Tradition." In *Education and Society in Late Imperial China, 1600–1900*, edited by Benjamin A. Elman and Alexander Woodside, 257–91. Berkeley: University of California Press, 1994.

Brooks, Peter. *The Melodramatic Imagination: Balzac, Henry James, Melodrama, and the Mode of Excess*. New Haven, CT: Yale University Press, 1976.

 | HTTPS://DOI.ORG/10.1163/9789004693357-010

Burke, Seán. *Authorship: From Plato to the Postmodern: A Reader*. Edinburgh: Edinburgh University Press, 1995.

Butler, Judith. *Bodies That Matter: On the Discursive Limit of "Sex."* New York: Routledge, 1993.

Butler, Judith. *Gender Trouble: Feminism and the Subversion of Identity*. New York: Routledge, 1999.

Butler, Judith. *Undoing Gender*. New York: Routledge, 2004.

Butler, Judith. *Giving an Account of Oneself*. New York: Fordham University Press, 2005.

Butler, Judith, Ernesto Laclau, and Slavoj Zizek, eds. *Contingency, Hegemony, Universality: Contemporary Dialogues on the Left*. London: Verso, 2000.

Cai Yi 蔡毅, ed. *Zhongguo gudian xiqu xuba huibian* 中國古典戲曲序跋彙編. Jinan: Qilu shushe, 1989.

Chan, Wing-tsit, trans. *Instructions for Practical Living and Other Neo-Confucian Writings by Wang Yang-ming*. New York: Columbia University Press, 1963.

Chen Duansheng 陳端生. *Zaisheng yuan* 再生緣. Beijing: Huaxia chubanshe, 2000.

Chen Hong 陳洪. "'Honglou meng' mushi kaolun"《紅樓夢》木石考論. *Wenxue yu wenhua* 文學与文化 3 (2016): 24–35.

Chen, Toyoko Yoshida. "Women in Confucian Society – a Study of Three T'an-tz'u Narratives." PhD dissertation, Columbia University, 1974.

Chen Yinke 陳寅恪. "Han Yu and the Tang Novel." *Harvard Journal of Asiatic Studies* 1 (1936): 39–43.

Chen Yinke 陳寅恪. *Lun Zaisheng yuan* 論再生緣. Hongkong: Youlian chubanshe, 1959.

Chen Yinke 陳寅恪. "Du Yingying zhuan" 讀鶯鶯傳. In *Chen Yinke xiansheng lunwen ji* 陳寅恪先生論文集, vol. 2, 527–36. Taibei: Sanranxing chubanshe, 1974.

Cheng Junying 程俊英, ed. *Shijing zhuxi* 詩經注析. Beijing: Zhonghua shuju, 1999.

Cheng Qianfan 程千帆. *Tang dai jinshi xingjuan yu wenxue* 唐代進士行卷與文學. Shanghai: Shanghai guji chubanshe, 1980.

Cheng Shude 程樹德, ed. *Lunyu jishi* 論語集釋. Taibei: Tianwen shuju, 1973.

Cheng Yizhong 程毅中. *Tangdai xiaoshuo shihua* 唐代小說史話. Beijing: Wenhua yishu chubanshe, 1990.

Cheng Yizhong 程毅中. *Song Yuan xiaoshuo yanjiu* 宋元小說研究. Nanjing: Jiangsu guji chubanshe, 1998.

Chin, Ann-ping, and Mansfield Freeman, trans. *Tai Chen on Mencius: Explorations in Words and Meaning*. New Haven, CT: Yale University Press, 1990.

Chiren fu 癡人福. Guben xiaoshuo congkan 古本小說叢刊, vol. 4. Beijing: Zhonghua shuju, 1991.

Chunliu ying, Guben xiaoshuo jicheng edition. Shanghai: Shanghai guji chubanshe, 1992.

Chun liuying 春柳鶯. Guben xiaoshuo jicheng 古本小說集成. Shanghai: Shanghai guji chubanshe, 1992.

Clough, Patricia Ticineto, and Jean Halley, eds. *The Affective Turn: Theorizing the Social*. Durham, NC: Duke University Press, 2007.

Clunas, Craig. *Fruitful Sites: Garden Culture in Ming Dynasty China*. Durham, NC: Duke University Press, 1996.

Dai Zhen 戴震. *Dai Zhen quanshu* 戴震全書. Hefei: Huangshan shushe, 1994–1997.

de Bary, Wm. Theodore. *The Message of the Mind in New-Confucianism*. New York: Columbia University Press, 1989.

de Bary, Wm. Theodore. *Learning for One's Self: Essays on the Individual in Neo-Confucian Thought*. New York: Columbia University Press, 1991.

de Bary, Wm. Theodore, ed. *Self and Society in Ming Thought*. New York: Columbia University Press, 1970.

de Bary, Wm. Theodore, and Irene Bloom, eds. *Sources of Chinese Tradition*. New York: Columbia University Press, 1999.

Deng Yunxiang 鄧雲鄉. *Honglou fengsu tan* 紅樓風俗譚. Beijing: Zhonghua shuju, 2015.

Ding Xigen 丁錫根, ed. *Zhongguo lidai xiaoshuo xuba ji* 中國歷代小說序跋集. Beijing: Renmin wenxue chubanshe, 1996.

Dingqing ren 定情人. Shenyang: Chunfeng wenyi chubanshe, 1985.

Dong Zhongshu 董仲舒, ed. *Chunqiu fanlu* 春秋繁露. Sibu beiyao 四部備要.

Dudbridge, Glen, trans. *The Tale of Li Wa*. London: Ithaca Press for the Board of the Faculty of Oriental Studies, Oxford University, 1983.

Edwards, Louise P. *Men and Women in Qing China: Gender in The Red Chamber Dream*. Leiden: Brill, 1994.

Edwards, Louise P. "Painting Boundaries of Sex Segregation in Qing China: Representing the Family in *The Red Chamber Dream*." In *The Family Model in Chinese Art and Culture*, ed. Jerome Silbergeld and Dora C.Y. Ching, 339–72 (Princeton, NJ: Princeton University Press and P.Y. and Kinmay W. Tang Center for East Asian Art, 2013).

Elman, Benjamin A. *From Philosophy to Philology: Intellectual and Social Aspects of Change in Late Imperial China*. Cambridge, MA: Harvard University Press, 1984.

Epstein, Maram. *Competing Discourses: Orthodoxy, Authenticity, and Engendered Meanings in Late Imperial Chinese Fiction*. Cambridge and London: Harvard University Asia Center, 2001.

Epstein, Maram. *Orthodox Passions: Narrating Filial Love during the High Qing*. Cambridge, MA: Harvard University Asia Center, 2019.

Feng Menglong 馮夢龍. *Feng Menglong ji jianzhu* 馮夢龍集箋註. Edited by Gao Hongjun 高洪鈞. Tianjin: Tianjin guji chubanshe, 2006.

Feng Menglong 馮夢龍. *Qing shi* 情史. Changsha: Yuelu shushe, 2003.

Feng Qiyong 馮其庸, ed. *Chongjiao bajia pingpi Honglou meng* 重校八家評批紅樓夢. Nanchang: Jiangxi jiaoyu chubanshe, 2000.

Feng Youlan. *A History of Chinese Philosophy*. Translated by Derk Bodde. Princeton, NJ: Princeton University Press, 1953.

Fenghuang chi 鳳凰池. Guben xiaoshuo jicheng 古本小說集成. Shanghai: Shanghai guji chubanshe, 1990.

Foucault, Michel. *The History of Sexuality*. Translated by Robert Hurley. New York: Random House, 1978.

Foucault, Michel. *Ethics: Subjectivity and Truth*. Edited by Paul Rabinow. New York: The New Press, 1997.

Frye, Northrop. *Anatomy of Criticism: Four Essays*. Princeton, NJ: Princeton University Press, 1957.

Furth, Charlotte. *A Flourishing Yin: Gender in China's Medical History, 960–1665*. Berkeley: University of California Press, 1999.

Garber, Marjorie. *Vested Interests: Cross-Dressing and Cultural Anxiety*. London: Routledge, 2002.

Ge Hong 葛洪. *Xijing zaji* 西京雜記. Sibu congkan chubian 四部叢刊初編.

Ge Xiaoyin 葛曉音. "Lun Tang Song de guwen gexin yu rudao yanbian de guanxi" 論唐代的古文革新與儒道演變的關係. In *Han Tang wenxue de shanbian* 漢唐文學的嬗變, 156–179. Beijing: Beijing daxue chubanshe, 1990.

Geertz, Clifford. *The Interpretation of Cultures*. New York: Basic Books, 1973.

Giddens, Anthony. *Modernity and Self-identity: Self and Society in the Late Modern Age*. Cambridge: Polity Press, 1991.

Giddens, Anthony. *The Constitution of Society: Outline of the Theory of Structuration*. Cambridge: Polity Press, 1984.

Gu mingjia zaju 古名家雜劇. Guben xiqu congkan 古本戲曲叢刊, ser. 4, vols. 93–95. Shanghai: Shangwu yinshuguan, 1958.

Gu Yanwu 顧炎武. *Rizhi lu jishi* 日知錄集釋. Annotated by Huang Rucheng 黃汝成. Shanghai: Shanghai guji chubanshe, 2006.

Gu Yingtai 谷應泰. *Mingshi jishi benmo* 明史紀事本末. Shanghai: Shanghai guji chubanshe, 1994.

Gu zaju 古雜劇. Guben xiqu congkan, ser. 4, vols. 4–8. Shanghai: Shangwu yinshuguan, 1958.

Guo Moruo 郭沫若. *Guo Moruo gudian wenxue lunwen ji* 郭沫若古典文學論文集. Shanghai: Shanghai guji chubanshe, 1985.

Hall, Stuart. *Representation: Cultural Representations and Signifying Practices*. London: Sage, 1997.

Han Jingtai 韓經太. *Lixue wenhua yu wenxue sichao* 理學文化與文學思潮. Beijing: Zhonghua shuju, 1997.

Han Yu 韓愈. *Han Changli wenji jiaozhu* 韩昌黎文集校註. Edited by Ma Qichang 馬其昶. Shanghai: Gudian wenxue chubanshe, 1957.

Han Yu 韓愈. *Han Yu quanji jiaozhu* 韓愈全集校註. Edited by Qu Shouyuan 屈守元 and Chang Sichun 常思春. Chengdu: Sichuan daxue chubanshe, 1996.

Hanan, Patrick. "The Making of The Pearl-Sewn Shirt and The Courtesan's Jewel Box." *Harvard Journal of Asiatic Studies* 33 (1973): 124–53.

Hartman, Charles. *Han Yu and the T'ang search for Unity*. Princeton, NJ: Princeton University Press, 1986.

Hawkes, David, and John Minford, trans. *The Story of the Stone*. 5 vols. Harmondsworth: Penguin, 1973–1986.

He Xinyin 何心隱. *He Xinyin ji* 何心隱集. Beijing: Zhonghua shuju, 1960.

He Zhuo 何焯. *Yimen xiansheng ji* 義門先生集. Xuxiu siku quanshu 續修四庫全書. Shanghai: Shanghai guji chubanshe, 1995–2002.

Henderson, John B. *The Development of Decline of Chinese Cosmology*. New York: Columbia University Press, 1984.

Hessney, Richard. "Beautiful, Talented, and Brave: Seventeenth-Century Chinese Scholar-Beauty Romances." PhD dissertation, Columbia University, 1979.

Hightower, James. "Yuan Zhen and 'Yingying zhuan.'" *Harvard Journal of Asiatic Studies* 33 (1973): 90–123.

Hogan, Patrick Colm. *What Literature Teaches Us about Emotions*. Cambridge: Cambridge University Press, 2011.

Houqing lu 侯鯖録. Zhibuzuzhai congshu 知不足齋叢書, vol. 5.

Hsia, C.T. "Time and the Human Condition in the Plays of T'ang Hsien-tsu." In *Self and Society in Ming Thought*, edited by Wm. Theodore de Bary, 249–79. New York: Columbia University Press, 1970.

Hudie mei 蝴蝶媒. Guben xiaoshuo jicheng 古本小説集成. Shanghai: Shanghai guji chubanshe, 1994.

Hu, Minghui. *China's Transition to Modernity: The New Classical Vision of Dai Zhen*. Seattle: University of Washington Press, 2015.

Hu, Siao-chen. *Cainü cheye weimian: Zhongguo jindai nüxing xushi* 才女徹夜不眠：近代中國女性敘事文学的兴起. Taibei: Maitian chuban, 2003.

Hu Yinglin 胡應麟. *Shaoshi shanfang bicong* 少室山房笔叢. Beijing, Zhonghua shuju, 1958.

Hua Wei 華瑋. *Ming Qing funü zhi xiqu chuangzuo yu piping* 明清婦女之戲曲創作與批評. Taibei: Zhongyang yanjiu yuan Zhongguo wenzhe yanjiusuo, 2003.

Huang Lin 黃霖, ed. *Zhiyanzhai pingpi Honglou meng* 脂砚斋评批红楼梦. 2 vols. Jinan: Qilu shushe, 1994.

Huang Lin 黃霖 and Hang Tongwen 韓同文, eds. *Zhongguo lidai xiaoshuo lunzhu xuan* 中國歷代小説論著選. Nanchang: Jiangxi renmin chubanshe.

Huang, Martin W. *Literati and Self-Re/Presentation: Autobiographical Sensibility in the Eighteenth-Century Chinese Novel*. Stanford, CA: Stanford University Press, 1995.

Huang, Martin W. *Desire and Fictional Narrative in Late Imperial China*. Cambridge, MA: Harvard University Asian Center, 2001.

Huang, Martin W. *Negotiating Masculinities in Late Imperial China*. Honolulu: University of Hawai'i Press, 2006.

Huang, Ray. *1587, A Year of No Significance: The Ming Dynasty in Decline*. New Haven, CT: Yale University Press, 1981.

Huang Yanli 黃嫣梨, ed. *Nü sishu jizhu yizheng* 女四書集註義證. Hong Kong: Shangwu yinshuguan, 2008.

Huatu yuan 畫圖緣. Guben xiaoshuo jicheng 古本小說集成, vol. 88. Shanghai: Shanghai guji chubanshe, 1990.

Huntington, Rania. *Alien Kind: Fox and Late Imperial Chinese Narrative*. Cambridge, MA: Harvard University Asia Center, 2003.

Ichikawa Kan 市川勘. *Hanyu yanjiu xinlun: xixiang yu wenzhang chuangzuo* 韓愈研究新論：思想与文章創作. Taibei: Wenjin chubanshe, 2004.

Idema, Wilt L. "Female Talent and Female Virtue: Xu Wei's *Nu zhuangyuan* and Meng Chengshun's *Zhenwen ji*." In *Ming Qing xiqu guoji yantao hui lunwen ji* 明清戲曲國際研討會論文集, edited by Hua Wei 華瑋 and Wang Ailing 王瑷玲, 549–71. Taibei: Zhongyang yanjiuyuan Zhongguo wenzhe yanjiusuo, 1998.

Irimia, Mihaela, ed. *Literature and Cultural Memory*. Leiden: Brill, 2017.

Jameson, Fredric. *The Political Unconscious: Narrative as a Socially Symbolic Act*. Ithaca, NY: Cornell University Press, 1989.

Jankowiak, William. *Romantic Passion: A Universal Experience*. New York: Columbia University Press, 1997.

Jiang Songyuan 蔣松源, and Tan Banghe 譚邦和. *Ming Qing xiaoshuo shi* 明清小說史. Wuhan: Changjiang wenyi chubanshe, 1996.

Jinxiang ting 錦香亭. Zhengzhou: Zhongzhou guji chubanshe, 1994.

Jin Ping Mei cihua 金瓶梅詞話. ed. Mei Jie 梅節. Hong Kong: Xinghai wenhua, 1987.

Kafalas, Philip A. *In Limpid Dream: Nostalgia and Zhang Dai's Reminiscences of the Ming*. Norwalk: East Bridge, 2007.

Knoblock, John. *Xunzi: A Translation and Study of the Complete Works*. Stanford, CA: Stanford University Press, 1988, 1990, 1994.

Ko, Dorothy. *Teachers of the Inner Chambers: Women and Culture in Seventeenth-Century China*. Stanford, CA: Stanford University Press, 1994.

Kominami Ichirou 小南一郎. "Li A den no kouzou 李娃伝の構造." *Touhou gakuhou* 東方学報 62 (1990): 284–91.

Kong Shangren 孔尚任. *Taohua shan* 桃花扇. Beijing: Renmin wenxue chubanshe, 1959.

Lee, Haiyan. *Revolution of the Heart: A Genealogy of Love in China, 1900–1950*. Stanford, CA: Stanford University Press, 2007.

Legge, James, trans. *Liji: Book of Rites*. New Hyde Park, NY: University Books, 1967.

Legge, James, *The Chinese Classics, with a Translation, Critical and Exegetical Notes, Prolegomena, and Copious Indexes*, vol. 1: *Confucian Analects, the Great Learning, and the Doctrine of the Mean*. Taipei: SMC Publishing, 1991.

Li Ao 李翺. *Li Wengong ji* 李文公集. Sibu congkan 四部叢刊.

Li Jianguo 李劍國, ed. *Tang Wudai zhiguai chuanqi xulu* 唐五代志怪傳奇敘録. Tianjin: Nankai daxue chubanshe, 1993.

Li Jianguo 李劍國, ed. *Songdai chuanqi ji* 宋代傳奇集. Beijing: Zhonghua shuju, 2001.

Li, Qiancheng. *Fictions of Enlightenment: Journey to the West, Tower of Myriad Mirrors, and Dream of the Red Chamber*. Honolulu: University of Hawai'i Press, 2004.

Li, Qiancheng. *Transmutations of Desire: Literature and Religion in Late Imperial China*. Hongkong: The Chinese University of Hongkong Press, 2020.

Li Ruzhen 李汝珍. *Huitu Jinghua yuan* 繪圖鏡花緣. Facsimile reprint of the 1888 illustrated Shanghai Dianshizhai edition. Beijing: Zhongguo shudian, 1985.

Li Sai 李賽. "Shi lun caizi jiaren pai xiaoshuo" 試論才子佳人派小說. *Ming Qing xiaoshuo luncong* 明清小說論叢 1 (1984): 49–83.

Li, Wai-yee. *Enchantment and Disenchantment: Love and Illusion in Chinese Literature*. Princeton, NJ: Princeton University Press, 1993.

Li, Wai-yee. "Mixture of Genres and Motive for Fiction in 'Yingying's Story.'" In *Ways with Words: Writing about Reading Texts from Early China*, edited by Pauline Yu, Peter Bol, Stephen Owen, and Willard Peterson, 185–92. Berkeley: University of California Press, 2000.

Li Yu 李漁. *Li Yu quanji* 李漁全集. Hangzhou: Zhejiang guji chubanshe, 1992.

Li Zhi 李贄. *Li Zhi wenji* 李贄文集. Beijing: Shehui kexue wenxian chubanshe, 2000.

Li Zhihong 李志宏. *Mingmo Qingchu caizi jiaren xiaoshuo xushi yanjiu* 明末清初才子佳人小說敍事研究. Taibei: Da'an chubanshe, 2008.

Liang jiaohun 兩交婚. Guben xiaoshuo congkan 古本小說叢刊, vol. 23. Beijing: Zhonghua shuju, 1991.

Lin Lan Xiang 林蘭香. Beijing: Zhonghua shuju, 2003.

Liu, James J.Y. *Chinese Theories of Literature*. Chicago: University of Chicago Press, 1975.

Liu Kairong 劉開榮. *Tangdai xiaoshuo yanjiu* 唐代小說研究. Hong Kong: Shangwu yinshuguan, 1964.

Liu Xie 劉勰. *Wenxin diaolong* 文心彫龍. Beijing: Zhonghua shuju, 1998.

Liu Yiqing 劉義慶. *Shishuo xinyu* 世說新語. Edited by Xu Zhen'e 徐震堮. Beijing: Zhonghua shuju, 1999.

Liu Yongqiang 劉勇強. *Zhongguo gudai xiaoshuo shi xulun* 中國古代小説史敘論. Beijing: Beijing daxue chubanshe, 2007.

Lou, Yulie 樓宇烈. "Tang Xianzu zhexue sixiang chutan" 湯顯祖哲學思想初探. In *Tang Xianzu yanjiu lunwen ji* 湯顯祖研究論文集, 152–73. Beijing: Zhongguo xiju chubanshe, 1984.

Lu Jiuyuan 陸九淵. *Lu Xiangshan quanji* 陸象山全集. Beijing: Zhongguo shudian, 1992.

Lu, Tina. *Persons, Roles, and Mind: Identity in "Peony Pavilion" and "Peach Blossom Fan"*. Stanford, CA: Stanford University Press, 2001.

Lu, Tonglin. *Rose and Lotus: Narrative of Desire in France and China*. New York: State University of New York Press, 1991.

Lu Xun 魯迅. *Zhongguo xiaoshuo shilüe* 中國小説史略. Beijing: Renmin wenxue chubanshe, 1975.

Lu Xun 魯迅, ed. *Tang song chuanqi ji* 唐宋傳奇集. Tianjin: Tianjin guji chubanshe, 2002.

Lunyu yizhu 論語譯註, ed. Yang Bojun 楊伯峻. Beijing: Zhonghua shuju, 1980.

Luo, Manling. "Discourse Formation in Tang Tales: Literati Identity Construction and the Writing of *Chuanqi*." PhD dissertation, Washington University at St. Louis, 2004.

Luo, Manling. *Literati Storytelling in Late Medieval China*. Seattle: University of Washington Press, 2015.

Luo Rufang 羅汝芳. *Mingdao lu* 明道錄. Taibei: Kuangwen shuju, 1987.

Lutz, Catherine A. *Unnatural Emotion: Everyday Sentiments on a Micronesian Atoll and Their Challenge to Western Theory*. Chicago: University of Chicago Press, 1988.

Ma, Qian. *Feminist Utopian Discourse in Eighteenth-Century Chinese and English Fiction: A Cross-Cultural Comparison*. Burlington: Ashgate, 2004.

Mair, Victor H. "Scroll Presentation in the T'ang Dynasty." *Harvard Journal of Asiatic Studies* 38, no. 1 (1978): 35–60.

Mann, Susan. *Precious Records: Women in China's Long Eighteenth Century*. Stanford, CA: Stanford University Press, 1997.

Mao Xiaotong 毛校同, ed. *Tang Xianzu yanjiu ziliao huibian* 湯顯祖研究資料彙編. Shanghai: Shanghai guji chubanshe, 1986.

Mather, Richard B., trans. *A New Account of the Tales of the World*. Ann Arbor: Center for Chinese Studies Publications, University of Michigan, 2001.

McMahon, Keith. *Causality and Containment in Seventeenth-Century Chinese Fiction*. Leiden: Brill, 1988.

McMahon, Keith. *Misers, Shrews, and Polygamists: Sexuality and Male-Female Relations in Eighteenth-Century Chinese Fiction*. Durham, NC: Duke University Press, 1995.

McMahon, Keith. *Polygamy and Sublime Passion: Sexuality in China on the Verge of Modernity*. Honolulu: University of Hawai'i Press, 2010.

Meng Chengshun 孟稱舜, ed. *Gujin mingju hexuan* 古今名劇合選. Guben xiqu congkan, ser. 4, vols. 101–120. Shanghai: Shangwu yinshuguan, 1958.

Meng Chengshun 孟稱舜. *Jiaohong ji* 嬌紅記. Shanghai: Shanghai guji chubanshe, 1988.

Meng Chengshun 孟稱舜. *Meng Chengshun xiqu ji* 孟稱戲曲集. Chengdu: Bashu shushe, 2006.

Meyer-Fong, Tobie. "Packaging the Men of Our Times: Literary Anthologies, Friendship Networks, and Political Accommodation in the Early Qing." *Harvard Journal of Asiatic Studies* 69, no. 1 (2004): 5–56.

Owen, Stephen. *Readings in Chinese Literary thought*. Cambridge, MA: Harvard University Press, 1992.

Owen, Stephen. *The End of the Chinese "Middle Ages": Essays in Mid-Tang Literary Culture*. Stanford, CA: Stanford University Press, 1996.

Parker, Patricia. *Inescapable Romance: Studies in the Poetics of a Mode*. Princeton, NJ: Princeton University Press, 1979.

Ping shan leng yan 平山冷燕. Beijing: Renmin wenxue chubanshe, 1987.

Plaks, Andrew. *Archetype and Allegory in the Dream of the Red Chamber*. Princeton, NJ: Princeton University Press, 1976.

Plamper, Jan. "The History of Emotions: An Interview with William Reddy, Barbara Rosenwein, and Peter Stearns." *History and Theory* 49, no. 2 (May 2010): 237–65.

Qingmeng tuo 情夢柝. Shanghai: Shanghai guji chubanshe, 1990.

Qiu Jiangning 邱江寧. *Qingchu caizi jiaren xiaoshuo xushi moshi yanjiu* 清初才子佳人小說敍事模式研究. Shanghai: Sanlian shudian, 2005.

Qiu Xinru 邱心如. *Bi sheng hua* 筆生花. Zhengzhou: Zhongzhou guji chubanshe, 1984.

Qiu Zhaoao 仇兆鰲. *Du shi xiang zhu* 杜詩詳註. Beijing: Zhonghua shuju, 1979.

Qu you 瞿佑. *Jiandeng xinhua* 剪燈新話. Shanghai: Shanghai guji chubanshe, 1981.

Renjian le 人間樂. Shenyang: Chunfeng wenyi chubanshe, 1990.

Rosaldo, Michelle Z. *Knowledge and Passion: Illongot Notions of Self and Social Life*. Cambridge: Cambridge University Press, 1980.

Rosaldo, Michelle Z. "Toward an Anthropology of Self and Feeling." In *Culture Theory: Essays on Mind, Self, and Emotion*, ed. Richard A. Shweder and Robert A. LeVine, 137–57 (Cambridge: Cambridge University Press, 1984).

Rosaldo, Renato. *Culture and Truth: The Remaking of Social Analysis*. Cambridge, MA: Beacon Press, 1989.

Rosenlee, Li-Hsiang Lisa. *Confucianism and Women: A Philosophical Interpretation*. New York: SUNY Press, 2006.

Rouzer, Paul. *Articulated Ladies: Gender and the Male Community in Early Chinese Texts*. Cambridge, MA: Harvard University Asian Center, 2001.

Santangelo, Paolo, and Gabor Boros, *The Culture of Love in China and Europe*. Leiden: Brill, 2020.

Seno Tachihiko 妹尾達彥. "Todai kohanki no chouan to denki shosetsu – 'Li A den' no bunseki o chuushin to shite" 唐代後半期の長安と伝奇小説一李娃伝の分析を中心として. In *Hino Kaizaburou Hakase shouju kinen lonshuu: chuugoku shakai seido bunkashi no shomondai* 日野開三郎博士頌壽紀念論集：中國社會．制度．文化史の 諸問題, 476–512. Fukuoka: Chuugoku shoten, 1987.

Shang Wei. *Rulin Waishi and Cultural Transformation in Late Imperial China*. Cambridge, MA: Harvard University Asia Center, 2003.

Shao Jingzhan 邵景詹. *Mideng yinhua* 覓燈因話. Guben xiaoshuo jicheng 古本小說集成. Shanghai: Shanghai guji chubanshe, 2017.

Shisan jing zhushu 十三經注疏. Taibei: Xin wenfeng chuban gongsi, 2001.

Sieber, Patricia. *Theaters of Desire: Authors, Readers, and the Reproduction of Early Chinese Song-Drama, 1300–2000*. New York and Hampshire: Palgrave Macmillan, 2003.

Sima Qian 司馬遷. *Shiji* 史記. Beijing: Zhonghua shuju, 1972.

Smith, Joanna F. Handlin. "Gardens in Ch'i Piao-chia's Social World: Wealth and values in Late Ming Kiangnan." *Journal of Asian Studies* 51 (1992): 55–81.

Song Dexi 宋德熹. "Tangdai de jinü" 唐代的妓女. In *Zhongguo funü lunji xuju* 中国妇女論集續集, edited by Bao Jialin 鮑家麟, 67–121. Taibei: Daoxiang chubanshe, 1991.

Su Jianxin 蘇建新. *Zhongguo caizi jiaren xiaoshuo yanbianshi* 中國才子佳人小説演變史. Beijing: Shehui kexue wenxian chubanshe, 2006.

Sun Kaidi 孫楷第. *Zhongguo tongsu xiaoshuo shumu* 中國通俗小説書目. Beijing: Guoli Beiping tushuguan, 1933.

Sun Xidan 孫希旦. *Liji jiejie* 禮記集解. Beijing: Zhonghua shuju, 1987.

Sung, Marina Hsiu-wen. "The Narrative Art of Tsai-sheng-yuan – a Feminist Vision in Traditional Confucian Society." PhD dissertation, University of Wisconsin, Madison, 1988.

Tan Zhengbi 譚正璧, and Tan Xun 譚尋, eds. *Pingtan tongkao* 評彈通考. Beijing: Zhongguo quyi chubanshe, 1985.

Tang Xianzu 湯顯祖. *Mudan ting* 牡丹亭. Beijing: Renmin wenxue chubanshe, 1998.

Tang Xianzu 湯顯祖. *Tang Xianzu quanji* 湯顯祖全集. Edited by Xu Shuofang 徐朔方. Beijing: Zhonghua shuju, 1999.

Taylor, Charles. *Human Agency and Language*. Cambridge: Cambridge University Press, 1985.

Taylor, Charles. *Sources of the Self: The Making of the Modern Identity*. Cambridge, MA: Harvard University Press, 1989.

Tsai, S.-C. Kevin. "Ritual and Gender in the 'Tale of Li Wa.'" *Chinese Literature: Essays, Articles, Reviews* 26 (Dec. 2004): 99–127.

Van Zoeren, Steven. *Poetry and Personality: Reading, Exegesis, and Hermeneutics in Traditional China*. Stanford, CA: Stanford University Press, 1991.

Wanru yue 宛如約. Shenyang: Chunfeng wenyi chubanshe, 1987.

Wang Fuzhi 王夫之. *Chuanshan quanshu* 船山全書. Changsha: Yuelu shushe, 1988–1996.

Wang Gen 王艮. *Mingru Wang Xinzhai xiansheng yiji* 明儒王心斎先生遺集. Beijing: Zhonghua shuju, 1911.

Wang Jide 王驥德. *Qulu* 曲律. Zhongguo gudian xiqu lunzhu jicheng 中國古典戲曲論著集成, vol. 4. Beijing: Zhongguo xiju chubanshe, 1959.

Wang, John C.Y. *Chin Sheng-t'an*. New York: Twayne Publishers, 1972.

Wang, Qingping. "The Commercial Production of the Early Sing Scholar-Beauty Romance." PhD dissertation, Stanford University, 1998.

Wang Shifu 王實甫. *Xin jiaozhu guben Xixiang ji* 新校註古本西廂記. Edited by Wang Jide 王驥德. Facsimile reprint of the Wanli (1614) edition held in Zhongguo guojia tushuguan. Beijing: Beijing tushuguan chubanshe, 2004.

Wang Shifu 王實甫. *Xixiang ji* 西廂記. Edited by Zhang Yanjin 張燕瑾. Beijing: Renmin wenxue chubanshe, 2007.

Wang Xianqian 王先謙. *Xunzi jijie* 荀子集解. Beijing: Zhonghua shuju, 1988.

Wang Xiaochuan 王曉傳, ed. *Yuan Ming Qing sandai jinhui xiaoshuo xiqu shiliao* 元明清三代禁毀小說戲曲史料. Beijing: Zuojia chubanshe, 1958.

Wang Yangming 王陽明. *Chuan xi lu* 傳習錄. Zhengzhou: Zhongzhou guji chubanshe, 2008.

Wang Yangming 王陽明. *Chuan xi lu zhushu* 傳習錄注疏. Shanghai: Shanghai guji chubanshe, 2012.

Wang Yangming 王陽明. *Chuan xi lu lanwaishu* 傳習錄欄外書. Shanghai: Shanghai guji chubanshe, 2017.

Watson, Burton, trans. *Records of the grand historian of China*. New York: Columbia University Press, 1961.

West, Stephen H. "Text and Ideology: Ming Editors and Northern Drama." In *Ming Qing xiqu guoji yantao hui lunwen ji* 明清戲曲國際研討會論文集, edited by Hua Wei 華瑋 and Wang Ailing 王璦玲, 235–84. Taibei: Zhongyang yanjiuyuan Zhongguo wenzhesuo, 1988.

West, Stephen, and Wilt Idema, trans. *The Moon and the Zither: The Story of the Western Wing*. Berkeley and Los Angeles: University of California Press, 1991.

Widmer, Ellen. *The Beauty and the Book: Women and Fiction in Nineteenth-Century China*. Cambridge, MA: Harvard University Asia Center, 2006.

Widmer, Ellen. "Between Worlds: Huang Zhouxing's Imaginary Garden." In *Trauma and Transcendence in Early Qing Literature*, ed. Wilt Idema, Wai-yee Li, and Ellen Widmer, 277–79 (Cambridge, MA: Harvard University Asian Center, 2006).

Wu Cuncun 吴存存. "Pingmin de qingge – cong wan Qing beifang pingmin changben kan xiaceng nüxing dui xingbie he xingai wenti de liji yu qidai" 平民的情歌——從晚清北方平民唱本看下層女性對性別和性愛問題的理解與期待. *Xiqu yu suwenxue yanjiu* 9 (2021): 18–39.

Wu Cuncun 吴存存. "Chunyi ce zhong de liangpian gaixie xiaoshuo" 春意冊中的兩篇改寫小說. *Zhongguo wenhua* 52 (2020): 91–103.

Wu Cuncun 吴存存. "Suzhou Dialect, Social Status, and Gender in *Sancaifu*, a Rediscovered Mid-Qing *Chuanqi* Play." *Chinoperl: Journal of Chinese Oral & Performing Literature* 39, no. 1 (2020): 7–30.

Wu Cuncun and Mark Stevenson, eds. *Wanton Women in Late-Imperial Chinese Literature: Models, Genres, Subversions and Traditions*, Leiden: Brill, 2017.

Wu, I-Hsien. *Eroticism and Other Literary Conventions in Chinese Literature: Intertextuality in "The Story of the Stone"*. Amherst, NY: Cambria Press, 2017.

Wu, Yenna. *The Chinese Virago: A Literary Theme*. Cambridge, MA: Council on East Asian studies, Harvard University, 1995.

Xia Jingqu 夏敬渠. *Yesou puyan* 野叟曝言. Beijing: Renmin wenxue chubanshe, 1985.

Xiao Chi. *The Chinese Garden as Lyric Enclave: A Generic Study of The Story of the Stone*. Ann Arbor: Center for Chinese Studies Publications, University of Michigan, 2001.

Xiuping yuan 繡屏緣, Guben xiaoshuo jicheng 古本小說集成. Shanghai: Shanghai guji chubanshe, 1994.

Xu Dajun 徐大軍. *Yuan zaju yu xiaoshuo guanxi yanjiu* 元雜劇與小說關係研究. Zhengzhou: Henan renmin chubanshe, 2006.

Xu Shichang 徐世昌. *Qingru xuean* 清儒學案. Beijing: Zhonghua shuju, 2008.

Xu Zong 許總, ed. *Lixue wenyi shigang* 理學文藝史綱. Nanjing: Jiangsu jiaoyu chubanshe, 2001.

Yang Binbin, *Heroines of the Qing: Exemplary Women Tell Their Stories*. Seattle: Washington University Press, 2016.

Yin Shizhen 尹世貞. *Langhuan ji san juan* 瑯嬛記三卷. Jinan: Qilu shushe, 1995.

Yin Zhanhua 尹占华. "'Yingying zhuan' shi Yuan Zhen ziyu – jian yu Wu Wenbin Xiansheng Shangque"《鶯鶯傳》是元稹自寓——兼與吳伟斌先生商榷. *Xibei shida xuebao* 西北師大學報 48, no. 4 (2001): 65–69.

Yisu 一粟 ed. *Honglou meng ziliao huibian* 紅樓夢資料彙編. Beijing: Zhonghua shuju, 1964.

Yu, Anthony. *Rereading the Stone: Desire and the Making of Fiction in the Dream of the Red Chamber*. Princeton, NJ: Princeton University Press, 1997.

Yu Gang 俞鋼. *Tangdai wenyan xiaoshuo yu keju zhidu* 唐代文言小說与科舉制度. Shanghai: Shanghai guji chubanshe, 2004.

Yu jiao li 玉嬌梨. Beijing: Zhonghua shuju, 2000.

Yu Yingshi 余英時. *Honglou meng de liangge shijie*《紅樓夢》的兩個世界. Taibei: Lianjing chubanshe, 1978.

Yu Yingshi 余英時. *Zhongguo jinshi zongjiao lunli yu shangren jingshen* 中國近世宗教倫理與商人精神. Taibei: Lianjing chuban shiye gongsi, 1987.

Yu Yingshi 余英時. *Lun Dai Zhen yu Zhang Xuecheng – Qingdai zhongqi xueshu sixiangshi yanjiu* 論戴震与章學誠——清代中期學術思想史研究. Beijing: Sanlian shudian, 2000.

Yu zhiji 玉支磯. Shenyang: Chunfeng wenyi chubanshe, 1983.

Yu Zhiyuan 于植元. "Lin Lan Xiang lun" 林蘭香論. *Ming Qing xiaoshuo luncong* 明清小說論叢 1 (1984): 190–213.

Yuan Hongdao 袁宏道. *Yuan Zhonglang quanji* 袁中郎全集. Shanghai: Shijie shuju, 1935.

Yuan Xingpei 袁行霈, ed. *Zhongguo wenxue shi* 中國文學史. Beijing: Gaodeng jiaoyu chubanshe, 1999.

Yuchuan yuan 玉釧緣. Haerbin: Heilongjiang renmin chubanshe, 1987.

Zaju xuan 雜劇選. Guben xiqu congkan 古本戲曲叢刊, ser. 4, vols. 96–98. Shanghai: Shangwu yinshuguan, 1958.

Zang Maoxun 臧懋循, ed. *Yuanqu xuan* 元曲選. Beijing: Zhonghua shuju, 1989.

Zeitlin, Judith T. *Historian of the Strange: Pu Songling and the Chinese Classical Tale*. Stanford, CA: Stanford University Press, 1993.

Zeitlin, Judith T. "Shared Dreams: The Story of the Three Wives' Commentary on the Peony Pavilion." *Harvard Journal of Asiatic Studies* 54, no. 1 (1994): 127–79.

Zeitlin, Judith T. *The Phantom Heroine: Ghosts and Gender in Seventeenth-Century Chinese Literature*. Honolulu: University of Hawai'i Press, 2007.

Zhang Dai 張岱. *Taoan mengyi* 陶庵夢憶. Shanghai: Shanghai guji chubanshe, 1982.

Zhang Hua 張華. *Bowu zhi* 博物誌. Sibu beiyao 四部備要.

Zhang Jun 張俊, "Lun Lin Lan Xiang yu Honglou meng jiantan lianjie Jin Ping Mei yu Honglou meng de lianhuan" 論林蘭香與紅樓夢兼談連接金瓶梅與紅樓夢的連環. *Ming Qing xiaoshuo luncong* 明清小說論叢 5 (1987): 63–84.

Zhang Shuxiang 張淑香. *Yuan zaju zhong de aiqing yu shehui* 元雜劇中的愛情與社會. Taibei: Da'an chubanshe, 1991.

Zhao Yongbing 赵咏冰. "Daizhe jiaoliao de shengming zhi wu – cong Zaisheng yuan kan chuantong Zhongguo nüxing xiezuo de kunjing" 帶着腳鐐的生命之舞——從〈再生緣〉看傳統中國女性寫作的困境. *Ming Qing xiaoshuo yanjiu* 明清小說研究 2 (2005): 244–54.

Zhou Jianyu 周建渝. *Caizi jiaren xiaoshuo yanjiu* 才子佳人小說研究. Taibei: Wenshizhe chubanshe, 1998.

Zhou Yukai 周裕鍇. *Songdai shixue tonglun* 宋代詩學通論. Chengdu: Bashu shushe, 1997.

Zhu Gang 朱剛. *Tang Song "guwen yundong" yu shidafu wenxue* 唐宋"古文運動"与士大夫文學. Shanghai: Fudan daxue chubanshe, 2013.

Zhu Xi 朱熹. *Sishu jizhu* 四書集註. Changsha: Yuelu shushe, 1987.

Zhu Xi 朱熹. *Zhuzi yulei* 朱子語類. Changsha: Yuelu shushe, 1997.

Zhu Xi 朱熹. *Sishu zhangju jizhu* 四書章句集註. Shanghai: Shanghai guji chubanshe, 2006.

Zhu Xi 朱熹. *Huian xiansheng Zhu wengong wenji* 晦案先生朱文公文集. Beijing: Beijing tushuguan chubanshe, 2006.

Zhu Zhiyuan 朱志遠, "Banqiao zaji de zuozhe Yuhuai yu Cao Yin jiaoyou kao"《板橋雜記》的作者余懷與曹寅交遊考. *MingQing xiaoshuo yanjiu* 明清小說研究, 3 (2008): 280–88.

Zou Zizhen 鄒自振. *Tang Xianzu zonglun* 湯顯祖綜論. Chengdu: Bashu shushe, 2001.

Index

Page numbers followed by *n* indicate footnotes.

 | HTTPS://DOI.ORG/10.1163/9789004693357-011

www.ingramcontent.com/pod-product-compliance
Ingram Content Group UK Ltd.
Pitfield, Milton Keynes, MK11 3LW, UK
UKHW020822290926
15470UKWH00003B/1312

9 789004 693340